YEARBOOK OF MORPHOLOGY 1998

Yearbook of Morphology

YEARBOOK OF MORPHOLOGY 1998

Edited by

GEERT BOOIJ

Vrije Universiteit,
Amsterdam, The Netherlands

and

JAAP VAN MARLE

Dutch Royal Academy of Sciences,
Amsterdam, The Netherlands

KLUWER ACADEMIC PUBLISHERS

BOSTON / DORDRECHT / LONDON

A C.I.P. Catalogue record for this book is available from the Library of Congress.

ISSN 0922-3495
ISBN 0-7923-6035-4

Published by Kluwer Academic Publishers,
P.O. Box 17, 3300 AA Dordrecht, The Netherlands.

Sold and distributed in North, Central and South America
by Kluwer Academic Publishers,
101 Philip Drive, Norwell, MA 02061, U.S.A.

In all other countries, sold and distributed
by Kluwer Academic Publishers,
P.O. Box 322, 3300 AH Dordrecht, The Netherlands.

Printed on acid-free paper

Printed in the Netherlands.

Table of Contents

Prototypical inflection: implications for typology[1]

GREVILLE G. CORBETT

1. INTRODUCTION

A category often held to be prototypically inflectional, namely number, proves less uniform cross-linguistically in its inflectional status than was once thought (Booij 1993, 1996; Van Marle 1996).[2] We therefore examine a series of hypotheses as to its status in section 2. We then take a typological view: number has been the basis for some seemingly robust typological claims and yet these too are problematic (section 3). They can be rescued by clarifying the domain of morphology to which the different claims apply. This leads back to the nature of inflection, with the conclusion that the 'obligatoriness' criterion for inflection requires greater prominence than in some recent accounts. (section 4). This criterion also allows us to make progress in understanding facultative number (section 5) and minor numbers (section 6).

2. NUMBER AS AN INFLECTIONAL CATEGORY

In discussions of inflectional morphology, the category chosen for illustration tends to be number. It is used by Bloomfield (1933: 222-224), Stump (1990: 98) and Matthews (1991: 53), to name just three. And it is, after all, one of the phi-features.

But what does it mean to say that a particular category, in this case number, is inflectional? At this stage we shall take for granted the definition of 'inflectional'. We will come back to that and to the division into contextual and inherent inflection. We will first investigate a list of reasonable hypotheses, the sort of hypotheses that writers may have had in mind when they chose number as the category for illustrating inflectional morphology, that is to say, possible interpretations of the claim that number is inflectional. The aim is not to disprove only hypotheses which are clearly articulated in the literature, but rather to investigate plausible weakenings of an apparently reasonable hypothesis, in order to show how far we must move from that hypothesis if we are to account for the category of number.

Hypothesis 1: All languages have the category of number and it is inflectional

At least the first part of this claim is widely accepted. For instance: "All languages have pronominal categories involving at least three persons and two numbers" (Greenberg 1963; Universal 42).

This reasonable claim appears to be incorrect. Let us consider Pirahã, the only remaining member of the Mura family, spoken in 1997 by some 220 people along the Maici River (Amazonas, Brazil). It has been described by Everett (1986) on the basis of fourteen months of intensive contact with the Pirahã, updated (1997) after five years of fieldwork. He states (1986: 217): "there are no plural forms in Pirahã".

Geert Booij and Jaap van Marle (eds), Yearbook of Morphology 1998, 1-22.
© 1999 *Kluwer Academic Publishers. Printed in the Netherlands.*

Greville G. Corbett

This holds even for pronouns, whose free forms are as follows (1986: 280):

first person	ti
second person	gíxai
third person	hiapióxio

Table 1: Personal pronouns in Pirahã

"There are no special plural forms for these pronouns." This means that *hiapióxio* (third person) can be plural or singular, as this example shows (1986: 282):

(1)   hiapióxio   soxóá   xo-ó-xio
            3RD   already   jungle-LOC-DIR
            (i) 'He already went to the jungle' or
            (ii) 'They already went to the jungle'

There are ways of expressing what in other languages would be plurality, by conjoining, for instance (1986: 281):

(2)   ti   gíxai   pí-o   ahá-p-i-í
            1ST   2ND   also-OBL   go-IMPRF-PROX-COMPLETE.CERT
            'You and I will go (i.e. we will go)'
            [abbreviations: OBLique, PROXimate, CERTainty]

There are other means for expressing the notion of plurality:[3] the associative/comitative postposition *xigí* and various quantifiers. But this does not mean that the language has a number category; after all, English can express duality through the use of *two* and *both*, but this does not mean that English has a dual. The grammar of English does not need to refer to a value 'dual'. Similarly in Pirahã, from Everett's description, the grammar has no need to refer to a value 'plural'. We conclude that Pirahã has no number category.

    Kawi (Old Javanese) is reported to have been similar to Pirahã in this respect, in not having plural nouns or pronouns, but marking number by conjoining pronouns or by quantifiers such as 'many' and 'all' (Becker & Oka 1974: 232).

    From now on we shall consider only languages with a number category, and assume this in our hypotheses.

Hypothesis 2: Where number is found it will be inflectional

This weakening of the original claim allows for there to be languages without number, but claims that where it is found, number will always be inflectional. It too is false, there is no universal list specifying that categories must be of a particular type. In fact genuine verbal number (rather than nominal number found on verbs by agreement) is typically derivational (Durie 1986; Mithun 1988a, 1988b). Verbal number has been claimed to exist in many languages. It is particularly widespread in North America; it is also found in the South Central Dravidian group of languages of southern India (Steever 1987) and in many languages of Africa (Brooks 1991), the Chadic group being particularly well documented (Newman 1990: 53-87). A major analysis of the subject is that of Durie (1986); Frajzyngier (1985) was a forerunner and Mithun (1988a) gives a diachronic perspective. Nor should the work of Jensen (1952: 17-20) be forgotten; he noted the distinctiveness of verbal number and gathered data from different language families.

The meaning of verbal number is still not well researched; and the difficulty is compounded by the fact that the terminology is not standardized. For example, Eulenberg discussing a reduplicated verb in Hausa says that it represents:

> a derivational category widespread among Nilo-Saharan and Afro-Asiatic languages, though rather marginal in Niger-Congo. This category is variously known as the *intensive, habitative, frequentative, repetitive,* or *plural* verb. ... it has the general meaning of a repeated action, an action simultaneously performed by several agents, an action performed on more than one object, or various combinations of these "plural" meanings (Eulenberg 1971:73).

There are two main types of verbal number: **event number** and **participant number**. We will consider an example of event number here, and an example of participant number (from Georgian) below. Event number can be illustrated from Hausa (a Chadic language, Chadic being one of the branches of Afro-Asiatic); the data are from Eulenberg (1971: 73-74):

(3)   naa   aikee   su[4]
       I.COMPL   send   them

(4)   naa   a"aikee   su
       I.COMPL   send.PL   them

Note that both have a singular subject and a plural object. Example (3) has a simple verb, but (4) has a verb with partial reduplication, which marks it as 'intensive' or 'plural'. Example (3) can be used with the meaning 'I sent them at the same time to the same place' and (4) would not be appropriate there. Both examples could be used with the following meanings:

(i)   I sent them at the same time to different places
(ii)   I sent them at different times to the same place
(iii)   I sent them at different times to different places

Thus the plural verb *a"aikee* indicates that the sending was not simple; rather it involved more than one time or more than one place - more than one 'sending-event'. Its use is not obligatory, however. The important thing is that the use of the 'plural' verb here indicates the number of sendings; it is an instance of verbal number.

Hypothesis 3: For a given language, number will be either inflectional or not inflectional (but not both)

This claim is false: there is not necessarily one answer for a given language: number may be both inflectional and derivational. We can conveniently show this, together with disproving the following, weaker claim.

Hypothesis 4: For a given lexical class, number will be either inflectional or not inflectional (but not both)

Surprisingly, perhaps, inflectional and derivational number may co-occur on a single item. We shall see this in examples involving the participant type of verbal number, in the South Caucasian language Georgian (Aronson 1982: 243, 406-407, quoted in Durie 1986):

(5)   ivane   še-mo-vid-a   da   da-ǰd-a
        John   PRV-PRV-enter-AOR.3.SG   and PRV-sit.SG-AOR.3.SG
        'John entered and sat down'(PRV = preverb, AOR = aorist)

(6)   čem-i   mšobl-eb-i   še-mo-vid-nen
        my-AG   parent-PL-NOM   PRV-PRV-enter-AOR.3.PL

        da   da-sxd-nen
        and PRV-sit.PL-AOR.3.PL
        'My parents entered and sat down'
        [AG indicates an agreement marker; the ending *-i* is syncretic, covering nominative singular and plural, and genitive singular and plural]

The verbs agree in number in a straightforward way. This is nominal number expressed on the verb by agreement. It is inflectional. Additionally, though, the verb 'sit' (unlike the verb 'enter') is one of those which has different derived forms according to whether one person sits *(daǰd-)*, or more than one *(dasxd-)*. The choice can be seen as a case of verbal number, determined by semantic considerations. Now consider what happens when there is a numeral phrase. Numerals require a singular noun *(megobari* 'friend', the plural would be *megobr-eb-i)* and the resulting phrase controls singular agreement:

(7)   čem-i   sam-i   megobar-i   še-mo-vid-a
        my-AG   three-AG   friend.SG-NOM   PRV-PRV-enter-AOR.3.SG

da   da-sxd-a
and   PRV-sit.PL-AOR.3.SG
'My three friends entered and sat down'

Singular agreement is found on both verbs. Yet the second, which has two forms according to the number of participants, shows the plural verbal form *dasxd-*, since more than one participant is involved in the action. In other words, the verb is plural in terms of verbal number, but this does not determine the agreement, which is singular. Thus in Georgian we have derivational and inflectional number together. And they can take different values.

Our rejection of hypotheses 2-4 has depended on the notion of verbal number. Some might not accept that the verbal opposition in the Hausa and Georgian examples above is an instance of the category of number. It could be argued that this was a case of aspect. Repeated versus non-repeated action is a classic aspectual distinction. There is a clear link between aspect and nominal number: if a language marks repeated action in some way, this is much more likely to be found when plurality is involved than without it (in the real world, a single person is, for instance, unlikely to send a single package repeatedly). Alternatively we might analyze the Hausa example as showing distributivity. The examples of participant number (as in Georgian) are perhaps harder to discount. However, for those who would restrict number to nominal number (including nominal number expressed on the verb by agreement), it still does not follow that hypotheses 2-4 hold. They will be disproved using different evidence along with claim 5 below.

Hypothesis 5: At least for the nominals in a given language, taking them together, number will be either inflectional or not inflectional (but not both)

We might expect that if there is inflectional nominal number, it will occur through-out the nominals. This claim too, is false. There can be splits within the nominals. This has been known for some time, but the theoretical consequences have generally not been thought through. There are several examples; we will take a less usual one, namely Marind, which belongs to the family of the same name and has about 7000 speakers in southern Irian Jaya. The data, originally from Drabbe (1955: 19-20), are given here as presented in Foley (1986: 78, 82-83).[5] Marind has four genders (which we designate I-IV in the examples), and nouns are assigned to them as follows: gender I is for male humans, gender II for female humans and animals, gender III is mainly for plants and trees, while the semantic residue makes up gender IV. First we see examples of genders I and II:

(8) e-pe   anem   e-pe   akek   ka
     I-the male.person   I-the light.I be
     'the man is light'

(9) u-pe   anum   u-pe   akuk   ka
     II-the female.person   II-the light.II be
     'the woman is light'

(10) u-pe   ŋgat   u-pe   akuk   ka
     II-the dog   II-the light.II be
     'the dog is light'

The agreement is prefixed on *-pe* 'the' but infixed in the adjective *ak-k* 'light'. In the plural, the forms are these:

(11) i-pe   anim   i-pe   akik   ka
     PL-the person.PL   PL-the light.PL be
     'the people are light'

(12) i-pe   ŋgat   i-pe   akik   ka
     PL-the dog   PL-the light.PL be
     'the dogs are light'

There is just one plural agreement form for genders I and II. *Anum* 'man' has the plural *anim*; while *ŋgat* 'dog/dogs' does not change morphologically. Though not marking number itself, *ŋgat* when plural takes plu-ral agreements.

For genders III and IV, the forms are these:

(13) e-pe   de   e-pe   akak   ka
     III-the wood   III-the light.III be
     'the wood is light'

(14) i-pe   behaw   i-pe   akik   ka
     IV-the pole   IV-the light.IV be
     'the pole is light'

Nouns of genders III and IV, those which are 'below' animals, have no distinct plural forms and no plural agreement forms. (Note that the gender IV marker is the same as the plural marker for genders I and II.)

This is one instance of a more general claimed regularity. Smith-Stark (1974) proposed this version of the Animacy Hierarchy:

speaker > addressee > kin > rational > human   > animate > inanimate
(1st person (2nd person
pronouns)   pronouns)

Figure 1: The Smith-Stark (Animacy) Hierarchy

He claimed that when plurality 'splits' a language, some top segment of the hierarchy will be involved in plural marking. For some languages there is a relatively clear split within the nominals, for others it is much less clear, with optional marking available at some positions on the hierarchy. What matters here, however, is that it is quite normal for nominals at different points on the hierarchy to behave differently with regard to number.

It is tempting to claim that number is inflectional for the count nouns of a language. However, this use of 'count' leads to circularity, if it means no more than the nouns which have inflectional number. To avoid circularity we would need to show that items denoted by nouns below the count noun threshold of the particular language, are not counted. This is certainly not the case for the Miya examples discussed below (see expecially example (16)).

The Marind data suggest new hypotheses, in that the examples include marking of number both on the noun and through agreement. The first type of marking is an instance of 'inherent' inflection, while agreement shows that the number of the noun (through the noun phrase of which it is the head) also has a role in contextual inflection (Booij 1996: 28). The relation between inherent and contextual inflection provides at least two hypotheses to consider, one leading to the other.

Hypothesis 6: For all the nominals in a given language, number will be a category of inherent inflection or it will have a role in contextual inflection

The Marind data are sufficient to disprove this hypothesis. Nominals below the animacy threshold are outside the number system, both in terms of marking number and in terms of agreement. We are not dealing with isolated exceptions but with a substantial proportion of the noun inventory. This suggests a further hypothesis:

Hypothesis 7: For each use of each nominal the value of the number category for inherent inflection must match the value for its role in contextual inflection

This makes the reasonable claim that those nominals for which number marking is available will match those which can head noun phrases controlling number agreement. Thus there will be a single cut-off point on the Animacy Hierarchy. If it were true, it would mean that for investigating number in nominals the inherent/contextual distinction was not relevant. However, we shall see that even this claim does not hold.

We might think of British English *committee* type nouns here, since they allow plural agreement while standing in the singular. However, these are a special case in that their agreements need not be consistent (*this committee, after long deliberation, have decided ...*).[6]

There is a more clear-cut counter-example. The relevant data are found in the West Chadic language Miya (Schuh 1989); the split involves obligatory/optional number marking and obligatory/excluded agreement. Number is involved in agreement and hence is relevant to syntax; furthermore: "Potentially, any noun may be pluralized morphologically" (Schuh 1989: 173). Hence by almost any definition the language has inflectional number. Let us look at its distribution.

Nouns are of two genders, masculine and feminine; males are masculine, females feminine, and non-sex differentiables can be either. Agreement targets (and many different items agree) have three agreement forms: masculine singular, feminine singular and plural. This may be illustrated by one of the demonstrative pronouns:

	singular	plural
masculine	nákə́n	níykín
feminine	tákə́n	

Table 2: The demonstrative 'this' in Miya (Schuh 1989: 172, 176)

In addition there is an animate/inanimate distinction: the animate nouns are those which denote "all humans, most, if not all, domestic animals and fowl, and some large wild animals". Large wild animals are the "grey area". The remaining nouns are inanimate (1989: 175). This distinction is relevant for number marking in that animate nouns must be marked for plurality when appropriate ((15a) is acceptable but not (15b)):

(15a) təvàm   tsə́r   cf: (15b) * 'ám   tsə́r
       woman.PL   two   woman.SG   two
       'two women'   'two women'

For inanimates, on the other hand, marking is optional:

(16a) zəkïyáyàw   vàatlə̀   cf: (16b) zəkïy   vàatlə̀
       stone.PL   five   stone.SG   five
       'five stones'   'five stones'

Animate plural nouns take plural agreements:

(17)   níykín   təvàm

this.PL woman.PL
'these women'

Inanimate nouns, however, even if they are marked as plural, do not take plural agreement; they take agreement according to their gender in the singular:

(18) nákə́n viyáyuwáwàw
this.M.SG fireplace.PL (*viyàyúw* 'fireplace' is masculine)
'these fireplaces'

(19) tákə́n tlə́rkayáyàw
this.F.SG calabash.PL (*tlə́rkay* 'calabash' is feminine)
'these calabashes'

Thus the status of number is different for animate and inanimate nouns. Marking of number is obligatory for animates but optional for inanimates. Number is syntactically relevant, since it is an agreement category; however, while agreement in number with animates is obligatory, plural agreement with inanimates is impossible. And, most interestingly, agreement with inanimate plurals does occur, but in gender and not in number. This shows that there is an agreement rule for inanimates where we might have expected to find number agreement, but where the latter fails to occur. Thus inanimate nouns have inherent number, marked optionally, but this number does not have a role in contextual inflection. The value of the number category for inherent inflection need not match the value for its role in contextual inflection and hypothesis 7 is shown to be false.

At least, we might think, the mismatch will always be this way:

Hypothesis 8: For the nominals in a given language, where the role of the number category differs for inherent inflection and contextual inflection, the role of inherent inflection will extend lower down the Animacy Hierarchy than that of contextual inflection.

This proves to be another reasonable but false supposition. Consider Merlan's (1983) account of Ngalakan, a language of the Gunwinjguan group, which had around 25 speakers in the late 1970's, at Bulman and Ngukurr in Arnhem Land, Australia. Here too, marking of number on the verb is sensitive to position on the hierarchy:

> ... in Ngalakan explicit non-singular marking on the noun is limited; nouns not explicitly marked as non-singular can be cross-referenced as non-singular, but this possibility is limited almost entirely to human and sometimes animate nouns. Non-singular reference of inanimate NPs is generally not explicitly marked in the verb, and is largely to be understood from the larger context of discourse (Merlan 1983: 90).

Greville G. Corbett

The implication of the interaction of number with the Animacy Hierarchy is that the status of number as an inflectional category is much less straightforward than generally imagined. It really is not a simple inflectional feature (+/- plural) ready to have a role in the syntax. It is also worth mentioning here that, to keep things simple, discussion has been restricted to singular and plural. Other values of the number category add whole layers of complexity: it is not the case that, for example, in a singular-dual-plural system what is true for the plural will be true for the dual. They can vary independently. We shall have to face some of these additional complexities shortly. And we have not been specific yet about 'inflectional'; the cases discussed have been chosen as 'consensus cases' where different definitions of inflectional (in the broad sense to cover both inherent and contextual) converge on the same result.

However, after several hypotheses which have been proved false, it is time to suggest a new one which it is hoped will prove correct:

Hypothesis 9: For the nominals in a given language, where the role of the number category differs for inherent inflection and contextual inflection, there may be counter-examples to the requirement of the Animacy Hierarchy in terms of inherent inflection but not in terms of contextual inflection.

We can illustrate the effect of this constraint from English, where the number split is very low on the hierarchy, being found within the inanimates. Nouns like *sheep* are therefore exceptional in terms of number marking:

(20)   This sheep has been cloned.

(21)   These sheep have been cloned.

Since sheep are animate, the noun should mark number. The noun is irregular in terms of inherent inflection,[7] but regular in terms of its role in contextual inflection (it takes plural agreement). Imagine a new lexical item *peesh* (a cloned sheep). It could not be the grammatical reversal of *sheep*:

(22)   This peesh has been fed. [Hypothetical]

(23)   This peeshes has been fed. [Hypothetical, claimed impossible]

At first sight, the hypothetical system which is claimed to be impossible looks rather like that which is found in Miya. The difference is that in Miya there are two splits, different for noun marking and agreement, but both in accord with the Animacy Hierarchy. English *sheep* is not part of a regular split but is a lexical exception. Exceptions of this type are allowed, while the converse, like the hypothetical *peesh*, are not.

3. THE TYPOLOGY OF NUMBER

Let us now approach the number category from a different angle, considering what the possible values are. The typology of number values proves quite challenging (Corbett 1992). Consider the often cited Number Hierarchy:

singular   >   plural   >   dual >   trial

Figure 2: the Number Hierarchy

This goes back to Greenberg's universal 34: 'No language has a trial number unless it has a dual. No language has a dual unless it has a plural' (Greenberg 1963). There are at least two problems. First, certain languages are exceptions in that they are claimed (in a way we will define) to have a plural but no singular (Greenberg wisely did not include the singular, though most subsequent versions of the hierarchy do). Second, it makes the wrong predictions for 'facultative number'.

Let us consider the problem of facultative number first. The South Slavonic language Slovene has singular, dual and plural, but the status of these three values is rather different. The dual is not obligatory in the way that the plural is in Slovene:

> Normally, dual forms are used in pronouns and in verbal forms whenever two actual referents are involved, be they explicitly mentioned or only implicit. However, in non-pronominal noun phrases with, for example, body parts that come in pairs like 'eyes' and 'feet', dual forms tend to be used only when the quantifiers 'two' or 'both' are explicitly stated in the context, and are replaced by the plural when this quantifier is unstated, even if a pair of referents are obviously implicit ... (Priestly 1993: 440-441).

Priestly gives the following example:

(24)   nóge   me   bolijo
       foot.PL 1ST.SG.ACC hurt.PL
       'my feet hurt'

This is a fully appropriate utterance for a normal biped. It is assumed that two feet are referred to, and the dual is not required. (Note again how number varies within the nominals.) A plural in Slovene may be for reference to just two real world entities.[8]

Where the dual is facultative, as in Slovene, the plural may be used in its place, as predicted by the hierarchy. Now consider Ngan'gityemerri (a Daly language with two dialects, Ngan'gikurunggurr and Ngan'giwumirri, and with 100 speakers, 300 miles SW of Darwin, Australia). It has singular, dual, trial and plural. The dual must be used to refer to two entities, the plural must be used for four and more. For three entities, the trial is used when the fact of there being three is salient (for example, at the first mention in discourse) but otherwise the plural is used for three (Reid 1990). Thus when the trial is facultative, as in Ngan'gityemerri, it is not, of course, the dual which is used, which would be the prediction from the hierarchy, but the plural.

This part of the problem can be overcome by replacing the hierarchy with a set of binary choices, as follows (for other values of the number category, such as greater and lesser paucals, see Corbett in preparation):

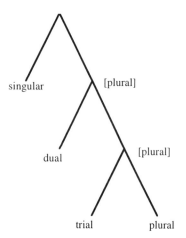

Figure 3: Representation of some possible number systems

This analysis represents possible number inventories just as well as the hierarchy: languages adopt varying top sections of the system. Unlike the hierarchy, it can be extended to include the paucal, and it copes perfectly with facultative numbers. Thus having a facultative trial means that the last branch (decision) is an optional one. We represent this system as follows:

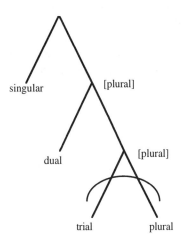

Figure 4: System with facultative trial

The arc indicates the choice which can be 'ignored'. When the last choice is not taken, the remaining system is singular - dual - plural, and then the plural is used for reference to three individuals.

Let us go back to our first problem, that of languages claimed to have 'no singular', to see whether we can extend the approach based on binary branches to cover this too. At first sight a language with a plural but no singular is a contradiction. What is meant is languages in which the absence of plural marking does not necessarily imply singular, merely the lack of specific number marking. Such systems are widely found, for varying parts of the noun inventory. According to Dick Hayward (personal communication) Cushitic languages normally have a form which is outside the number opposition, a form by which the meaning of the noun can be expressed without reference to number. We shall call this 'general number'. Other terms have been used: Jespersen (1924: 198) writes of the "want of a common number form (i.e. a form that disregards the distinction between singular and plural)". Hayward (1979) introduced the term 'unit reference', the German tradition is to use 'transnumeral', as in Biermann (1982). We follow Andrzejewski (1960) in using the term 'general'. We frequently find that this general form is the same as the singular for some nouns, and the same as the plural for others, though there will be fewer of these. There are rare languages like Bayso with a unique general form (Corbett & Hayward 1987). The usual situation, with general identical to singular, can be illustrated from the Cushitic language Arbore (Hayward 1984: 159-183). We find pairs like the following:

(25)   *general*   *plural*
        kér 'dog(s)'   ker-ó 'dogs'
        garlá 'needle(s)'   garlá-n 'needles'

Greville G. Corbett

It is important to stress that, though the morphology may appear comparable to English or Dutch, the semantics of the forms is quite different: *keró* guarantees more than one dog, while *kér* does not imply only one: it might be one, it might be more than that. (There are other, less frequent number pairings in Arbore.)

In analysing such systems, we could extend the tree upwards, and treat number itself as facultative (as indicated by the arc):

Figure 5: General number (first attempt)

This alluring solution fails. General and singular regularly share a form, in language after language. The unique general form is very rare. Hence we would be predicting use of a form which is rarely available. A more helpful representation of the system perhaps is given in figure 6:

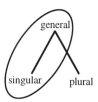

Figure 6: System with general/singular versus plural

Note: The ellipse is used to signal that two potential meanings share a single form.

This shows a second type of problem: if we try to claim that the plural is facultative, then we get exactly the wrong pattern of overlapping: it is not consistent with the patterns found with the clear facultative numbers, in which it was precisely the plural that was used in place of facultative numbers (dual or trial).

We should accept that the systems with singular/general forms are more radically different than our proposal suggested: here it is the whole category of number which is optional. If the plural value is optional, in a singular-plural system, then number as a category is optional. We should therefore consider next the problem of obligatoriness.

4. OBLIGATORINESS AND INFLECTION

If we take obligatoriness as a characteristic of inflection (such that the absence of a marker is significant: English *cat* is singular not general), then these general number systems can be seen as having derivational rather than inflectional number. They do not form part of the more complex systems we have been considering (though they do obey some of the same constraints).

Obligatoriness has a strange position within morphology: some take it as so important and obvious a criterion that it needs no justification, while others leave it to one side. Instances of discussions of the inflection/derivation distinction where it is not a criterion include: Anderson (1985: 162-4, 1992: 75-82), Corbett (1987: 327-329) and Stump (1990: 98). It is mentioned by Scalise (1988: 563) but it is not one of the ten main criteria he discusses. The history of the notion is discussed in Percov (1996: 40), who traces it back to Jakobson, who followed Boas, who had been preceded by Maspero. It is included in Plank's set of criteria (1994) and is discussed by Van Marle (1996: 67). A clear statement can be found in Bybee (1985: 27):

> The second major criterion distinguishes inflectional from derivational morphology, and in some cases, inflectional from syntactic expression. This criterion is obligatoriness. An inflectional category is obligatorily marked every time a stem category to which it applies appears in a finite clause.

She in turn (1985: 81) refers back to Greenberg (1954: 215-216).

If we adopt obligatoriness (specifically of the category, not of a particular number value) as criterial for an inflectional category (including within it both inherent and contextual inflection), then inflectional number systems can be elegantly constrained.[9] The problem of 'plural without singular' means that we have a derivational form, which - at first at least - is not subject to our constraints. The branching structures which we propose (Corbett in preparation) serve to constrain the possible *inflectional* number systems. They allow:

singular	dual	plural	
singular	dual	paucal	plural
singular	dual	trial	plural

and others, but not, for instance:

*	singular	trial	plural

However, though we have saved the typology, we have done so at the expense of apparently excluding some frequently occurring systems, as being derivational. And yet these systems do not vary randomly. In fact, the possible values permitted are similar to those in inflectional systems, and the nominals involved are also predictable. Where for nominals we find an obligatory (inflectional) system and an optional (derivational) system coexisting, the inflectional system will always be for some top segment of the Animacy Hierarchy and the derivational system for a lower segment.

Thus in the Cushitic language Qafar (Dick Hayward, personal communication), the personal pronouns are restricted to use for humans, there is a singular-plural opposition and it is obligatory (inflectional). For nouns denoting humans too, the plural is used for referring to more than one. But for other animates and nouns lower on the Animacy Hierarchy, the plural is optional (derivational); in other words there is a singular/general versus plural system. And this claim about derivational number fits with other facts about the language: people have to think what the plurals are. There are competing forms, and speakers will disagree on whether a particular noun has a plural or not.

There is a nice paradox here. We know that the inflectional/derivational line is hard to draw. But by doing so here we clarify the typological problem considerably.

5. FACULTATIVE NUMBER

There is a potentially confusing factor in all this, namely facultative number. The position of a facultative number (or more than one, as in Longgu and Marshallese) within the system is constrained by the branching structures we proposed (which we now claim are for obligatory inflectional number). Yet facultative is clearly not obligatory. The point is that in languages with facultative number, the number category is marked obligatorily. Consider this typical paradigm:

	singular	dual	plural
NOM	kót	kóta	kóti
ACC	kót	kóta	kóte
GEN	kóta	kōtov	kōtov
DAT	kótu	kótoma	kótom
INST	kótom	kótoma	kōti
LOC	kótu	kōtih	kōtih

Table 3: Paradigm of Slovene *kót* 'corner' (Priestly 1993: 400-402)

For every use of a noun in Slovene, the expression of number is obligatory (hence inflectional). There is no form which allows the expression of number to be avoided.

Within this system, a particular value (the dual) is facultative. Thus number as a whole in such a system is obligatory, while a particular value (the dual) is facultative.

In the light of earlier claims, there is a further constraint to be placed on facultative numbers:

> If within a given number value there is an obligatory-facultative split, the items higher on the Animacy Hierarchy must mark the number value obligatorily and those lower on the Hierarchy will mark it facultatively.

That is, we are claiming that there could not be a language similar to Slovene in all respects except that use of the dual was obligatory with nouns but facultative with pronouns.

6. MINOR NUMBERS

Finally, certain 'minor numbers', specifically those like the Hebrew dual (Corbett 1996) drop neatly into place (some others need further work). They are typically inflectional relics, available for subsets of the noun inventory (hence these nouns are overdifferentiated). In Modern Hebrew the number of nouns for which the dual is normally available is something under a dozen (David Gil, personal communication, compare Ritter 1995: 409-412). They are typically terms for measures of time, for instance *ħodšayim* 'two months' (but there are also some measures of time without a dual).[10] The nouns with a dual, then, clearly do not form a top segment of the Animacy Hierarchy. They make up one of several such sets of potential exceptions analysed in Corbett (1996) and termed 'minor numbers'. Nouns in a minor number involve a proportion of the nouns of a given language which is relatively small by comparison to those involved in the major number(s), where being a major number involves splitting the noun inventory, taking some top segment of the Animacy Hierarchy.

There is a second restriction on the dual by comparison to the plural in Modern Hebrew: it is found only in noun morphology (inherent inflection), and not in the agreement of the verb, as the following examples show (David Gil personal communication):

(26)   ha-yom   ʕavar   maher
     DEF-day   pass.PAST.3.SG.MASC quickly
     'the day passed quickly'

(27)   ha-yom-ayim ʕavru   maher
     DEF-day-DUAL pass.PAST.3.PL quickly
     'the two days passed quickly'

(28)   ha-yam-im   ʕavru   maher
        DEF-day-PL   pass.PAST.3.PL   quickly
        'the days passed quickly'

For agreement with a controller headed by a noun in the dual, the plural is used, as in (27). (Note that in (28), plurality is marked both by the form of the stem and by the ending.) Thus the dual in Modern Hebrew involves inherent inflection but is not relevant for contextual inflection (it does not differ from the plural for inflection). It is thus the mirror image of English nouns like *sheep*. Instead of having a missing form, these nouns have an additional form; they too are irregular in terms of number marking (inherent number) but regular in terms of agreement (they do not have a role for contextual inflection different from that of the plural). They thus conform to our hypothesis 9.

These minor numbers are certainly not unconstrained (Corbett and Mithun 1996). The possible minor number values are drawn from the inventory of major numbers. That is, a number which can operate as a minor number will be found in another language operating as a major number. (Modern Hebrew has a minor dual: there are, of course, plenty of languages with a normal dual.)

Furthermore, a language with a minor number must have a number system which would match an otherwise attested system of major numbers (e.g. singular - dual - plural as opposed to the unattested *singular - trial - plural) both with the minor number included and without it. This is clearly true of Modern Hebrew: the system including the minor number is an attested one, and if the dual were excluded, then the system is again a common one (singular - plural).

7. CONCLUSION

We conclude that number is far from being a straightforward inflectional category. Several reasonable hypotheses, some widely held I suspect, proved false. However, taking the criterion of obligatoriness for inflectional systems as central has allowed us to make substantial progress in the typology of the category of number. This was specifically in the areas of general number, the problem of exceptions to the Animacy Hierarchy (examples exceptional with relation to inherent number but not to number relevant to contextual inflection), facultative number and minor numbers. This progress is itself an argument for treating the criterion of obligatoriness as more important than has been the case in recent discussions of inflectional morphology.

NOTES

[1]   The support of the British Academy and of the ESRC (grants R000236063 and R000222419) is gratefully acknowledged. I also wish to thank Norman Fraser and Andrew

Hippisley for helpful comments on a draft. A version was read at the First Mediterranean Morphology Meeting (Mytiline 1997) and the first part is to appear in the Proceedings. I am grateful to participants at the meeting, especially Wendy Sandler, for useful questions and suggestions, as well as to two anonymous referees.

2   Others who have discussed the status of number include Kuryłowicz (1964: 16-17), who makes a distinction within inflectional forms of the same word between those which vary only in syntactic value (as with case) and those which differ semantically (as with number), and Beard (1982), who adopts the opposite position to the common one, in arguing against an inflectional interpretation of number. Interestingly, in a brief discussion Dressler treats it as not prototypically inflectional (1989: 6). A recent psycholinguistic perspective is provided by Baayen, Lieber and Schreuder (1997).

3   More generally, in our discussions of whether a particular language has number, and for which word classes, we should bear in mind that number may be expressed indirectly, for example through distributivity, in order not to be misled by phenomena of this type.

4   *naa* 'I' is in a form marking completive aspect (COMPL); the verb is *aikaa* 'to send' but the *-aa* ending changes to *-ee* because of the presence of a pronominal object.

5   As yet I have unfortunately been unable to gain access to a copy of the original.

6   Such examples of inconsistent agreements are not rare; see Corbett (1998) for further cases.

7   Note that such nouns are different from those (like *lion* ~ *lions*) for which there is a plural inflection available but which is not used in certain circumstances (see Allan 1976).

8   The same was true of Classical Greek (Diver 1987).

9   For discussion of problems with the criterion see, for instance, Maslova (1994). Percov (1996) gives an extended discussion and argues that inflectional and obligatory are independent notions. Number is central to the argument. However, he appears to assume that number must be inflectional, hence if number is not always obligatory, then obligatory and inflectional are distinct.

10   Tobin (1988, 1990: 100-50) lists over 100 items with a dual; however, he does not distinguish the few nouns with a genuine dual (in opposition to a singular and a plural) from the larger number with a 'pseudo-dual', that is, a form which is historically a dual but which now functions as a plural (in opposition to a singular only). It is worth noting too that the Hebrew dual is facultative (David Gil, personal communication).

REFERENCES

Allan, Keith. 1976. "Collectivizing". *Archivum Linguisticum* 7, 99-117.

Anderson, Stephen R. 1985. "Inflectional Morphology". In Timothy Shopen (ed.), *Language Typology and Syntactic Description, III: Grammatical Categories and the Lexicon.* Cambridge: Cambridge University Press, 150-201.

Anderson, Stephen R. 1992. *A-Morphous Morphology.* Cambridge: Cambridge University Press. (Cambridge Studies in Linguistics 62)

Andrzejewski, B. W. 1960. "The Categories of Number in Noun Forms in the Borana dialect of Galla". *Africa* 30, 62-75.

Aronson, Howard I. 1982. *Georgian: a Reading Grammar.* Columbus, Ohio: Slavica.

Baayen, Harald, Rochelle Lieber and Robert Schreuder. 1997. "The Morphological Complexity of Simplex Nouns". *Linguistics* 35, 861-877.

Beard, Robert. 1982. "The Plural as a Lexical Derivation". *Glossa* 16, 133-48.

Becker, A. L. and I. Gusti Ngurah Oka. 1974. "Person in Kawi: Exploration of an Elementary Semantic Dimension". *Oceanic Linguistics* 13, 229-255.

Biermann, Anna. 1982. "Die grammatische Kategorie Numerus". In Hansjakob Seiler and Christian Lehmann (eds), *Apprehension: Das sprachliche Erfassen von Gegenständen: I: Bereich und Ordnung der Phänomene*. Tübingen: Narr, 29-43.

Bloomfield, Leonard. 1933. *Language*. New York: Holt, Rinehart and Winston.

Booij, Geert. 1993. "Against Split Morphology". In Geert Booij and Jaap van Marle (eds),*Yearbook of Morphology 1993*. Dordrecht: Kluwer, 27-49.

Booij, Geert. 1996. "Inherent versus Contextual Inflection and the Split Morphology Hypothesis". In Geert Booij and Jaap van Marle (eds), *Yearbook of Morphology 1995*. Dordrecht: Kluwer, 1-15.

Brooks, Bryan. 1991. "Pluractional Verbs in African Languages". *Afrikanistische Arbeitspapiere* 28, 157-68. (Cologne)

Bybee, Joan. 1985. *Morphology: a Study of the Relation between Meaning and Form* . Amsterdam: Benjamins. (Typological Studies in Language 9)

Corbett, Greville G. 1987. "The Morphology/Syntax Interface: Evidence from Possessive Adjectives in Slavonic". *Language* 63, 299-345.

Corbett, Greville G. 1992. *A Typology of Number Systems*. European Science Foundation Programme in Language Typology: Theme 7, Noun Phrase Structure: Working Paper no. 15.

Corbett, Greville G. 1996. "Minor Number and the Plurality Split". *Rivista di Linguistica* 8, 101-122

Corbett, Greville G. 1998. "Agreement in Slavic [Online]". (Available: http://www.indiana.edu/~slavconf/linguistics/index.html [January 1998])

Corbett, Greville G. in preparation. *Number*. Cambridge: Cambridge University Press.

Corbett, Greville G. and Richard J. Hayward. 1987. "Gender and Number in Bayso". *Lingua* 73, 1-28.

Corbett, Greville G. and Marianne Mithun. 1996. "Associative Forms in a Typology of Number Systems: Evidence from Yup'ik". *Journal of Linguistics* 32, 1-17.

Diver, William. 1987. "The Dual". *Columbia University Working Papers in Linguistics* 8, 100-14.

Drabbe, P. 1955. "Spraakkunst von het Marind". *Studia Instituti Anthropos* 11. [Cited from Foley 1986]

Dressler, Wolfgang U. 1989. "Prototypical Differences between Inflection and Derivation". *Zeitschrift für Phonetik, Sprachwissenschaft und Kommunikationsforschung* 42, 3-10.

Durie, Mark. 1986. "The grammaticization of number as a verbal category". In Vassiliki Nikiforidou, Mary VanClay, Mary Niepokuj and Deborah Feder (eds), *Proceedings of the Twelfth Annual Meeting of the Berkeley Linguistics Society: February 15-17, 1986*. Berkeley, California: B. L. S., University of California, 355-70. .

Eulenberg, John B. 1971. "Conjunction Reduction and Reduplication in African Languages". In Chin-Wu Kim and Herbert Stahlke (eds), *Papers in African Linguistics*. Edmonton: Linguistic Research, 71-80. (Current Inquiry into Language and Linguistics 1)

Everett, Daniel. 1986. "Pirahã". In Desmond C. Derbyshire and Geoffrey K. Pullum (eds),

Handbook of Amazonian Languages: I. Berlin: Mouton de Gruyter, 200-325.

Everett, Daniel. 1997. Pirahã. Unpublished presentation. (ESRC Research Seminar Series "Challenges for Inflectional Description" - III, University of Surrey 13.5.1997).

Foley, William A. 1986. *The Papuan Languages of New Guinea.* Cambridge: Cambridge University Press.

Frajzyngier, Zygmunt. 1985. "Ergativity, Number, and Agreement". In Mary Niepokuj, Mary Van Clay, Vassiliki Nikiforidou and Deborah Feder (eds), *Proceedings of the Eleventh Annual Meeting of the Berkeley Linguistics Society, February 16-18, 1985.* Berkeley, California: B. L. S., University of California, 96–106.

Greenberg, Joseph H. 1954. "A Quantitative Approach to the Morphological Typology of Languages". In Robert F. Spencer (ed.), *Method and Perspective in Anthropology: Paper in Honor of Wilson D. Wallis.* Minneapolis: University of Minnesota Press, 192-220. [Reprinted in Keith Denning and Suzanne Kemmer (eds) 1990, *On Language: Selected Writings of Joseph H. Greenberg.* Stanford: Stanford University Press, 3-25.]

Greenberg, Joseph H. 1963. "Some Universals of Grammar with Particular Reference to the Order of Meaningful Elements". In Joseph H. Greenberg (ed), *Universals of Language.* Cambridge, Massachusetts: MIT Press, 73-113.

Hayward, Richard J. 1979. "Bayso Revisited: some Preliminary Linguistic Observations-II". *Bulletin of the School of Oriental and African Studies, University of London* 42, 101–32.

Hayward, Dick [= R. J. Hayward] 1984. *The Arbore Language: A First Investigation: Including a Vocabulary.* Hamburg: Buske. (Cushitic Language Studies 2)

Jensen, H. 1952. "Die sprachliche Kategorie des Numerus". *Wissenschaftliche Zeitschrift der Universität Rostock, Reihe Gesellschafts- und Sprachwissenschaften* 1, 2.1-21.

Jespersen, Otto. 1924. *The Philosophy of Grammar.* London: Allen & Unwin.

Kuryłowicz, Jerzy .1964. *The Inflectional Categories of Indo-European.* Heidelberg: Carl Winter.

Marle, Jaap van. 1996. "The Unity of Morphology: on the Interwovenness of the Derivational and Inflectional Dimension of the Word". In Geert Booij and Jaap van Marle (eds), *Yearbook of Morphology 1995.* Dordrecht: Kluwer, 67-82.

Maslova, E. S. 1994. "O kriterii objazatel'nosti v morfologii". *Izvestija Akademii Nauk: Serija literatury i jazyka* 53: 3, 44-50.

Matthews, Peter H. 1991. *Morphology.* Cambridge: Cambridge University Press. Second edition. [First edition: 1974]

Merlan, Francesca. 1983. *Ngalakan Grammar, Texts and Vocabulary.* Canberra Department of Linguistics, Research School of Pacific Studies, Australian National University. (Pacific Linguistics, series B, no. 89)

Mithun, Marianne. 1988a. "Lexical Categories and the Evolution of Number Marking". In Michael Hammond and Michael Noonan (eds), *Theoretical Morphology: Approaches in Modern Linguistics.* San Diego: Academic Press, 211-234.

Mithun, Marianne 1988b. "Lexical Categories and Number in Central Pomo". In William Shipley (ed.), *In Honor of Mary Haas: From the Haas Festival Conference on Native American Linguistics.* Berlin: Mouton de Gruyter, 517-537.

Newman, Paul. 1990. *Nominal and Verbal Plurality in Chadic.* Dordrecht: Foris. (Publications in African Languages and Linguistics 12)

Percov, N. V. 1996. "Grammatičeskoe i objazatel'noe v jazyke". *Voprosy jazykoznanija*

4, 39-61.

Plank, Frans. 1994. "Inflection and Derivation". In R. E. Asher (ed.), *Encyclopedia of Language and Linguistics.* Volume 3. Oxford: Pergamon Press, 1671-1678.

Priestly, T. M. S. 1993. "Slovene". In Bernard Comrie and Greville G. Corbett (eds), *The Slavonic Languages.* London: Routledge, 388-451.

Reid, Nicholas J. 1990. "Ngan'gityemerri: A Language of the Daly River Region, Northern Territory of Australia". Unpublished PhD thesis, Australian National University, Canberra.

Ritter, Elizabeth. 1995. "On the Syntactic Category of Pronouns and Agreement". *Natural Language and Linguistic Theory* 13, 403-443.

Scalise, Sergio. 1988. "Inflection and Derivation". *Linguistics* 26, 561-581.

Schuh, Russell G. 1989. "Number and Gender in Miya". In Zygmunt Frajzyngier (ed.), *Current Progress in Chadic Linguistics: Proceedings of the International Symposium on Chadic Linguistics: Boulder, Colorado, 1-2 May, 1987.* Amsterdam: Benjamins, 171-181. (Current Issues in Linguistic Theory 62)

Smith-Stark, T. Cedric. 1974. "The Plurality Split". In Michael W. La Galy, Robert A. Fox and Anthony Bruck (eds), *Papers from the Tenth Regional Meeting, Chicago Linguistic Society, April 19-21, 1974.* Chicago: Chicago Linguistic Society, 657-71.

Steever, Sanford B. 1987. "The Roots of the Plural Action Verb in the Dravidian Languages". *Journal of the American Oriental Society* 107, 581-604.

Stump, Gregory T. 1990. "Breton Inflection and the Split Morphology Hypothesis". In Randall Hendrick (ed.), *The Syntax of the Modern Celtic Languages.* San Diego: Academic Press, 97-119. (Syntax and Semantics 20)

Tobin, Yishai. 1988. "Sign: Context: Text-theoretical and Methodological Implications for Translation: the Dual Number in Modern Hebrew: a Case in Point". In Reiner Arntz (ed.), *Textlinguistik und Fachsprache: Akten des Internationalen übersetzungswissenschaftlichen AILA-Symposions: Hildesheim, 13.-16. April 1987.* Hildesheim: Georg Olms, 449-468. (Studien zu Sprache und Technik 1)

Tobin, Yishai. 1990. *Semiotics and Linguistics.* London: Longman.

Linguistic & International Studies,
University of Surrey
Guildford, Surrey, GU2 5XH, United Kingdom

e-mail: g.corbett@surrey.ac.uk

The status of tense within inflection

MARIANNE MITHUN

0. INTRODUCTION

One of the most frequently cited examples of a prototypical inflectional category is tense. Yet the motivation for classifying tense as inflectional varies according to the criteria proposed to delineate inflection from derivation. Inflection has often been taken as a cluster concept composed of characteristics such as those detailed in Bauer (1983), Scalise (1988) and Plank (1994). Categories may thus be inflectional to varying degrees, depending on the number of pertinent characteristics they exhibit. Sometimes a single characteristic has been seen as criterial, such as obligatoriness or relevance to the syntax. The definition of syntactic relevance depends in turn on the particular view of syntax assumed.

The status accorded tense within the domain of inflection has varied as well. Anderson (1992: 82-3) distinguishes four types of inflection:

a) configurational (case)
b) agreement (number concord on English verbs)
c) phrasal (genitive on English noun phrases, tense on verbs)
d) inherent (gender on Latin nouns).

Booij (1994, 1996) distinguishes just two:

a) contextual (number agreement on Dutch verbs)
b) inherent (number on Dutch nouns, tense on verbs).

Anderson's first three types, configurational, agreement, and phrasal (a-c), are subsumed under Booij's contextual type (a). The types they label inherent are essentially the same (Booij 1994: 28). Tense occupies different positions within the two schemas, however. Anderson classifies tense as phrasal (c) because it is a property that is "assigned to a larger constituent within a structure" (the clause) but "realized on individual words" (verbs). Booij concurs that tense has scope over a whole clause, but classifies it as inherent, because "the tense of the verb is not deter-mined by syntactic structure" (1994: 30).

A significant feature of inherent inflection noted by Booij is the fact that it can interact with derivation, an observation that argues against split models of morphology. Booij's model also allows a more specific formulation of the nature of the boundary between inflection and derivation. Contextual inflection, defined as "that kind of inflection that is dictated by syntax" (1996: 2), differs cleanly from derivation, while inherent inflection may differ from derivation to varying degrees.

For many languages, the various criteria for inflection yield the same categorization of tense markers. For some, however, they do not, providing us a better vantage

Geert Booij and Jaap van Marle (eds), Yearbook of Morphology 1998, 23-44.
© 1999 *Kluwer Academic Publishers. Printed in the Netherlands.*

point from which to compare their utility. Such a situation will be illustrated here with material from Central Alaskan Yup'ik, a language of the Eskimo-Aleut family. It will be shown that Booij's schema accounts well for the sometimes surprising patterning of tense markers synchronically and diachronically in the language.

1. TENSE IN CENTRAL ALASKAN TUP'IK

At first glance, Yup'ik appears to exhibit a regular paradigmatic inflectional tense system similar to those of many European languages. Examples are drawn here from the speech of the Charles family of Bethel Alaska, particularly Nick Charles, Elena Charles, George Charles, Elizabeth Charles Ali, and John Charles. (Additional descriptions of the system are in Mithun 1995, 1998, 1999, and Snyder 1996.) I am especially grateful to Elizabeth Ali and George Charles for their help in transcribing and discussing the material.*

(1)   Basic tense suffixes

ayagtua
ayag-tu-a
go-INDICATIVE.INTRANSITIVE-1SG
'I'm going'

ayallruunga
ayag-llru-u-nga
go-PAST-INDICATIVE.INTRANSITIVE-1SG
'I went'

ayakatartua
ayag-qatar-tu-a
go-IMMINENT.FUTURE-INDICATIVE.INTRANSITIVE-1SG
'I'm going to go'

ayaciqua
ayag-ciqe-u-a
go-FUTURE-INDICATIVE.INTRANSITIVE-1SG
'I'll go'

In much spontaneous speech, the use of the suffixes appears quite straightforward, essentially matching tense distinctions in English. Present tense verbs are unmarked for tense, while those referring to past events carry the past suffix *-llru-* and those referring to future events carry the imminent future *-qatar-* 'going to' or the general future *-ciqe-* 'will'.

(2) Use of tense suffixes in conversation (Elizabeth Ali, speaker):

Wiinga	*tang*	*kaikapailrianga.*
wiinga	tang	kaig-qapiar-lria-nga
I	see	be.hungry-very-PARTICIPIAL-1SG

'You see, I'm very hungry.

Atsalurpainek	*kiimek*	*tuai*	*nerellruunga.*
atsar-lugpiar-nek	kii-mek	tuai	nere-llru-u-nga
berry-authentic-ABL.PL	only-ABL	that.is	eat-<u>PAST</u>-IND.INTR-1SG

I only <u>ate</u> salmonberries.

Palugatartua.
palu-<u>qatar</u>-tu-a
starve-<u>IMMINENT.FUTURE</u>-IND.INTR-1SG
I'm <u>going to</u> starve.

Carrakuinermek	*tauggaam*	*cikiquvnga*	*tuai*
carrar-kuiner-mek	tauggaam	cikir-ku-vnga	tuai
little.bit-small.amount-ABL	but	give-COND-2SG/1SG	well

But if you give me just a little bit,

quyapairciqua.
quya-pair-<u>ciqe</u>-u-a.
be.thankful-very-<u>FUTURE</u>-IND.INTR-1SG
I <u>will</u> be most grateful.'

While Yup'ik tense marking often seems quite systematic, on many occasions it might seem haphazard at best. Verbs relating past events, for example, often lack past tense suffixes. The passage in (3) below came from a family breakfast table conversation. Mrs. Charles, the mother of the family, is an excellent, gifted Yup'ik speaker.

(3) Apparent optionality (Elena Charles, speaker):

Last fall-gguq	*maaten-gguq*
last fall=gguq	maaten=gguq
last fall=HEARSAY	when=HEARSAY

'Last fall when

Frankynguk	*tekituk*
Franky-ngu-k	tekite-u-k
Franky-ASSOC-DU	arrive-IND.INTR-3.DU

Franky and his companion arrived (no tense)

campaput   *yungqe<u>llru</u>yaaqelliniuq*
campaq-aput   *yuk-ngqerr-<u>llru</u>-yaaqe-llini-u-q*
camp-1PL/3SG   person-have-<u>PAST</u>-actually-apparently-IND.INTR-3SG
they realized that there had been (<u>PAST</u>) people at our camp.

upa<u>llru</u>lliniluteng
upag-<u>llru</u>-llini-lu-teng
change.residence-<u>PAST</u>-apparently-SUB-3PL
They had moved (<u>PAST</u>)

carayiim   *piateng.*
carayag-m   *pi-a-ateng*
bear-ERG   do-CONSEQUENTIAL-3SG/R.PL
because a bear was bothering them (no tense).

Franky-gguq   *bother-neritellinilutek.*
Franky=gguq   *bother-nrite-llini-lu-tek*
Franky=HEARSAY   bother-not-apparently-SUB-3DU
But Franky said that they (he and his companion) were not bothered (no tense).

Kiimek   *Franky-nkuk*   *aya<u>llru</u>uk.*
kii-mek   *Franky-nku-k*   *ayag-<u>llru</u>-u-k.*
alone-ABL   Franky-ASSOC-DU   go-<u>PAST</u>-IND.INTR-3DU
Franky and his companion had gone (<u>PAST</u>) up there by themselves.'

There is no tense marking on the verbs 'arrive' or 'bother', even though both the arrival and the bothering took place in the past.

The Yup'ik tense markers are not absolute, as in English, but relative. In languages like English, the deictic center of the tense system is generally the moment of speech. Past tense markers indicate a time before the moment of speech, and future tense markers a time after it. In Yup'ik the deictic center may be the moment of speech, as in (2) above, but within narrative, even short anecdotes, the deictic center is the narrative time. Events happening along the timeline of the narrative are unmarked for tense. A past tense marker specifies a time before the current narrative moment, and a future tense marker a time after it. The reference time in (3) is Franky's arrival at the camp and his subsequent stay. The past tense suffixes on 'there had been people' and 'they had moved' specify a time before Franky's visit, before the narrative moment. The clause stating that Franky and his friend were not bothered by a bear is unmarked for tense, because it is simultaneous with narrative time, the visit to the camp. A past tense suffix appears in the last line to specify a time preceding the visit, namely the trip up.

An example of a relative future can be seen in (4). Most of the events related in the narrative took place along the narrative timeline, so they are unmarked for tense. The final line, however, 'I would be squashed', projects an event after the narrative moment.

(4) Relative future (Elena Charles, speaker):

Tuntuviik	*taukuk*	*wavet*
tuntuvag-ek	*tauku-k*	*wavet*
moose-DU	those.visible.stationary-DU	to.here

'Those two moose here,

tangerraqlua	*angyam*	*caniani*
tangerr-aqe-lu-a	*angyar-m*	*cani-ani*
watch-repeatedly-SUB-R/1SG	boat-ERG	area.beside-3SG/3SG.LOC

were looking at me (no tense) near the boat.

Wiinga-gg	*tangvagkegka*
wiinga=gga	*tangvag-ke-gka*
I=as.for	watch-PARTICIPIAL-1SG/3DU

As for me, I was watching them (no tense).

Tuai	*tuntuviik*	*ukuk*
tuai	*tuntivag-ek*	*uku-k*
and	moose-DU	these.approaching-DU

And if these two moose

taingareskaggnek
tai-ngarte-ku-agnek
come-suddenly-CONDITIONAL-3.DU
came suddenly (no tense)   …

tuai	*yaavet*	*qerciqua*
tuai	*yaavet*	*qerte-ciqe-u-a*
so	to.yonder	squashed-FUTURE-IND.INTR

then I would be squashed (FUTURE).'

The pattern is reminiscent of the historical present in English. In Yup'ik however, narrative time must be assumed as the point of reference, because the tense system is a relative one. It is a matter of grammar. In English, the historical present is simply a stylistic option, a possible exploitation of an absolute tense system for stylistic effect. Of course one may evolve into the other diachronically.

A shift in the point of reference to narrative time is not necessarily signalled by any formal means in Yup'ik. There need not be an overt past tense marker to shift the point of reference away from the speech time. Often, of course, time is established at the beginning of a narrative in one way or another, with adverbials or lengthier explanations. The passage in (4) above, for example, opened with 'Last fall'. In the same way, shifts in the point of reference back to the moment of speech are not necessarily marked.

Even in the course of telling narratives, however, speakers do not always maintain a single point of temporal reference. Speakers often step out of the narrative world for a moment to add comments from their present vantage point. Such a shift can be seen in (5). Mrs. Charles was telling of a time when a large moose had been shot and four people had to bring it a long distance to the boat. As long as events followed the narrative timeline, there was no tense marking. In the last line however, Mrs. Charles stepped outside of the narrative to provide an evaluative comment from her current standpoint.

(5) Shift in perspective (Elena Charles, speaker):

> *Kapeluku*   *menuitqapairluku.*
> *kape-lu-ku*   *menuite-qapiar-lu-ku*
> cut-SUB-R/3SG   be.tidy-very-SUB-R/3S
> 'We cut it very cleanly (no tense).

> *Atraugurluku*   *nangeluku*
> *atrar-ute-gur-lu-ku*   *nange-lu-ku*
> go.down-with-repeatedly-SUB-R/3SG   use.up-SUB-R/3SG
> We kept bringing down pieces (no tense) until it was finished (no tense)

> *tuntuvacugpuk*   ...
> *tuntuvag-cug-puk*
> moose-ugly.old-3D/3SG
> our big old moose

> *Anglanitullruunga*   *caknek*
> *anglani-tu-llru-u-nga*   *caknek*
> enjoy-customarily-PAST-IND.INTR-1SG   very.much
> I used to enjoy myself (PAST) very much.'

Mrs. Charles opened an account of another excursion by describing the scenery. As the narrative unfolded, there was no past tense marking. After a pause and a murmur from the audience, she made the statement in (6), this time with a past tense suffix.

(6) Shift in perspective (Elena Charles, speaker):

> 'We went again (no tense) to see (no tense) Qitenguq. You see, we could not

catch game (no tense). And those two accompanied us (no tense), those two from up there, Peter Aluska and another, travelling (no tense) with their own boat ... and Bob Qilang.' (Mmm).

Yunerillruuq		*tauna.*
yunerir-llru-u-q		*tauna*
die-PAST-IND.INTR-3SG		that

'He died (PAST TENSE), that one.

Ayiimek	*tuai*	*mululutek.* ...
ayag-a-mek	*tuai*	*mulu-lu-tek*
go-CONSEQUENTIAL-3R.DU	so	be.late-SUB-3.DU

The two left late [but at least they arrived, and the weather was good ...]'

The dying clearly did not take place prior to the narrative time, when the two men were coming along in their boat. Mrs. Charles left the narrative time to mention the death of Mr. Qilang; the past tense on 'he died' situates his death prior to the moment of speaking, not the narrative. She then resumed her narrative with no special signal and no tense marking.

Discussions of past habitual events, unlike narratives, generally exhibit systematic past tense marking on each clause. This is because there is no narrative time-line, no sequence of events.

(7) Past habituals (Elena Charles, speaker):

Ayagllermegni	*nunanirqelallruuq.*
ayag-ller-megni	*nunanirqe-la-llru-u-q.*
go-CONTEMPORATIVE.PAST-1DU	be.pleasant-HABITUAL-PAST-IND.INTR-3SG

'When we travelled, it used to be beautiful (past habitual).

Ayakarrarrlemegni	*qamani*
ayag-qarraar-ller-megni	*qama-ni*
go-at.first-CONTEMPORATIVE.PAST-1DU	upriver-LOC

When we first travelled in there

uitalallruukuk	*qaivani*	*Iituliggegmi.*
uita-la-llru-u-kuk	*qaiva-ni*	*Iituliggeg-mi*
stay-HABITUAL-PAST-IND.INTR-1PL	upriver-LOC	Iituli-LOC

we would stay (PAST HABITUAL) far in there at Iituli.

Allaneq-am	*ikanitengnaqlallruuq*
allaner=am	*ikani-te-ngnaqe-la-llru-uq*
stranger=EMPH	across.there-go.to-try-HAB-PAST-IND.INTR

A stranger used to try to stay over there (PAST HABITUAL)

Marianne Mithun

qikertarraremi
qikertar-rrar-mi
island-little-LOC
on a little island.

Wiinga-am	*tauna*	*assikngamku*
wiinga=am	*tauna*	*assike-nga-mku*
I=EMPH	that	like-CONSEQUENTIAL-1SG/3SG
Because I liked that place		

tuantelallruukuk	*kiigamegnuk*
tuan-te-la-llru-u-kuk	*kiiga-megnuk*
there-go.to-HABITUAL-PAST-IND.INTR-1DU	alone-1DU
we used to stay there (PAST HABITUAL) by ourselves.'	

The clauses in this passage represent related comments around a theme, rather than the progression of a sequence of events.

Once the relative nature of the Yup'ik tense system is understood, it appears straightforwardly inflectional, according to most of the usual criteria for inflection. The tense suffixes do not appear to create new lexemes: verbs remain verbs, denoting the same concepts. The tense suffixes affect none of the features cited by Scalise (1988: 568) as alterable by derivation only: syntactic category, conjugation class, subcategorization features, or selectional features. They are fully productive, applicable to all verbs. They are unconstrained by anything comparable to Aronoff's blocking, by which tense marking on certain stems would be avoided because of the prior existence of synonyms. Their allomorphy is regular, phonologically rather than lexically conditioned. Their semantic contribution is transparent and predictable, as well as sufficiently abstract. Tense markers are also inflectional by Plank's criterion of relationality (1994: 1673), "specifying the temporal relation between the proposition and the speech act". Tense qualifies as inflectional even by the more elusive commutability criterion: there are no monomorphemic stems in Yup'ik that could replace a stem plus tense suffix. Furthermore, there are no independent words that could replace a tense suffix in a clause, though of course there are adverbials that cooccur with tense markers. The classification of the Yup'ik tense suffixes as inflectional is buttressed by the fact that tense is a commonly recurring inflectional category cross-linguistically.

The Yup'ik system does raise interesting questions about one feature often considered definitive alone for the distinction between inflection and derivation: obligatoriness.

2. OBLIGATORINESS

Among the characteristics of inflectional categories, the feature of obligatoriness has often been taken as criterial. Bybee (1985: 81) remarks, for example:

> One of the most persistent undefinables in morphology is the distinction between derivational and inflectional morphology. While linguists seem to have an intuitive understanding of the distinction, the objective criteria behind this intuition have proved difficult to find. The most successful criterion is *obligato-riness*, applied to the definition of derivation and inflection by Greenberg 1954. Obligatory categories force certain choices upon the speaker.

An analysis of the Yup'ik tense suffixes as obligatory entails the recognition of a meaningful zero; the lack of a tense suffix must be identified as signalling time as well, either present or, more preciely, 'time simultaneous with the deictic center'. Such a characterization seems to accord with what we have seen of the Yup'ik tense markers so far. Yet further examination of natural Yup'ik speech shows that verbs sometimes occur without tense marking when they represent events not simultaneous with the deictic center. The passage in (8) describes a sequence of events that occurred along the narrative timeline, appropriately unmarked for tense: getting up, drinking coffee, going down, stopping, shooting. But when Ayaginar spoke, we might have expected a past tense within his utterance: 'They must have caught a moose.'

(8) Unmarked tense (Elena Charles, speaker):

> 'In the morning we woke up and it was raining. We had coffee and those two men, our companions, came up to have coffee too. Then your daddy said to them, "Now over there, to the side of us, dock at the edge of the lake and look to see if there is game". The two left and after some time they suddenly stopped, and they shot their guns. Ayaginar [the father] said:

Cakma	*tuai*	*tuntuturtuk*
cakma	tuai	tuntu-tur-tu-k
down.there.obscured	so	moose-catch-IND.INTR-3DU

"They must have caught a moose down there (unmarked tense)."'

He himself was not telling a narrative, but rather making a simple observation, so we would anticipate that the deictic center for him would be the moment of speech. The sounds of the shots had already faded by the time he spoke. Yet his comment carried no tense marking.

An investigation of the use of such verbs without tense suffixes might suggest that the Yup'ik point of temporal reference covers a larger span of time than its English counterpart. The different tense forms of the verb *nalkute-* 'find' can be com-

Marianne Mithun

pared in (9).

(9) Tense on *nalkute-* 'find' (George Charles, speaker):

nalkutaqa	'I'm finding it'	(unmarked)
nalkute̲l̲lruaqa	'I found it'	(*-llru-* PAST)
nalkkutqataraqa	'I'm about to find it'	(*-qatar-* IMMINENT FUTURE)
nalku̲ciiqaqa	'I'll find it''	(*-ciiqe-* FUTURE)

Mr. Charles reports that if he and a friend were out looking for a lost knife, and he suddenly spied it, he could use the unmarked (present) tense as he was bending over to pick it up: *nalkutaqa* 'I'm finding it'. If he and his friend were some distance apart, so that after picking up the knife he had to make his way over to where the friend was searching, he could still use the same verb several minutes later to announce his good luck. If the two men were far from home and then spent most of the day returning, he could use the same unmarked verb to announce his success to his wife that evening. If his mother had been asleep when he returned, he could even use the unmarked verb to tell her the news the following morning. Mrs. Ali concurred, commenting, "To her, it's still lost until you tell her". Immediately after the announcement, the mother could turn to her own husband and use the past tense: *nalkute̲l̲lruullinia* 'he apparently found it'. The Yup'ik unmarked present tense thus seems appropriate for a span of time encompassing not only the moment of speech, but as the preceding day and night as well.

But the difference is more interesting. Scurrying around the kitchen preparing dinner, I might realize that I have mislaid my knife. Discovering it a few moments later, Mrs. Ali notes that I could use the unmarked *nalkutaqa* just as I caught sight of it. Now if my husband had been on his way out when I began searching for the knife, but he returned 15 minutes later to find me engrossed in a book, having completed dinner preparations, I would have to use the past tense to announce my discovery: *nalkutellruaqa* 'I found it'. This time the Yup'ik unmarked present tense seems to cover a span no longer than 15 minutes.

Similar patterns emerge with other verbs. The different tense forms of the verb *ayag-* 'go, leave' were seen in (1). Mrs. Ali explains that the unmarked present tense *ayagtuq* 'she is leaving' could be used as a guest is at the door saying goodbye. It could also be used for what would seem to be an immediate past, as when you come into a room looking for our guest: 'she just left'. After a few minutes, the past tense *ayag-llru-uq* 'she left' must be used. Yet under other circumstances, the present is perfectly appropriate after a longer duration. Mrs. Charles could use it when she watched her daughter leave for boarding school, even after the bus was well out of sight. As with the verb 'find', the unmarked present is appropriate for what appears to be the imminent future as well. Mrs. Ali recalled that as she and her sisters were sitting in the steam bath recently, she used the unmarked present *ayagtua* 'I'm leaving' to announce that she was going to back down to the house to cook. The future need not be immediate. As Mrs. Ali was packing her suitcase the night before leaving home after a month-long visit, her mother used the same unmarked present tense verb: *ayagtuq* 'Well, she's leaving'.

The unmarked tense category does not of course indicate a specific span of time. It is used to convey immediacy, for what is portrayed as immediate rather than displaced experience. What is included within the realm of immediate experience can vary to a certain extent with the situation and the desire of the speaker. When Ayaginar spoke in (8) above, he was portraying the shooting of the moose as part of the current situation. The same was true of Mr. Charles announcing the discovery of his knife even after a day had passed, and of Mrs. Charles bemoaning the departure of her daughter, both the night before she left and for some time after her disappearance. English shows a somewhat similar use of the present progressive for imminent futures (*I'm leaving*) but the similarity does not extend to past events. Yup'ik speakers systematically use the unmarked present for past punctual events that have current relevance. In similar situations an English speaker could use a perfect: 'I've found my knife', 'she's left', 'they've caught a moose'. The fact that the unmarked present forms cover both past and future events indicates that it is neither a perfect nor an imminent future marker, but simply a marker of immediate relevance.

Once the relative nature of the tense system is understood, and the absence of an overt tense suffix is recognized as meaningful, it becomes clear that tense is indeed obligatory in the language.

3. PARADIGMATICITY

Closely related to the issue of obligatoriness and meaningful zeroes is paradigmaticity. We expect inflectional categories to be expressed by a relatively small set of terms that constitute a closed class, and to be mutually exclusive. There are several more Yup'ik tense suffixes than those discussed so far. The suffix *-arkau-* is translated variously 'will eventually', 'should', 'is supposed to'. The suffix *-niar-* is used if there is uncertainty about the time or means by which a future event will occur. When Mrs. Ali proposed a summer visit to her mother Mrs. Charles, they began to talk of the things they could do.

(10) Future *-niar-* (Elena Charles, speaker):

Assir<u>arkau</u>guq	*maavirrsukuvet,*
assir-<u>arkau</u>-gu-q	*maa-virte-yu-ku-vet*
good-<u>will.eventually</u>-IND.INTR-3SG	here-go.to-be.able.to.well-COND-2SG
'It <u>will be</u> good, when you come,	

> *kuvyacuar<u>niar</u>tuku*
> *kuvya-yuar-<u>niar</u>-tu-kuk*
> fish.with.net-in.case-<u>UNCERTAIN.FUTURE</u>-IND.INTR-1DU
> we two <u>will</u> go dipnetting.'

Another future marker *-ki-* is used only with the optative mood to yield a delayed imperative: *tai-<u>ki</u>-na*! 'Come (later)!'. The existence of a slightly larger inventory is of course not problematic in itself for the classification of tense as inflectional.

The Yup'ik tense suffixes constitute a relatively closed class, immune to borrowing, but it is not impervious. New tense markers have come into the language in an interesting way, through suffix compounding. There is, for example, a negative future *-ngaite-*, formed from the compounding of a now unidentifiable element plus the negative *-ngite-*.

(11) Negative future (Elena Charles, speaker):

> *Pin<u>gaita</u>agten!*
> *pi-<u>ngaite</u>-a-agten*
> do-<u>NEGATIVE.FUTURE</u>-IND.TR-3DU/2SG
> 'They <u>will not</u> attack you!'

Another compound negative future suffix *-nrilki-*, composed of the negative *-nrite-* and delayed future *-ki-*, is used with the optative mood. A suffix *-niarar-*, which contains the future *-niar-* is translated 'to be going to soon'. The fact that new markers may enter the system should not be problematic for a classification of tense as inflectional. All grammatical systems evolve over time. What is interesting is the extent to which the creation of a new category affects the system as a whole, since it is purportedly paradigmatic and markers should be mutually exclusive. The creation of new markers by suffix compounding is not in fact disruptive, since reanalyzed verbs still have just one tense marker.

The tense markers are not, however, clearly mutually exclusive. Past and future suffixes can cooccur within the same verb, as in (12) and (13).

(12) Imminent future + past (George Charles, speaker):

> *aya<u>katall</u>ruunga*
> *ayag-<u>qatar-llru</u>-u-nga*
> go-<u>IMMINENT.FUTURE-PAST</u>-IND.INTR-1SG
> 'I was going to go'

(13) Past + future (George Charles, speaker):

> *aya<u>llruciq</u>ua*
> *ayag-<u>llru-ciqe</u>-u-a*
> go-<u>PAST-FUTURE</u>-IND.INTR-1SG
> 'I will have gone'

Semantic scope relations are reflected in the order of the suffixes. The first verb *ayaqatallruunga* 'I was going to go' represents an imminent event (inner formation 'about to go'), the whole set in past time (outer past suffix *-llru-*). The second verb *ayallruciqua* 'I will have gone' represents a past event (inner formation 'went') viewed from the future (outer future suffix *-ciqe-*). The existence of such forms does not necessarily constitute evidence against the paradigmaticity of the tense markers, however, if the complexes are analyzed as additional members of the system in their own right: *-qatallru-* and *-llruciqe-*. It is significant that the alternative orders are not possible: there is no **ayaciqellruunga* (go-FUTURE-PAST-IND.INTR-1SG) and no **ayallruqatartua* (go-PAST-IMM.FUTURE-IND.INTR-1SG).

4. RELEVANCE TO THE SYNTAX: AGREEMENT

A number of authors have cited a different feature as criterial for inflection: relevance to the syntax. This criterion has important implications for models of linguistic structure such as that of Anderson, in which inflection is accomplished by syntactic rules rather than by processes localized within a separate morphological component. Booij (1994, 1996) has proposed that not all categories that would be considered inflectional by other criteria are relevant to syntax, and that the distinction can be captured by recognizing two types of inflection, contextual inflection, "that kind of inflection that is dictated by syntax, such as person and number markers on verbs that agree with subjects and/or objects, agreement markers for adjectives, and structural case markers on nouns", and inherent inflection, "the kind of inflection that is not required by the syntactic context, although it may have syntactic relevance" (1996: 2). He notes that "inherent inflection is more similar to derivation, and it may feed word formation, unlike contextual inflection, which is peripheral to inherent inflection. Language acquisition and language change also appear to reflect this distinction" (1996: 3). As noted earlier, Anderson and Booij differ in how they categorize tense. For Anderson, tense is relevant to the syntax because it is a property "assigned to a larger constituent within a structure" (the clause) but "realized on indi-vidual words". Booij concurs that tense has scope over a whole clause, but classifies it as inherent, because "the tense of the verb is not determined by syntactic structure" (1994: 30).

If we were to find a system with tense agreement, we would have a clear case of contextual inflection. Yup'ik appears to offer just such a system. Tense can be marked on Yup'ik nouns as well as verbs.

(14) Tense on nouns

    uillra   *akutarkat*
    ui-ller-a   *akutar-kar-t*
    husband-PAST-3SG/3SG   Eskimo.ice.cream-FUTURE-PL
    'her former husband'   'future Eskimo ice cream'

Tense suffixes on nouns and verbs can cooccur within a sentence, suggesting the possibility of agreement.

(15) Co-occurrence of noun and verb tense

    uillra   *sugtullruuq*
    Ui-ller-a   *sugtu-llru-u-q*
    husband-PAST-3SG/3SG   tall-PAST-INDICATIVE-3SG
    'Her husband was tall.'

A closer look soon reveals, however, that the noun and verb suffixes operate in different domains. The verb suffixes situate events in time, while the noun suffixes situate referents. They need not match within a clause.

(16) No agreement: past tense (Elizabeth Ali, speaker):

    Uillra   *sugtuuq*
    ui-ller-a   *sugtu-u-q*
    husband-PAST-3SG/3SG   tall-INDICATIVE-3SG
    'Her former husband is tall.'

(17) No agreement: future tense (Elena Charles, speaker):

    Qallalluki   *piuratuaput*
    qallate-lu-ki   *piurar-tu-a-put*
    boil-SUB-R/3PL   continue-customarily-IND.TR-1PL/3PL
    'We bring them a boil, those (fish) that will be made into

    akutarkat
    akutar-kar-t
    mixture-FUTURE-PL
    Eskimo ice cream.'

There is of course frequent correspondence between sentence adverbials and tense.

(18) Adverbials of past time with past tense (Elizabeth Ali, speaker):

<u>*unuaq*</u>   <u>*ak'a*</u>   *ayagnill<u>ruu</u>nga*
<u>*unuaq*</u>   <u>*ak'a*</u>   *ayagnir-<u>llru</u>-u-nga*
this.past.morning   past   begin-<u>PAST</u>-IND.INTR-1SG
'This morning I started

erinan   *niilluku*
erina-n   *niite-lu-ku*
voice-2SG/3SG   hear-SUB-R/3SG
hearing your voice ...'

(19) Adverbial of future time with future tense (Elena Charles, speaker):

<u>*waniku*</u>   *taugaam*   *dockaq*   *ikna*
<u>*waniku*</u>   *taugaam*   *dockaq*   *ikna*
after.awhile   however   dock   one.across.there

paq<u>ciiqaqa</u>
paqete-<u>ciiqe</u>-gar-ka
check-<u>FUT</u>-IND.INTR-1SG/3SG

'But <u>after awhile</u> I'<u>ll</u> go check out the dock across there.'

The co-occurrence could be taken as the result of either grammatical mechanisms or simply the fact that speakers tend to say things that make sense. In any case, there is little formal evidence that Yup'ik tense should be considered contextual in the stronger sense of Booij.

5. INTERACTION WITH DERIVATION

Booij has proposed that inherent inflection, unlike contextual inflection, can interact with derivation. It is here that the Yup'ik case becomes especially interesting.

Yup'ik contains an unusually large inventory of suffixes, among them a set that can affect argument structure by adding an agent. They include not only causatives, but also suffixes like *-ni-* 'claim that', *-yuke-* 'think that', and *-nayuke-* 'think that maybe'. They are in some ways like evidentials, except that they are not simply adverbial, like typical hearsay or inferential evidentials (Yup'ik *=gguq* and *-llini-*). They actually introduce a claimer or thinker. If the derived verb is inflected intransitively, it specifies that the person cast as the absolutive thinks something about himself or herself. If it is inflected transitively, it specifies that the person cast as the ergative thinks something about another, cast as the absolutive.

(20) Derivational suffix *-ni-* 'say that' (Elizabeth Ali, speaker):

> *Ayagtuq*
> ayag-tu-q
> leave-IND.INTR-3SG
> 'He's leaving'

> *Ayag<u>ni</u>uq*
> ayag-<u>ni</u>-u-q
> leave-<u>say</u>-IND.INTR-3SG
> 'He <u>says</u> he (himself) is leaving'

> *Ayag<u>ni</u>at*
> ayag-<u>ni</u>-a-at
> leave-<u>say</u>-IND.TR-3PL/3SG
> 'They <u>say</u> he's leaving.'

Tense markers can appear with derived verbs of claiming and thinking. A past tense suffix, for example, may follow the derivational suffix of saying to put the entire claiming event expressed by the derived verb stem in the past, as in (21).

(21) Past claim (Elizabeth Ali, speaker):

> *Ayag<u>ni</u>llruat*
> ayag-<u>ni</u>-<u>llru</u>-u-at
> leave-<u>say</u>-<u>PAST</u>-IND.TR-3PL/3SG
> 'They said he was leaving.'

Tense markers may also precede the derivational suffix of saying. The past tense suffix in (22) puts the event claimed in the past.

(22) Claim about the past (Elizabeth Ali, speaker):

> *Aya<u>llru</u>niat*
> ayag-<u>llru</u>-<u>ni</u>-a-at
> leave-<u>PAST</u>-<u>say</u>-IND.TR-3PL/3SG
> 'They say he left.'

Tense suffixes may even occur both before and after the derivational suffix of saying.

(23) Past claim about previous event (Elizabeth Ali, speaker):

Aya<u>llru</u>ni<u>llru</u>at
ayag-<u>llru</u>-ni-<u>llru</u>-a-at
leave-<u>PAST</u>-<u>say</u>-<u>PAST</u>-IND.TR-3PL/3SG
'They said he had left.'

The tense markers can and do interact with the derivational morphology.

The capacity of tensed verbs to serve as the input to derivational processes has consequences for related features considered characteristic of inflection. The tense markers are not always 'outer' affixes, occurring at the margins of words. As we can see from examples (22) and (23), tense affixes can appear inside of derivational affixes, closer to the root. The tense suffixes could also be said not to have an invariant order with respect to other suffixes: as seen above, they occur sometimes before and sometimes after the derivational suffix *-ni-*. They could even be said to apply recursively, that is, to their own output, with the mediation of suffixes like *-ni-*.

The situation is actually just what would be predicted by Booij's scenario. Yup'ik tense would be classified as inherent derivation.

> Inherent inflection is the kind of inflection that is not required by the syntactic context, although it may have syntactic relevance. Examples are the category number for nouns, comparative and superlative degree of the adjective, and tense and aspect for verbs ... Inherent inflection is more similar to derivation, and it may feed word formation, unlike contextual inflection, which is peripheral to inherent inflection. Language acquisition and language change also appear to reflect this distinction. (Booij 1996: 2-3)

Booij notes further that "contextual inflection tends to be peripheral with respect to inherent inflection" (1996: 11). The morphology of nouns and verbs in Yup'ik and other Eskimoan languages is traditionally presented as consisting of three parts:

BASE	(POSTBASES)	ENDING

The language is uniquely suffixing. All nouns and verbs consist of one base (root), any number of optional postbases, and one and only one obligatory ending. On nouns, the ending specifies number and case. (Singular, dual, and plural number are distinguished, and ergative, absolutive, ablative, allative, locative, vialis, and aequalis cases.) If the noun is possessed, the ending encodes the possessor and possessed in a transitive pronominal suffix. On verbs, the ending consists of two parts: a mood marker and a pronominal suffix complex. The moods are indicative, interrogative, optative, participial, subordinative, and a set of 'connective' moods: contemporative 1 ('when in the past'), contemporative 2 ('while'), precessive ('before'), concessive ('although'), contingent ('whenever'), consequential ('because'), and conditional ('if, when in the future'). The pronominal suffix complex specifies the core arguments of the clause, one for intransitives and two for transitives.

The endings would qualify as inflectional suffixes by any criteria. They are obligatory and paradigmatic, they comprise a closed set, they are fully productive and applicable to all stems, they show only phonologically conditioned allomorphy, and they contribute predictable meanings. Their order is invariant, and they are not recursive. They do not feed derivation. They would generally be considered contextual inflection. On nouns they specify case and number in portmanteau forms, and case is obviously highly contextual syntactically. On verbs, the mood suffixes function to relate clauses to the larger discourse event (indicative, interrogative, optative) or to each other (participial, subordinative, connectives). The pronominal suffixes specify the core argument of the clause. To a great extent, Yup'ik morphology thus shows a structure in accord with Booij's division of inflection into inherent and contextual types. Those categories that would be classified as contextual inflection are always word-final, while others that would be classified as inherent, particularly tense, are word-internal.

6. THE SHIFTING OF CATEGORIES OVER TIME

Yup'ik also shows us that morphological categories do not necessarily occupy fixed positions between derivation and inflection. They may slide along the continuum over time, in various directions. The past tense suffix *-llru-* is not reconstructed for Proto-Eskimo (Fortescue, Jacobson, and Kaplan 1995). Jacobson 1984 derives it from a compounding of the nominal past tense suffix *-ller-* plus the verbalizing suffix *-u-* 'be'. The suffix *-ller-* can be attached to either noun stems or verb stems, but it always derives a noun stem: 'former N', 'the one that Ved'. It is thus a past nominalizer, always including a specification of past tense. (The uvular fricative *r* automatically appears as a uvular stop *q* word-finally.)

(24) Historic elements of past *-llru-*: *-ller-* + *-u-* (Jacobson 1984: 491, 488):

angyaq	'boat'
angya<u>lleq</u>	'former boat, that which was a boat'
angyara	'his boat'
angya<u>llra</u>	'his former boat'
	'that which was his boat but is either no longer a boat, or no longer his'
ayag-	'to leave, go'
aya<u>lleq</u>	'the one who left'

angyaq   'boat'
angyauguq   'it is a boat'

The derivational leanings of the modern past tense suffix *-llru-* might be explicable in part as relics of its earlier source, literally 'to be the one that V-ed'.

Markers may apparently slide along the continuum between derivation and inflection in either direction. The suffix *-ller-* also appears as an etymological element in a number of other suffixes, some highly derivational. It has been compounded with the suffix *-(ng)un-* 'supply of', for example, to yield a new suffix *-nguteller-* 'empty container which held N'.

(25) Element of new derivation (Jacobson 1984: 583):

ciku   'ice'
cikuutelleq   'empty container which held ice'

kayanguq   'egg'
kayanguutelleq   'empty egg carton'

kaassaq   'gasoline'
kaassautelleq   'empty gas can'

Of special interest is the separate evolution of the past tense nominalizer *-ller-* into a modern inflectional suffix (ending), the past contemporative mood *-ller-* 'when (in the past)'. Its use can be seen in example (7), repeated here in part.

(7) Past contemporative *-ller-* 'when (in the past)' (Elena Charles, speaker):

Ayagllermegni   *nunanirqelallruuq.*
ayag-ller-megni   *nunanirqe-la-llru-u-q.*
go-CONTEMPORATIVE.PAST-1DU be.pleasant-HABITUAL-PAST-IND.INTR-3SG
'**When** we travelled, it used to be beautiful.

Ayakarrarrlemegni   *qamani*
ayag-qarraar-ller-megni   *qama-ni*
go-at.first-CONTEMPORATIVE.PAST-1DU upriver-LOC
<u>When</u> we first travelled in there

uitalallruukuk   *qaivani*   *Iituliggegmi.*
uita-la-llru-u-kuk   *qaiva-ni*   *Iituliggeg-mi*
stay-HABITUAL-PAST-IND.INTR-1PL upriver-LOC   Iituli-LOC
we would stay far in there at Iituli.'

The mechanism by which the derivational past nominalizer was reinterpreted as an inflectional connective mood is clear. As a nominalizer, it formed nouns that could be inflected for number, case, and possession, just like other nouns. The intransitive pronominal suffixes that appear with the modern inflectional past contemporative mood resemble those that appear with locative endings on verbs.

(26) Noun with possessor and case:

> *angyaatni*
> *angyar-atni*
> boat-3PL/3SG.LOCATIVE
> 'at/in their boat'

(27) Past contemporative mood (Elizabeth Ali, speaker):

> *tangvagkai*   *ayallratni.*
> *tangvag-ke-ai*   *ayag-ller-atni*
> watch-PARTICIPIAL-3SG/3PL   leave-PAST.CONTEMPORATIVE-3PL
> 'He watched them as they were leaving (at their leaving).'

It is clear, however, that contemporatives like *ayallratni* 'as they were leaving' are no longer nominals. If the form is accompanied by another noun identifying the persons leaving, it is in the absolutive case, consistent with the intransitive status of 'leave', rather than the ergative case that would identify a possessor.

(28) Past contemporative with absolutive noun (Elizabeth Ali, speaker):

> *angun*   *ayallrani*
> *angun*   *ayag-ller-ani*
> man.ABSOLUTIVE   leave-PAST.CONTEMPORATIVE-3SG
> 'as the man (ABSOLUTIVE) was leaving'

> *angutem*   *angyaani*
> *angute-m*   *angyar-ani*
> man-ERGATIVE   boat-3SG/3SG.LOCATIVE
> 'in the man's (ERGATIVE) boat'

In transitive verbs, the traces of the nominal source are disappearing. The past contemporative mood is usually (though not always) followed by the same verbal transitive pronominal suffixes that appear with other connective moods.

7. CONCLUSION

Yup'ik tense marking provides us with an example of a system that would be perplexing for traditional accounts of inflection, but that is predicted by the proposal by Booij (1994, 1996) for separating contextual from inherent inflection. Once the relative nature of the system is understood, and it is seen that speakers exploit the unmarked present to convey a sense of immediacy, the system shows most marks of prototypical inflection. Tense suffixes do not create new lexemes: verbs remain verbs with essentially the same meanings, and syntactic category, conjugation class, subcategorization features, and selectional features remain intact. The markers are fully productive, and their semantic contributions are transparent and predictable. They are obligatory and paradigmatic. On the other hand, the tense suffixes can interact with derivation. This is just the constellation of features proposed by Booij to characterize inherent inflection. At the same time, a closer look at the shallow history of the suffixes themselves reminds us that the position of markers along a continuum from derivation to inflection is not necessarily fixed for all time. A single suffix *-ller-* has been seen to evolve in a variety of directions, from derivational to more derivational, to inherent inflection, and to contextual inflection.

NOTE

* Mark Aronoff and Paul Kiparsky made helpful comments on several points discussed here. Work on Yup'ik was made possible by grants from the Academic Senate, University of California, Santa Barbara. The transcription used here is in the practical orthography developed by the Alaska Native Language Center in Fairbanks. Stops are plain: *p, t, c* = *[č], k, q*. There is a series of voiced fricatives *v, s* = *[z], l, y, g* = *[ɣ], ug* = *[ɣʷ], r* = *[ʁ], ur=[ʁʷ]*, and a series of voiceless fricatives *vv* = *[f], ss* = *[s], ll* = *[ɬ], gg* = *[x] w* = *[xʷ], rr=[x], urr = [xʷ]*. Nasals are *m, n, ng=[ŋ]*. There are three prime vowels *i, a, u* and schwa, spelled *e*.

The following abbreviations are used for glosses:

Cases		Moods	
ERG	ERGATIVE	IND.INTR	INDICATIVE.INTRANSITIVE
ABS	ABSOLUTIVE	IND.TR	INDICATIVE.TRANSITIVE
ALL	ALLATIVE	INTERR	INTERROGATIVE
ABL	ABLATIVE	OPT	OPTATIVE
LOC	LOCATIVE	SUB	SUBORDINATIVE
VIA	VIALIS	PRT	PARTICIPIAL
AEQ	AEQUALIS	CNTP	CONTEMPORATIVE
		PRE	PRECESSIVE
Person		CNC	CONCESSIVE
1	FIRST PERSON	CNTG	CONTINGENT
2	SECOND PERSON	CNSQ	CONSEQUENTIAL
3	THIRD PERSON	COND	CONDITIONAL
R	CO-REFERENTIAL		

REFERENCES

Anderson, Stephen. 1992. *A-Morphous Morphology*. Cambridge: University Press.

Bauer, Laurie. 1983. *English Word-formation*. Cambridge, Mass: MIT.

Booij, Geert. 1994. "Against Split Morphology". In Geert Booij and Jaap van Marle (eds), *Yearbook of Morphology 1993*. Dordrecht: Kluwer, 27-49.

Booij, Geert. 1996. "Inherent versus Contextual Inflection and the Split Morphology Hypothesis". In Geert Booij and Jaap van Marle (eds), *Yearbook of Morphology 1995*. Dordrecht: Kluwer, 1-15.

Bybee, Joan. 1985. *Morphology*. Amsterdam: John Benjamins.

Fortescue, Michael, Steven Jacobson, and Lawrence Kaplan. 1995. *Comparative Eskimo Dictionary*. Fairbanks: Alaska Native Language Center.

Greenberg, Joseph. 1954. "A Quantitative Approach to the Morphological Typology of Language". *International Journal of American Linguistics* 26, 178-194.

Jacobson, Steven. 1984. *Yup'ik Eskimo Dictionary*. Alaska Native Language Center.

Mithun, Marianne. 1995. "The Codification of Time on the Pacific Rim of North America". Symposium on Time and Language, National Museum of Ethnology, Osaka, Japan.

Mithun, Marianne. 1998. "The Codification of Time on the Pacific Rim of North America". In Yasuhiko Nagano (ed.), *Time, Language, and Cognition*. Osaka, Japan: National Museum of Ethnology, 251-280.

Mithun, Marianne. 1999. *The Languages of Native North America*. Cambridge.

Plank, Frans. 1994. "Inflection and Derivation". *Encyclopedia of Lg and Ling*. 3, 1671-1678.

Scalise, Sergio. 1988. "Inflection and Derivation". *Linguistics* 22, 561-581.

Snyder, Jill. 1996. "A Discourse-based Analysis of Tense in Central Alaskan Yup'ik". In Marianne Mithun (ed.), *Prosody, Grammar, and Discourse in Central Alaskan Yup'ik*. Santa Barbara, California: Department of Linguistics, University of California, Santa Barbara: 55-63. (Santa Barbara Papers in Linguistics 7)

Department of Linguistics
University of California, Santa Barbara

e-mail: mithun@humanitas@ucsb.edu

On the boundaries of inflection and syntax: Greek pronominal clitics and particles*

IRENE PHILIPPAKI-WARBURTON AND VASSILIOS SPYROPOULOS

1. INTRODUCTION

A fundamental concern of linguistic theory is the identification of its basic units. The unit of *word*, as traditionally conceived, unites all levels of linguistic description; Lexicon, where words are both stored and derived; Syntax, the principles that govern the organisation of words into phrases, and Phonology, where words provide the frame for a number of phonological phenomena. The fact that words constitute the meeting point of all three levels makes them sensitive to the different demands of these levels and for this reason words constitute an excellent domain of study in the search for establishing the borders of these levels and their effects on each other.

In traditional treatments of inflection the relationship between syntax and inflection is recognised, but the categories expressed within the inflectional section of the word are accorded no independent syntactic status. In such a treatment, the words stored or formed in the Lexicon/Morphology (*grammatical words*) are precisely the forms which enter the syntactic component. In the current Minimalist Program (MP henceforth) Chomsky (1993, 1995) adopts a strict lexicalist position, whereby the words enter syntax fully inflected (derived either in the Lexicon or in a separate morphological component), while syntax, whose functional categories terminate in grammatical abstract features (*formal features*), checks and licences those aspects of the inflection which need to harmonise with the syntactic properties of the construction in which the inflected words are entered. Thus, in the MP the word is a unit which has both an independent morphological definition and a clear syntactic role. Its morphological identity derives from the fact that it is formed by morphological processes, while its syntactic status is shown by the fact that syntax contains movement operations which revolve around this unit. This interpretation of word is much closer to the spirit of traditional grammar.

However, a precise definition of word becomes problematic when we consider the status of elements such as clitics and particles, which behave like affixes in some ways but also like full words in others. We will try to show that the intermediate character of these elements in Modern Greek is due to the fact that, on the one hand, they constitute full *grammatical words* in the Lexicon, entering the syntactic component as independent syntactic units through the operations of *Selection* and *Numeration*, but on the other, during the syntactic derivation, they combine with other full grammatical words to create a new syntactic unit which we call *syntactic word* following Di Sciullo and Williams (1987).[1] In other words, we will argue that for Greek the object clitic pronouns and the future/mood particles *na* and *θa* start as separate and independent lexical entries but end up as 'affixes' in the syntactic component. We will try to support this position by focusing on the following spe-

Geert Booij and Jaap van Marle (eds), Yearbook of Morphology 1998, 45-72.
© 1999 *Kluwer Academic Publishers. Printed in the Netherlands.*

cific questions:

a) What is the status of the auxiliary verb (V$_{aux}$ henceforth) *exo* 'I have' which combines with the *non-finite*[2] verb form (V$_{non-finite}$ henceforth) *γrapsi* restricted to appear only in combinations with *exo* as in *exo γrapsi* 'I have written' to form the perfect aspect/tense?

b) What is the status of the object clitic pronouns in Greek? These elements cannot be hosted within a functional head, since they do not have a grammatical function, and yet in some ways behave like affixes (cf. Zwicky and Pullum 1983; Zwicky 1985)?

c) What is the status of the preverbal particles in Greek which express grammatical information (as heads of certain functional categories) similar to those expressed by bound morphemes, but which seem to be neither clear affixes nor full words?

We will proceed by presenting the variety of verb constructions formed either monolectically or by the combinations of one or more of the elements listed above starting from those with auxiliary *exo*.

2. THE AUXILIARY *EXO*

The categories that affect both the monolectic and the periphrastic verb forms with *exo* are *aspect*, *voice*, *person* and *number*, *subject agreement* and *tense*. The monolectic verb (i.e. when there is no auxiliary) carries the morphological exponents of the grammatical categories mentioned, as shown in (1). But when the auxiliary is present then tense, person and number are marked on the V$_{aux}$, whereas voice and aspect are marked on the V$_{non-finite}$, (2):

(1)	γraf-o	Imperf.Act.Non-Past.1st.Sg:	'I write'
	eγrap-s-a	Perf.Act.Past.1st.Sg:	'I wrote'
	γraftik-e	Perf.Pass.Past.3rd.Sg	'He/she/it was written'

(2)	ex-o (Non-Past.1st.Sg)	γrapsi (Perf.Act)	'I have written'
	ex-i (Non-Past.3rd.Sg)	γrafti (Perf.Pass)	'It has been written'
	ix-e (Past.3rd.Sg)	γrafti (Perf.Pass)	'It had been written'

Following the assumptions of the MP that morphological information relevant to syntax is represented in the syntactic component as abstract formal features in the head of the relevant functional categories and that the organisation of these categories more or less represents the order of their exponents[3], we can conclude that the clause structure of Greek is the following:

(3)   INFL   (*exo*)   VOICE   ASPECT   VP[...V...]

Note that the presence of the auxiliary *exo* divides the functional categories into two groups. The underlying representation in (3) can explain why $V_{non\text{-}finite}$ has morphology that indicates voice and aspect only, and why it is V_{aux} that shows inflection with tense and subject agreement. In formal terms we follow the analysis advanced by Kayne (1993), and we suggest that V_{aux} is a separate verb head which takes as a complement a verbal non-finite small clause with $V_{non\text{-}finite}$ as its main element. The functional categories of Voice and Aspect are associated with this small clause, whereas the INFL belongs to the main clause. $V_{non\text{-}finite}$ cannot be related to INFL because the lexical projection V_{aux} constitutes a Barrier for Head Movement (*Head Movement Constraint*; Travis 1984; Chomsky 1986; Rizzi 1990):

(4) $[_{INFLP}$ INFL $[_{VP}$ $V_{aux}[exo]$ $[_{VOICEP}$ VOICE $[_{ASPP}$ ASP $[_{VP}$ $V_{non\text{-}finite}]]]]]$

However, such an analysis is based on the assumption that the auxiliary *exo* is an independent lexical element for both syntax and morphology. The question which this raises is the extent to which empirical and/or other evidence can be provided to support this lexical status of the auxiliary. Independent support of this analysis is necessary because it can be claimed that *exo* should be analysed instead as an affix on its hosting verb. The affix analysis can derive support from the observation that *exo* is used to express the *perfect* (Aspect/Tense) and in its content, therefore, it is a verbal grammatical category and as such it is more naturally expressed by morphologically bound elements. Furthermore, its position between the [+/-Perfective] aspect on its right and [+/-Past] tense on its left, both affixal, may reinforce the suggestion that it fulfils the role of a grammatical category and that it too should be affixal. It may thus be suggested that the periphrastic perfect expressions (*exo ɣrapsi, exis ɣrapsi* etc.) should be analysed as members of the verb paradigm, entering the syntax as single items (syntactic atoms).

We propose to reject the affixal analysis for the auxiliary *exo* for Greek by providing further evidence in support of our claim that it is lexically separate. The evidence is as follows:

a) The two parts of the periphrasis carry independent stress.

(5)   éxo ɣrápsi   'I have written'

Given that according to the phonological constraints of Greek each word has one and only one main stress, this evidence shows that we are dealing with two separate lexical items.

b) The two elements of the periphrasis often appear syntactically separated by whole phrasal constituents, such as adverbials (6) or DPs (7):[4]

(6) a.   i maria   me   exi   *poles fores* stenoxorisi
         [the Mary]-NOM   I-ACC   have-3rdSg many times upset
         'Mary has upset me many times'

b. i maria   ixe   *kapote*   milisi   me   to niko
    [the Mary]-NOM   had-3rdSg some time spoken   with [the Nick]-ACC
    'Mary had spoken with Nick once'

(7) a. exi   *o nikos*   sinandisi ton aδelfo   su?
        Have-3rdSg [the Nick]-NOM   met   [the brother]-ACC you-GEN
        'Has Nick met your brother?'
    b. arketes fores exi   *ke o nikos*   θimosi   mazi tis
        many times   has-3rdSg and [the Nick]-NOM got angry with her
        'Nick has got angry with her too on many occasions'

c) A single V_{aux}, as in (8), may be followed by two co-ordinated $V_{non\text{-}finite}$
forms reinforcing the idea that V_{aux} is lexically separate:

(8)   exo   epanilimena *episimani ke   tonisi* ...
      have-1stSg repeatedly   noted   and stressed ...
      'I have repeatedly remarked and stressed ...'

If V_{aux} was excorporated, as suggested by one of the reviewers, (see note 4), we
would expect two instances of V_{aux} provided by the two verbs. The single occurrence
of V_{aux} shows that it is a separate lexical item. This is naturally accounted for by the
structure proposed above in (4). There is only one V_{aux} in the main clause with two
co-ordinated complement non-finite verbal clauses.

On the basis of the evidence presented above we conclude that the most straightforward analysis is the one which interprets *exo* as a separate lexical head of the category Verb and the subcategory [Aux], selecting for a clausal unit with the non-finite
main verb. On the other hand, *exo*, not being a core representative of the lexical category verb, does not have the full complement of grammatical properties nor does it
have a theta-grid. These deficiencies bring it closer to a grammatical formative and
this is reflected by its role and its position in the construction. The interesting fact is
that the functional categories INFL, Aspect, Voice, which we found combined in the
inflectional ending of the monolectic forms in a fairly fused way, appear here as lexically separate.

The connection between syntax and morphology, in the periphrastic forms
discussed above, is fairly direct in that the properties of the one level seem to support
and justify those of the other. However, the situation becomes more complex when
we consider further combinations of verbs plus a variety of other modifications such
as pronoun clitics and the mood and negation particles.

3. OBJECT CLITIC PRONOUNS

Pronominal clitics in Greek in many respects resemble those of the Romance languages in that they are not sensitive to second-position constraints, they are enclitic to all non-finite forms and the imperative and proclitic to all other finite forms, they form clitic clusters[5] and they can appear doubled by a DP. These elements have been studied a great deal and there is a rich literature concerning the issue of their status (for an overview see Spencer 1991; Halpern 1998). Two alternative proposals have been advanced: i) One analysis considers them affixes, equivalent to the agreement inflection markers (Jaeggli 1982, 1986; Borer 1984, Lyons 1990; Dobrovie-Sorin 1990; Suñer 1988; for a slightly different approach see Anderson 1992, 1993; Beard 1995), base generated in their surface position licensing a pro in the argument position. ii) The second view considers them independent syntactic units, lexical items, which are base generated in the argument position and they sub-sequently move to adjoin to a functional category becoming thus cliticised on to their host. (Kayne 1975, 1989, 1991; Uriagereka 1995, among others). Spencer (1991) and Halpern (1998) discuss these two approaches and point out their strengths and weaknesses. It is not possible in the space of this paper to examine the details of these views. Besides we feel that it is not necessary that the analysis will be the same for all languages. If there is a grammaticalisation process by which strong pronouns end up as agreement markers (Bybee 1985, Bynon 1992, Bybee, Perkins and Pagliuca 1993) we expect to find the pronominal clitics at different stages of this process in different languages.

In the present study we will defend the view (see Warburton 1977; Philippaki-Warburton 1994a contra Joseph 1988) that pronominal clitics in Greek are lexically separate from the verb head; they enter the syntactic component as the arguments of the verb and subsequently move and attach on to their hosting verb. Crucial evidence derives from the so called *clitic-doubling* constructions which seem to pose the most serious problem for the movement analysis. We will show that in such constructions in Greek the doubled DPs are not arguments but clitic left or right dislocated elements. This constitutes strong syntactic evidence for the movement analysis of pronominal clitics in Greek, which will be also reinforced by morphological and phonological evidence.

3.1. Syntactic evidence

i) Object clitics in Greek are optional elements, unlike typical agreement markers which are usually obligatory, and their appearance is not constrained by grammatical factors but by stylistic reasons: to free the object argument and to mark the structure for object topicalisation (Philippaki-Warburton 1985, 1987; Tsimpli 1995; see also Bresnan and Mchombo 1987 for a similar conclusion in Chichewa).

ii) The hypothesis that when both object clitics as well as their corresponding DPs are present the latter are not true arguments but dislocated elements (topics) in an adjunct position is reinforced by the fact that these lexical DPs cannot receive the main stress of the sentence, and that they cannot be focalised (see Philippaki-Warburton 1985; Tsimpli 1995)

(9) a. xθes   aγorasa   *to vivlio   tu Chomsky*
        yesterday bought-1stSg [the book]-ACC [the Chomsky]-GEN
        'Yesterday, I bought *the book by Chomsky*'

    b. *xθes*   to   aγorasa   to vivlio   tu Chomsky
        yesterday   IT-ACC   bought-1stSg [the book]-ACC [the Chomsky]-GEN
        'It was *yesterday* that I bought the book by Chomsky'

    c. to vivlio tu Chomsky to aγorasa *xθes*
        'The book by Chomsky, I bought it *yesterday*

    d. * xθes to aγorasa *to vivlio tu Chomsky*

This shows that in the presence of clitics the lexical object DPs form part of the background, peripheral information. There is further syntactic evidence related to this discussed in Tsimpli (1995), which clearly shows that the existence of a clitic makes the doubled DP an adjunct.[6] The conclusion from such evidence seems to be that when a clitic is present the object argument position cannot be occupied by a DP and, therefore, the doubled DP, when present, cannot be the object argument.

Related to the above is the fact that in the presence of its clitic a lexical object DP cannot normally undergo wh-movement within a single clause. Compare (10a) with (10b):

(10) a. pjo   vivlio   aγorases?
        [which book]-ACC bought-2ndSg
        'Which book did you buy?'

     b. * pjo   vivlio   to   aγorases?
        [which book]-ACC it-ACC   bought-2ndSg

Given that wh-movement leaves a coindexed trace at the argument position with which the moved wh-item forms a chain, the irregularity of (10b) follows from the fact that in these sentences a wh-trace cannot occupy the argument position. This fact seems to be associated with the incompatibility of the presence of a clitic and an argument doubled DP. On the contrary, the movement analysis of pronominal clitics makes the right predictions here. The clitic is generated at the argument position and then moves to adjoin to the verb head leaving behind a trace. The doubled DP cannot be generated in an already occupied position so it becomes an adjunct (see also Aoun 1985).[7]

Against our proposal it can be argued that the incompatibility of a doubled DP in argument position with a clitic is due to the fact that the clitic absorbs the case so that the argument position is caseless and as such it cannot host a DP which must therefore be interpreted as an adjunct. Despite the fact that clitics have been suggested to be case absorbers (Borer 1984), such a hypothesis is not without problems and it has been criticised even by some of the advocates of the affixal approach to pronominal clitics (see Jaeggli 1986; Suñer 1988; Lyons 1990, and the discussions in Spencer 1991 and Halpern 1998). Moreover, such an analysis would imply that the clitic licenses a caseless *pro* in the argument position, a theoretically undesirable result (see Rizzi 1982; Chomsky 1981). Suñer (1988) presents empirical evidence that the clitic does not absorb case, even if it is analysed as an affix, and so the argument position is case marked in clitic-doubling constructions too. This is appropriate for her data because she has evidence from extraction possibilities, that the doubled DP behaves as an object argument when present. However, in Greek, as we have argued above, a doubled DP is never an argument but an adjunct. We may thus conclude that the movement analysis of clitics with a trace in argument position and adjunct DPs when present, makes the right predictions for the syntactic characteristics of the clitic-doubled (more precisely clitic-dislocation) structures in Greek.

iii) Another undesirable consequence of the view that clitic pronouns in Greek are affixes is the fact that not only the monolectic verb forms will need to enter the syntactic component with clitic prefixes (*to-eɣrapsa*), but the auxiliary *exo*, which we have argued to be lexically independent from the verb, will also have to be featured in the lexicon prefixed with clitics (*to-exo* ɣrapsi) because object clitics precede the auxiliary. This situation is not only uneconomical but it also runs into descriptive problems because to chose the correct number and type (io, do) of the clitic prefixed on *exo*, in a particular syntactic context, we will have to take into consideration not the subcategorisation properties of the auxiliary itself (since it is completely transparent) but the subcategorisation properties of the main verb which we have shown must enter the syntactic component as a separate lexical item. This is shown in the following data:

(11) a. eɣrapsa   to ɣrama
         wrote-1stSg [the letter]-ACC
         'I wrote the letter'
     b. *to   exo   ɣrapsi (to ɣrama)*
         it-ACC have1stSg written (the letter)
         'I have written it'

(12) a. * xamoɣelasa   to niko
         smiled-1stSg   [the Nick]-ACC
         '*I have smiled Nick'
     b.* *ton   exo   xamoɣelasi*
         him-ACC have-1stSg smiled
         '*I have smiled him'

These examples show that for the auxiliary *exo* to appear prefixed with the do clitic the main verb must be transitive. Furthermore a do clitic may be prefixed on auxiliary *exo*, if the main verb is in the active voice but it cannot be present when the same verb is in the passive voice.

(13) a. * γraftika   to γramma
         write-1stSg.Past.Pass [the letter]-ACC
      b. * *to   exo   γrafti*
         it-ACC have-1stSg   written-Pass

In an analysis where the [clitic+*exo*] constitute a single lexical unit the unacceptability of (*13b) would appear unjustified because the auxiliary itself remains unaltered in its single transitive form in both voices. What this shows is that the presence and the choice of clitic pronouns prefixed on to the auxiliary <u>exo</u> is crucially dependent on the main verb and not the auxiliary. This dependence will require complicated restrictions to be stated, if clitics are interpreted as affixes, and more seriously it will fail to explain that the crucial factor for the presence or absence of clitics preceding the auxiliary is the fact that these clitics originate in the syntax as the internal objects of the main verb.

3.2. Morphological evidence

The object clitic pronouns in Greek clearly reveal morphophonologically the full complement of features of person, number, and gender and case and this renders them identical to pronouns, while the feature of case treats them in fact as the arguments proper of the verb (cf. the complexity test by Zwicky (1985: 288): "Words are frequently morphologically complex ... affixal units rarely are"). This conclusion is strengthened by the fact that the morphological variation of the clitics follows almost completely the regular morphological pattern also followed by the corresponding stronger pronominal forms. Compare the strong pronominal forms of *aftos* 'this, he' (14a), and the strong forms of the first and second person pronominals *ego* 'I' and *esi* 'you' (15a) with the corresponding clitic forms (14b-15b):

(14)	Masc.Sg.GEN:	a. aftu	b. tu
	ACC:	a. afton	b. ton
	Masc.Pl.GEN:	a. afton	b. tus (dialectal: ton)
	ACC:	a. aftus	b. tus

(15)	1st.Sg.ACC:	a. emena	b. me
	2nd.Sg.ACC:	a. esena	b. se
	1st.Pl.ACC:	a. emas	b. mas
	2nd.Pl.ACC:	a. esas	b. sas

Within an analysis which treats clitics as affixes the case variation and the similarity of the morphological exponents of person, number, gender and case, with those of the stronger pronouns will be a strange coincidence. On the contrary, these phenomena are natural and the expected ones within our analysis which considers them as syntactically independent pronouns with the full complement of pronominal features including gender and case.

3.3. Phonological evidence

i) Stress: In Greek each grammatical word (in the traditional narrow sense) carries one stress only. Furthermore each stress must occur on one of the last three syllables. This constraint is referred to as the *antepenultimate stress rule* or the *trisyllabic rule*.[8] Derivationally and inflectionally (again in the narrow sense) related words may show differences in the position of the stress as shown in the following examples:

(16) a. vunó   'mountain'
     b. vunaláki
         vuno-DIMINUTIVE   'little mountain'

(17) a. NOM: máθima 'lesson'   b. GEN: maθímatos
     c. γráfo   d. γrafómuna
         write-1st.Sg.Pres.Act.Imperf.   write-1st.Sg.Past.Pass.Imperf.
         'I write'   'I was being written'

We see that to satisfy the trisyllabic rule the stress is moved one syllable to the right. This is the strategy that applies within the unit of grammatical word, i.e. within any member of the morphological paradigm, but not to forms containing clitics. Instead when one or two clitics are attached to a grammatical word (as enclitic) increasing the length of the form and creating units which violate the trisyllabic rule a new stress is added to the second syllable from the end of the new unit, as is the case of imperatives in (18).

(18) a. δjávase
         read-2ndSg.Imper.perf.
         'Read'
     b. δjávasé   to
         read-2ndSg.Imper.perf. it-ACC
         'Read it'

This shows that cliticisation is a different process from inflection proper and that it operates after inflection has been completed. It takes place in a larger domain than a word domain, in the sense of the relevant tests in Zwicky (1985: 288). This phenomenon is naturally handled within a theory that recognises that the effect of clitics on the stress takes place within the syntax after combining clitics with their hosts. On the other hand, a theory which treats clitics as affixes will have to resort to establishing different cycles both of which will have to operate on lexical entries but following different principles. Such an analysis has the weakness that it offers no explanation for these differences.[9]

ii) Euphonic *-e*: In Greek there is a very strong preference for open syllables in word-final position. When a word terminates in final *-n*, there is a tendency for a euphonic *-e* to be added after it in order to obtain a word final open syllable:

(19) a. irθan   → irθane   'they came'
     b. milun   → milune   'they speak'
     c. ton peδjon → ton peδjone 'of the children'

Although not all words ending in *-n* will add a euphonic *-e*, those that do are clearly motivated by this preference for word final open syllable. Affixes on the other hand have no need for such a constraint nor do they show any such tendency. And yet clitic pronouns may appear with such final euphonic *-e*.

(20) a. ton-e   θelume
         he-ACC   want-1stPl
         'We want him'
     b. δen tin-e   fovate
         not she-ACC   afraid-3rdSg
         'He is not afraid of her

This again shows that clitics are perceived as independent words in spite of their attachment on to the host in other respects.

3.4. The analysis of object clitic structures in Greek

The evidence presented above, derived from all levels of description, argues strongly that the object clitic pronouns in Greek are not affixes on the verb but constitute separate syntactic units (syntactic atoms). Pronominal clitics in Greek have the syntactic and morphological properties of grammatical words stored in the lexicon or derived in the morphological component before they enter syntax. However, they are phonologically reduced and this creates the need for them to move and adjoin to an appropriate host, this being the INFL head, creating an INFL^{0max} (see Kayne 1991 and Chomsky 1995).

4. PARTICLES

4.1. Their forms and their functions

In addition to clitic pronouns a verb may be preceded by one of the two negative morphemes and one of the two mood/tense particles. These are: *θa* whose prototypical use is to express futurity; *na* which marks the subjunctive mood; the negative particle for the indicative is *δe(n)*, while for the subjunctive it is *mi(n)*. The possible combinations are shown below:

(21) a. δen to   eγrapsa
        not it-ACC   wrote-1stSg
        'I did not write it'
   b. δen θa   to   γrapso
        not will it-ACC write-1stSg
        'I will not write it'
   c. δen θa   to   ixa   γrapsi
        not will   it-ACC have-1stSg written
        'I would not have written'
   d. na   min to   γrapsis
        SUBJ not it-ACC write-2ndSg
        'You should not write it'
   e. na   min to   ixes   γrapsi
        SUBJ not it-ACC had-2ndSg written
        'You should not have written it'

The analysis which will be assumed here is the following (Philippaki-Warburton 1994b, 1996): *na* is a subjunctive mood marker generated under a Mood (MD) functional category.[11] The particles *δen* and *min* are generated under a NEG functional category. We note that Rivero & Terzi (1995), and Drachman (1994), analyse *θa* as part of the Mood projection, as an alternative to *na*, and place it before negation, giving the order in (22):

(22)   MD   NEG ....
        θa   δen
        na   min

However, this analysis requires an additional rule to invert *θa* and *δen* in order to obtain the actual surface order with *δen* preceding *θa* as in (21b, c). We find the analysis in (22) counterintuitive because the rule of the subsequent reversal seems unmotivated and formally peculiar. We suggest instead that the difference between the position of *δen* before *θa*, on the one hand, but *min* after *na*, on the other, indicates differences in the mood status of *θa*, which, according to our analysis, is prototypically a future tense exponent within the indicative[11] while *na* is clearly a subjunctive mood exponent. So we propose, following Philippaki-Warburton (1996), that *θa* is generated under a different functional category (let us call it FT for Futurity) as in (23):

(23)   MD   NEG   FT
    a. Ind.   [0] δen   θa to γrapsis
    b. Sub.   [na] min   to γrapsis

The two maximal combinations forming the two alternative groupings are represented in (24):

(24)   MD   NEG   FT   INFL *exo* VOICE ASPECT V
    a. Ind.   [0] [δen]   [θa] io.cl do.cl
    b. Sub.   [na] [min]   --- io.cl do.cl

Irrespective of the specific details of the analysis of these particles we must now come to the question relevant to the issue of the interface between syntax and morphology, namely whether these particles should be analysed as affixes of the verb or as independent and separate syntactic elements (syntactic atoms). Zwicky (1985) argues that particles do not form a recognisable class of items but are reducible to either full words or affixes. However Greek particles (and object clitics) provide evidence against this view. We will show that these particles have an intermediate status, like clitic pronouns, although the particles differ from clitics in the following respects: a) particles carry functional content whereas clitics have referential properties, b) particles are hosted under functional heads, whereas clitics are lexical and c) particles do not move whereas clitics move from their original position on to a host.

4.2. The intermediate status of particles

4.2.1. Particles as affixes

One argument that particles are affixes is based on the fact that these elements appear morphophonologically attached on to the verb so that the combination [particle+ verb] constitutes a single phonological unit in that there is only one stress on such a string, as shown by the brackets in (25) below:

(25) a. o nikos   [θa féri]   ta lefta   avrio
         [the Nick]-NOM will bring-3rdSg [the money]-ACC   tomorrow
         'Nick will bring the money tomorrow'
     b. θelo   [na min γrápsis]   to γrama
         want-1stSg SUBJ not write-2ndSg   [the letter]-ACC
         'I do not want you to write the letter'

Furthermore, the morphophonological phenomena which apply across the boundaries of particles and their host match more closely those that operate within single grammatical words. This affix view is further strengthened by the fact that the unity of these strings is not only phonological but also syntactic, as shown by the following observations:

a) The particles represent grammatical (functional) elements which modify the head, in the same way that affixal functional categories do.

b) There are syntactic phenomena which apply to such strings (i.e. particle+verb or particle+clitic+verb) treating them as single syntactic units, larger than the grammatical word, in the narrow sense of this term, but smaller than the phrase.

(i) Nothing can intervene between the particles and the verb form (with the exception of pronominal clitics).

(ii) The focalisation of the verb involves movement (either overt or covert)[12] of the whole verb group to the head Fc of a Focus Phrase (FcP) leaving the object DP behind, as seen in (26).

(26) a.   o nikos   [θa δosi]   ta lefta
           [the Nick]-NOM   will give-3rdSg   the money-ACC
           'Nick will give the money
     b.   *θa δosi* o nikos ta lefta
     c. * θa o Nikos δosi ta lefta
     d.   o nikos   [δe θa δosi]   ta lefta
           [the Nick]-NOM   not will give-3rdSg [the money]-ACC
           'Nick will not give the money'
     e.   *δe θa δosi* o Nikos ta lefta
     f. * *δosi* o Nikos ta lefta δe θa

It is obvious that what is focalised/moved is the whole string [particle+verb], and not the verb alone; if focalisation is a syntactic operation then it can be concluded that the string[particle+verb] forms a syntactic unit. [13]

(iii) The syntactic unity of [particle+verb] is also supported if we apply the test of sentence fragments (Radford 1988). Consider the following:

(27) a. ti   su   ipe   [na   min   kanis]?
         what-ACC   you-GEN   said-3rdSg SUBJ   not   do-2ndSg
         'What did he tell you not to do?'
     b.   [na   min fiγo]
           SUBJ   not go-1stSg
          'Not to leave'
     c.* fiγo
           go-1stSg

In (27) we see that when a question concerns the verb, the answer cannot consist simply of the filler for the verb *kano* 'do' (*27c), but has to contain also the appropriate particles (27b) and this leads us to consider this grouping as a single syntactic word.[14]

iii) Similar results are obtained by the test of co-ordination:

(28) a. * θa erθo   avrio   ke fiγo   meθavrio
        will come-1stSg tomorrow   and leave-1stSg the day after tomorrow
     b. θa erθo   avrio   ke θa fiγo   meθavrio
        will come-1stSg tomorrow and will leave-1stSg the day after tomorrow
        'I will come tomorrow and leave the day after tomorrow'

Such evidence shows that the string [particle+verb] is a syntactic unit and that the verb, when it is modified by particles, is not syntactically independent enough to be able to enter into a co-ordination.[15]

We conclude that the evidence presented above shows that the combination of particles plus verb forms a single unit both for phonological but also for syntactic reasons and this could be said to strengthen the proposal that particles are affixes. If all affixation, including the attachment of particles on to their host, is to be treated in the Lexicon/Morphology before entering syntax, the evidence presented above would lead to the conclusion that the verb groupings such as *δen θa γrafo, na min γrapsi*, etc. should be represented as single lexical entries (syntactic atoms), members of the verb paradigm (morphological objects). However in spite of the strong arguments in its favour this conclusion must be rejected because there is strong evidence against the affixal view, as we will argue below.

4.2.2. Particles as independent syntactic elements

i) Firstly, if we accept all the arguments offered earlier that auxiliary *exo* is a separate lexical entry from that of main verb, we must also reject the view that particles are affixes, because their treatment as affixes will entail that they should appear as affixes both on the monolectic verb forms but also on the forms of the auxiliary *exo*, as in (29). This duplication is rather redundant and, although this argument on its own may not be too damaging to the affixal view, in combination with all the other arguments adduced here, adds support to our analysis.

(29) a.   [θa fiγo]
          will leave-1stSg
          'I will leave'
     b.   [na fiγo]
          SUBJ leave-1stSg
          '... that I leave'
     c.   [θa exo]   fiγi
          will have-1stSg   left
          'I will have left'

    d.   [na exo]   fiɣi
        SUBJ have-1stSg left
        '... that I have left'

ii) More seriously if we accept the evidence that object clitics are separate syntactic units and thus independent lexical entries, we must reject the view that particles are affixes, because an analysis that treats clitics as separate lexical entries and particles as affixes will involve particles prefixed on to clitics, as in (30) below:

(30) a.   [θa to]   γrapso
          will it-ACC   write-1stSg
          'I will write it'
     b. [θa tu]   γrapso
          will he-GEN write-1stSg
          'I will write to him'
     c. [θa tu   to]   exo   γrapsi
          will he-GEN it-ACC have-1stSg written
          'I will have written it to him'

This creates a great deal of redundancy and moreover it fails to capture the obvious generalisation that the particle belongs to the verb itself and not to the auxiliary and much less to the object clitic pronoun.

    iii) If particles are to be treated as affixes we must also treat as affixes the negative particles *δen* and especially *min*, because the particle *na* precedes negative *min*. Thus if *na* is an affix either *min* is also an affix or we end up with the same situation as with *exo* and the clitics discussed above.

    From the above discussion we conclude that particles have also an independent syntactic status, and, therefore, must be considered separate independent entries for the Lexicon and the syntactic Numeration and Derivation. Additional support for this conclusion derives from the fact that particles can be nominalised by the use of the definite article, e.g. *ta θa ke ta min* 'The wills and the nos'.

4.2.3. The paradox of the intermediate status of particles

We can now draw the conclusion that particles are separate independent syntactic items (that is *grammatical words* or *syntactic atoms*), which enter the syntax as independent syntactic elements and not as affixes, but somehow they end up united with the verb form with which they are closely related. Thus, the string [particle+ verb], though not a unit in the Lexicon and in the morphological paradigm, becomes a unit in the syntactic component. The challenge is to find a formal account of this phenomenon.

5. A FORMAL ACCOUNT OF THE INTERMEDIATE STATUS OF CLITICS AND PARTICLES

We argued above that the whole of the verb group consists of a lexical entry for the grammatical word of the verb plus a number of reduced grammatical elements which also constitute separate entries at the Morphology/Syntax interface. This conclusion, however, leaves unaccounted for the evidence that these verb groupings behave as single units for the purposes of some phonological but also syntactic phenomena. For the phonological phenomena the problem is not serious, because it may be argued that these operate in terms of the phonological word which is formed after the syntax at PF. But the phenomenon of verb focus, for example, which has been strongly argued to be a syntactic rule, seems to apply to the unit formed either by the verb alone, if no other modification is present, or by any combination of [particle +clitic+verb] or [particle+clitic+auxiliary[16]/verb]. This raises the question of how our theory can capture the fact that these elements form a single syntactic unit for the purposes of some syntactic phenomena.

The solution, which we believe will satisfy both types of properties of these elements is one which formally recognises two different types of word (see also Di Sciullo and Williams 1987). *Primary words*, or *grammatical words* (the *morphological objects* or *syntactic atoms* in Di Sciullo and Williams' terms), are those which enter the syntax as separate entries. These are the units of the Morphology/Syntax interface and the units that enter the syntactic component through the operation of Numeration. These include the inflectionally complete members of the narrowly defined verb paradigm, as well as those words which are either monomorphemic (particles, clitics), or derivationally derived. Another type of word, which we may call *secondary* or *syntactic word* is formed subsequently after the interface. This unit consists of such reduced lexical elements as particles and clitics in combination with the grammatical word that constitutes the head of the construction. The syntactic word is, furthermore, the unit which is the input to both PF and LF, i.e. the unit at Spell-Out. The questions that are raised now are the following:

    i)   How do particles combine into a single syntactic word with the verb?
    ii) Where precisely does this union take place?

Some theoretical details are in order here: In the MP functional/grammatical information is projected on the syntactic structure by means of functional heads. These heads consist of certain grammatical features to be satisfied either by verb-movement (*operation attract/move*) or by merging a functional word (*operation merge*), mostly a particle (Chomsky 1995). In Greek, Voice, Aspect, INFL and MD (when imperative) are satisfied by means of verb-movement; their morphophonological exponents are affixed on to the verb stem (verb head) in the Lexicon/ Morphology component before syntax. This is what we refer to as grammatical word. In the syntactic derivation the V^0 is attracted by these functional heads and moves to adjoin to them in order to check out their features. Thus, head movement of the V^0 to a functional head F^0 results in left adjunction of the former to the latter creating a complex head which is labelled as F^{0max}, since the head of the projection is still the relevant functional category F.[17] On the other hand, NEG, FT and MD (subjunctive) are satisfied by means of merging a particle (the negative *δen* and *min*, the future *θa*, and the subjunctive *na*). No verb movement is required, and actually it is banned as unmotivated (Last Resort). The theory thus predicts that there is no motivation for the syntactic unity of the verbal group.

However, we presented evidence showing clearly that the verbal group constitutes a syntactic unit for some syntactic operations (focalisation, sentence fragments, co-ordination). In order to solve this problem we propose a merging operation,[18] which unites all these elements in the syntactic component. According to the strict syntactic theoretical frameworks, such as the MP, the only syntactic operation is Move α. We therefore suggest that the merging operation required for the Greek particles is in fact an instance of Move α and more specifically of head movement. It is similar to the so called Incorporation (Baker 1988), which also unites two independent syntactic units in one (for example the N object with the V head). We call this merging operation Move-Incorporate. Furthermore, we observe that cliticisation and incorporation are syntactic operations in the sense that they i) respect certain syntactic economy constraints on movement (for cliticisation see Kayne 1989, 1991; for incorporation see Baker 1988) and ii) they apply on full grammatical words which enter the syntax as independent items.

It may be argued that our analysis is facing a theoretical problem. According to the restricted theory of the MP, movement is motivated by the economy principle of *Last Resort* and it is thus restricted to take place only in order to satisfy certain functional features on morphologically empty functional heads. Our rule *Move- Incorporate*, however, involves full lexical items and not simply features on lexical heads and this may be undesirable. To overcome this problem we suggest that the reason that particles become morphophonologically dependent on the verb is the fact that they are elements which modify the verb grammatically. This means that particles require the support of a verb head and in that sense they are very similar to affixes. This grammatical affinity can be formally captured by assuming that the particles carry the functional feature [+V] which needs to be satisfied in the syntactic component, in the same way as an empty functional head expressing a bound morpheme must satisfy its feature content. Thus, particles are grammatical words that do not carry a categorial feature but a functional one, like any empty functional head. Given these assumptions we propose that the derivation proceeds as follows:

All the functional information coming from the Lexicon is satisfied either by moving the verb all the way up to the functional heads attracted by their abstract features, or by inserting a particle under the relevant functional head. If the derivation contains a clitic, at some point of the derivation, the clitic will move to the INFL-V head. It will adjoin at this point and will thus create an $INFL^{0max}$. On the other hand, if a structure contains particles they will be marked by the functional feature [+V]. Thus a verb group structure will be as in (31):

(31)	MD^0	Neg^0	FT^0	$INFL^{0max}$
	+V	+V	+V	+V
	na	min		to γrapso
		δen	θa	to γrapso

A merging operation will now apply moving the unit containing the grammatical word for the verb (the head word) to the next F^0 category until one single word unit is created. Thus $INFL^{0max}$ will be attracted by *θa* and it will move to incorporate to it creating the node FT^{0max} (*θa-to-γrapso*). Then the negative particle *den* will attract the FT^{0max}, which will move to incorporate to the NEG^0 creating a NEG^{0max} consisting of the NEG^0 plus FT^{0max} (*δen-θa-to-γrapso*) and so on.

We have presented the merging operation *Move-Incorporate*, which acts in a syntactic way, subsumed in fact under the *Operation Move*. However we must now clarify the differences between Move-Incorporate, relevant to the merging of independently existing lexical items, and the standard Move α, which operates in order to check functional information represented as features on the heads of affixal functional categories. The differences are as follows:

(i)   The features which motivate the Move-Incorporate are associated with independently existing lexical items and not with morphologically empty functional nodes.

(ii)   Move-Incorporate is relevant to X^{0max} and not to X^0, i.e. it moves only the full maximum zero projection and not only a part of it.

(iii)   Move-Incorporate results in right adjunction with the host grammatical word, whereas Move results in left adjunction.[19]

(iv)   The motivation for Move-Incorporate is not to eliminate the functional features of an empty head, but to eliminate the functional feature [+V] of a particle which formally captures its grammatical affinity to a verb head.

6. CONCLUSION

In the present study we investigated the morphological and syntactic properties of the Greek verb group. The fact that this group behaves as a single syntactic unit in certain syntactic operations raises a number of theoretical questions regarding the notion word because of the evidence which indicates that these elements (clitics and particles) also exhibit properties of independent words. To reconcile the two types of evidence we were led to propose that the theory should recognise two types of words operating within syntax. On the one hand, we have the unit *grammatical word*, as the lexical unit, created by certain morphological processes before syntax. This unit consists of a stem and a number of affixal formatives carrying grammatical 'functional' information and it is the unit that enters the syntactic component by Select and Numeration. In addition we propose that there is a unit *syntactic word*, which is formed by a merging operation in the syntactic component. This unit consists of a main lexical head (a grammatical word) plus a number of reduced elements such as clitics and particles. The reduced character of these elements forces them to merge before PF with the element they modify grammatically. Thus, our analysis provides more support to the Di Sciullo & Williams' (1987) distinction between *syntactic atom* and *syntactic word*. However, we propose a very different way of capturing the formation of this syntactic word. We might add that a third type of word, namely the *phonological word* will also need to be recognised in order to account for both types of phonological units those that are syntactically motivated but also those phonologically single units whose constituent elements do not have syntactic relation and are not relevant to syntactic phenomena (simple clitics in Zwicky's terms such as clitics in Ancient Greek, the possessive in English, etc.).

In our theory which draws a distinction between grammatical and syntactic word the debate among various analyses revolving around the lexical vs. affixal character of clitics and particles is resolved. The phonological, morphological and syntactic facts which point to the lexical independence of these items are satisfied by their original lexical status. On the other hand, their morphophonological dependence on their host is satisfied by the cliticisation and incorporation rules which are triggered by a) their functional role to grammatically modify their host and b) the fact that they are morphophonologically reduced. Thus the paradox of their conflicting properties is resolved and explained.

NOTES

*   This is a revised version of a paper presented at the First Mediterranean Conference of Morphology (Lesvos 1997). We would like to thank the organisers of that conference and the participants for their comments on our work. We also thank two anonymous reviewers for their stimulating and constructive comments. Vassilios Spyropoulos also thanks the State Scholarship Foundation of the Hellenic Republic for the financial support of his studies.

1   Di Sciullo and Williams (1987) suggest a distinction between i) the *morphological atom*, i.e. any word complete in terms of morphology (inflection and derivation), ii) the *syntactic atom*, i.e. any word, or better unit, that can be inserted under an X0, and thus can function as a head in syntax, and iii) the *syntactic word*, i.e. a unit of two or more syntactic atoms. This unit has the characteristics of an X0, but its components are also accessible to syntactic rules, that is to say they are syntactic atoms. In this paper we expand the notion of syntactic word to cover cases in which two heads form a syntactic unit (word), and thus we provide more evidence for the suggested distinction.

2   In the analyses of the Aux-V construction of other languages (e.g. Kayne 1993) the verb form that follows the auxiliary is called participle. In the case of Greek, however, this term is not satisfactory since there are distinct verb forms which have the status of a participle. Thus this verb form is referred to simply as *non-finite* (Holton, Mackridge and Philippaki-Warburton 1997).

3   See the discussion on the *Mirror Principle* (Baker 1985, 1988) and its relevance for the postulation and ordering of the functional categories involved in the syntactic structure of the clause (Speas 1991 and Thrainsson 1996). This does not mean, however, that we advocate a syntactic analysis of the inflection as proposed by the standard theory of Principles and Parameters (Pollock 1989). On the contrary, we agree with many studies pointing out the inadequacy of an Item and Arrangement model to account for the complex morphological processes of inflection (Matthews 1972; Anderson 1992; Sells 1995, and for Greek Joseph and Smirniotopoulos 1993; Ralli 1998). However, the necessity for including the functional categories in syntax is justified on the grounds that they contribute significantly to a better description of syntactic phenomena such as the requirement of flexibility in the order and the need for more positions to be present in the syntactic representation, (see Webelhuth 1995; Kayne 1994), differences in the ordering possibilities of the verb with other elements in the clause (Pollock 1989), the licensing of certain adverbials, etc.

4   It has been pointed out to us by a reviewer that the separability of the auxiliary exo may be accounted for in terms of a process of *excorporation*. According to this view the periphrasis *exo γrapsi* enters the syntactic component as a single lexical item. Subsequently, one part of this, namely *exo*, moves separately to some other position creating the discontinuity we observe in (6-7). However we feel that the rule of excorporation as it has been formulated by Roberts (1991), as an operation by which a head (lexical) which has been adjoined to another head, (lexical or functional) moves out attracted by a higher functional head for checking reasons, leaving the first incorporating head behind, is not relevant to these constructions. We cannot see how our case can fit to this formulation of excorporation. But even if we broaden the definition of excorporation to fit these cases it is difficult to see how we can formulate the excorporation rule to effect the single lexical item V (its internal structure would be $[_V V_{aux}\text{-}V_{non\text{-}finite}]$) by attracting only the V_{aux} part since, the closer element to attract is the whole verb complex (the larger V element). Moreover such an operation will violate one of the main tenets of syntactic theory since Chomsky (1970) and Jackendoff (1972), that syntactic rules cannot effect the internal structure of lexical items. These theoretical objections are reinforced by the observation that each of the two verbal forms, V_{aux} and $V_{non\text{-}finite}$ carry different morphosyntactic marking. If these morphosyntactic features are related to certain functional categories in the clause structure, then it is difficult to see how the V_{aux} section of a single verb unit $[_V V_{aux}\text{-}V_{non\text{-}finite}]$ will skip some of these functional categories, leaving them behind to be checked by Vnon-finite. Such a separate movement of the Vaux part would constitute violation of the Head Movement Constraint (Travis 1984).

5   Anticipating the discussion about the lexical versus affixal status of the Greek pronominal clitics, we note here that clitic clusters in Greek are more straightforward combinations of independent elements than the corresponding Romance. In Greek too there are some restrictions on the possible combinations of clitics, but these are fairly simple and they can be easily captured by means of postsyntactic morphological filters (Warburton 1977). On the other hand, in Greek unlike Romance, there are no other special irregularities in the morphophonology of the clitics. For these reasons we feel that the existence of these limited restrictions does not constitute evidence for their affixal status (see also Bonet 1991 for a similar conclusion for Greek; she also provides a postsyntactic morphological analysis of the complex restrictions and irregularities that apply to the Romance clitic clusters by advocating a movement analysis of clitics).

6   These arguments include: i) the doubled DP has no stable position, ii) multiple clitic-doubled DPs can occupy a position even out of the domain of their clause, iii) there are instances of chain violation constructions where the DP corresponding to the clitic appears in the nominative while the clitic is in the accusative, etc.

7   We must note however that, although the constructions in (10a) are the normal and most frequent ones, while (10b) are ungrammatical, the latter may become more acceptable if the sentence is extended with, for example, some adverbial as in (i).

(i)   a. ? pjo vivlio   to   aγorases   xθes?
         [which book]-ACC it-ACC bought-2ndSg yesterday
         'Which one was the book that you bought yesterday?'
      b.   pjo vivlio$_i$ to$_i$ aγorases t$_i$ xθes

Such evidence may seem to undermine our analysis and to support the analysis which treats the clitic as an affix and the gap in object position as a *pro*. However, this evidence is rather weak because constructions as those in (i) are the more marked ones and the more rare ones and more significantly because the wh-constituent in such constructions is not straightforwardly questioned but has a topic reading. Thus (ia) means: 'of the various books you are holding (or I see on your desk) about which one is it the case that you bought it yesterday'. It is possible, therefore, to argue that the structure of (ia) is (ib), where the wh-DP is a left dislocated element, analogous to:

(ii)   to jani   ton   iδa   xθes
          [the John]-ACC he-ACC   saw-1stSg yesterday
          'As for John, I saw him yesterday'

where the dislocated DP requires coindexation with the element [clitic ...t]. For more on this issue see Anagnostopoulou (1994), Androulakis (1998), Theofanopoulou- Kontou (1986-7).

8   See Warburton (1971), Joseph and Philippaki-Warburton (1987), Holton, Mackridge and Philippaki-Warburton (1997).

9   For rules capturing these stress phenomena see an early differentiation between grammatical vs. phonological word in Warburton (1971) and in Nespor and Vogel (1986) among others.

10   Cf. its analysis as a complementiser as suggested by Agouraki (1991) and Tsoulas (1994).

11   The reason for considering θa a particle within the indicative is the fact that it co-occurs with the negative marker δen which is specific to indicative. The position of the negative before rather than after it constitutes a further evidence that we do not have a mood of the same type as the deontic one. However, it must be pointed out that θa, as the exponent of the future tense, refers to a reality which is not a true fact at the time of the utterance. The verifiability of the truth of a future clause is projected to a future time. This means that the truth conditional semantics of clauses with future tense are not as direct and this allows clauses with θa to also express a number of modalities such as possibility, probability, the irrealis etc. All these modalities, however, fall outside the [+/-deontic] oppostion which characterises the subjunctive/non-subjunctive major division. The particle θa in its less prototypical use falls with the epistemic subvariety of the [-deontic]

mood, i.e. the epistemic subvariety of the indicative. This is true for the future indicative in other languages too, including Ancient Greek.

12   See Brody (1990).

13   An anonymous reviewer has pointed out that focalisation may be considered a PF phenomenon and that therefore this evidence may simply support an analysis where the groupings of [particle+verb] are phonological rather than syntactic words. Against this alternative view we would like to point out the evidence available that focalisation, though closely associated with PF, is indeed a syntactic operation which involves movement either in overt or in covert syntax. The fact that focalisation applies to either full phrases or to heads and that these two syntactic units do not form a natural class is not a strong argument for a PF interpretation of focalisation especially since wh-movement also applies to phrases or heads and yet it is clearly a syntactic phenomenon. It has been pointed out in fact (Tsimpli 1998) that focalisation and wh-movement pattern in very similar ways in that they belong to syntactic operations which involve operator movement either in overt or covert syntax. This is shown by the fact that focalisation creates weak crossover effects and it also interacts with other operators. Moreover focalisation respects the bounding conditions on movement (see Tsimpli 1995). All this points to the conclusion that focalisation is a syntactic operation which moves the focalised element to a Focus functional category and which can apply either to phrases moving them to the [Spec, FP] or to heads moving them to the [F0, F']. It is natural therefore to assume that this rule 'sees' elements which are syntactic units. This evidence supports our analysis that the combination [particle+verb] forms a single word (it is clearly not a phrase) irrespective of the fact that this unit also receives the focal stress marking at PF.

14   It has been brought to our attention by one of the reviewers that this sort of deletion may also be considered a PF phenomenon where an answer to a preceding question is a full sentence underlyingly which then gets reduced in the PF to the focused phonological word. According to this interpretation our data simply show that [particle+verb] form a phonological but not necessarily a syntactic word. Our answer to this is as follows. In Greek the combinations which form the phonological words follow the syntactic constituency, i.e. only syntactic units, as far as we know, can become phonological words and thus this test will not decide on the issue at hand. The evidence from other languages (e.g. English) is also not conclusive. Thus, on the one hand, it is not possible to have a sentence fragment consisting of a subject followed by an encliticised form of the auxiliaries *be* and *have*, as shown in the following examples:

(i)   Question: Who's speaking to Mary?
          Answer in full sentence: John is speaking to Mary
          PF cliticisation: John's speaking to Mary
          Answer in terms of phonological word: * John's
          Answer in terms of syntactic word: John

On the other hand, it is possible to have a sentence fragment consisting of a verb such as *want* combined with the infinitive particle *to*:

(ii) a.   I want to leave early
      b.   I wanna leave early

  c.   I wanna

It would seem therefore that this phenomenon is much more complex and needs further investigation.

15   It must be noted that one of the reviewers offers an alternative PF analysis of this type of constructions (ia) which involves the claim that their underlying syntactic representation may be analogous to (ib):

  (i) a.   θa   foviθi   ke θa   milisi
            will be afraid-3rdSg and will speak-3rdSg
            'He will be afraid and he will speak'
       b.   θa [foviθi ke milisi]

Later, the argument goes, at PF the particle *θa* must cliticise on to the nearest verb and given that there are two such verbs the particle distributes to both of them. Thus the co-ordination construction in (ia) is the result of such a PF phenomenon. It seems to us that the PF solution is more complicated than the one we offer and in addition there is strong empirical evidence against it. Our objections are based on the following facts. Consider the construction in (ii) which contains not only particle *θa* but also the negative particle *δen*.

  (ii)   δe θa foviθi   ke   δe θa   milisi
            not will be afraid-3rdSg and not will   speak-3rdSg
            'He will not be afraid and he will not speak'

This example can also be successfully analysed in terms of an underlying representation where both particles *δen θa* modify the co-ordinate construction as shown in (iii):

  (iii)   δe θa [foviθi kai milisi]

with subsequent duplication of both the negative *δen* and the future *θa* at PF as suggested by the reviewer. However consider now the expression in (iv):

  (iv)   δe θa foviθi   ke θa milisi
            not will be afraid-3rdSg and will speak-3rdSg
            'He will not be afraid and he will speak'

which has a different meaning in that the negation modifies only the first verb while *θa* modifies both of them. In this example if we are to follow the PF duplication analysis we will have to extract particle *θa* which will then at FP distribute to both the verb forms. But if *θa* is to be represented as modifying the co-ordination [*foviθi ke milisi*], since *δen* precedes *θa*, we must also place *δen* before *θa* as in (v):

  (v)   δen θa [foviθi ke milisi]

and the PF distribution rule will then automatically distribute both the δ*en* and the θ*a* on both verbs resulting in the wrong meaning:

(vi)   δe θa foviθi   ke δe θa milisi
        not will be afraid-3rdSg and not will speak-3rdSg
        'He will not be afraid and he will not speak'

Thus the PF solution of the co-ordination facts runs into problems because there are more than one particles in a sequence and because the two verbs of the co-ordination may be differently modified by these particles.

16   The auxiliary being of the category verb behaves exactly as the main verb does when there is no auxiliary present. To put it in another way the particles and the clitics attach onto the auxiliary when present to form one syntactic word with it.

17   At this point it would be useful to clarify the difference between the terms X^0 and X^{0max}. According to the recent claims of the theory of phrase structure (Chomsky 1995) the minimal projection of a category is the head of its phrase. This head is termed X^0. When another head Y^0 being attracted by X^0 comes to adjoin to it the result will be a complex head which carries the same label as the X. This complex head is a new object, a new projection of the original X^0 and if no other head comes to adjoin it will be the maximum projection X^{0max} of the zero level. Such a formulation is reminiscent of the proposals put forward by many morphologists (e.g. Selkirk 1982; Lieber 1992; Di Sciullo 1997) that there is internal structure below word level (the zero level) in terms of X-bar Theory (different bar levels). However we do not want to relate these two claims at this point; the distinction between X^0 and X^{0max} is in fact a different formulation for the traditional head adjunction, it has been invented in order to distinguish the two syntactic objects (a single head and a complex head), and it does not refer to the internal structure of the words (note also that the MP advocates a Strict Lexicalist approach by which the internal structure of word is not visible to the syntactic component). According to the traditional formulation of adjunction when a category Y was adjoined to another category X the result was again a category X, i.e. adjunction did not result in a different level projection. In the minimalist program adjunction creates a different syntactic object which constitutes a different projection but at the same level, and therefore the terminological distinction between X^0 and X^{0max} facilitates the theoretical distinction between single and complex heads.

18   Marantz (1988) also proposes a merging operation by means of rebracketing. He assumes that this merging operation is in fact an instance of affixation, which requires strict adjacency and which can apply at any level of the derivation (morphology, syntax, phonology). His proposal can apply to our case as well. Thus, we can assume that what unites all these elements is a merging operation of the type of affixation which operates in the syntax (syntactic affixation). We have no principled objection to this alternative. However, if we are willing to stick to the main claims of the MP for strict modularity, then it is difficult to see how to include an operation of affixation in the syntactic component. Our analysis is an attempt to offer a syntactic formulation of such a merging operation. Another merging operation has been proposed by Di Sciullo and Williams (1987), which cannot apply to the cases we examine here. They deal mostly with syntactic words deriving from the union of phrases, like the Romance compounds, i.e. phrases which behave as single units in the syntactic component. Their proposal is a renaming of the XP

constituent as X^0. However, our cases concern the unity of two (or more) heads creating another head and for this situation we need a different kind of operation.

[19] There may appear to be problem with this formulation, since the normal position for an adjunction is to the left (both Move α and Incorporation results in left adjunction). We have no definite explanation for this fact but we can make the following suggestions: i) Given the fact that this rule is a merging operation and not a clear instance of Move α (stereotypical syntactic operation) we may assume that it is not able to affect the linear order provided by the syntactic structure (as in the case of the merging operation proposed by Marantz 1988). ii) If Williams' assumptions for the *Righthand Head Rule* (Williams 1981) applies to the formation of syntactic words as well, the right adjunction of the verb seems to be motivated by the need for the resulting word (particle+verb) to be also of the category verb. I.e. the verb form being adjoined to the right is the right hand constituent of the syntactic word and thus it is the head of the construction so that the whole syntactic word is now of the category of verb.

REFERENCES

Agouraki, Georgia. 1991. "A Modern Greek Complementiser and its Significance for Universal Grammar". *UCL Working Papers in Linguistics* 3, 1-24.

Anagnostopoulou, Elena. 1994. *Clitic Dependencies in Modern Greek*. Ph.D. dissertation, University of Salzburg.

Anderson, Stephen. 1992. *A-morphous Morphology*. Cambridge: Cambridge University Press.

Anderson, Stephen. 1993. "Wackernagel's Revenge: Clitics, Morphology and the Syntax of Verb-Second Position". *Language* 69, 68-98.

Androulakis, Anna. 1998. "Wh- and Direct Object Clitics Revisited". In Joseph, Horrocks and Philippaki-Warburton (eds), 131-167.

Aoun, Joseph. 1985. *A grammar of Anaphora*. Cambridge Mass.: MIT Press.

Baker, Mark. 1985. "The Mirror Principle and Morphosyntactic Explanation". *Linguistic Inquiry* 16, 373-415.

Baker, Mark. 1988. *Incorporation: A Theory of Grammatical Function Changing*. Chicago: University of Chicago Press.

Beard, Robert. 1995. *Lexeme-Morpheme Base Morphology*. New York: State University of New York Press.

Bonet, Eulalia. 1991: "Morphology after Syntax: Pronominal Clitics in Romance". Ph.D. Dissertation, MIT.

Borer, Hagit. 1984. *Parametric syntax. Case studies in Semitic and Romance Languages*. Dordrecht: Foris.

Bresnan, Joan and Sam A. Mchombo. 1987. "Topic, Pronoun, and Agreement in Chichewa". *Language* 63, 741-82.

Brody, Michael. 1990. "Some Remarks on the Focus Field in Hungarian". *UCL Working Papers in Linguistics* 2, 201-26.

Bybee, Joan L. 1985. *Morphology: a Study of the Relation between Meaning and Form*. Amsterdam: J. Benjamins.

Bybee, Joan L., Revere Perkins and William Pagliuca. 1994. *The Evolution of Grammar: Tense, Aspect and Modality in the Languages of the World*. Chicago: The University of Chicago Press.

Bynon, Theodore. 1992. Pronominal Attrition, Clitic Doubling and Typological Change. *Folia Linguistica Historica* 13, 27-63.

Chomsky, Noam. 1957. *Syntactic Structures*. The Hague: Mouton.

Chomsky, Noam. 1970. "Remarks on Nominalization". In R. Jacobs and P. Rosenbaum (eds), *Readings in English Transformational Grammar*. Waltham, MA: Blaisdell, 184-221.

Chomsky, Noam. 1981. *Lectures on Government and Binding*. Dordrecht: Foris.

Chomsky, Noam. 1986. *Barriers*. Cambridge Mass.: MIT Press

Chomsky, Noam. 1993. "A Minimalist Program for Linguistic Theory". In K. Hale and S. J. Keyser (eds), *The view from Building 20*. Cambridge Mass.: MIT Press, 1-52.

Chomsky, Noam. 1995. *The Minimalist Program*. Cambridge Mass.: MIT Press.

Di Sciullo, Anna Maria. 1997. "On Word-structure and Conditions". In A. M. Di Sciullo (ed.), *Projections and Interface Conditions: Essays on Modularity*. Oxford: Oxford University Press, 3-27.

Di Sciullo, Anna Maria and Edwin Williams. 1987. *On the Definition of Word*. Cambridge Mass.: MIT Press.

Dobrovie-Sorin, Carmen. 1990. "Clitic-doubling, Wh-movement and Quantification in Romanian". *Linguistic Inquiry* 21, 351-97.

Drachman, Gaberel. 1994. "Verb Movement and Minimal Clauses". In Philippaki-Warburton, Nikolaidis and Sifianou (eds).

Halpern, Aaron L. 1998. "Clitics". In A. Spencer and A. M. Zwicky (eds), *The Handbook of Morphology*. Oxford: Blackwell, 101-122.

Holton, David, Peter Mackridge and Irene Philippaki-Warburton. 1997. *Greek: a Comprehensive grammar of the modern language*. London: Routledge.

Jackendoff, Ray S. 1972. *Semantic Interpretation in Generative Grammar*. Cambridge Mass.: MIT Press.

Jaeggli, Osvaldo. 1982. *Topics in Romance Syntax*. Dordrecht: Foris.

Jaeggli, Osvaldo. 1986. "Three Issues in the Theory of Clitics: Case, Doubled NPs and Extraction". In H. Borer (ed), *The Syntax of Pronominal Clitics. Syntax and Semantics 19*. New York: Academic Press, 15-42.

Joseph, Brian. 1988. "Pronominal Affixes in Modern Greek: the Case against Clisis". *CLS* 24, 203-15.

Joseph, Brian, Geoffrey Horrocks, and Irene Philippaki-Warburton. 1998. *Themes in Greek Linguistics II*. Amsterdam: J. Benjamins

Joseph, Brian and Irene Philippaki-Warburton. 1987. *Modern Greek*. London: Routledge.

Joseph, Brian and Jane C. Smirniotopoulos. 1993. "The Morphosyntax of the Modern Greek Verb as Morphology and not Syntax". *Linguistic Inquiry* 24, 388-98.

Kayne, Richard. 1975. *French syntax*. Cambridge Mass.: MIT Press.

Kayne, Richard. 1989. "Null Subjects and Clitic Climbing". In O. Jaeggli and K. Safir (eds), *The Null Subject Parameter*. Dordrecht: Kluwer, 239-261.

Kayne, Richard. 1991. "Romance Clitics, Verb movement and PRO". *Linguistic Inquiry* 22, 647-686.

Kayne, Richard. 1993. "Toward a Modular Theory of Auxiliary Selection". *Studia Linguistica* 4, 3-31.

Kayne, Richard. 1994. *The Antisymmetry of Syntax*. Cambridge Mass.: MIT Press.

Marantz, Alec. 1988. "Clitics, Morphological Merger and the Mapping to Phonological

Structure". In M. Hammond and M. Noonan (eds), *Theoretical Morphology: Approaches in Modern Linguistics*. San Diego: Academic Press, 253-270.

Lieber, Rochelle. 1992. *Deconstructing Morphology. Word Formation in Syntactic Theory*. Chicago: Chicago University Press.

Lyons, Christopher. 1990. "An Agreement Approach to Clitic-doubling". *Transactions of the Philological Society* 88, 1-57.

Matthews, Peter. H. 1972. *Inflectional Morphology*. Cambridge: Cambridge University Press.

Nespor, Marina and Irene Vogel. 1986. *Prosodic Phonology*. Dordrecht: Foris.

Philippaki-Warburton, Irene. 1985. "Word Order in Modern Greek". *Transactions of the Philological Society*, 114-43.

Philippaki-Warburton, Irene. 1987. "The Theory of Empty Categories and the Pro-drop Parameter in Modern Greek". *Journal of Linguistics* 23, 289-318.

Philippaki-Warburton, Irene. 1994a. "Verb Movement and the Distribution of Clitic Pronouns". In Philippaki-Warburton, Nikolaidis and Sifianou (eds), 53-60.

Philippaki-Warburton, Irene. 1994b. "The Subjunctive Mood and the Syntactic Status of the Particle *na* in Modern Greek". *Folia Linguistica* 28, 297-328.

Philippaki-Warburton, Irene. 1996. "Functional Heads and Modern Greek Syntax". Paper presented at the GLOW Workshop on Current Issues in Modern Greek Syntax, Athens.

Philippaki-Warburton, Irene, Katerina Nikolaidis and Maria Sifianou (eds). 1994. *Themes in Greek Linguistics: Papers from the First International Conference on Greek Linguistics*. Amsterdam: J. Benjamins.

Pollock, Jean-Yves. 1989. "Verb Movement, Universal Grammar and the structure of IP". *Linguistic Inquiry* 20, 365-424.

Radford, Andrew. 1988. *Transformational Grammar*. Cambridge: Cambridge University Press.

Ralli, Angela. 1998. "On the Morphological Status of inflectional Features: Evidence from Modern Greek". In Joseph, Horrocks and Philippaki-Warburton (eds), 51-74.

Rivero, Maria Luiza and Arhonto Terzi. 1995. "Imperatives, V-movement and Logical Mood". *Journal of Linguistics* 31, 135-146.

Rizzi, Luigi. 1982. *Issues in Italian Syntax*. Dordrecht: Foris.

Rizzi, Luigi. 1990. *Relativized Minimality*. Cambridge Mass.: MIT Press.

Roberts, Ian, 1991. "Excorporation and Minimality". *Linguistic Inquiry* 22, 209-18.

Selkirk, Elizabeth. 1982. *The Syntax of Words*. Cambridge Mass.: MIT Press.

Sells, Peter. 1995. "Korean and Japanese Morphology from a Lexical Perspective". *Linguistic Inquiry* 26, 277-325.

Speas, Peggy. 1991. "Functional Heads and the Mirror Principle". *Lingua* 84, 181-214.

Spencer, Andrew. 1991. *Morphological Theory: an Introduction to Word Structure in Generative Grammar*. Oxford: Blackwell.

Suñer, Margarita. 1988. "The Role of Agreement in Clitic-doubled Constructions". *Natural Language and Linguistic Theory* 6, 391-434.

Theofanopoulou-Kontou, Dimitra. 1986-7. "Kenes katigories ke klitika sti NE: I periptosi tu amesu antikimenu" (Empty categories and clitics in MG: the object case). *Glossologia* 5-6, 41-68.

Thrainsson, Hoksuldur. 1996. "On the (Non)-Universality of Functional Categories". In W. Abraham, S. D. Epstein, H. Thrainsson and J.-W. Zwart (eds), *Minimal Ideas: Syntactic Studies in the Minimalist Framework*. Amsterdam: J. Benjamins, 253-81.

Travis, Lisa. 1984. *Parameters and Effects of Word Order Variation*. Ph.D. dissertation,

MIT

Tsimpli, Ianthi Maria. 1995. "Focusing in Modern Greek". In K.É. Kiss (ed.), *Discourse Configurational Languages*. Oxford: OUP, 176-207.

Tsimpli, Ianthi Maria. 1998. "Individual and Functional Readings for Focus, Wh- and Negative Operators: Evidence from Greek". In Joseph, Horrocks and Philippaki-Warburton (eds), 197-227.

Tsoulas, Georges. 1994. "Checking Theory, Subject Extraction, and the Theory of Movement". In Philippaki-Warburton, Nikolaidis and Sifianou (eds), 93-100.

Uriagereka, Juan. 1995. Aspects of the Syntax of Clitic Placement in Western Romance. *Linguistic Inquiry* 26, 79-123.

Warburton, Irene. 1971. "Rules of Accentuation in Classical and Modern Greek". *Glotta* 48, 107-121.

Warburton, Irene. 1977. "Modern Greek Clitic pronouns and the 'Surface Structure Constraints' Hypothesis". *Journal of Linguistics* 13, 259-81.

Webelhuth, Gert. 1995. "X-bar Theory and Case Theory". In G. Webelhuth (ed.), *Government and Binding theory and the Minimalist Program*. Oxford: Blackwell, 15-95.

Williams, Edwin. 1981. "On the Notions 'Lexically Related' and 'Head of a Word'". *Linguistic Inquiry* 12, 203-38

Zwicky, Arnold. M. 1985. "Clitics and Particles". *Language* 61, 283-305.

Zwicky, Arnold M. and Geoffrey Pullum. 1983. "Cliticization and Inflection: English *n't*". *Language* 59, 502-13.

Department of Linguistic Science
The University of Reading
Whiteknights, PO Box 218
Reading RG6 6AA
United Kingdom

e-mail:
I.Philippaki-Warburton@reading.ac.uk
V.Spyropoulos@reading.ac.uk

Transpositions and argument structure*

ANDREW SPENCER

1. INTRODUCTION

Considerable attention has been devoted in the recent literature to the morphosyntax of deverbal action nominalizations (Comrie and Thompson 1985; Grimshaw 1990; Rozwadowska 1997; Zubizarreta 1987; see Koptjevskaja-Tamm 1993 for a typological survey), especially those that give rise to so-called 'mixed categories' (Lefebvre and Muysken 1988), in which a nominalization shows some of the categorial properties of a noun and some of the properties of a verb. Rather less attention has been directed towards other types of morphological category which share some of the general features of nominalizations such as participles and relational adjectives. A participle is a verb form which shows the external syntax of an adjective, while a relational adjective can be thought of as a noun form showing the external syntax of an adjective. In a great many languages the only significant effect of the process is to shift the word from one syntactic category to another. Beard (1995), who has discussed these types of process in some detail, refers to this as 'transposition'.

One reason why transpositions can pose theoretical problems is that they exhibit the properties both of inflection and derivation (Haspelmath 1996). Like canonical cases of inflection they can be highly productive, they introduce no meaning change, [1] and nominalizations and participles often involve morphology which relates them to the inflectional paradigm of the verb rather than to any derivational category. On the other hand, by definition transpositions change syntactic category, often thought to be a hallmark of derivational morphology. However, we should feel uncomfortable about regarding transpositions as derivational. The principal function of derivational morphology is to create new lexemes and a derived lexeme typically has a more complex semantic representation than its base. However, there is, by definition, no meaning change with transpositions. Haspelmath (1996) has argued that inflection should be allowed to change category, precisely because participles and regular nominalizations (masdars) appear to be inflectional. However, he also suggests that there is a cline between inflection and derivation, so it is not clear whether we could specify the degree to which participles, nominalizations or relational adjectives represent inflection rather than derivation. Overall, I conclude that transpositions pose a problem for morphosyntactic theory which has not been adequately addressed.

There is a parallel here with certain types of argument structure alternation. It is widely recognised that argument structure representations and alternations are primarily the result of semantic conditions on well-formedness (where this may include notions of event structure or aspectuality). Nonetheless, many theorists argue for a morphosyntactic level at which the basic argument structure of a predicate is represen-

Geert Booij and Jaap van Marle (eds), Yearbook of Morphology 1998, 73-101.
© 1999 *Kluwer Academic Publishers. Printed in the Netherlands.*

ted, in addition to a level of semantic representation (Booij 1992; Grimshaw 1990; Levin and Rappaport Hovav 1995; Williams 1981; for general discussion see Sadler and Spencer 1998). Jackendoff (1990) denies the need for a separate level of representation but instead introduces A-annotations for elements of semantic representation which perform essentially the same job. A related model is that of Hale and Keyser's (1993) level of Lexical Relational Structure, in which the syntactic category labels are used to denote conceptual categories corresponding to entities, properties, relations and events. A level with essentially the same functions as a-structure is postulated in a number of studies within the framework of Lexical Functional Grammar (cf. especially Alsina 1996 and also Bresnan 1999; Butt 1995; Mohanan 1995). This additional level acts as an interface between semantics and morphosyntax and essentially codes those aspects of semantic representation which are grammaticalized.

By far the most attention has been devoted to verb argument structure and one of the main functions of the argument structure representation is to distinguish those verb alternations which do not involve any (idiosyncratic) change in meaning from those that do. The meaning-preserving alternations are then regarded as operations over argument structure (often called predicate-argument structure, or PAS), while the meaning-changing alternations are treated as operations over the underlying semantic structure, often referred to as Lexical Conceptual Structure, or LCS (cf. Sadler and Spencer 1998). The verbal argument structure is a (possibly structured) list of those semantic participants which are obligatorily represented in the morphosyntax, for instance, the indirect object, direct object and subject of a ditransitive verb. These elements are often called semantic roles, thematic roles or θ-roles. For simplicity I shall call them argument structure roles. In such theories there is then a theory of the mapping which relates the semantic content to the argument structure roles and a mapping theory which relates the argument structure roles to morphosyntactic notions such as subject, object, oblique participant and so on.

In some frameworks additional argument structure roles have been proposed. Higginbotham (1985) proposes a theory of the mapping from argument structure to morphosyntax ('theta-discharge' in his terminology) in which elements in the syntax are bound, identified with or marked by elements in the argument structure of a predicate. In particular, Higginbotham's (1985) reworking of Davidson's (1967) views on event structure proposes that the argument structure of a verb includes a position corresponding to the notion of 'event' and that this position is accessible to modification by adverbials and the tense operator. In a similar vein, Williams' (1981) original model of argument structure included a 'referential' role 'R' for nouns, which is coindexed with the argument structure roles of verbs when the verb discharges those roles onto a complement or subject. I shall place the symbols for the 'R' and 'E' roles in angled brackets, <R>, <E>, and jointly refer to them as 'semantic function roles', to distinguish them from the rather different type of argument structure roles which act as place holders for semantic participants. Finally, it is generally assumed that adjectives represent one- or two-place predicates which have argument structure roles akin to those of verbs. An adjective is thus a little like a verb, but without the event role.

These assumptions are summarized in the amalgam shown in (1), which I shall treat as a 'traditional' view on argument structure:

(1)   'Traditional' argument structure representations for transitive verb, noun, adjective (Higginbotham 1985, Williams 1981):[2]

shoot	<E, Ag, Th>
lion	<R>
tall	<Th>
proud(-of)	<Exp, Th>

Most theorists tend to assume that argument structure roles simply reflect positions and not the semantic content of those positions. It is irrelevant to my present purposes how we view the content of argument structure roles so I will retain these labels for mnemonic purposes.

On this picture, the category of adjective differs from that of noun or verb in that it lacks a semantic function role of its own. However, I argue that all major categories have a semantic function role. On the 'traditional' account, verbs are predicates which enjoy a privileged position with respect to anchoring the event in time, while nouns are predicates which have a privileged function with respect to reference. But adjectives are simply predicates which take one or two arguments. This fails to capture the fundamental semantic purpose of an adjective, which is to serve as an attributive modifier. I shall therefore argue that adjectives, too, have a semantic function role, which I shall notate as <A> (for 'attribute'). Thus, (1) is rewritten as (2):

(2)   Revised argument structure representations for transitive verb, noun, adjective:

shoot	<E, Ag, Th>
lion	<R>
tall	<A, Th>
proud(-of)	<A, Exp, Th>

I explain how the <A> role operates in section 2. It will be clear that in the general case we can determine the syntactic class of a predicate trivially by observation of its semantic function role. Indeed, in Spencer (1998) I argue that purely syntactic category features (such as [(N, (V]) are superfluous and that we solve some rather puzzling problems of lexical category membership if we define action nominalizations and the like purely in terms of operations over semantic function roles. However, that claim is orthogonal to the theme of this paper.

The semantic function roles encapsulate the semantic functions of eventive predication, reference and attribution, but on the morphosyntax side they also trigger (or license) the occurrence of functional features which reflect these meanings. Thus, the <E> role is associated with auxiliaries, particles or inflections for tense, aspect, mood and so on. In some languages only finite verb forms license overt subjects, and so the <E> role can then be thought of as being implicated in the assignment of syntactic case and subject agreement. The <R> role is associated with quantification and determination features, and presumably also with the expression of nominal cases (notably the syntactic ones, Nominative/Accusative, Ergative/Absolutive, but also perhaps Dative and Genitive). The <A> role is associated principally with agreement features, especially gender, case, number, definiteness.[3] Adjectives are also used predicatively, of course, and often bear the same morphology as attributively used adjectives. However, I shall follow the standard assumption that the attributive usage is prior. For the sake of simplicity I shall assume that the <A> role can also trigger predicative features in such cases, though I shall only briefly touch on the relationship between attributive and predicative adjectives when I come to discuss periphrastic constructions involving participles. The relationship between attributive and predicative modifiers is an under-researched issue in contemporary theories and would repay a separate study (see Ackerman and LeSourd 1997 for an interesting discussion of the notion of 'predicate' which bears on these matters).

In addition to the revision in (2) I shall argue that it is possible on a language-specific basis to insert additional semantic function roles into these representations, thereby 'demoting' the original semantic function role. Thus, we can have the following derived representations:

(3) a. shoot   <E, Ag, Th>   the hunter shot the lions
     b. shooting   <R, E, Ag, Th>   the shooting (of the lions by the hunter)
     c. shooting   <A, E, Ag, Th>   the hunter shooting the lions (was Tom)

(4) a. lion   <R>
     b. leonine   <A, R>

(5) a. tall   <A, Th>   a tall tree
     b. tallness   <R, A, Th>   the tallness of the tree

(6) a. proud(-of) <A, Exp, Th>   (parents) proud of their children
     b. pride   <R, A, Exp, Th>   the parents' pride (in their children)

Clearly, this defines precisely the class of transpositions. The derived word acts as though it belongs principally to the syntactic class associated with the new semantic function role, but a deverbal category, in particular, will often retain some of the features associated with the old semantic function role, and will, of course, retain the argument structure roles of the original predicate as shown in (3). Thus, in many languages participles or action nominalizations are distinguished for time reference or aspect, though they don't predicate with respect to time reference in the same way that finite forms do. Given that the old semantic function role seems to be subordinated with respect to the new role, I shall speak loosely of the old role being 'demoted', with the proviso that this may mean anything from retaining nearly all its properties to being more or less invisible, depending on the language. In section 4.2 I refine the notation in (3) to reflect this.

Section two provides a summary of how attributive modification is supposed to work. In section three I illustrate the proposals with a comparison between noun-noun compounding in English and attributive modification by relational adjectives. In section four I discuss participles and deverbal nominalizations. In section 4.1 I show how the current account solves a conceptual problem surrounding the argument structure status of passive participles in Russian. In section 4.2 I show how simple assumptions about the hierarchical organization of argument structure can account for argument structure realization in action nominals. I conclude with a brief discussion of some of the more general implications of these proposals.

2. ATTRIBUTIVE MODIFICATION

When an adjective such as *tall* modifies a noun such as *tree* it is generally assumed that the resulting expression is mapped onto a semantic representation which says, in effect, that the referent is at once a tree and tall, as shown in (7):

(7) a. tall tree
    b. $tall<A,Th_i>$ $tree<R_i>$
    c. $\lambda x[\textbf{tall}'(x) \ \& \ \textbf{tree}'(x)]$

In English it is difficult to express syntactically the second argument of a two-place adjective, but we can see the realization of argument structure in an adjective which is typically postnominal, *responsible*:

(8) a. man responsible for the accident
    b. $responsible<A,Ag_i,Th>$, $man<R_i>$, $accident<R>$
    c. $\lambda x[\textbf{responsible-for}'(x,y) \ \& \ \textbf{man}'(x) \ \& \ \textbf{accident}'(y)]$

The noun which is modified by the adjective is always assigned the argument structure role which appears first in the list. This corresponds to a notion of 'external argument' or, perhaps less controversially, 'most prominent argument' (cf. Grimshaw 1990, and also Zwarts 1992: 63). This is reflected in the coindexation shown in (8b). However, this is not quite what we want. The simple coindexation in (7b, 8b) is effectively what Higginbotham (1985) introduces for simple assignment of argument structure roles to subjects and objects, but we wish to code the additional fact that the predicates *tall* and *responsible* are attributes. This is the whole point of the <A> role. Let us therefore adopt the convention that the <A> role is coindexed with the most prominent role of its argument structure array, and that the <A> is then also co-indexed (via a different indexing mechanism, represented here as an asterisk)[4] to the expression being modified. This means we revise the representations for the lexical entries of the adjectives to (9, 10):

(9) tall<A^*_i,Th_i>

(10) responsible<A^*_i,Ag_i,Th>

We then revise representations (7b, 8b) to (11, 12):

(11) tall<A^*_i,Th_i> tree<R*>

(12) responsible<A^*_i,Ag_i,Th_j>, man<R*>, accident<R_j >

Thus, the prominent Ag role of *responsible* is linked to the <R> role of *man*, but indirectly, via the attribution relation. The second argument of the adjective is then coindexed in the normal manner of complements (though it is not, of course, realized in the normal manner of a verb complement, a matter for language specific realizational principles).

This use of the <A> role becomes particularly important when we compare verbs with participles. Thus, we need to be able to ensure that (7) is grammatical, but not (13):

(13) a. * fall tree
   b. fall<E,Th_i> tree<R_i>

If we simply allowed attribution to be handled by coindexation of the argument structure role, Th, with the <R> role of *tree*, then it would remain unclear why (13a) is ungrammatical. However, on the current assumptions, (13b) can only correspond to an expression in which *fall* is predicated of *tree* (*the tree fell* or whatever). In order to be used as an attributive modifier the verb would have to acquire the <A> role, as in (14):

(14) a. falling tree
   b. falling<A^*_i,E,Th_i> tree<R*>
   c. $\lambda x[E(x)$ & **fall′**(x) & **tree′**(x)]

This expresses the idea that *falling* is an attribute morphosyntactically, but because the argument structure still includes an <E> role, the expression can still denote an event and thus has largely the semantics of an expression such as *the tree falls/is falling*. (The semantic representation in (14c) is given for illustration only and is not supposed to represent a definitive stance on the nature of semantic representations).

3. A REVISED THEORY OF ARGUMENT STRUCTURE FOR ADJECTIVES

The question of how modification is to be represented is far from simple. The questions to be answered include the following:

(15) a. What is the relationship between restrictive and non-restrictive modification?
  b. What is the relationship between attributive and predicative modification (*the tall tree* vs. *the tree is tall*)?
  c. How is the semantics of expressions such as *small elephant, large ant, fake banknote, former President* to be handled?
  d. What is the relationship between adjectival modification and modification in compounding. In particular what is the relationship between modification by a relational adjective and modification by a bare noun (*atomic bomb* vs. *atom bomb*)?
  e. What is the relationship between adjectives denoting properties and other types of adjectives such as (deverbal) participles and (denominal) relational adjectives?

I shall leave question (15a) for future research. I touch upon question (15b) in section 4.1 below for expositional reasons, but without giving serious justification to my analysis. Question (15c) refers to a well-known problem in semantics: why is it that a small elephant/large ant is not necessarily a small/large entity, and why is it that 'X is a fake banknote/former President' cannot entail 'X is a banknote/ President'? This set of problems is addressed in some detail in Higginbotham (1985), where he introduces the notion of 'autonymous' adjectives, which are capable of taking in their scope the whole phrase and not just the noun they modify. It is possible that his solution can be imported into the account I present below. However, this would require a separate study. Accordingly, in this section I will concentrate on questions (15d, e). I begin by briefly comparing noun-noun compounds in English with relational adjectives.

3.1 Compounds and relational adjectives

What is the relationship between the head (*bomb*) and non-head (*atom*) of an endocentric compound such as *atom bomb*? How do we ensure that *atom* is taken as a modifier of *bomb*? One crucial point is that we can't simply coindex the <R> roles of the two nouns $atom{<}R^i_1{>}$ $bomb{<}R^i_2{>}$, for this would denote an entity which is at once an atom and a bomb. I propose that the compound construction itself is associated with an unspecified predicate, ρ, which asserts some pragmatically defined relationship (cf. Downing 1977) between two nouns (which I shall regard as a relationship between two sets of properties represented as lambda-expressions, for the sake of simplicity). This is illustrated in (16):

(16) $\lambda\rho\lambda x[[\textbf{bomb}'(x)] \ \& \ \rho(\lambda w[w=x], \lambda y[\textbf{atom}'(y)])]$

The details of this representation are not crucial. All that matters is that we have some way of capturing the idea that an atom bomb is a bomb such that there is some relationship between the property of being an atom and the property of being that bomb. The semantic interpretation of a sentence containing such a compound must therefore provide the modifier with the representation shown in (17):

(17) $\lambda P\lambda\rho\lambda z[P(z) \ \& \ \rho(\lambda w[w=z], \lambda y[\textbf{atom}'(y)])]$

We might wish to say that the constructional meaning of a compound noun is given explicitly in (18), where the asterisk is again used to denote attribution:

(18) $N_1<R_1>$ in the construction $[N_1<R*_1>, N_2<R*_2>]$ corresponds to
         $\lambda P\lambda\rho\lambda z[P(z) \ \& \ \rho(\lambda w[w=z], \lambda y[\textbf{noun}_1'(y)])]$ where $\textbf{noun}_1'$ is the
         denotation of N_1

However, we can directly capture the notion of attribution by claiming that the morphosyntactic effect of the compound construction is to add an <A> role which is not lexically present on the modifying noun. Thus, we can revise (18) to (19):

(19)   The argument structure representation of a compound $N_1 \ N_2$ is
         interpreted as:
         $<R_1>, <R_2> \ \Rightarrow \ <A*_i,R_1,Th_i> <R*_2>$
         This corresponds to
         $\lambda P\lambda\rho\lambda z[P(z) \ \& \ \rho(\lambda w[w=z], \lambda y[\textbf{noun}_1'(y)])](\lambda x[\textbf{noun}_2'(x)])$
         where $\textbf{noun}_1'$, $\textbf{noun}_2'$ denote N_1, N_2 respectively

This means that the representation for *atom bomb* will be (20), which after λ-conversion collapses to (16):[5]

(20) $\lambda P\lambda\rho\lambda z[P(z) \ \& \ \rho(\lambda w[w=z], \lambda y[\textbf{atom}'(y)])](\lambda x[\textbf{bomb}'(x)])$

It is important to note that the representation yielded by (20) is read off a syntactic structure. We do not create a separate 'adjectival' lexeme every time we use a noun as modifier in a compound. In fact, both the semantic representation (LCS) and the argument structure of the noun remain unaltered in lexical representations.[6]

3.2 Attributive adjectives

I have said that adjectives have a special <A> role which mediates the semantic effect of attribution. From what has been said about compounding it should be clear how we handle the semantics of adjectives. All we need to assume is a principle along the lines of (21) (for a one-place adjective):

(21)   adj<A^*_i,Th_i> translates as
         $\lambda Q \lambda x[\mathbf{adj}'(x) \& Q(x)]$

where **adj**′ is the meaning of 'adj'. Applied to *tree* (translation $\lambda z[\mathbf{tree}'(z)]$) an adjective such as *tall* will give (22):

(22) $\lambda Q \lambda x[\mathbf{tall}'(x) \& Q(x)](\lambda z[\mathbf{tree}'(z)])$ $\Rightarrow$
         $\lambda x[\mathbf{tall}'(x) \& \lambda z[\mathbf{tree}'(z)](x)]$ $\Rightarrow$
         $\lambda x[\mathbf{tall}'(x) \& \mathbf{tree}'(x)]$

This handles 'ordinary' qualitative adjectives such as *tall, pretty*, as well as non-gradable adjectives such as *married* (and perhaps even *fake, former* and so on; see commentary to (15d) above). It will also handle derived adjectives such as *milky, girlish, cat-like, readable*, and so on. The relationship between, say, *cat-like* and *cat* is a matter of semantics rather than argument structure: *cat-like* has a semantic representation very roughly [LIKE[CAT]], which corresponds straightforwardly to an adjective.

What of relational adjectives such as *atomic*? We might wish to say that the relationship between the relational adjective *atomic* and the noun *atom* results from an operation over the semantic representation of the noun. We could, for instance, say that *atomic* has some predicate, say, REL in its semantic representation meaning 'related to', giving [REL[ATOM]]. However, an element such as REL itself wouldn't really contribute anything to the semantic representation of the adjective.[7] To call something an *atomic bomb* is to claim some relationship between the property of being that bomb and the property of being an atom, rather than attributing 'atomicity' to *bomb*. But this is exactly the pragmatically determined relation ρ used to define the constructional meaning of compounds. Hence, the relational adjective should be derived directly from the noun at the level of argument structure, in such a way that the noun acquires an attributive semantic function role which then coindexes with the base noun's <R> role, as shown in (23):

(23)   atomic: atom<A^*_i,R,Th_i>

This can now be interpreted in the same way as the modifier in a compound noun, as in (24):

(24)   noun<A^*_i,R,Th_i> translates as
         $\lambda P \lambda \rho \lambda x[P(x) \& \rho(\lambda w[w=x], \lambda y[\mathbf{noun}'(y)])]$

In other words, the interpretation of relational adjectives is the lexical equivalent of the pragmatically defined relation in compounds. The meaning of *atomic bomb* is now derived as in (25), essentially as for *atom bomb*:

(25) a. atom$<A^*_i,R_1,Th_i>$ bomb$<R^*_2>$ $\Rightarrow$

    b. $\lambda P\lambda\rho\lambda x[P(x)$ & $\rho(\lambda w[w=x], \lambda y[\textbf{atom}'(y)])](\lambda x[\textbf{bomb}'(x)])$ $\Rightarrow$

    c. $\lambda\rho\lambda x[\textbf{bomb}'(x)$ & $\rho(\lambda w[w=x], \lambda y[\textbf{atom}'(y)])$

Note that the basic interpretation of *atomic* is identical to that of the noun from which it derives. For this reason, the formulae in (25b,c) make reference to the property $\lambda y[\textbf{atom}'(y)]$ and not the property $\lambda y[\textbf{atomic}'(y)]$. The adjectival morphology is nothing more than a reflection of the changed argument structure of the noun, and not the bearer of a semantic constant, such as the *-like* of *cat-like* or the *-y* of *milky*. In this sense, then, the derivation of a relational adjective creates a distinct form of a nominal lexeme rather than creating a distinct adjectival lexeme.[8] Beard (1995: 189) argues that there are no grounds for treating relational adjective formation as derivational morphology proper, because there is no conceivable relationship between the various meanings expressed and the affixation used for it. For him, this means that the process of forming the adjective must involve nothing more than a switch of category features. His argument carries over: if relational adjective formation is not a form of lexical derivation, then there must be some level other than the semantic level of LCS at which it occurs. My claim is that that level is argument structure.

4. ALTERNATIONS AFFECTING THE <E> ARGUMENT - MIXED CATEGORIES

Transpositions from noun to adjective are accomplished by adding the <A> role of an attribute as the new semantic function role, effectively 'demoting' the <R> role. The new semantic function role will then trigger a host of adjectival functional features, specifically agreement, largely or completely displacing the functional features of nouns (though there is much to be said about the way this happens in individual cases). In this section I briefly sketch a treatment of transpositions from verb to adjective (participles) and verb to noun (deverbal nominalization), in which an <A> or <R> role is added and the verb's eventuality role, <E> is demoted.

4.1 Participles

Participles pose a serious problem for traditional conceptions of inflection and derivation because on the one hand they seem to belong to a verb lexeme, but on the other they inflect as adjectives. Thus, they appear to be a case of category changing inflection. I shall discuss this problem from the perspective of Russian participles, basing myself on Babby (1993, 1997) (cf also Beard 1995: 195f). Russian participles are interesting because they reflect voice, tense and aspect. Russian verbs are regularly paired into perfective aspect indicating a completed action, and imperfective indicating repeated or habitual actions, or action in progress (amongst other things). In addition, there are two morphological tenses, a past tense and a non-past (interpreted as present with imperfective verbs and as future with perfectives). Russian has active/passive voices. The passive is regularly formed by a past passive participle with perfective verbs, but with imperfectives a form historically deriving from a reflexive is used. The reflexive imperfective passive has all the participial forms of any other intransitive imperfective verb.

In (26) I provide a list of participial forms for a typical transitive verb.

(26)   Russian participles: *delat'/sdelat'* 'make (IMPF/PF)'

Active:

PAST	NON-PAST	
dela-vš(-ij)	delaj-ušč(-ij)	IMPF
s-dela-vš(-ij)	--------------------	PF

Passive:

PAST	NON-PAST	
------------------	delaj-em(-yj)	IMPF
s-dela-n(-n-yj)	--------------------	PF

The formatives in parentheses are default (MASC SG) adjectival agreement markers, and the parenthetical -*n*- formative of the past passive participle is used when the participle is used attributively. In other conjugations the past passive participle formative appears as -*en* on the surface and for this reason the participle is often referred to as the '-*en* participle' and the morphological operation deriving it as '-*en* affixation'.

Participles enjoy some properties typical of verbs and other properties associated with adjectives. These are summarized in (27) (the point can be made for a whole host of languages, of course, including many other Indo-European ones):

(27)   *Verb properties*
        (i)   preservation of argument structure

    (ii) realization of complements (including 'quirky case' assignment)

    (iii) preservation of reflexive suffix -*sja*

    (iv) preservation of (some) tense/aspect-like properties (PAST/NON-PAST, IMPF/PF)

    (v) modification by aspectual adverbials 'still', 'already', 'no longer' etc.

(28)   *Adjective properties*
    (i)   external inflection as adjectives
    (ii) use as attributive/predicative modifiers
    (iii) conversion to nouns

Properties (27i, ii) and (28i, iii) can be illustrated by the present active participle from verbs of controlling such as *upravljat´* 'govern', *rukovodit´* 'supervise', *komandovat´* 'command'. These govern complements in the instrumental rather than the accusative, as shown in (29):

(29)   komandovat´ vos´m-oj armi-ej
          to.command eighth-INSTR army-INSTR
          'to command the Eighth Army'

The participle shows the same behaviour:

(30)   oficer komanduj-ušč-ij vos´m-oj armi-ej
          officer command-PRESPRT-MASC.SG.NOM eighth-INSTR army-INSTR
          'the officer commanding the Eighth Army'

The participle can be converted to a type of agentive noun, by a very productive process in Russian. In (31) we see such a noun in the form of a compound (linked by a meaningless intermorph -*o*- of the kind found in Greek compounding):

(31)   glavn-o-komand-ujušč-ij vos´m-oj armi-ej
          chief-O-command-PRESPRT-MASC.SG.NOM eighth-INSTR army-INSTR
          'Commander-in-Chief of the Eighth Army'

Properties (27i-iv) and (28i, ii) are illustrated by (32, 33), in which the verb *ščitat´sja* takes an adjectival complement as a secondary predicate to the subject:

(32)   Èti fakty ščitaj-ut-sja bessporn-ymi
          These facts consider-PL-SJA uncontroversial-INSTR.PL
          'These facts are considered uncontroversial'

(33)   fakty ščitaju-šč-ie-sja bessporn-ymi
          facts consider-PRESPRT-PL-SJA uncontroversial-INSTR.PL

'facts which are considered uncontroversial'

There is considerable unclarity about the status of the tense/aspect distinctions in Slavic participles and the extent to which they correspond to the tense/aspect distinctions of finite forms. However, the crucial point for our purposes is that participles denote events which have a particular time reference with respect to the main clause and which are differentiated for aspect in much the same way as finite verb forms, something which is never true of adjectives not derived from verbs.

As I pointed out in section one, the grammar associates sets of functional features with argument structure representations. Typical associations are those of (34):

(34)   verb<E,x,y> $\Rightarrow$ [TNS, ASP, ...], [AGR], [NOM, ACC]
        noun<R> $\Rightarrow$ [NUM] [CASE]
        adj<A*$_1$,x$_1$> $\Rightarrow$ [COMPARISON], [AGR$_A$], [AGR$_P$], ...

(where x, y stand for argument structure positions, [NOM, ACC] refers to the assignment of case to subjects/objects, [AGR$_A$] stands for attributive agreement features and [AGR$_P$] stands for predicative agreement features). For simplicity let us follow Babby (1993) in treating the passive alternation as the suppression of the external argument, x, rendering it 'implicit' (shown by placing it in parentheses):

(35)   verb<E,x,y> $\Rightarrow$ verb[PASS]<E,(x),y>
        $\lambda x[\lambda y[\textbf{verb}'(y)](x)]$ $\Rightarrow$ $\exists x[\lambda y[\textbf{verb}'(y)](x)]$

This is an argument structure operation and the LCS of the verb does not undergo any change. This means that the passive can be input to further processes, say, participle, gerund, or nominal formation (as a language-particular feature).

In Babby's (1993) approach *-en* suffixation gives rise to a verb form. However, it is a form which has adjectival inflectional features. Babby argues (1993:9) that since (only) true adjectives form comparatives and manner adverbials they must be categorially distinct from participles, and that this difference should best be reflected in terms of "...a more finely grained decomposition of the lexical categories into categorial features...". Given the discussion of various types of adjectives above, and especially of relational adjectives, this conclusion does not follow. In particular, relational adjectives (which are abundant in Russian) have neither comparative forms nor manner adverbial derivates, but I presume Babby would still regard them as categorially adjectives, rather than some sort of subcategory of noun. Thus, there remains an important question over the categorial identity of participles.

In its predicative use in forming passives, the past passive participle is often regarded as a verb form with suppressed external argument, and hence essentially an unaccusative verb form. The internal argument is then linked to subject position, triggering subject-predicate agreement with the auxiliary verb 'be'. This is seen in (37), the passive form of (36):

(36)   Devuška s -delal-a   uprazženenie
        girl.NOM PF-did   -AGR   exercise.ACC
        'The girl did the exercise'

(37)   Upražnenie byl-o   s -dela-n -o   (devušk-oj)
        Exercise   was-AGR PF-do -PPP-AGRp (girl-INSTR)
        'The exercise was done (by the girl)'

However, when furnished with an additional *-n-* formative, the participle can also be used attributively:

(38)   upražnenie s -dela-n -n   -oe   (devušk-oj)
        exercise   PF-do -PASTPRT-ADJ-AGR$_A$ (girl-INSTR)
        'the exercise done (by the girl)'

Babby sees this as a problem for argument structure realization. He assumes that all attributive modifiers must have an external argument in order to modify. However, passive participles lack an external argument (being passive) even though the passive participles (both past and present) can be used attributively as well as predicatively. Babby thus argues that there must be a process associated with the *-n-* formative of past passive participles and the *-m* formative of present passive participles which externalizes the internal argument. However, he categorically denies (p. 23) that this creates an adjective. On the contrary, he stresses that the participles, whether attributive or predicative, are forms of the verb paradigm.

Given the assumptions already outlined we can consider participle formation to be an operation over argument structure representations, independent of voice. An <A> role is introduced, coindexed with the most prominent argument. In the case of an active participle this will be the verb's external argument, otherwise it will be the next accessible argument, namely the internal argument. This is illustrated in (39):

(39)   Participle formation:

        $\text{verb}<E,x,y>$ $\Rightarrow$ $\text{verb}<A^*_i,E,x_i,y>$ active
        $\text{verb}<E,(x),y>$ $\Rightarrow$ $\text{verb}<A^*_i,E,(x),y_i>$ passive

Since the <E> role has been demoted by the <A> role, the participle is non-finite in the syntax.

For clarity I set out how the features are distributed on the participial and finite forms of verbs. Ignoring much detail, the picture is essentially as shown in (40, 41). In (40) we see how a finite form links argument structure to functional features. I indicate feature licensing by superscripting:

(40) a.   *delajet* 'does 3SG, IMPF'   b. *s-delajet* 'will do 3SG, PF'

          $\langle E^i, x^j, y^k \rangle$ $\langle E^i, x^j, y^k \rangle$

TNS^i: PRES	TNS^i: PRES
ASP^i: IMPF	ASP^i: PF
AGR^j: 3SG	AGR^j: 3SG
NOM^j	NOM^j
ACC^k	ACC^k

I have indicated the aspect features coindexed with the <E> role of the verb's argument structure, reflecting the common assumption that aspect is syntactically relevant (see Schoorlemmer 1995 for a detailed exploration of this view for Russian).

In (41) we see the active participles. The subscripts indicate the link between the <A> role and the prominent argument of which the participle is predicated:

(41) a. *delaj-ušč-* (PRES IMPF)   b. *s-dela-vš-* (PAST PF)

       $\langle A^*_1, E^i, x_1, y^j \rangle$ $\langle A^*_1, E^i, x_1, y^j \rangle$

        TNS^i: PRES   TNS^i: PAST

ASP^i: IMPF	ASP^i: PF
ACC^j	ACC
AGR$_A$	AGR$_A$

Here we have a tense and aspect distinction, though not one that is directly relevant to main clause predication, hence it does not affect clausal finiteness. These features are not accessible to clause level tense operators or whatever, and this is reflected in the fact that they are not coindexed with the semantic function role at argument structure but rather are licensed through the demoted <E> argument. This allows us to capture the fact, emphasized by Babby, that the participles are still forms of a verb lexeme and the LCS of the verb has not changed.[9]

In (42) we see concrete examples of how this works for an active present participle:

(42)   devuška delajušč-aja upražnenie
        girl doing-FEM.SG exercise
        'The girl doing the exercise'
        devuška<R_1> delat´<E,x,y> upražnenie <R_2> $\Rightarrow$
        devuška<R^*_1> delat´<A^*_i,x_i,y_j> upražnenie <R_2j> $\Rightarrow$
        $\lambda y[\lambda x[$**delajušč**´$(y)(x)]($**devuška**´$)]($**upražnenie**´$)$

In (43) we see the passive participles:

(43) a.   *delaj-em-* (PRES IMPF)
          <E,x,y> $\Rightarrow$ passive
          <E,(x),y> $\Rightarrow$ participle formation

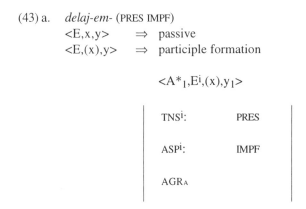

                    <$A^*_1,E^i,(x),y_1$>

TNS^i:	PRES
ASP^i:	IMPF
AGR$_A$	

     b.   *s-dela-n-* (PAST PF)
          <E,x,y> $\Rightarrow$ passive
          <E,(x),y> $\Rightarrow$ participle formation

                    <$A^*_1,E^i,(x),y_1$>

TNS^i:	PAST
ASP^i:	PF
AGR$_A$	

Finally, it is worth briefly commenting on the predicative use of the participles. In (38) above we saw a typical passive clause formed by the auxiliary *be* and the predicative form (without *-n-*) of the *-en* participle. This construction can be handled as follows. First we must decide how to represent a predicatively used adjective in combination with the copula, as in *The exercise was difficult*. The copula will be given the argument structure in (44a) and the adjective will have the argument structure of (44b):

(44) a.　was<E,Th$_i$,Pred$_j$>

　　 b.　difficult<A*$_j$,Th$_j$>

The argument 'Pred' corresponds to the complement of the copula, and the Theme argument will be discharged to the subject. Predication via a copula is then achieved by identifying the index of the adjective with that of the copula, as in (45):

(45)　　was<E,Th$_i$,Pred$_{i,j}$>　　difficult<A*$_j$,Th$_j$>

The complete sentence then results from predicating (45) of the subject, to give (46):

(46)　　The exercise<R$_i$>　　was<E,Th$_i$,Pred$_{i,j}$>　　　difficult<A*$_j$,Th$_j$>

I shall assume that the auxiliary is essentially the copula with an <E> role which is not specified for subtype (durative event, stative and so on). The specification of event type comes from the verb itself via the participle. This is clear when we notice that the copula is a stative verb and statives are almost invariably imperfective, yet this type of passive is perfective. Thus, if we say that the auxiliary is like the stative copula except in being unspecified for stativity we can explain this anomaly as well as the fact that the passive auxiliary is transparent to the eventuality class of the main verb. On the other hand, the tense is derived from the auxiliary, for although the participle is called a past passive participle, its morphology signals aspect rather than tense and it is itself tenseless. It is not possible to form a present passive using a participial construction, so that we must conclude that the TENSE category lacks specification in these participles. The predicate as a whole then has to inherit its TENSE/ASPECT feature specifications from both components of the predicate (cf. Börjars, Vincent and Chapman 1997, who use similar underspecification in their treatment of the cognate Latin construction). This result is presented in (47, 48):[10]

(47)　　　　　　　$<E^i,x^j{}_1,Pred_{1,2}>$　　　　$<A*_2,E^k,(x),y^m{}_2>$
　　　　　　　　　bylo　　　　　　　　　　　s-dela-n-o

TNS^i: PAST	TNS:
ASP^i:	ASP^k: PF
AGR^j	AGR$^m{}_p$
NOM^j	

(48)　　$\lambda y \exists x [$**sdelan**$'(y)(x)](\textbf{upražnenie}')$

Notice that we do not need to say that a participle has to be furnished with an external argument in order to be used either attributively or predicatively. The argument structure operation which derives an adjective-type argument structure from the argument structure of the verb can remain oblivious to this distinction, provided it can have access to the most prominent (remaining) theta role. Also, I have not attempted to associate the extra *-n-* formative of the attributive form with any kind of external argument formation. This is because no external arguments are needed in order to account for these constructions. But notice that Babby's own account is suspect anyway. First, he needs the morpholexical rule of externalization only for attributive participles. The predicatively used participles found in the finite passive construction apparently remain unaccusative, even though Babby (1993: 21) has earlier quoted a variety of sources claiming that predicative adjectives, no less than attributive adjectives, "...involve assignment of AP's external theta-role to a sister constituent...". Second, Babby himself points out that a similar process of externalization is necessary for the present passive participles, and these lack the additional *-n-* formative. Finally, not all past passive participles take the *-n-* formative under any circumstances, namely, those in *-t* (*izbi-t-yj* 'beaten up' from *izbit ´*). I conclude, therefore, that the *-n-* formative is a parochial indicator of attributive function for a certain morphological class of past passive participles and has nothing to do with argument structure alternations.[11]

4.2 Nominalizations

A particularly problematic case of category shift is the eventive deverbal (action) nominalization. On standard feature systems [N, V] features switch values.[12] But in any case, unless the switch of features can be shown to follow from something or to lead to desirable effects any theory which codes transpositions simply as the 'toggling' of syntactic features (cf. Beard 1995) is effectively just providing a description of the phenomenon.

The nominal retains the verb's argument structure and continues to denote an event. Moreover, in many circumstances the nominal marks its arguments in the way that verbal arguments (including subject and direct object) are marked. The obvious analysis is to assume that the <E> role of the verb is demoted and superseded by <R> as shown in (49):[13]

(49)   the shooting of the lions by the hunter
        shooting $<R,E,x_i,y_j>$ (hunter $<R_i>$, lions $<R_j>$)

The difficulty with nominalizations comes when we ask what the morphosyntactic realization of the nominal is. There is an event position, though it no longer functions as the semantic function role. We have seen that in participles this position may still be specified by verbal functional features such as tense and aspect. This is much less common with nominalizations. However, just as the <A> role of participles determines the syntactic behaviour of the participle (as canonical noun modifier) and the functional features it is associated with (adjectival ones), so the

<R> role of the nominalization triggers functional features such as determination, syntactic case assignment to complements, and so on. Nominalizations may also assume case forms themselves and function as gerunds (e.g. many Caucasian languages, Chukchee, cf. Spencer 1995) or as case-marked 'infinitival' complements (e.g. Finnish). Which features are acquired is a language-specific property (though there are strong universal tendencies, examined by Koptjevskaja-Tamm 1993).

One particularly intriguing phenomenon is the way in which a nominalization retains more of its verb-like features within the VP nexus while higher up the projection the functional features are those of a noun. This is illustrated in the paradigm given in (50):

(50) a.   Tom's shooting of the lions
    b.   Tom's shooting the lions
    c.   Tom shooting the lions
    d. * Tom shooting of the lions

Example (50a) is the Poss-Gen or Poss-of nominal, (50b) is the Poss-*ing* nominal and (50c) is the Acc-*ing* gerund. The missing case (50d) would be an example of Koptjevskaja-Tamm's (1993) 'SENT-Poss' type.

This pattern of argument licensing is not surprising given that the whole point of a nominal is to be a noun for the purposes of NP external syntax. The nominal can, however, afford to remain a verb deeper inside its own phrase. However, this doesn't actually explain why structures such as (50d) should be almost vanishingly rare typologically. Koptjevskaja-Tamm (1993) notes only three cases. In two (Tongan and Samoan) the subject nominal is marked with the Ergative case postposition. However, this marker has, arguably, developed fairly recently from the marker of the implicit argument of a passive, at a time when the languages had an accusative rather than an ergative system. If this is so, we might prefer to say that the Ergative case marker was really the equivalent of English *by* in *the shooting of the lions by the hunter*. The other example is from Classical Arabic, in a construction which is apparently excluded in the modern standard, and which is therefore rather difficult to investigate.

As a simple way to account for this patterning I propose a more articulated version of argument structure than the simple listing of participants given hitherto. The idea that argument structure representations have a hierarchical structure is familiar from frameworks such as that of Levin and Rappaport Hovav (1995), who follow a popular tradition of distinguishing a set of internal arguments (the direct and indirect internal arguments, corresponding in the syntax to direct and indirect objects) and an external argument. The same idea is also found in Hale and Keyser's (1993) reinterpretation of argument structure (their Lexical Relational Structure). The position of the external argument is rather controversial, and I shall sidestep the tricky problem of explaining exactly how it is best represented by adopting the notational convention of Williams (1981) and simply underline it. This means that the argu-ment structure of a simple transitive predication will be (51):

(51)   E

A nominalization is treated here as the name of an event, or more generally of a situation (presupposing an ontology for natural language in which situations can be thought of as things). The simplest way of representing this is (52):

(52)   R

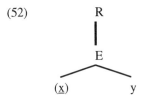

The <E> role is treated as a dependent of the <R> role, while the internal argument, y, is a dependent of <E> (and hence indirectly of <R>). The external argument is typically implicit, and this is shown by putting it in parentheses. Clearly this type of structure will be applicable to participles too, with <A> replacing <R> in (52), reflecting the fact that a participle is simply a verb with the semantic function of attributive modification as in (53):

(53) A^*_i

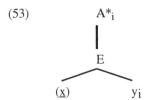

Such a representation is more perspicuous than that which we would obtain if we simply adopted the coindexing notation for attributive modifiers (see note 4), since it clearly reflects the fact that we have an adjective derived from a verb rather than a verb derived from an adjective. Likewise, a relational adjective will have an argument structure in which an <A> role governs the <R> role.

In all cases the morphosyntactic behaviour of the resulting expression is governed principally by the governing semantic function role, though to varying degrees. In a nominalization of type (50a) we have a situation in which the <R> predominates, determining the external syntax of the nominal and also the expression of all arguments. In Type (50b), the <E> role is able to govern the expression of the internal argument (the direct object) but not the external argument. This is the 'mixed category' in the usual sense of the term (though it should be recognized that all constructions which have more than one semantic function role are to some extent 'mixed'). Finally, in type (50c) the expression of arguments is governed entirely by the <E> role, though the expression as a whole may function as a nominalization in the syntax, for instance, in being the complement of a preposition: *We were surprised at Tom shooting the lions*. What is excluded is a situation in which the <R> role determines the expression of the lowest argument (the internal argument) and then the <E> role is permitted to determine the expression of the external argument or to determine the external syntax of the nominalization (Type (50d), since this would contradict the government relations entailed by the process of nominalization.[14]

This is illustrated in the simplified syntactic trees shown in (54). Here I have indicated which semantic function role determines the morphosyntax at each bar-level. The syntactic category labelling is somewhat arbitrary - what counts is which features are licensed by which semantic function roles:

(54) a.

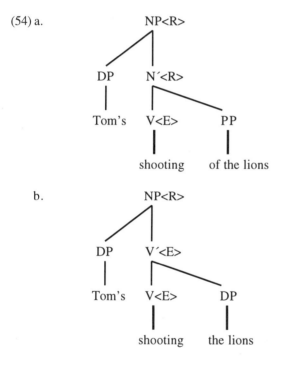

b.

c.

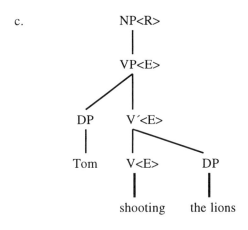

d.

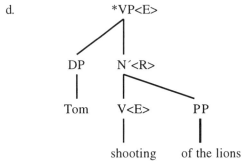

In compound tenses it is the auxiliary verb which is nominalized, giving rise to the two possibilities shown in (55, 56):

(55) a. Tom's having shot the lions
b. Tom having shot the lions

(56) a.

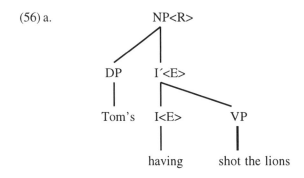

b.

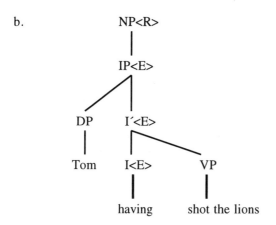

5. CONCLUSIONS

I have shown how widespread assumptions about the argument structure representations of predicates for the three major classes of noun, verb and adjective can provide us with a simple account of transpositions, provided we take seriously the idea that argument structure includes a semantic function argument. I propose that nouns, verbs and adjectives have a role <R>, <E> and <A>, representing the semantic functions of reference, event denotation and attributive modification. Relational adjectives and participles have the structure <A,R>, <A,E>, which is interpreted semantically as the use of a noun/verb as attribute. Deverbal nominalizations have the structure <R,E>, denoting the name of an event. Unlike some (e.g. Zwarts 1992) I claim that all members of major categories have such a role, and that these roles govern the expression of morphosyntactic functional features. In addition, some members have more than one role. Transpositions of syntactic category occur when one of the semantic roles is overlaid over the basic role, thereby 'demoting' the latter. Both semantic function roles may license the expression of functional categories, but it is the governing role which determines the external syntax. I argue that natural assumptions about the hierarchical organization of such semantic function roles helps explain why certain types of 'mixed' category seem not to be found.

The model proposed here prompts a number of extensions, particularly with respect to deverbal and deadjectival nominalizations. In addition, one can ask to what extent property nominalizations of adjectives can be treated this way: for instance, it seems plausible to regard the argument structure of *redness* as <R,A,Th> derived by simple transposition from red <A_i,Th_i>. More problematical, however, would be the suggestion that the <E> role can be the governing role in transpositions. Thus, could we treat denominal verbs such as *to saddle (a horse)* or *to shelve (the books)* as belonging to the argument structure class <E,R> (as is implicit in Hale and Keyser's 1993 analysis)? This seems unlikely, since such verbs always have additional and unpredictable components of meaning determined by semantic, cultural or pragmatic factors (Kiparsky 1997). Similarly, it is not obvious how we could treat inchoative and causative deadjectival verbs as <E,A,Th> and <E,A,Ag,Th> respectively, without having to add inchoative or causative predicates to the semantic representation. The problem with the <E> role is obviously that some way has to be found to establish what the arguments would be of such a derived predicate, and in general, this cannot be done automatically, without lexical stipulation of the semantics.

On the other hand, we can ask to what extent the process is recursive. For instance, in many languages (e.g. Russian) it is possible for an adjective, including a participle to be used as a noun, so does this mean we can motivate a structure <R,A, E,Ag,Th>? Nothing seems to rule out this possibility, and I assume it is realized for at least some combinations of semantic function role.

More generally, the analysis raises interesting questions about the notion of the lexeme: is a deverbal nominalization always a member of the same lexeme as the base verb, and if so does this make it an inflected form (like the various 'gerunds' and 'masdars' found as part of the verb paradigms in the descriptions of many languages)? It also raises questions about the nature of the ontology presupposed by such argument structure representations. For instance, what principles govern the attributive relationship stated here in argument structure terms and the kinds of semantic representations or logical forms we need to posit for attributes? What kind of ontology has to be proposed in order to make sense of the idea that a deverbal nominalization is the name of a situation?

NOTES

*   I am grateful to the Economic and Social Research Council for supporting some aspects of the research reported here, Project no. R000236115. I am grateful to Keith Brown for detailed discussion of a number of aspects of these ideas. Thanks also to Greg Stump and Steven Lapointe for helpful discussion, and to Marina Zaretskaya for discussion of some of the Russian examples, and to an anonymous referee for very detailed and thoughtful criticism. Versions of these ideas have been presented at the Workshop on Inflection, 8th Morphology Conference, Vienna, 6th February, 1996, and the Associação Portuguesa de Lingüística, University of Lisbon, 1 October 1997. The paper has benefited from the comments of participants in the Research Workshop in Argument Structure at the Department of Language and Linguistics, University of Essex, participants at the Workshop on Inflection, 8th Morphology Conference, Vienna, 6th February, 1996, the audience at the Linguistics Association of Great Britain, Spring 1997 meeting (8 April), University of Edinburgh, and the participants in the 18 April 1997 meeting of 'Challenges for Inflection Description', funded by the ESRC, particularly Roger Evans and Gerald Gazdar, and the Lexical Functional Grammar 97 meeting, University of California San Diego, especially Joan Bresnan, Phil LeSourd, Joan Maling and Nigel Vincent. I would particularly like to thank the organizers of the First Mediterranean Conference on Morphology for their invitation to present these ideas to that meeting. Default disclaimers apply.

1   What is meant here, of course, is 'lexical meaning', so that we are not obliged to treat

arrive and *arrived* as two distinct lexemes simply because *arrived* appears to mean something like PAST[ARRIVE]. It can be argued that inflection never changes meaning in the sense of affecting the semantic representation of the individual lexeme. Rather, a form like *arrived* is a morphological form which corresponds to a V or VP (or clausal) node in the syntax bearing the syntactic feature [Past]. Such a node will then normally be interpreted as indicating past tense semantically, though not always, as in sequence of tense cases such as 'I had originally thought she arrived tomorrow (but in fact she arrives next week)'.

2   I use the following abbreviations: A = Attributive semantic function role; ACC = Accusative (case); ADJ = Adjective; Ag = Agent (argument role); AGR = Agreement; ASP = Aspect; DAT = Dative (case); E = Event semantic function role; Exp = Experiencer (argument role); IMPF = imperfective; INSTR = Instrumental (case); LCS = Lexical Conceptual Structure; MASC = Masculine; NOM = Nominative (case); NUM = Number; PAS = Predicate-Argument Structure; PASTPRT = Past passive participle; PF = perfective; PL = Plural; PRES = Present; PRESPRT = Present participle; R = Referential semantic function role; SG = Singular; Th = Theme (argument role); TNS = Tense

3   Zwarts (1992) also proposes to extend the notion of semantic function role to adjectives (and prepositions), but he choses to reflect the notion of gradability for this. This, of course, is not a semantic function for many adjectives and this is in keeping with Zwarts' claim, rejected here, that some major lexical category members lack a semantic function role altogether. For further discussion of this see Spencer (1998). For further discussion of the possible semantic function role of prepositions see Zwarts (1992) and Rauh (1997). I remain agnostic as to whether prepositions have a semantic function role, since it is not clear to me what kind of syntactic category they represent.

4   For the simplest cases we could dispense with the additional <A> role and just make use of the asterisk for indexing (as indeed is effectively done in Higginbotham 1985), and rely on the lack of <R> or <E> role to trigger adjective functional features. However, when we come to consider participles and other transpositions we will see that the transparency of the <A> role notation is rather useful. Ultimately, however, these are notational questions. The crucial point is Higginbotham's (1985) idea that event structure and attribution (as well as referentiality) be reflected in argument structure in some way.

5   This will work for all nouns including proper nouns, as in *London fog*. Accounting for the appearance of proper nouns in compounds is problematical on a theory such as that of Zwarts (1992), on which proper nouns lack a semantic function role altogether.

6   It is interesting to speculate whether noun incorporation could be handled in a similar way. In a complex predicate such as *bear=kill* we assume a constructional process which makes *bear* into an attribute of the event (cf. Di Sciullo and Williams 1987; Spencer 1995), roughly, *bear*<A*$_i$,R$_i$> *kill*<E*,Ag,Th>. We could then interpret this using a semantics such as that proposed by van Geenhoven 1997.

7   I should confess that English is a poor language with which to illustrate relational adjectives. Because modification by nouns is achieved by compounding in Germanic languages, the relational adjective is a recent interloper, having appeared in the language with Romance and Greek loans. There is therefore a strong tendency to interpret even Romano-Greek relational adjectives as gradable adjectives. Thus, a syntactician might say to me: 'Your theory is too morphological'. However, in a language such as Russian, which has much less compounding and in which nouns have to be transposed into adjectives to serve as modifiers, it would be impossible to translate such a sentence literally: '*Tvoja teorija - slíškom morfologičeskaja'.

8   In Spencer (1998) I show how this provides a very simple account of morpho-semantic mismatches such as *East German (economy)*: *East* modifies *Germany* to form a lexicalized expression and the (partially suppletive) relational adjective derived from *(East) Germany* is *(East) German*. This is straightforward if *German* is (in this usage) an exponent of the same lexeme as *Germany*, as on the present account. If *German* is a separate lexeme, then *East* has to modify something which doesn't exist, namely the deleted *-y* of *Germany*. Arguably, we could also handle the remarkable Sorbian examples discussed by Corbett (1987: 303) in which a possessive determiner agrees with the possessive adjective derived from a noun as though it were agreeing with a noun in the genitive case as in (i):

(i)   moj-eho   wučer-ow -ej   dźowc   -e
        my-MASC.SG.GEN. teacher-ADJ-FEM.DAT.SG daughter.FEM-DAT.SG
        'to our teacher's daughter'

Categories don't come much more mixed than this. However, we could arguably treat the possessive adjective stem *wučerow-* as a form of the *noun* lexeme (despite the fact that it inflects as an adjective) and allow the possessive pronoun to agree with it as though the possessive adjective morphology were effectively the genitive case of the noun.
9   There are a number of interesting and difficult issues surrounding these claims, which I can't address in this paper. In particular, while finiteness features can be described as inflectional and mediated through syntax, it is not obvious how this can be true for the tense/aspect features of participles. The meaning imparted by tense/aspect morphology thus takes on more the character of a semantic modification of the lexeme itself, rather than being interpreted through syntactic features. But this would make participles appear to belong to a derivational rather than an inflectional category. This is a matter which has not been investigated very thoroughly in the literature.
10   The question arises as to why the copula can't combine with other participles, such as the present active, say, to give other grammatical forms (*byl delajuščij* 'was doing' and so on). The simple answer to this is that the meanings which would be expressed by such forms are already expressed by the simple non-past form. Whether the absence of such paradigms can be made to fall out of anything deeper I don't know. Note also that it is only the shorter form of the participle, not the form with the *-n-* formative, that can form periphrastic passives (cf. *upražnenie bylo sdelanno*). This derives from the fact that the *-n-* form is purely attributive, while the periphrastic construction is obviously predicative. However, it remains unclear how exactly we should state in lexical entries that a given form can only be used predicatively or attributively.
11   This analysis of the analytic passive shares certain features with the treatment of the periphrastic Latin perfect passive given in Börjars, Vincent and Chapman (1997). However, although I am sympathetic to their overall strategy, I do not follow the specific analysis of Börjars et al. One difficulty is that the passive participle has a number of the syntactic properties of an adjective (it coordinates with non-participial adjectives, for instance) and this isn't reflected in any obvious way in Börjars et al.'s discussion. In the treatment outlined here the categorial status of the participle as an adjective is derivable from the argument structure representation, and it is precisely this which triggers the appearance of purely adjectival agreement features on what should be a verb form. In Börjars et al.'s account it is a mystery why participial constructions should have the syn-

tax of adjective phrases.

12   This is not the case on Wunderlich's (1996) theory of syntactic features, but then Wunderlich would be forced to assume that participle formation involves (non-monotonic) feature changing, which is supposed to be disallowed in his system.

13   As suggested in (3) deadjectival nominalizations work in the same way, by giving a nominal such as *redness* a representation red<R,A,Th(x)>. Since the <A> role is not the most prominent of the semantic function roles it fails to determine the external syntax and in particular the derived noun can't be used as an attributive modifier (except in compounds, of course). A number of interesting technical questions remain, however, which can't be addressed here.

14   An important question concerns the syntactic category of transpositions, particular 'mixed' nominalizations. Lapointe (1993), for example, argues for dual lexical categories, a double-headed syntactic category labelling which can reflect the nominal and verbal properties of such constructions. The approach argued for here shares much with Lapointe's, though his syntactic categories remain purely distributional labels, lacking specific content, unlike the semantic function classes distinguished here. In addition, he has to stipulate that dual lexical categories arise only from derivation, which is an automatic consequence of the analysis presented here. Further, the present analysis makes it a straightforward matter to accommodate the Poss-Gen nominalization (type (47(a)) using the same machinery, whereas it is not obvious how this would emerge from the dual lexical category analysis. The present analysis also allows for further specification of a derived category, for instance, the nominalization of a participle, but it is not clear how this can be achieved on the dual lexical category account. Finally, the present account does not require us to alter assumptions about endocentricity, merely to refine our understanding of the ways in which the components of structured lexical entries license functional features and other aspects of morphosyntax.

REFERENCES

Ackerman, Farrell and Philip LeSourd. 1997. "Toward a Lexical Representation of Phrasal Predicates". In Alsina et al. (eds), 67-106.

Alsina, Alex. 1996. *The Role of Argument Structure in Grammar. Evidence from Romance*. Stanford: CSLI Publications.

Alsina, Alex, Joan Bresnan and Peter Sells (eds). 1997. *Complex Predicates*. Stanford: CSLI Publications.

Babby, Leonard H. 1993. "A Theta-theoretic Analysis of -EN Suffixation in Russian". *Journal of Slavic Linguistics* 1, 3-43.

Babby, Leonard H. 1997 "Nominalization, Passivization and Causativization. Evidence from Russian". *Die Welt der Slaven* XLII, 201-251.

Beard, Robert. 1995. *Lexeme Morpheme Base Morphology*. Stony Brook, NY: SUNY Press.

Booij, Geert. 1992. "Morphology, Semantics and Argument Structure". In I. M. Roca (ed.), *Thematic Structure: Its Role in Grammar*. Dordrecht: Foris, 47-64.

Börjars, Kersti, Nigel Vincent and Carol Chapman. 1997. "Paradigms, Periphrases and Pronominal Inflection: a Feature-based Account". In Geert Booij and Jaap van Marle (eds), *Yearbook of Morphology 1996*. Dordrecht: Kluwer Academic Publishers,

  155-180.
Bresnan, Joan. 1999. *Lexical Functional Syntax*. Oxford: Blackwell Publishers.
Butt, Miriam. 1995. *The Structure of Complex Predicates in Urdu*. Stanford University:
  Center for the Study of Language and Information
Comrie, Bernard and Sandra A. Thompson. 1985. "Lexical Nominalization". In Timothy
  Shopen (ed.), *Language Typology and Syntactic Description. Vol. III Grammatical
  Categories and the Lexicon*. Cambridge: Cambridge University Press, 349-398.
Corbett, Greville G. 1987. "The Morphology-Syntax Interface". *Language* 63, 299-345.
Davidson, Donald. 1967. "Truth and Meaning". *Synthese* 17, 304-323.
Di Sciullo, Anna-Maria and Edwin Williams. 1987. *On the Definition of Word*.
  Cambridge, Massachusetts: MIT Press.
Downing, Pamela. 1977. "On the Creation and Use of English Nominal Compounds",
  Language 55, 810-42.
Geenhoven, Veerle van. 1998. "On the Argument Structure of Some Noun Incorporating
  Verbs in West Greenlandic". In Miriam Butt and Wilhelm Geuder (eds), *The Projection
  of Arguments: Lexical and Compositional Factors*. Stanford: CSLI Publications,
  225-263.
Grimshaw, Jane. 1990. *Argument Structure*. Cambridge, Massachusetts: MIT Press.
Hale, Kenneth and S. Jay Keyser. 1993. "On Argument Structure and the Lexical
  Expression of Syntactic Relations". In Kenneth Hale and S. Jay Keyser (eds), *The
  View From Building 20: Essays in Linguistics in Honor of Sylvain Bromberger*.
  Cambridge, MA: MIT Press, 53-110.
Haspelmath, Martin. 1996. "Word-class-changing Inflection and Morphological Theory".
  In Geert Booij and Jaap van Marle (eds), *Yearbook of Morphology 1995*. Dordrecht:
  Kluwer Academic Publishers, 43-66.
Higginbotham, James. 1985. "On Semantics", *Linguistic Inquiry* 16, 547-621.
Jackendoff, Ray S. 1990. *Semantic Structures*. Cambridge, MA: MIT Press.
Kiparsky, Paul. 1997. "Remarks on Denominal Verbs". In Alsina et al. (eds), 473-500.
Koptjevskaja-Tamm, Maria. 1993. *Nominalizations*. London: Routledge.
Lapointe, Steven. 1993. "Dual Lexical Categories and the Syntax of Mixed Category
  Phrases". In A. Kathol and M. Bernstein (eds), *Proceedings of the East Coast States
  Conference on Linguistics 1993*, 199-210.
Lefebvre, Claire and Pieter Muysken. 1988. *Mixed Categories*. Dordrecht: Kluwer Aca-
  demic Publishers.
Levin, Beth and Malka Rappaport Hovav. 1995. *Unaccusativity*. Cambridge, MA: MIT
  Press.
Mohanan, Tara. 1995. *Argument Structure in Hindi*. Stanford: CSLI Publications.
Rauh, Gisa. 1997. "Lokale Präpositionen und referentielle Argumente". *Linguistische
  Berichte* 171, 415-440.
Rozwadowska, Bożena. 1997. *Towards a Unified Theory of Nominalizations. External and
  Internal Eventualities*. Wrocław: Wydawnictwo Uniwersytetu Wrocławskiego.
Sadler, Louisa and Andrew Spencer. 1998. "Morphology and Argument Structure". In A.
  Spencer and A. Zwicky (eds), *Handbook of Morphology*. Oxford: Blackwell
  Publishers, 206-36.
Schoorlemmer, Maaike. 1995. *Participial Passive and Aspect in Russian*. Utrecht:
  Onderzoeksinstituut voor Taal en Spraak.
Spencer, Andrew. 1995. "Incorporation in Chukchi". *Language* 71, 439-89.

Spencer, Andrew. 1998. "The Redundancy of Lexical Categories". In *If you see what I mean. Essays on Language, Presented to Keith Brown on the Occasion of his Retirement in 1998*. Essex Research Reports in Linguistics, Special Issue, 14-33.

Williams, Edwin. 1981. "Argument Structure and Morphology". *The Linguistic Review* 1, 18-114.

Wunderlich, Dieter. 1996. "Lexical Categories". *Theoretical Linguistics* 22, 1-48.

Zubizarreta, Maria Luisa. 1987. *Levels of Representation in the Lexicon and in the Syntax*. Dordrecht: Foris.

Zwarts, Joost. 1992. *X'-Syntax - X'-Semantics: On the Interpretation of Functional and Lexical Heads*. Utrecht: Onderzoeksinstituut voor Taal en Spraak.

Department of Language and Linguistics
University of Essex
Colchester, CO4 3SQ
UK.

e-mail: spena@essex.ac.uk

On Italian derivatives with antesuffixal glides*

ANNA M. THORNTON

1. INTRODUCTION

The Italian denominal adjectival suffixes *-ale*, *-oso*, *-ario*, and the denominal verbal suffix *-are*,[1] sometimes appear preceded by orthographic <i> or <u>, which can be realized as high vowels /i,u/ or glides /j,w/ (cf. (1a)). A glide realization is almost exceptionless in the case of the front vowel, while the realization of the back vowel is more subject to individual and diaphasic variation (see Marotta 1987 for discussion). Nothing of what I will say in the following hinges on whether the segment which occurs between root and suffix is a vowel or a glide; therefore, following my own usage, I will consider these segments glides. Examples of words showing the alternation under discussion are given in (1b). As the data in (1b) show, both glides can appear, apparently unpredictably, in contexts (1bii-iii) which are virtually identical from the segmental point of view to the ones in which no glide appears (1bi).

(1)   Pretheoretical overview of the data to be discussed

a.   Suffixes

-ale/-iale/-uale	$[[\ X \ ]_N + \text{suffix} \ ]_A$
-oso/-ioso/-uoso	"
-ario/-iario/-uario	"
-are/-iare/-uare	$[[\ X \ ]_N + \text{suffix} \ ]_V$

b.   Examples of derivatives[2]

-ale	i.	strad+a	ii.	mond+o	iii.	grad+o
		strad+ale		mond+i+ale		grad+u+ale
-oso	i.	ferr+o	ii.	mister+o	iii.	mostr+o
		ferr+oso		mister+i+oso		mostr+u+oso
-ario	i.	second+o	ii.	fond+o	iii.	cens+o
		second+ario		fond+i+ario		cens+u+ario
-are	i.	sched+a	ii.	distanz+a	iii.	accent+o
		sched+are		distanz+i+are		accent+u+are

What conditions govern the presence vs. absence of the glides in derivatives of the kind presented in (1b)?

I will show that, in spite of the superficial similarity of the contexts in which the two glides appear, their distribution is governed by fairly different conditions.

Geert Booij and Jaap van Marle (eds), Yearbook of Morphology 1998, 103-126.

The back glide /w/ is part of a root allomorph that is developed by bases conforming to a certain schema (in the sense of Bybee and Slobin 1982; Bybee and Moder 1983; cf. § 3). This analysis has consequences for the choice between two alternative models of Italian denominal derivation, as I will briefly show in § 4.

The front glide /j/ appears mostly after bases ending in certain suffixes; although its overall distribution in the Italian lexicon can still be accounted by means of two schemata à la Bybee (cf. § 5), its behaviour in neologic creations (§ 6) is better captured by positing a morphologically conditioned readjustment rule which operates when the suffix *-ale* attaches to bases containing certain other suffixes (§ 7). The analysis of derivatives with /j/, therefore, shows that the devices needed to account for productive lexeme formation processes can be different from those used for the analysis of existing complex words.

2. THE CORPUS

The present research is based on a corpus containing all the derivatives in *-iale, -uale, -ioso, -uoso, iario, -uario, -iare, -uare* present in a reverse dictionary of Italian,[3] and in five dictionaries of Italian neologisms of the Eighties.[4] The number of words with each final shape in the corpus is shown in (2):

(2)   Number of words with each final shape in the corpus

iale	uale	ioso	uoso	iario	uario	iare	uare
95	49	19	27	15	17	29	12

For convenience, a rough number of derivatives with each of the suffixes under discussion not preceded by any glide is given in (3).[5]

(3)   Rough number of derivatives with *-ale, -oso, -ario, -are* not preceded by glides

-ale	-oso	-ario	-are[6]
±850	±540	±360	±900?

Clearly, the derivatives which display a glide between the root of the base and the suffix are the exception rather than the rule. Our task, then, is to find out what conditions determine the appearance of the glides.

We will discuss the derivatives with the front glide and those with the back glide separately.

3. DERIVATIVES WITH /w/[7]

3.1. Data

Historically, most of the bases of these derivatives go back to Latin fourth declension nouns, whose stem ended in - *u* (4a); there are, however, a number of derivatives from bases of other kinds, as the data in (4b-e) show:

(4)   Bases of derivatives with /w/ (total = 82)
        Derivatives already existing in Latin are <u>underlined</u>.
        Neologisms are in **boldface**.

    a.   Descendants of Latin fourth declension nouns (-*u* stems) (total = 48)
        Examples:

accento 'stress'	→ accentuale 'accentual', accentuare 'to accentuate'
arco 'bow, arch'	→ <u>arcuare</u> 'to bend', <u>arcuato</u> 'bent, arched'
caso 'case'	→ <u>casuale</u> 'casual; relating to case'
evento 'event'	→ eventuale 'contingent'
lusso 'luxury'	→ lussuoso 'luxurious'
porto 'harbour'	→ portuale, portuario 'relating to a harbor', <u>portuoso</u> 'having many harbors'

        ...

    b.   Descendants of Latin nouns alternating between fourth and second declension (total = 8)
        Examples:

tumulto 'riot'	→ <u>tumultuoso</u> 'tumultuous'
punto 'point'	→ puntuale 'punctual'

        ...

    c.   Descendants of Latin nouns of the second declension (-*o* stems) (total = 18)
        Examples:

santo 'saint'	→ <u>santuario</u> 'sanctuary'
mostro 'monster'	→ <u>mostruoso</u> 'horrible'
talento 'talent'	→ **talentuoso** 'talented'
delitto 'crime'	→ delittuoso 'criminal'

        ...

    d.   Descendants of Latin nouns of the third declension (-C stems) (total = 4)

monte 'mount'	→ <u>montuoso</u> 'mountainous'
ponte 'bridge'	→ pontuale 'relating to bridges' (rare)
voluttà 'pleasure'	→ <u>voluttuoso</u>,<u>voluttuario</u> 'voluptuous'
bound root mens- 'month'	→ <u>mensuale</u> 'monthly' (rare, antiquated)

e. New bases (not attested in Latin according to Lewis and Short)
    brevetto 'patent'   → **brevettuale** 'concerning patents'
    contorno 'contour'   → **contornuale** 'concerning contours'
    per cento 'per cent'   → percentuale 'percentual, percentage'
    rapporto 'relationship'   → **rapportuale** 'concerning relationships'

The bases exemplified in (4) do not share any morphological property, except for a clear preponderance of nouns of masculine gender (only two bases, *voluttà* and *mano* 'hand', are feminine). We will comment later on the relevance of this feature.

3.2. Segmental conditions

From the segmental point of view, it is striking that the overwhelming majority of the bases (95,1%) have a root[8] ending in a coronal anterior segment.[9]

However, a root ending in a coronal anterior segment does not automatically yield the insertion of /w/ before one of our suffixes, as the data in (5) show:

(5)   Rough number of derivatives from bases with a root ending in a coronal anterior segment and without /w/ between root and suffix

-ale	-oso	-ario
>300	~100	>100

Examples:

fato 'fate'   → *fatale* 'fatal'
dialetto 'dialect'   → *dialettale* 'dialectal'
naso 'nose'   → *nasale* 'nasal'
colosso 'colossus'   → *colossale* 'colossal'
cultura 'culture'   → *culturale* 'cultural'
spirito 'humour'   → *spiritoso* 'humorous'
sasso 'stone'   → *sassoso* 'full of stones'

Thus, having a root ending in a coronal segment seems to be at most a necessary, but by no means a sufficient, condition to yield a derivative with a /w/ between root and suffix. Therefore, it cannot be incorporated into a phonological rule or a readjustment rule.

3.3. The schema

I propose that this condition functions rather as a schema, in the sense of Bybee and Slobin (1982) and Bybee and Moder (1983). These authors introduce the concept of schema in relation to the past tenses of English irregular verbs. These past tense forms

> are rote-learned and stored in the lexicon, but this does not prevent speakers from formulating generalizations about these forms. These generalizations are not in the form of rules that derive one thing from another by changing features. Thus we will not call them rules, but will rather refer to them as SCHEMAS. A SCHEMA is a statement that describes the phonological properties of a morpho-logical class [...]. It is not a constraint which rigidly specifies what can and can-not occur, but it is rather a much looser type of correlation [...] (Bybee and Slobin 1982: 267).

Bybee and Slobin (1982: 279) exemplify their notion of schema with a class of English verbs whose past tense has the shape in (6):

(6)   æŋ(k)] _{verb}
     past

They comment that "the schema defines a prototype of the category (in the sense of Rosch and Mervis 1975), in that *sing* or *drink* are the best exemplars – but *swim* and *begin* may also belong to the category because they end in nasals, although not velar nasals" (Bybee and Slobin 1982: 279).

The theory of Bybee and colleagues, then, is that a schema defines the prototype of a category that functions as a natural class, i.e., a schema defines/describes a class by referring to its prototype, which is defined on the basis of its phonological shape. The phonological shapes of the members of the class form a series of family resemblances rather than sharing a discrete set of features. The "most common and best exemplars" of the class conform to the schema, i.e., to the prototype.

Using this notion of schema, and the idea that morphological classes, like natural categories, can be defined not by a necessary and sufficient set of features but by their clustering around a prototype, we could say that there is a prototypic shape of the bases of derivatives displaying /w/ before one of the suffixes in (1a); bases which differ from the prototype by one feature only often still behave like the prototype, i.e., belong to the class of bases which display a /w/ in derivatives containing one of the suffixes in (1a), while progressively more distant bases display progressively less often the /w/ before these suffixes.

The prototype of bases displaying /w/ is shown in (7):

(7)   Base ends in /Ct/

i.e., base ends in $C_1 C_2$
                              $|$
                         [- Continuant]
                         [- Sonorant]
                         [- Voice]
                         Coronal
                         [+Anterior]

Bases differing from the prototype by one or more features are schematized in (8):[10]

(8)   Shape of the base   Feature(s) differing from the prototype

a.   Base ends in /Cs/   [+ Continuant] C_2
b.   Base ends in /Vt/   V instead of C_1
c.   Base ends in /Vs/   [+ Continuant] C_2, V instead of C_1
d.   Base ends in /Cn/   [+ Sonorant] C_2
e.   Base ends in /Ck/ C_2 is not Coronal
   ...

The number and percentage of bases of each type in the corpus are shown in (9).

(9)

Final shape	Number of bases	Percentages	Cumulative percentage
/Ct/	51	61.4	61.4
/Cs/	10	12.0	73.4
/Vt/	9	10.8	**84.2**
/Vs/	3	3.6	
Other	10	12.0	

It is clear that the majority of bases that have a root allomorph ending in /w/ either correspond to the prototype or differ from it by only one feature. A chi-square test was run to determine whether the distribution of the bases in the first three rows in (9) differed significantly from what could be expected given the number of bases with the relevant shape in the language. It turns out that the difference between the prototype and the /Cs/ shape is not significant (χ^2 (1) = 0,69, p = n.s.), while the difference between the prototype and the /Vt/ shape is highly significant (χ^2 (1) = 22,81, p <.001).

This leads to the hypothesis that there is a hierarchy among the features characterizing the prototype: having a C_1 before C_2 is more important than having exactly /t/ as C_2, and the feature [Coronal] is more important than the feature [- Continuant].[11]

Even more striking in their conformity to the prototype are the data which result from taking into account only the bases of the 'new' derivatives with /w/, i.e., the bases of those derivatives that did not exist in Latin (according to Lewis and Short). These data are shown in (10).

(10)   Number and percentage of new derivatives from bases
         with different final shapes

Final shape of the base	Number of derivatives	Percentage	Cumulative percentage
/Ct/	41	66.1	66.1
/Cs/	9	14.5	80.6
/Vt/	6	9.7	**90.3**
Other	6	9.7	

It seems that the likelihood for a base to develop a /w/ final root allomorph is directly proportional to the closeness of the base to the prototype defined by the schema in (7), and decreases abruptly for bases differing from the prototype by more than one feature, again with certain features being more important than others in defining the shape of the prototype.

The characteristics recognized by Bybee and Slobin in the schemas for English irregular past tenses and considered by these authors as general characteristics of all morphological schemata are listed in (11):

(11)   Characteristics of the schemas for English irregular past tenses

(a) Their defining properties are phonological and can range over more than one segment.

(b) Classes of items covered by schemas are defined in sets of family resemblances, not by sets of strictly shared properties.

(c) Though schemas do not in themselves change features, they are used in lexical selection; and they may serve as the basis of new formations occasionally, either in speech errors [...] or in so called analogical formations [...] (Bybee and Slobin 1982: 285).

The schemata we have established to describe the class of bases that may develop a /w/ final root allomorph, which is then used before one of the suffixes in (1a), have the characteristics (11b) and (11c); as far as characteristic (11a) is concerned, although the definition of our schema is primarily phonological, some other conditions seem to play a role: the bases should be masculine,[12] and should not contain the suffix *-mento*, although it has the appropriate phonological shape. [13] The generalization in (12) holds both in the attested lexicon and in neologisms:

(12)   -mento   →   -mentale   *-mentuale
         e.g.
         ornare   →   ornamento   →   ornamentale   *ornamentuale
         fondare →   fondamento →   fondamentale   *fondamentuale

Furthermore, there is another characteristic which distinguishes the schema we have established to describe the set of bases that may develop a /w/ final root allomorph from Bybee and Slobin's schemata. Bybee and Slobin claim that schemata are product-oriented generalizations: one of their schemata "does not relate a base form to a derived one, as a rule does, but describes only one class of forms (the product class, in terms used by Zager 1980)" (Bybee and Slobin 1982: 267). Our schema in (7), on the contrary, is not product-oriented but base oriented (or 'source-oriented', in Zager's terms): the relevant conditions are defined over the base and not over the derivative (or at least, there is no gain in defining them over the derivative).

It seems, therefore, that the study of the Italian bases which employ a /w/ final root allomorph before certain suffixes has led us to widen the concept of morphological schema, to include also source-oriented generalizations that define classes of bases rather than classes of outputs.

4. A MODEL OF ITALIAN DENOMINAL DERIVATION

Some observations are in order here about the actual mechanics of the derivation of denominal lexemes which display a /w/ between root and suffix.

It is customary to refer to Italian nouns through a citation form which ends in a vowel. In denominal derivatives, however, the final vowel of the base's citation form does not appear. This vowel is lacking not only in derivatives with /w/ before the suffix, but in all the derivatives we are considering (cf. 1bi), and in fact in all Italian denominal derivatives. To explain why this is so, we must consider in full the working of Italian denominal (and deadjectival) derivation.

Some models of Italian derivation (notably that of Scalise 1983, 1984) claim that denominal and deadjectival derivation in Italian takes as a base an 'abstract word' homophonous with the citation form of the lexeme (the singular of nouns, and the masculine singular of adjectives). When a vowel-initial suffix is added, the final vowel of the base, if unstressed, is deleted by a vowel deletion rule characterized as in (13):

(13)   V   → Ø / ___ + V
         [- stress]
         (Scalise 1984: 68)

Other authors, however, (notably, Peperkamp 1995) observe that practically all denominal and deadjectival suffixes of Italian are vowel-initial, so that rule (13) must operate in practically all instances of denominal or deadjectival derivation in Italian. This is rather uneconomical; an account of Italian denominal and deadjectival derivation in which the root of a nominal or adjectival lexeme is assumed as the actual base to which suffixes attach is therefore preferable.

Further evidence that the base of denominal and deadjectival derivation in Italian is the root is provided, according to Peperkamp (1995: 214-215), by the behavior of -*cino* and -*cello*, two consonant-initial allomorphs of the diminutive suffixes -*ino* and -*ello*. "These allomorphs are selected with bases that end in a sequence -*on* plus vowel" (Peperkamp 1995: 215), and in the output the root of the base appears: *leon-e* → *leoncino* 'lion → DIM.', *poltron-a* → *poltroncina* "armchair → DIM.'. If suffixes were to attach to bases containing the final vowel, there would be no way to explain the lack of the vowel in these outputs, as the vowel deletion rule only applies with vowel initial suffixes, and sequences like *leonecino, *poltronacina* are not ruled out by any phonotactic constraint (cf. the existing words *lumicino* 'small light', *Terracina* (toponym)). "If, on the other hand, the base of suffixation is the root, we can simply state that bases in -*on* select for the allomorph -*cino* and -*cello* and no vowel deletion needs to apply" (Peperkamp 1995: 215).

The assumption that Italian denominal and deadjectival derivation takes as bases abstract words that end in a vowel and are homophonous with free forms seems to have arisen out of a misunderstanding of Aronoff's (1976) word-based hypothesis. As Aronoff (1994) has made clear, the hypothesis that derivational morphology is word-based must be understood in the sense that it is lexeme-based, and not in the sense that the base must be (homophonous with) a word used as a free form. Aronoff (1994: 7) explicitly states: "I especially did not mean that the base or stem for a word formation rule had to be a complete word or free form, only that the base should be a lexeme and the stem some form of a lexeme". A model of Italian denominal and deadjectival derivation which assumes the lexeme's root as base is then fully compatible with Aronoff's (1994) model of lexeme-based morphology.

In such a model, the lexical entries for Italian nouns might be organized around roots, and look like the ones in (14):

(14)   A possible format of the lexical entries for Italian nouns

Root	/kas-/	/libr-/	/fjor-/
Syntactic info.	N, fem	N, masc	N, masc
Semantic info.	'house'	'book'	'flower'
Morphological info.	class 2	class 1	class 3
	sg. -a	sg. -o	sg. -e
	pl. -e	pl. -i	pl. -i

If a noun has root allomorphy, this can be represented as in (15):

(15)   Representation of *uomo* (pl. *uomini*) 'man'

Root 1	/wɔm-/
Root 2	/'wɔmin-/
Syntactic info.	N, masc
Semantic info.	'man'
Morphological info.	class 1
	sg. -o, select root 1
	pl. -i, select root 2

In representations like those in (14) and (15), the citation form does not appear; the surface forms of both singular and plural can be computed on the basis of the morphological information provided.[14]

This model of Italian denominal derivation has welcome consequences for our analysis of derivatives with /w/. We have assumed that lexical items whose root conforms to the schema in (7) develop a root allomorph ending in -*u*, which is then selected as the base to which one of the suffixes in (1) attaches.[15] The possibility of having more than one root allomorph, with conditions stating the distribution of each, is required independently, as we have seen in (15). There is therefore no principled reason to exclude the presence of a /u/ final root allomorph, in addition to the bare root, in the representation for certain words, as in (16):

(16)   Representation of *monte*

Root 1:	/mont-/
Root 2:	/montu-/
Syntactic info.	N, masc
Semantic info.	'mountain, mount'
Morphological info.	class 3
	sg. -e
	pl. -i
	Select root 2 with -*oso*, ...
	Select root 1 elsewhere

Notice that if a vowel deletion rule such as (13) existed, the final /u/ of Root 2 would never have a chance to surface, as it would be deleted when followed by a vowel-initial suffix. Instead, in our account of Italian denominal derivation, we define Root 2 as a root allomorph employed with certain suffixes and, as derivation is root based and no vowel deletion rule exists, the /u/ surfaces, changing to /w/ for certain speakers (cf. § 1, *supra*), so that, e.g., *montuoso* can be syllabified either as /mon.tu.'o.so/ or as /mon.'two.so/.

5. DERIVATIVES WITH /j/

I have been able to collect 118 bases which have at least one derivative in which one of the suffixes in (1a) is preceded by /j/. There is no strong historical relation among these bases, comparable to the descent from nouns belonging to the Latin IV declension for the bases of derivatives with /w/.

5.1. Two schemata

The best way to account for all the derivatives with /j/ between root and suffix attested in the Italian lexicon seems to be the hypothesis of the existence of phonologically defined schemata, as in the case of derivatives with /w/. There are two schemata, shown in (17), which can define the bases which yield derivatives with /j/.

(17)   Schemata of the bases which yield /j/ derivatives

   a.   **"ts" schema**

   Prototype: Base ends in $C_1 C_2$[16]   i.e., base ends in /Cts/

$$\widehat{\qquad\qquad}$$

[- Continuant]	[+ Continuant]
[- Sonorant]	[- Sonorant]
[- Voice]	[- Voice]
Coronal	Coronal
[+Anterior]	[+Anterior]

   Examples: *esistenza* → *esistenziale, razza* → *razziale*
   Shapes differing from the prototype by one or more features:

Base ends in /Ct/	lack of the [+ Continuant] unit
Base ends in /Cs/	lack of the [- Continuant] unit
Base ends in /Vts/	V instead of C_1
Base ends in /Vt/	lack of the [+ Continuant] unit, V instead of C_1
Base ends in /Vs/	lack of the [- Continuant] unit, V instead of C_1

Examples: *veste* → *vestiario*

b. **"r" schema**

Prototype: Base ends in   V   C   i.e., base ends in /Vr/
                                        |
                                   [+ Sonorant]
                                   [+ Continuant]
                                   [+ Voice]
                                   Coronal
                                   [+Anterior]
                                   [- Lateral]

Examples: *ministero* → *ministeriale*, *imprenditore* → *imprenditoriale*

Shapes differing from the prototype by one or more features:

Base ends in /Vl/   [+ Lateral] C
Base ends in /Cr/   C instead of V before /r/
...
Examples: *umile* → *umiliare*, *nobile* → *nobiliare*

The table in (18) shows the number and percentage of bases with each final shape.

(18)

Final shape	Number of bases	Percentage	Cumulative percentage
a. /Cts/	55	46.6	46.6
/Ct/	8	6.8	53.4
/Cs/	2	1.7	**55.1**
Other	3	2.4	
b. /Vr/	29	24.6	24.6
/Vl/	6	5.1	29.7
/Cr/	2	1.7	**31.4**
			86.5

A chi-square test shows that the difference between the number of bases in the prototype and in the second and third row in (18a) respectively is highly significant (/Cts/ vs. /Ct/: χ^2 (1) = 129,73, p < .001; /Cts/ vs. /Cs/: χ^2 (1) = 20,47, p < .001).

The table in (19) shows the number and percentage of new derivatives with /j/ from bases of different final shapes:

(19)

	Final shape	Number of derivatives	Percentage	Cumulative percentage
a.	/Cts/	77	62.6	62.6
	/Ct/	1	0.8	63.4
	/Cs/	1	0.8	64.2
	/Vts/	1	0.8	**65.0**
	/Vt/	1	0.8	/
	/Vs/	1	0.8	/
b.	/Vr/	24	19.5	19.5
	/Vl/	6	4.9	24.4
	/Cr/	2	1.6	**26.0**
				91.0

Here again, bases conforming to the prototype are the vast majority.

Now that we have seen the schemata at work with derivatives which display a /j/, we can compare them with the schema at work with /w/ derivatives. The interesting point is that there are certain phonological configurations that could be members of classes defined by two different schemas, yielding root allomorphs with different glides. For example, bases ending in /Ct/, besides conforming to the prototype of the class defined by the schema in (7), are also good members of the class defined by the schema in (17a), differing from the prototype for this class in only one feature, the lack of a [-continuant] unit; bases ending in /Cs/ differ from bases ending in /Ct/ (prototype of the class defined by the schema in (7)) only in the feature [+continuant], and from bases ending in /Cts/ (prototype of the class defined by the schema in (17a)) by the lack of the [-continuant] unit. The prediction, in such a case, would be that we should find, at least occasionally, derivatives from bases of these shapes with both glides. This prediction is borne out by data such as those in (20):

(20)	/Cs/ base	derivative with /j/	derivative with /w/
	asse 'axis'	assiale 'axial'	—
	sesso 'sex'	—	sessuale 'sexual'

5.2. Morphological conditions

As we have just seen, phonologically defined schemata account well for the appearance of /j/ between stem and suffix in certain derivatives. Therefore, we could offer an account parallel to the one given for the appearance of /w/: the bases defined by the schemata in (17) develop a root allomorph ending in /j/ which is then selected to be used with the suffixes in (1a).

It is worth considering, however, that many of the bases of these derivatives end in one of the suffixes -*tore*, -*anza*, -*enza*, as shown in (21):

(21)   Number of bases in -*tore*, -*anza*, -*enza* which have one or more /j/ derivatives

-tore	(deverbal suffix forming agent nouns)	15
-anza	(deadjectival/deverbal suffix forming quality nouns)	5
-enza	” ”	48

Thus, we could hypothesize that at least in these cases it is the suffix in the base which is responsible for the appearance of the glide, and we could try to write a readjustment rule inserting /j/ after these suffixes. But there are two problems with this account. In the first place, about half of the derivatives with /j/ remain unexplained, as they do not come from bases with these suffixes; some examples are given in (22):

(22)	Base	Derivative
	ministero 'ministry'	ministeriale 'ministerial'
	mondo 'world'	mondiale 'world-wide'
	razza 'race'	razziale 'racial'
	grande 'big'	grandioso 'grand'
	umile 'humble'	umiliare 'to humiliate'
	terzo 'third'	terziario 'tertiary'

More crucially, there are counterexamples to the generalization that bases with the suffixes in (21) yield a derivative with /j/. These counterexamples are shown in (23):

(23)   Derivatives from bases in *-anza, -enza, -tore* without /j/
(neologisms are in **boldface**)

-ale: semenzale, influenzale, pastorale, elettorale, dottorale[17]

-oso: burbanzoso, baldanzoso, speranzoso, **vacanzoso**

-ario: scadenzario

-are: burbanzare, fidanzare, speranzare, quietanzare, incombenzare,
piacenzare, cadenzare, scadenzare, mordenzare, agenzare,
urgenzare, influenzare, addottorare

Therefore, it is not possible to predict the occurrence of /j/ before one of our suffixes on morphological grounds, at least if we want to predict the distribution of /j/ in the whole Italian lexicon.

6. PRODUCTIVITY

In this section we will look at the neologisms formed with our suffixes, to see whether the glides appear with new derivatives.

While the formation of denominal verbs in *-are* seems to be slightly, if at all, productive in contemporary Italian (cf. Iacobini and Thornton 1992: 32), all three adjectival suffixes are productive in a Schultinkian sense, i.e., new words are formed with them. Among neologisms, however, we find glide final root allomorphs employed essentially only in the formation of *-ale* derivatives. The table in (24) gives an outline of the data.

Anna M. Thornton

(24)   Neologisms with the suffixes *-ale*, *-oso* and *-ario*

	-ale	glide+ale	-oso	glide+oso	-ario	glide+ario
Neologisms from prototypic bases						
Ct	giuntale comportamentale apprendistale frattale	rapportuale gestuale fattuale oggettuale progettuale conflittuale autoportuale	—	talentuoso	eccedentario divertimentario	—
Cts	—	adolescenziale dirigenziale tangenziale emergenziale coscienziale consulenziale vertanziale coesistenziale	vacanzoso incazzoso	—	—	—
Vr	cantautorale! figurale congiunturale (anticongiunturale) infrastrutturale	manageriale teenageriale datoriale amatoriale genitoriale monitoriale settoriale autoriale	caciaroso ceroso paperoso	—	carcerario	—
Neologisms from non-prototypic bases						
	epocale camionale decisionale promozionale coitale ... (Total: 43)	bardottiale	palloso quattrinoso malavitoso ... (Total: 14)	—	budgetario evoluzionario comunitario ... (Total: 16)	—

Contrary to what has been observed in the attested lexicon, no glide-final root allomorph is employed to create new derivatives in *-ario*; in two cases (*carcerario, eccedentario*), there is no glide in derivatives from a base which corresponds to the prototype of one of the classes defined by the schemata we have discovered.[18] With *-oso*, the /Ct/ schema for /w/ seems active, and the /Cts/ schema for /j/ seems inactive (there are two derivatives, *vacanzoso* and *incazzoso* that have no glide in spite of the fact that their bases fit the schema). As to the status of the /Vr/ schema, the three derivatives which display a glideless root allomorph in the relevant segmental conditions (*caciaroso, ceroso, paperoso*), are from feminine bases (*caciara* 'noise (dialectal)', *cera* 'wax' and *papera* 'slip of the tongue' (literally, 'duck'), respectively). It might be that feminine bases are excluded from the schema, as was the case with the /Ct/ schema. In any case, *-ario* and *-oso* neologisms from prototypic bases are so few that the evidence for or against the productivity of the schemata with them is hardly conclusive.

With *-ale*, all three schemata seem active,[19] and neologisms in *-ale* without glide from bases which match the prototype of one of the schemata are extremely rare and can in most cases be accounted for.

Among neologisms from bases apparently conforming to the prototype of the /Ct/ schema, *giuntale* is from a feminine base (*giunta*), and as we have seen, masculine gender constitutes a condition defining the /Ct/ schema; *comportamentale* is from a noun in *-mento*, not fitting the schema because of the restriction in (12); *apprendistale* is from *apprendista* 'apprentice', a noun that can be both masculine and feminine, and in any case ends in *-a*, an ending typical of feminine nouns. It might be that a /w/ root allomorph is not created in this case because the base is formally too similar to a feminine base. Finally, *frattale* is a loanword from English *fractal* and/or French *fractal*.

Among neologisms from bases matching the /Vr/ schema, *figurale, infrastrutturale* and *congiunturale* are from feminine bases, and *anticongiunturale* is a prefixed derivative from *congiunturale*. It is possible that masculine gender is a condition to be added also to the definition of the prototype of the /Vr/ schema, as derivatives from feminine bases that match the phonological definition of this schema also fail to display the glide with *-oso*, as we have seen. *Cantautorale* (from *cantautore* 'singer-author', a blend from *cantante* 'singer' and *autore* 'author') is a real counterexample, as there is no glide in a derivative from a base ending in *-tore*, while all the other derivatives with /j/ from bases in the /Vr/ schema are from nouns in the Agentive/Instrumental suffix *-tore* or from English bases with the comparable suffixes *-er, -or* (*manageriale, teenageriale*,[20] *monitoriale*). No neologism in *-ale* from a base matching the /Cts/ schema appears without /j/, but all the neologic derivatives in this schema are from bases in *-enza* .

The schemata we have discovered for /j/, therefore, seem to be active mostly in the derivation with the most productive suffix in our set, *-ale*, and with this suffix they appear to be defined by a morphological condition (the base should end in the suffixes *-enza, -tore, -er* or *-or*) rather than by a purely phonological one.

7. DISCUSSION

Let us summarize our findings.

To account for derivatives with /w/, we have hypothesized that certain bases, whose root corresponds to a prototype described by the phonologically and morphologically definable, base-oriented schema in (7), may have or develop a root allomorph ending in /w/, which is employed in the derivation of adjectives in *-ale* and occasionally in *-oso*, and which is also observable in the attested lexicon in derivatives in *-ario* and *-are*. Productivity is scanty (only 7 neologisms), as expected with morphological processes regulated by a schema rather than by a rule.

Bybee and Moder, following Rosch, call our attention to the factor of 'cue validity' as predictor of the productivity that a morphological class defined by means of a schema can attain. According to Rosch, "cue validity is a probabilistic concept: the validity of a given cue X as a predictor of a given category Y [...] increases as the frequency with which cue X is associated with category Y increases, and decreases as the frequency with which cue X is associated with categories other than Y increases" (Rosch 1978: 30).

In the case of the category of bases which display a root allomorph ending in /w/, the cue validity of the schema we have established is very low, as most of the bases that match the prototype in the language do not in fact display a glide-final root allomorph. There are almost 2000 masculine nouns whose root ends in /Ct/, and only 51 have a root allomorph with final /w/.

Thus, the schema for root allomorphs with final /w/ is not very productive, but, like some of the schemata discovered by Bybee and colleagues, can "serve as the basis of new formations occasionally" (Bybee and Slobin 1982: 285, cf. (11) above). There are in fact a few neologisms in *-uale* and *-uoso* from bases that conform to the prototype, as we have seen in (24), and in a pilot test I have been able to elicit oral production of *-uale* derivatives from bases which do not have an established adjectival derivative in the language and whose phonological shape conforms to the schema in (7).

As for cases in which a /j/ appears, different analyses are possible. If we want to take into account the whole Italian lexicon, the analysis will be parallel to that offered for /w/ derivatives: certain bases, conforming to one of the two phonologically defined schemata in (17), may have or develop a root allomorph ending in /j/, which is employed in derivatives with one of the suffixes in (1a).

But another analysis is possible for derivatives in *-iale*. Let us consider the data in (25), which show the number of derivatives in *-ale* (excluding neologisms) with and without /j/ from bases in *-anza, -enza,* and *-tore*:

(25)   Number of derivatives in *-ale* (excluding neologisms) with and without
        /j/ from bases in *-anza, -enza,* and *-tore*

	-anza	*-enza*	*-tore*
with /j/	4	42	14
without /j/	–	2	2

From the data in (25), we can see that the presence of one of the three suffixes *-anza*, *-enza* and *-tore* has high cue validity in predicting that a derivative in *-ale* will display a /j/ before this suffix, as there are very few counterexamples to this generalization. If, then, we hypothesize the existence of morphologically defined schemata such as the ones in (26), which define a base containing one of these suffixes as prototypic for derivatives in -/jale/, such schemata would have a high cue validity, contrary to the low cue validity of the purely phonologically defined schemata in (17).

(26)   Morphologically defined schemata of bases which have /jale/ derivatives

    a.   Base ends in -*anza*
    b.   Base ends in -*enza*
    c.   Base ends in -*tore*

The morphologically defined schemata in (26) are not mutually exclusive with the phonologically defined ones in (17). Of course, there is overlapping between the sets of bases captured by the morphologically defined schemata in (26a-b) and the phonologically defined schema in (17a), and by the schema (26c) and the schema (17b). But the interesting point is that the two sorts of schemata have different cue validity: this is quite low for the phonologically defined schemata in (17), but quite high for the morphologically defined ones in (26).

According to Bybee's (1988) approach, in which the difference between rules and schemata is not qualitative but purely quantitative, in that "rules are highly reinforced representational patterns or schemata" (Bybee 1988: 135), we would predict that a 'highly reinforced' schema, i.e., a schema with high cue validity, such as the ones in (26), is almost non-distinct from a rule. And in fact, this is the case: remember that with -*ale* all but one of the neologisms from bases conforming to the morphologically defined schemata in (26) display the /j/, and conversely, only one neologism displaying the /j/ (*bardottiale* < *Bardot* /bar'do/) is not derived from a base defined by one of the schemata in (26). This almost categorical behaviour is typical of a productive lexeme formation rule.

So, if we do not aim at generating the whole Italian lexicon, but limit our aim only to the characterization of productive processes, the establishment of a morphological condition is possible. As we have seen (cf. (24) above), /j/ appears in neologisms only in derivatives with -*ale* from bases ending in the suffixes -*enza*, -*tore* or English -*er*, -*or*. In this case, we might analyze the data both as cases of morphologically governed base allomorphy (as in (27a)) or of morphologically governed suffix allomorphy (as in (27b)):

(27)   Two possible analyses for the appearance of /j/ in neologisms with -*ale*

    a. $+\text{tor}]_N \rightarrow +\text{tori}]_N \,/\underline{\quad}+\text{ale}]_A$
             $+\text{enz}]_N \rightarrow +\text{enzi}]_N \,/\underline{\quad}+\text{ale}]_A$
        ...
    b. $+\text{ale}]_A \rightarrow +\text{jale}]_A \,/ +\text{tor}]_N \quad +\underline{\quad}$
                     $+\text{enz}]_N$
                     $+\text{er}]_N$
                     $+\text{or}]_N$

Up to a point, the decision between analyses (27a) and (27b) is arbitrary, as both correctly describe the facts.

Analysis (27a) would be preferred on historical grounds, as the source for the observed allomorphy is in the fact that the Latin suffix *-entia* yielded derivatives in *-entialis*, and the Latin suffix *-torius* (*+tor+ius*) yielded derivatives in *+torialis*, which then formed the model for analogical creations in *-enziale*, *-toriale* from Italian bases in *-enza*, *-tore*.

Analysis (27b) would be preferred on economic grounds, as it reduces the number of allomorphic entities in the language (only the suffix *-ale* would have an allomorph, vs. the four suffixes *+tore*, *+enza*, *+er* and *+or*).

8. CONCLUSION

In this paper I have described the conditions that govern the appearance of /w/ and /j/ before certain derivational suffixes of Italian. The back glide /w/ can appear when the base conforms to a schema which is mainly phonologically defined (cf. (7) above). The same schema accounts well for the appearance of /w/ both in derivatives that have been part of the Italian lexicon for a long time and in the few neologisms that display this glide. In the case of derivatives with /j/, on the contrary, we have to separate the acccount given for the bulk of derivatives attested in the Italian lexicon from the account which is possible to give for the formation of neologisms. While two phonologically defined schemata à la Bybee (cf. (17) above) account well for the whole set of existing derivatives with /j/, the set of neologisms can be analyzed better by positing a readjustment rule that inserts /j/ between base and suffix in certain morphologically defined contexts (cf. (27) above). In Bybee's approach, in which rules are simply highly reinforced schemata, the conditions governing the appearance of /j/ in neologisms can still be considered schemata. Nevertheless, there is a strong contrast between these schemata and the schema which accounts for the appearance of /w/. The two sorts of schemata occupy the opposite ends of a continuum: the /w/ schema has low cue validity and is used only occasionally in the production of new derivatives, while the /j/ schemata that account for neologisms have high cue validity and are productive: virtually all new derivatives whose base conforms to one of these schemata display /j/. These schemata, therefore, are nondistinct from rules.

The study of derivatives with /w/ and /j/ has shown that the devices available for the analysis of the attested lexicon can be different from those used in accounting only for productive processes. In other words, word formation rules are not the only devices availabe for word analysis. Schemata have proved themselves useful in the analysis of attested Italian derivatives with antesuffixal /w/ and /j/ which cannot be generated by rules.

NOTES

*   This paper was read at the First Mediterranean Conference of Morphology, Mytilene (Greece), September 19-21, 1997. I wish to thank Alessandro Laudanna for helping me with statistical analyses, Federica Casadei and Maria Grossmann for providing useful references, Barbara Weiden Boyd for checking my English, and, last but not least, Geert Booij and two anonymous referees for their helpful suggestions. Thanks also to Cippa, Paola, Alessandro, Mimmo, Enrico, Simone, Luigi, Miriam, Zipe and Felice for taking part in my test and for producing many occasional derivatives with /w/ from prototypic bases.

1   *-are* is used here as a convenient citation form (homophonous with the infinitive ending) to identify a process of conversion of nouns into first conjugation verbs (distinguished by the thematic vowel *-a-*). By no means should it be implied, however, that I take the infinitive (inflectional) ending as having category-changing power. The actual process at work can be analyzed in two ways: either as the addition of a zero suffix *-0-a,* which forms verbs from adjectives and nouns, and is associated with the first verbal conjugation (as proposed in Thornton 1990), or (along the lines of Aronoff 1994) as a case of lexeme formation rule whose overt correlates are the assignment to the *-a-* inflectional class (first conjugation) and sometimes the selection of a given base allomorph (cf. *infra*, § 3.3).

2   Representation is in the standard orthography of Italian. The boundary symbol '+' is used pretheoretically in (1), simply to show the result of a blind segmentation procedure.

3   Based on the merging of Zingarelli (1983) and Garzanti (1987), two dictionaries of usage including around 100.000 words each (courtesy of Tullio De Mauro).

4   Quarantotto (1987), Cortelazzo & Cardinale (1989), Vassalli (1989), Forconi (1990), Lurati (1990).

5   These data are based on a reverse dictionary of an abridged dictionary of Italian, containing about 45.000 lemmata (Ratti et al. 1989).

6   It is difficult to determine the number of denominal verbs in *-are* because in a reverse dictionary they are not set apart from underived verbs in *-are,* which are the majority of Italian verbs. In BDVDB (Thornton, Iacobini and Burani 1994, 1997) denominal verbs in *-are* are 187 out of a total of 1007 verbs in *-are*, that is 18.6%. Projecting from this percentage, I have estimated the number of denominal zero-suffixed *-are* verbs in a 45.000 lemmata dictionary, which lists about 5000 verbs in *-are*, at about 900.

7   Derivatives with /w/ are also discussed by Rainer (1998, to appear).

8   In what follows, I will call 'root' that part of a word which remains when the word is stripped of its inflectional ending. In many cases, this entity is not monomorphemic; therefore, some linguists object to calling it a 'root', and prefer to call it a 'stem'. In the framework of Italian morphology, however, this terminology could be misleading. It has been argued (by Dressler and Thornton 1991) that Italian verbal morphology must be described by positing, for each verb, two base allomorphs, called 'base radicale' and 'base tematica', each of which is used in a number of inflectional, derivational and compounding processes. The 'base radicale' is the verb's root, while the 'base tematica' (or simply 'tema') is the verb's root followed by a thematic vowel, which is different for each conjugation (e.g., for the three verbs *parlare, vedere, sentire* 'to speak/talk, to see, to hear/feel', the roots are *parl-, ved-, sent-*, and the 'temi' are *parla-, vede-, senti-*). A common and traditional English translation for 'tema' is 'stem'. So the word 'stem', in the framework of Italian morphology, implies the presence of a thematic vowel in the entity referred to. I believe that there is a basic asymmetry between verbal and nominal morphology in Italian, because in nominal (and denominal) morphology there is no need to posit entities such as 'temi' or stems provided with a thematic vowel (*contra* Scalise 1993: 190; cfr. *infra*, § 4). There are, of course, entities which correspond to the definition of 'root' given

above, but are polimorphemic, both among nouns and among verbs. Dressler & Thornton (1991: 7) propose to call these entities 'derived roots', and define a derived root as a root derived from another one by means of a WFR. For example, the verb *gareggiare* 'to compete' is formed from the noun *gara* 'competition' by addition of the derivational suffix /eddʒ/, which forms verbs of the first conjugation: thus, the verb's stem (or 'tema', or 'base tematica') is *gareggia-* (which appears in the infinitive *gareggiare*, or in the imperfect indicative *gareggiavo*, etc.), while its root -- a derived root -- is /gareddʒ/, which appears in some present indicative and subjunctive forms, such as *gareggio, gareggi*. A parallel example from nominal morphology is the noun *sentimento* 'feeling': it is derived from the verb *sentire* 'to feel', which appears in its stem (or 'tema', or 'base tematica') *senti-*, by addition of the derivational suffix *ment-*, which forms nouns that belong to the inflectional class that has the ending *-o* in the singular and *-i* in the plural. Thus *sentiment-* is a derived nominal root, which in its turn appears in derivatives such as *sentimentale*. In this paper, both monomorphemic and derived nominal roots will be referred to simply as 'roots'.

9   Only the roots of the following bases do not end in a coronal segment:

Base	Derivatives
arc+o 'bow'	*arcuato, arcuare*
antic+o 'ancient'	*antiquario*
bound root *lac-* connected to *lago* 'lake'	*lacuale*
rip+a 'river bank'	*ripuario* (rare)

The three words whose roots end in /k/ are reflexes of words that belonged to the Latin fourth declension. *Ripa* is included only for the sake of completeness: in fact, its only derivative with /w/, *ripuario,* is rare and not in contemporary usage (while *ripario* is more usual, at least in the name of the river *Dora Riparia*), and *ripa* itself is not used in contemporary standard Italian, where it has been replaced by *riva*. It seems, then, that in contemporary usage only nouns ending in a coronal can acquire a root allomorph ending in /w/ (cf. the data in 4e); words that have such an allomorph even if their root does not end in a coronal are all inherited from Latin.

10   A base differs from the prototype by one feature if C_2 is either [+Continuant], [+Sonorant], [+Voice], non Coronal or [-Anterior], or if it is preceded by a V rather than by a C.

11   The existence of a hierarchy among the features defining the prototype of a class had already been discovered by Bybee and colleagues. Bybee (1988: 135) observes that in schemata "some features [are] more strongly represented than others". Bybee and Moder (1983) report experimental evidence that the features defining a class of English irregular monosyllabic verbs are ranked, in that the final consonant is the most important defining feature, followed by the initial consonant cluster, while the vowel counts very little in defining a nonce-form as part of the class.

12   No new derivatives with /w/ have appeared from feminine bases: *voluttuario* 'voluptuary', *voluttuoso* 'voluptuous', from fem. *voluttà* 'pleasure, voluptuousness', and *manuale* 'manual' from fem. *mano* 'hand' are inherited from Latin.

13   This is reminiscent of a negative morphological restriction in the sense of Aronoff (1976: 53).

14   However, there are psycholinguistic data that point to the fact that the citation form of nominal lexical items has a privileged status in the Italian mental lexicon (cf. Burani

1992 and references therein). Therefore, a less economical but psychologically more plausible model of Italian lexical entries might include the citation form along with one or more root allomorphs.

15 Geert Booij suggests that this could be interpreted as paradigmatically determined allomorphy.

16 The autosegmental representation of the affricate /ts/ in (19a) is not entirely correct from a technical point of view. It is adopted here for purposes of clarity. No violation of the OCP is implied.

17 Consider also the pair of synonyms *rettorale/rettoriale,* from *rettore* 'head of a University' (Sgroi 1997).

18 In the case of *divertimentario,* the glide is predictably absent because of the restriction involving the suffix *-mento* observed in (12).

19 There is also an occasional extension of /j/ to a non prototypic base (*Bardot* → *bardottiale*).

20 This word seems to be an Italian creation: *teenagerial* does not exist in English, as Mark Aronoff has observed in Mytilene.

REFERENCES

Aronoff, M. 1976. *Word-Formation in Generative Grammar.* Cambridge: The MIT Press.

Aronoff, M. 1994. *Morphology by Itself. Stems and Inflectional Classes.* Cambridge: The MIT Press.

Burani, C. 1992. "Patterns of Inflectional Errors with Reference to the Italian Adjectival System". *Rivista di Linguistica* 4 (2), 255-272.

Bybee, J.L. 1988. "Morphology as Lexical Organization". In M. Hammond and M. Noonan (eds), *Theoretical Morphology.* San Diego et alibi: Academic Press, 119-141.

Bybee, J.L. and D.I. Slobin. 1982. "Rules and Schemas in the Development and Use of the English Past tense". *Language* 58, 265-89.

Bybee, J.L. and C.L. Moder. 1983. "Morphological Classes as Natural Categories". *Language* 59, 251-270.

Cortelazzo, M. and U. Cardinale. 1989. *Dizionario di parole nuove 1964-1987.* Torino: Loescher.

Dressler, W.U. and A.M. Thornton. 1991. "Doppie basi e binarismo nella morfologia italiana". *Rivista di Linguistica* 3, 3-22.

Forconi, A. 1990. *Dizionario delle nuove parole italiane.* Milano: SugarCo.

Garzanti 1987 = *Il grande dizionario Garzanti della lingua italiana.* Milano: Garzanti.

Iacobini, C. and A.M. Thornton. 1992. "Tendenze nella formazione delle parole nell'italiano del ventesimo secolo". In B. Moretti, D. Petrini and S. Bianconi (eds), *Linee di tendenza dell'italiano contemporaneo.* Roma: Bulzoni, 25-55.

Lewis & Short = *A Latin Dictionary.* Oxford: OUP.

Lurati, O. 1990. *3000 parole nuove. La neologia negli anni 1980-1990.* Bologna: Zanichelli.

Marotta, G. 1987. "Dittongo e iato in italiano: una difficile discriminazione". *Annali della Scuola Normale Superiore di Pisa* 17, 847-887.

Peperkamp, S. 1995. "Prosodic Constraints in the Derivational Morphology of Italian". In G. Booij and J. van Marle (eds), *Yearbook of Morphology 1994.* Dordrecht:

Kluwer, 207-244.

Quarantotto, C. 1987. *Dizionario del nuovo italiano*. Roma: Newton Compton.

Rainer, F. 1998. "Paradigmatic Factors in the Irradiation of Allomorphy: The Reanalysis of the Latin Type MANUALIS in Italian". In G. Booij, A. Ralli and S. Scalise (eds), *Proceedings of the First Mediterranean Conference of Morphology*. Patras: University of Patras, 77-85.

Rainer, F. to appear. "I meccanismi di diffusione di allomorfi: il caso della rianalisi del tipo*man-u-alis* in italiano". In P. Benincà, A.M. Mioni and L. Vanelli (eds), *Fonologia e morfologia dell'italiano e dei dialetti d'Italia*. Roma: Bulzoni.

Ratti, D., L. Marconi, G. Morgavi and C. Rolando (eds) 1989. *Flessioni, rime, anagrammi: l'italiano in scatola di montaggio*. Bologna: Zanichelli.

Rosch, E. 1978. "Principles of Categorization". In E. Rosch and B.B. Lloyd (eds), *Cognition and Categorization*. Hillsdale, NJ: Erlbaum, 27-48.

Rosch, E. and C.B. Mervis. 1975. "Family Resemblances: Studies in the Internal Structure of Categories". *Cognitive Psychology* 7, 573-605.

Scalise, S. 1983. *Morfologia lessicale*. Padova: Clesp.

Scalise, S. 1984. *Generative Morphology*. Dordrecht: Foris.

Sgroi, S.C. 1997. "I derivati in *-iale* e in *-uale*: dai prestiti lessicali all'induzione di morfema". *Bollettino della Società di Linguistica Italiana (SLI)* XV (2), 95-97. Expanded version to appear in P. Benincà, A.M. Mioni and L. Vanelli (eds), *Fonologia e morfologia dell'italiano e dei dialetti d'Italia*. Roma: Bulzoni.

Thornton, A.M. 1990. "Vocali tematiche, suffissi zero e "cani senza coda" nella morfologia dell'italiano contemporaneo". In M. Berretta, P. Molinelli and A. Valentini (cds), *Parallela 4. Morfologia/Morphologie*. Tübingen: Narr, 43-52.

Thornton, A.M., C. Iacobini and C. Burani. 1994. *BDVDB. Una base di dati per il Vocabolario di base della lingua italiana*. Roma: Istituto di Psicologia del CNR (2nd ed., Roma: Bulzoni, 1997).

Vassalli, S. 1989. *Il neoitaliano. Le parole degli anni Ottanta*. Bologna: Zanichelli.

Zager, D. 1980. *A Real-time Process Model of Morphological Change*. Buffalo: SUNY Dissertation.

Zingarelli, N. 1983. *Vocabolario della lingua italiana*. XI ed. Bologna: Zanichelli.

Universita' Degli Studi - L'Aquila
Dipartimento Di Culture Comparate
Via Camponeschi 2
67100 L'Aquila

The nonuniform structure of Dutch N-V compounds*

PETER ACKEMA

1. INTRODUCTION

The structure of compounds perhaps does not appear to be the most exciting issue in morphological theory. Usually it is assumed that compounds are formed by adjoining one X^0 stem to another, resulting in a structure like (1).

(1)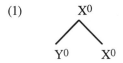

In this paper I argue that, for N-V compounds at least, this view on compounding needs to be adapted, in two respects. First, not all N-V compounds have the same structure. Second, the structure of an N-V compound can be more complex, but also less complex, than the one in (1). I will argue that this more flexible picture of the structure of N-V compounds can explain a correlation between the argument structure of such compounds and their syntactic behaviour. I will focus my attention on N-V compounds in Dutch.

Dutch N-V compounds can be divided along two lines. First, as with all verbal compounds in this language, there are separable and inseparable compounds. In the case of separable compound verbs (henceforth SCVs) the noun is stranded when the verb undergoes V2 in a main clause (see (2)). In the case of inseparable compound verbs (henceforth ICVs) the noun is taken along under V2 (see (3)).[1]

(2) a. Petra rijdt met veel plezier paard
      Petra rides with much pleasure horse
      'Petra has much pleasure in horseriding'
  b.* Petra paardrijdt met veel plezier
      Petra horserides with much pleasure

(3) a. Piet slaapwandelde de hele nacht
      Piet sleepwalked the whole night
      'Piet was sleepwalking the whole night long'
  b.* Piet wandelde de hele nacht slaap
      Piet walked the whole night sleep

The second distinction between two types of N-V compound that can be made concerns the thematic status of the noun with respect to the verb. In one type the noun corresponds to the verb's internal argument, which, if expressed syntactically, would be expressed by a direct object NP; see (4). In the other type, the noun does

Geert Booij and Jaap van Marle (eds), Yearbook of Morphology 1998, 127-158.
© 1999 *Kluwer Academic Publishers. Printed in the Netherlands.*

not correspond to an argument, but it receives a modifying interpretation, which, if expressed syntactically, would be expressed by an adjunct; see (5).

(4) Piet zette een heerlijk kopje koffie, hoewel hij bijna   nooit koffiezet
     Piet made a delicious cup of coffee, although he almost never coffeemakes
     'Piet made a delicious cup of coffee, although he almost never makes coffee'

(5) Iemand die buikspreekt   spreekt natuurlijk niet echt   met zijn buik
     someone who stomachspeaks speaks of course not really with his stomach
     'A ventriloquist does not really speak via his stomach of course'

One might think that this second distinction is not a real one. In general, the semantic relation between the noun and the verb in an N-V compound is very free. The interpretation of the noun as the internal argument of the verb might simply be one of the possibilities this semantic freedom allows for (see for instance Carstairs-McCarthy (1992: 118) for such an argument with respect to synthetic compounds in English).

I will argue, however, that the difference between argumental nouns and nonargumental nouns is a fundamental one in that it reflects a structural difference between the two types of N-V compound. This structural difference will account for a correlation that I will show exists between the thematic status of the noun and the syntactic behaviour of the N-V compound. This correlation is the following: if the noun is an argument of the verb, the N-V compound must be separable.

The paper is organized as follows. In section 2, an argument is made in favour of regarding SCVs as morphological constructs. Section 3 discusses the question what the difference between ICVs and SCVs is, if it is not one of morphology versus syntax. In section 4 the structure of N-V compounds with an argumental noun is discussed. It is shown that it follows from this structure, in combination with a general constraint on V2 in Dutch, that such compounds must be separable. In section 5 it is shown that, because of their structure, it should be impossible for the noun to be an argument in ICVs and that this turns out to be correct. In section 6 a potential problem for the analysis that is posed by N-V compounds in Frisian is discussed. Section 7 contains the conclusion.

2. THE MORPHOLOGICAL STATUS OF SCVs

It is not very controversial to assume that ICVs are morphological constructs and are not derived syntactically. But the syntactic or morphological status of SCVs in Dutch has been the subject of some debate. Especially particle verbs, where the same distinction between SCVs and ICVs occurs that was illustrated for N-V compounds in section 1, have come up for discussion.

Consider a separable particle verb like *opbellen* 'call up' (lit. 'upcall'):

(6) a.   (Ik denk) dat Jan   zijn moeder   opbelde
      (I think) that Jan   his mother   upcalled
      '(I think) that Jan called his mother'
  b.   Jan belde zijn moeder   op
      Jan called his mother   up
      'Jan called his mother'

Because the parts of an SCV can become separated as a result of a syntactic movement process, some authors argue that both parts of an SCV originate as distinct syntactic constituents. The compound then is derived via syntactic incorporation of the particle into the verb. An analysis along these lines is proposed by Hoekstra, Lansu and Westerduin (1987), who assume that the particle starts out as the head of a Small Clause complement to the verb:

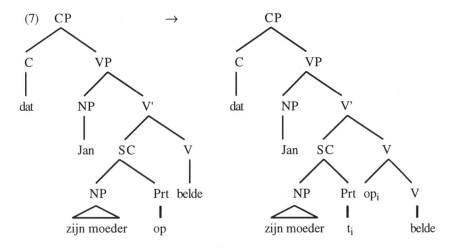

A similar analysis can of course be given for separable N-V compounds. These would then involve incorporation of the head of an NP complement to the verb (on a par with what Baker (1988) proposes for noun incorporation structures in polysynthetic languages). In (8) such a derivation is given for the SCV *brandstichten* 'fire-light'.

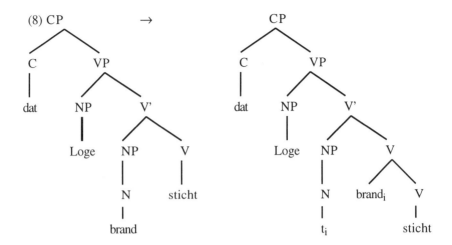

(8)

The advantage of such an analysis is that it straightforwardly explains why the noun is interpreted as the verb's internal argument.

Neeleman and Weerman (1993) argue, however, that separable particle verbs must be morphologically derived. The most straightforward argument for a morphological analysis of such verbs is that they can be input to further morphological derivation (see also Groos 1989 and Booij 1990). If the parts of such SCVs are generated as separate syntactic constituents, as in (7), this morphological activity can only be explained if all subsequent derivations (after incorporation of the particle) take place in syntax as well. Neeleman and Weerman show that the interactions between morphology and syntax needed in that case lead to unattested structures.

Like separable particle verbs, separable N-V compounds can be input to further derivation, as the examples in (9) show.

(9) a. ademhalen 'breath-get'   ademhaling 'breathgetting'
        brandstichten 'fire-light'   brandstichting 'firelightning'
        wraaknemen 'revenge-take'   wraakneming 'revengetaking'
        hulpverlenen 'aid-give'   hulpverlening 'aidgiving'
        oorlogvoeren 'war-wage'   oorlogvoering 'warwaging'
    b. kaartlezen 'map-read'   kaartlezer 'mapreader'
        komediespelen 'comedy-play'   komediespeler 'comedyplayer'
        notenkraken 'nut-crack'   notenkraker 'nutcracker'
        hulpverlenen 'aid-lend'   hulpverlener 'aidlender'
        actievoeren 'action-undertake'   actievoerder 'actionundertaker'
    c. rechtspreken 'right-speak'   rechtspraak 'rightspeech'
        pianospelen 'piano-play$_V$'   pianospel 'pianoplay$_N$'

It might seem that the righthand examples in (9a-c) are structured as in (11) rather than (10), i.e. that they are not derivations of compound verbs, but compounds with a deverbal noun as head.

(10)

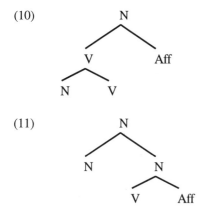

(11)

Although structures as in (11) exist as well, (10) does seem to be the most plausible structure for the examples under discussion.[2] This is indicated by the fact that the synthetic compounds preserve the possibly idiosyncratic meaning of the separable N-V compounds on the basis of which they are formed according to (10). For example, *ademhalen* 'breath-get' in (9a) means 'breathe' and *ademhaling* means 'respiration'; *komediespelen* 'comedy-play' in (9b) means 'simulate' and *komediespeler* means 'one who simulates'; and *rechtspreken* 'right-speak' in (9c) means 'administer justice' whereas 'rechtspraak' means 'administration of justice'. Given the structure in (10) this follows straightforwardly from a compositional semantics; given the structure in (11) some extra mechanism would be necessary to derive these facts.

Also, in some cases the deverbal noun that occurs as righthand part in (11) does not exist independently, as for instance with *haling in *ademhaling* or *neming in *wraakneming* in (9a). This argument is not compelling (cf. also Van Santen 1992), given that there are other cases of synthetic compounds for which neither the lefthand compound of (10) nor the righthand derivation of (11) exist independently. However, given that in the cases in (9) the N-V compound does exist independently, the structure in (10) again appears the more plausible one. The least we can say, then, is that the combined force of these two arguments makes it hard to maintain that separable N-V compounds can *not* undergo further derivation. (Also, if the argumentation below is correct, (11) is not a possible structure in the first place for cases in which the noun is the internal argument of the verb, like those in (9)).

As noted, the fact that further derivation of SCVs with for instance *-er* and *-ing* is possible can only be explained under a syntactic analysis if these derivations take place syntactically (after syntactic incorporation of the lefthand part of the compound) as well. It is unlikely that this is possible, however. A canonical instance of a syntactic incorporation structure in Dutch, namely the verb cluster that results from V-to-V raising in clauses with infinitival complements, as in (12) (cf. Evers 1975),

Peter Ackema

cannot be input to such derivation, as is shown in (13).[3]

(12) a. dat ik [Eva een lied t_i] hoor   fluiten$_i$
        that I   Eva a song   hear   whistle
        'that I hear Eva whistle a song'

     b. dat we [Loge een brand t_i] zien stichten$_i$
        that we Loge a fire   see light
        'that we see Loge start a fire'

(13) a. * horenfluiter
          hearwhistler
     b.* zienstichting
          seelighting

Hence, the fact that separable N-V compounds can be further derived is an argument in favour of their being morphologically derived.

Separable N-V compounds can not only be input to further derivation, but to further compounding as well:

(14)   koffiezetapparaat   paardrijdinstituut   brandstichtavontuur
          coffeemake-machine   horseride-institute   firelight-adventure

          houtzaagmolen   houtsnijkunst   broodbakwedstrijd
          woodsaw-mill   woodcut-art   breadbake-competition

At noted by Booij (1990: 51), this does not seem to be an argument for a morphological (V^0) rather than syntactic (VP) status of SCVs at first sight, because full XPs can occur as lefthand members in compounds in Dutch anyway (see for instance Hoeksema 1988, and Botha 1981 for discussion of similar data in Afrikaans). The NP-N compounds in (15), for instance, are grammatical neologisms.

(15) a. lekkere-koffieliefhebber $[_N[_{NP}$ lekkere koffie] $[_N$ liefhebber]]
          goodcoffeelover
     b. tropisch-houtwinkel $[_N[_{NP}$ tropisch hout] $[_N$ winkel]]
          tropicalwoodshop

However, it turns out to be impossible to have a VP consisting of a direct object plus verb as the lefthand member of a compound:[4]

(16) a. * lekkerekoffiezet-apparaat $[_N [_{VP}$ [lekkere koffie] zet] apparaat]
          goodcoffeemake-machine
     b.* tropischhoutzaag-molen $[_N [_{VP}$ [tropisch hout] zaag] molen]
          tropicalwoodsaw-mill

c. * grotebrandsticht-avontuur   [N [VP [grote brand] sticht] avontuur]
   greatfirelight-adventure

If VP-N compounds are indeed impossible, the examples in (14) indicate that SCVs are not VPs but V⁰s.⁵ Under a syntactic incorporation analysis for SCVs, as in (8), these facts can only be derived if the V^0 complexes so derived could be input to further compounding in syntax. But, as was the case with derivation, this is very unlikely, given that verb clusters that are derived by syntactic incorporation cannot possibly occur as lefthand member of a nominal compound (compare (17) with (12)-(13) and with (14)):

(17) a. * horenfluiten-ervaring
        hearwhistle-experience
     b. * zienstichten-getuige
        seelight-witness

So, SCVs appear to be morphological constructs. Nevertheless, they can be split in syntax. Because SCVs appear to have this dual syntactic and morphological behaviour, it has also been proposed that they belong to a special category that is somewhere in between morphology and syntax. Thus, they have been termed *samenkoppelingen* ('together-linkings') (Geerts et al. 1984; De Haas and Trommelen 1993), or *lexoïden* ('lexoids') (Model 1991) or they are said to have a special X-bar level in between V^0 and V' (Booij 1990). Elements belonging to such a special category (namely the SCVs) then are argued to behave like morphological constructs but to differ from them in that they can be split up by syntactic movement.

The argument for assigning SCVs such a special status usually is that, whereas SCVs appear to be morphological constructs (see above), they cannot possibly be real morphological constructs because they do not obey the principle of Lexical Integrity (see for instance Booij and Van Santen 1995: 120). However, instead of introducing an extra grammatical area in between syntax and morphology to accommodate SCVs, it is also possible to give up the idea that morphological constructs are subject to an absolute Lexical Integrity principle.

In fact, it can be shown that independently motivated restrictions on movement, in particular the ECP, can account for apparent Lexical Integrity effects with respect to movement, while at the same time allowing excorporation of the head of a compound. This result is obtained by invoking the well-known requirement that traces of nonreferential elements be antecedent-governed (see Rizzi 1990 and Cinque 1990). Simplifying things considerably, we can say that the nonhead of an SCV cannot be excorporated because the head of the compound will always be a minimality barrier for antecedent government of the trace of the nonhead:

(18)   * Y^0_i ... [$_{X0}$ t_i X^0]

This problem of course does not arise in case of movement of the head of the compound itself – hence, this is possible:[6,7]

(19)   ok X^0_i ... $[_{X0} Y^0 t_i]$

It can be concluded that SCVs are morphological constructs. Their separability can be explained under the assumption that morphology is not opaque to syntax. The same principles that apply to syntax apply to morphology, hence movement rules can affect morphological constructs. But since the conditions that restrict movement apply to morphology just as well, possible movement out of an SCV is limited to its head.

3. THE DIFFERENCE BETWEEN SCVs AND ICVs

If SCVs in Dutch are indeed morphological constructs a new problem arises: what is the difference between SCVs and ICVs, if it is not one of syntactic versus morphological derivation? It seems that both animals are morphological, but that one is more morphological than the other. Saying that, however, is not much of an answer.

An answer can be provided on the basis of the idea that morphological constructs have autonomous structures in the various modules of grammar. Thus, a morphological construct has a particular structure in the syntactic module and it has a particular structure in the phonological module. These structures are built by different principles and, crucially, they need not be isomorph. (A link between these structures must be established, of course, for instance by the type of correspondence rules proposed in Jackendoff 1997).

The idea that morphological constructs have autonomous phonological and syntactic representations is present at least since structuralism (cf. Hockett 1954) and has been used in various guises in the generative literature (see for instance Marantz 1984; Sproat 1985; Zubizarreta 1985; Sadock 1991; Halle and Marantz 1993; Beard 1995). I assume that in the syntactic module morphosyntactic structures are created in accordance with general syntactic wellformedness principles like X-bar principles. In the phonological module morphophonological forms are inserted that correspond to terminal nodes in the morphosyntactic structure. Crucially, there need not be a one-to -one relation between terminal nodes in the morphosyntactic tree and morphophonological stems and affixes.

An example of a deviation from a one-to-one correspondence is the process of morphological conversion. Don (1993) argues that the properties of this process can be made to follow from the hypothesis that a converted word is complex in the syntactic module (where the structure contains a stem position and an affix position) but simplex in the phonological module (where it consists of a stem form only). An element corresponding to the affix position in syntax is altogether lacking at PF. This is illustrated in (20) for the noun *run*, derived from the verb *run*; cf. Don (1993: 100).

(20)

```
              N
            /   \
        V      AFFIX        (morpho)syntax
        |        |
       RUN    NOMINAL
       ----------------
            run            (morpho)phonology
```

Given such a conception of morphology, the difference between SCVs and ICVs can be said to be the following. SCVs are complex structures in both syntax and phonology. ICVs, however, although phonologically complex, are simplexes in syntax. (In this respect ICVs are the mirror-image of cases of conversion). As an illustration, the structures of the SCV *paardrijden* 'horseride' and the ICV *slaap-wandelen* 'sleepwalk' are given in (21) and (22) respectively. (The morphosyntactic structure in (21) is to be made more precise below).

(21)

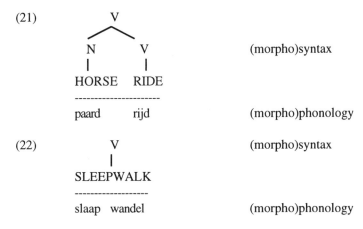

```
              V
            /   \
        N      V          (morpho)syntax
        |        |
      HORSE    RIDE
       ----------------
      paard     rijd       (morpho)phonology
```

(22)

```
              V              (morpho)syntax
              |
         SLEEPWALK
       ----------------
      slaap  wandel          (morpho)phonology
```

Several syntactic and morphological differences between the two types of compound verbs can be made to follow from this conjecture. For example, an inflectional prefix like participial *ge-* must occur in between noun and verb in case of SCVs but in front of the noun-verb sequence in case of ICVs:

(23) a. * gepaardreden   a'. paardgereden
        GE-horse-ridden   horse-GE-ridden
     b.   geslaapwandeld   b'.* slaapgewandeld
        GE-sleep-walked   sleep-GE-walked

The impossibility of (23b'), in contrast to (23a'), follows straightforwardly from the fact that *slaapwandelen* is a simplex verb in combination with the fact that *ge-* is a prefix, not an infix.

As discussed above, an important syntactic difference between ICVs and SCVs is that ICVs undergo V2 as a whole, whereas SCVs strand the noun (see (2) versus (3) in section 1). This fact can now be explained by invoking a general principle that has the effect of excluding complex heads in C. A principle that does this is proposed by Neeleman and Weerman (1993) and Neeleman (1994). They argue that the following 'complexity constraint' is operative in Dutch (the formulation in (24) is from Neeleman 1994: 304).

> (24)   COMPLEXITY CONSTRAINT
>   The head of an X^0 may not be complex, where a head is complex
>   iff it branches

Given that V2 is substitution in a functional head, presumably C^0, (24) is violated if a syntactically complex verb undergoes V2, since C^0 would have a complex head then (the complex verb). Therefore, SCVs cannot undergo V2 as a whole. Only the V-head in (21) can move to C without violating (24). ICVs, on the other hand, are syntactically simplex, hence they undergo V2 as a whole.[8]

A possible objection to analyzing ICVs as syntactic simplexes is that in some cases their semantics is still transparently related to the semantics of the two morphemes on the basis of which they have been formed. The meaning of *slaapwandelen* 'sleepwalk', for example, is derived from the meanings of *slaap* 'sleep' and *wandel* 'walk' in a way that complies with the Righthand Head Rule for complex words.[9]

However, this does not imply that the ICV in question cannot be a simplex synchronically speaking. Its apparently transparent semantics can be a remnant of its diachronic history. There are several ways in which inseparable N-V compounds can come into being. Separable N-V compounds can become inseparable (cf. Wurzel 1993). Another possibility is backformation from a synthetic compound or nominal infinitive (cf. Holmberg 1976). As argued here, SCVs are syntactically complex, and in all probability so are synthetic compounds. The meaning of the ICV and its apparent rightheadedness then are remnants of its diachronic history. This does not exclude that in the synchronic grammar it is listed as a simplex in the lexicon, with a non-compositional meaning.

The fact that in case of *slaapwandelen* people still see a relation with the two morphemes it seems to consist of is a consequence of the fact that these two morphemes are still listed in the lexicon, with their respective meanings, as well. This is a coincidence rather than a necessity, however. Next to an ICV like *radbraken* 'break on the wheel', for example, the verb *braken* 'break' on the basis of which this was once formed does not occur in the Dutch lexicon any more (there is another verb *braken* which means 'vomit' and is obviously unrelated to this ICV). Consequently, the semantics of *radbraken* is not at all transparent for a present day speaker of Dutch who does not have any knowledge of the history of this word. Only an historical linguist sees the 'rightheadedness' of this word.[10]

Before turning to the main subject of the paper, let me summarize the conclusions reached so far. Like ICVs, SCVs in Dutch are morphological constructs, not syntactic ones. The syntactic properties of a morphological construct are governed by general syntactic principles and its phonological properties by general phonological principles (i.e. there are no principles that specifically hold for morphological constructs only). The difference between SCVs and ICVs is the following: both types of compound verb are complex in the phonological module of grammar, but only SCVs are complex in the syntactic module as well. ICVs are simplexes in syntax.

In the next two sections I will argue that a striking difference in the interpretation of the noun in SCVs and ICVs respectively follows from these conjectures.

4. SCVs AND ARGUMENTAL NOUNS

As mentioned above, I assume that morphological structures are subject to the same principles that syntactic structures are subject to. If this is correct in general, this must be true not only for conditions on movement (see section 2), but for structural restrictions on Θ-assignment just as well. Now, a general condition on Θ-assignment in syntax is that assigner and assignee are sisters in the structure (cf. Chomsky 1986). With respect to the direct internal Θ-role, this means that this Θ-role is assigned by a head X^0 to its complement, as in (25).

(25)
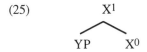

Therefore, if the direct internal Θ-role is to be assigned in morphology and if the same structural conditions on this assignment hold there, a head-complement structure must again be established. This means morphological phrase structure must parallel syntactic phrase structure, in the sense that a structural distinction between heads, complements, specifiers and adjuncts must be present. Here, I will adopt the phrase structure rules for morphology proposed in Ackema (1995), according to which heads in morphology are X^{-2} categories that project to X^0s, morphological complements then being sisters to X^{-2}, morphological specifiers being sisters to X^{-1} and morphological adjuncts of course occupying an adjunct position (cf. also Cinque 1993).

The configuration in (26), analogous to (25), must then be present if the direct internal Θ-role is to be assigned within a morphological construct.

(26)
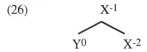

This means that an N-V compound in which the noun is the internal argument of the verb necessarily has a structure as in (27), otherwise Θ-assignment cannot take place.[11]

(27)

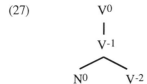

In other words, the structure of an N-V compound in which the noun is the internal argument of the verb is complex in the syntactic module of grammar.

If so, it is predicted that N-V compounds in which the noun is an argument are separable. This is because the condition in (24) is violated if V^0 in (27) is moved as a whole to C^0 (since C^0 would be headed by a complex V^0 then). A violation of (24) is avoided in the following way. First, N^0 adjoins to V^0, resulting in (28).[12]

(28)

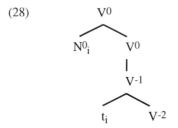

The lower V^0 in this structure can be excorporated (see section 2). If this lower V^0 is moved to C,[13] (24) is complied with if branches that do not dominate lexical material do not render an X^0 complex in the relevant sense. To this end the definition in (24) must be refined to (29).[14] (The additional facts that Neeleman (1994) derives from the complexity constraint, like the impossibility for SCVs to act as hosts for Verb Raising, still follow under this definition).

(29)   COMPLEXITY CONSTRAINT
         The head of an X^0 may not be complex, where a head is complex
         iff it branches into nodes that each dominate lexical material

The trigger for N^0-adjunction as in (28) hence is that the alternative derivation in which it does not take place crashes. Therefore, with respect to the interaction between N^0-adjunction and the condition in (29) we must assume a model in which global economy decides which structure surfaces.[15] Extra evidence for this view will be provided in section 6.

So, an N-V compound with an argumental noun is predicted to be necessarily separable. The reverse of this prediction is that, if an N-V compound is inseparable, the noun cannot be the internal argument of the verb. Θ-assignment is not possible in an ICV, since in a simplex structure like (22) there is nothing to which the Θ-role could be assigned.

We thus arrive at the following conjecture:

(30)   If N is an argument of V, N-V is separable

Note, by the way, that it need not necessarily be the case that in all SCVs the noun is the verb's argument (in other words, 'if' in (30) cannot be replaced by 'iff'). There can be compounds with a complex structure in which the noun is generated in adjunct position instead of argument position, as in (31).

(31)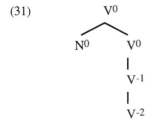

Note that in this case V^0 can be excorporated without prior N^0-movement being necessary, since (in contrast to SCVs with argumental nouns) the noun is generated directly in the position adjoined to V^0. (See also section 6.)

In order to establish the correctness of the prediction in (30), I will consider it from two angles. First, in the remainder of this section I will try to establish that those N-V compounds for which it can be argued on independent grounds that the noun is the verb's internal argument are indeed separable. Then in the next section it will be established that in inseparable compounds the noun indeed is not the verb's internal argument.

Let us consider N-V compounds with argumental nouns then. The clearest indication of argument-status of the noun in an N-V compound is detransitivization of the verb. If a verb that can take a syntactic internal argument can no longer do so when it occurs as the head of an N-V compound, this is straightforwardly accounted for by assuming that the N in the compound is assigned the verb's internal Θ-role. In that case, adding a syntactic direct object as well amounts to a violation of the Θ-Criterion (see also Rosen 1989).[16] Hence, the contrast between the (a) and the (b) examples in (32)-(33) indicates that the noun in the N-V compounds in the (b) examples is the verb's internal argument.

(32) a. Ik hoor dat Carla *(iets)   viert
         I hear   that Carla something celebrates
         'I hear that Carla celebrates something'

b. Ik   hoor   dat Carla (*iets)   feestviert
   I   hear   that Carla (something)   party-celebrates
   'I hear that Carla is having a party'

(33) a. Ik geloof   dat Loge *(iets)   sticht
        I believe   that Loge something lights
        'I think that Loge is starting something'
     b. Ik geloof   dat Loge (*iets)   brandsticht
        I believe   that Loge (something)   fire-lights
        'I think Loge is starting a fire'

Consider now the following lists of SCVs and ICVs respectively, taken from De Haas and Trommelen (1993: 133, 445-446) (with some additions of my own).

(34)   *SCVs*

ademhalen (breath-take) 'breathe'

brandstichten (fire-light) 'start a fire'

deelnemen (part-take) 'partake'

feestvieren (party-celebrate) 'have a
    party'

kaartlezen (map-read) 'read a map'

lesgeven (lesson-give) 'teach'

maathouden (measure-hold) 'keep time'

paardrijden (horse-ride) 'ride a horse'

plaatsvinden (place-find) 'happen'

rechtspreken (right-speak) 'administer
    justice'

schoolblijven (school-stay) 'stay at
    school during lunch'

autorijden (car-drive) 'drive a car'

collegelopen (course-walk) 'attend a
    course'

koffiezetten (coffee-set) 'make coffee'

komediespelen (comedy-play) 'simulate'

pianospelen (piano-play) 'play the piano'

televisiekijken (television-watch) 'watch tv'

dienstweigeren (service-refuse) 'refuse to
    go into military service'

gelukwensen (happiness-wish) 'congratulate'

standhouden (stand-keep) 'stand one's ground'

goededagzeggen (goodday-say) 'say hello'

goedemorgenwensen (goodmorning-wish)
    'wish a good morning'

goedenachtkussen (goodnight-kiss) 'kiss
    goodnight"

hulpverlenen (help-lend) 'render help'

broodbakken (bread-bake) 'bake bread'

Saabrijden (Saab-drive) 'drive a Saab'

PvdA-stemmen (PvdA-vote) 'vote for the
    PvdA'

(35)   *ICVs*

stofzuigen (dust-suck) 'vacuumclean'

beeldhouwen (statue-carve) 'sculpt'

slaapwandelen (sleep-walk) 'sleepwalk'

redetwisten (reason-argue) 'quarrel'

koorddansen (cord-dance) 'dance on the
    tight-rope'

grondverven (ground-paint) 'prime'

handwerken (hand-work) 'do needlework'

bloemlezen (flower-read) 'make an
    anthology'

rangschikken (rank-order) 'order'

heupwiegen (hip-rock) 'shake one's hips'

bekvechten (mouth-fight) 'quarrel'

zegevieren (victory-celebrate) 'win'

bloemschikken (flower-arrange) 'arrange flowers'

windsurfen (wind-surf) 'go windsurfing'

buikspreken (stomach-speak) 'ventriloquize'

kieskauwen (molartooth-chew) 'trifle with one's food'

radbraken (wheel-break) 'break upon the wheel'

stijldansen (style-dance) 'dance classic dances'

steengrillen (stone-grill) 'grill on a stone'

vingerverven (finger-paint) 'paint with one's fingers'

koekhappen (cake-bite) 'try to eat a cake that hangs from a line' (children's game)

wadlopen (shallow-walk) 'walk on the shallows'

hersenspoelen (brain-wash) 'brainwash'

dagdromen (day-dream) 'daydream'

Applying the detransitivization test illustrated in (32)-(33) shows that in the following members of these lists the noun is the verb's argument: *ademhalen, brandstichten, collegelopen, deelnemen, feestvieren, kaartlezen, maathouden, paardrijden, autorijden, Saabrijden, plaatsvinden, rechtspreken, koffiezetten, komediespelen, dienstweigeren, standhouden, hulpverlenen, broodbakken*.[17] In all these cases the head of the compound is a transitive verb, whereas the compound verb itself is intransitive.

To this list can be added those compounds that are formed on the basis of ditransitive verbs and that take only one syntactic internal argument (the other internal Θ-role hence being saturated by the lefthand N), like the one in (36b).

(36) a. Ik hoop dat Marie Piet iets   geeft
         I hope that Marie Piet something gives
         'I hope Marie will give Piet something'
     b. Ik hoop dat Marie Piet (*iets)   lesgeeft
         I hope that Mary Piet (something) lesson-gives
         'I hope Marie will be teaching Piet'

Such cases include *lesgeven* 'lesson-give', *gelukwensen* 'goodluck-wish', *goededagzeggen* 'goodday-say', *goedemorgenwensen* 'goodmorning-wish' and *goedenachtkussen* 'goodnight-kiss'.[18]

In fact, the list of N-V compounds with argumental nouns can be extended even further when considering cases like *televisiekijken* 'television-watch' and *pianospelen* 'piano-play'. At first sight, it appears that these have not been formed on the basis of transitive verbs that can take an internal argument of the relevant semantic type:[19]

(37) a. ?*Pires speelt een Steinway
           Pires plays   a   Steinway
           'Pires plays a Steinway'

b. ?*Frits kijkt   alle programma's
   Frits watches   all   programs
   'Frits watches all programs'

It can be argued, however, that these compounds too are the morphological realizations of a verb plus internal argument. The difference with the cases discussed
above is that in the syntactic structure that realizes these particular combinations of
head plus internal argument an extra element is present that must be deleted in the
morphological structure that realizes the same combination.

A case like *televisiekijken* is the morphological counterpart of a syntactic structure with a PP-complement to the verb (instead of an NP-complement):

(38)   Frits kijkt   naar alle programma's
        Frits watches   at   all   programs
        'Frits watches all programs'

In case of PP-complements, it is not the complete PP but the NP in the PP that is
the internal argument of the verb; the P is idiosyncratically selected by the verb to introduce this argument (cf. Neeleman 1997).

Now, it can be observed independently of the cases under discussion here that in
the morphological realization of the combination of a head plus argument or adjunct
sometimes elements can be left out that must be present in the syntactic realization
of the same combination. For instance, some syntactic idioms, like (39a), can be expressed morphologically, as in (39b).

(39) a.   Hij werkt met   zijn ellebogen
          he works with   his elbows
          'He pushes his way up'
     a'.* Hij werkt zijn ellebogen / * Hij werkt ellebogen
          he works his elbows /   he works elbows
     b.   Hij is een ellebogenwerker
          he is an   elbowsworker
          'He pushes his way up'
     b'.?*Hij is een metzijnellebogenwerker
          he is a   withhiselbowsworker

The syntactic structure contains material that in the morphological structure necessarily must be omitted. Yet they have the same idiomatic reading. This is straightforwardly explained if the idiomatic reading is associated with the combination of
head plus argument or adjunct (cf. Coopmans and Everaert 1988) and that both (39a)
and (39b) are realizations of the same such combination (cf. also Ackema and
Neeleman 1998).

Analogously, a compound like *televisiekijken* 'television-watch' plausibly is the morphological realization of the same verb plus internal argument combination as syntactic *naar de televisie kijken* 'at the television watch'. Note that the detransitivization test applies here as well: in contrast to *kijken*, *televisiekijken* cannot take a PP-complement (compare (40) with (38)).

(40) * Frits kijkt   naar alle programma's televisie
       Frits watches   at   all   programs   television

A similar case is the SCV *PvdA-stemmen* 'PvdA-vote', which corresponds to syntactic *op de PvdA stemmen* 'on the PvdA vote' with a PP-complement to *stemmen*.

The SCV *pianospelen* 'piano-play' is the morphological counterpart of syntactic *een piano bespelen* 'a piano *be*-play'. In this case, it is the verb's prefix that is not realized in the compound. This phenomenon too is not unique for this case. The process can be observed on a wider scale in Frisian, for which Dijk (1997: 103ff.) observes that a prefix or a particle is a hindrance for noun incorporation (although there are some exceptions) and that, as a remedy, it is possible to delete the prefix or particle. Two examples with *be-* are given in (41), from Dijk (1997: 122).

(41) a.   de   golle   *(be)ploaitsje
       the   haystack   pick
       'pick the haystack'
   a'.   golleploaitsje
       haystack-pick
   b.   in   draak *(be)plakke
       a   kite   stick
       'stick a kite'
   b'.   draakplakke
       kite-stick

Also, the detransitivization test gives a positive result for *pianospelen*, as it is intransitive, in contrast to both *bespelen* and *spelen*:

(42) a.   Pires bespeelt   een nieuw instrument
       Pires BE-plays   a   new   instrument
       'Pires plays a new instrument'
   a'.* Pires   speelt een   nieuw instrument piano
        Pires   plays a   new   instrument piano
   b.   Pires speelt   het 9e concert   van Mozart
       Pires plays   the 9th concerto   of   Mozart
       'Pires plays Mozart's 9th concerto'
   b'.* Pires speelt   het 9e concert   van Mozart piano
        Pires plays   the 9th concerto   of   Mozart piano

Cases like *televisiekijken* en *pianospelen* hence must be included in the list of

N-V compounds in which the noun is the verb's internal argument. This list then contains the following members:

(43)   *N-V compounds in which the noun is the verb's internal argument*
        ademhalen, brandstichten, deelnemen, collegelopen, feestvieren,
        huishouden, kaartlezen, maathouden, paardrijden, plaatsvinden,
        rechtspreken, autorijden, Saabrijden, koffiezetten, komediespelen,
        dienstweigeren, standhouden, hulpverlenen, broodbakken, lesgeven,
        gelukwensen, goededagzeggen, goedemorgenwensen, goedenacht-
        kussen, televisiekijken, PvdA-stemmen, pianospelen

When the list in (43) is compared to those in (34)-(35) we see that all members of (43) are SCVs, not one is an ICV. This clearly supports the conjecture in (30), which states that compound verbs with an argumental noun are necessarily separable.

5. ICVs AND NONARGUMENTAL NOUNS

Let us now consider the conjecture in (30) from the other side: in ICVs the noun cannot be an argument of the verb (as they are syntactically simplex). This appears to be correct as well in Dutch.

Consider the list of ICVs in (35). The first thing that can be noted is that a lot of ICVs are headed by an intransitive verb (for instance *slaapwandelen* 'sleep-walk', *redetwisten* 'reason-argue', *dagdromen* 'day-dream'). In these cases, then, the noun certainly is not an argument of the verb.

In fact, some minimal pairs can be constructed with verbs that have both an intransitive and a transitive variant, like *lopen* 'walk' and *rijden* 'ride'. It turns out that SCVs are headed by the transitive variant, whereas ICVs are headed by the intransitive variant:[20]

(44) a.   Anna loopt   twee   colleges tegelijk   (transitive)
           Anna walks   two   courses simultaneously
           'Anna takes two courses at once'
     a'.   Anna loopt   vanmiddag   college   (SCV)
           Anna walks   this afternoon course
           'Anna goes to a class this afternoon'
     a".* Anna collegeloopt   vanmiddag   (*ICV)
           Anna coursewalks   this afternoon
     b.   Wij lopen op het wad   (intransitive)
           we walk   on the shallow
           'We are walking on the shallow'
     b'.* Wij lopen met   veel plezier   wad   (*SCV)
           we walk   with   a lot of pleasure shallow

b".? Wij wadlopen   met veel   plezier   (ICV)
    we shallow-walk with a lot of pleasure
    'We love to walk on the shallows'

(45) a. Erika rijdt   een blauwe Saab   (transitive)
      Erika drives a   blue   Saab
      'Erika drives a blue Saab'
  a'. Erika rijdt   al   haar hele leven Saab   (SCV)
      Erika drives already her whole life   Saab
      'Erika has been a Saabdriver all her life'
  a".* Erika Saabrijdt   al   haar hele leven   (*ICV)
      Erika Saabdrives already her whole life
  b. De monteurs rijden in deze auto om hem te testen (intransitive)
      the repairmen drive in this car for him to test
      'The repairmen drive in this car in order to test it'
  b'.* De monteurs rijden al   hun   hele   leven test (*SCV)
      the repairmen drive already their whole life   test
  b".? De monteurs   testrijden al   hun   hele   leven (ICV)
      the repairmen   testdrive already their whole life
      'The repairmen have been testdrivers all their lives'

Similarly, some minimal pairs can be constructed by comparing verbs that take a PP-complement, introduced by a particular preposition, with verbs that are modified by a PP-adjunct that is introduced by the same preposition. In both cases the preposition is not realized in the corresponding compound (cf. section 4), but whereas the former are separable, the latter are inseparable:

(46) a. Frits kijkt   naar de televisie   (PP-complement)
      Frits watches   at   the television
      'Frits watches tv'
  a'. Frits keek   gisteren   televisie   (SCV)
      Frits watched   yesterday television
      'Frits watched tv yesterday'
  a".* Frits televisiekeek   gisteren   (*ICV)
      Frits televisionwatched yesterday
  b. De kinderen happen naar de koek   (PP-adjunct)
      the children bite   at   the cake
      'The children are trying to take a bite off the cake'
  b'.* De kinderen happen nou al de hele middag   koek (*SCV)
      the children bite   already the whole afternoon cake
  b". De kinderen koekhappen nou al de hele middag   (ICV)
      the children cakebite   already the whole afternoon
      'The children have been playing 'cake-bite' the whole afternoon'

(47) a.   Wim stemt op de PvdA   (PP-complement)
          Wim votes on the PvdA
          'Wim votes PvdA'
     a'. Wim stemt al   zijn hele   leven PvdA   (SCV)
          Wim votes already his whole life   PvdA
          'Wim has been a PvdA-voter all his life'
     a".* Wim PvdA-stemt al   zijn hele   leven   (*ICV)
          Wim PvdA-votes already his whole life
     b.   Bombini   danst   op een   koord   (PP-adjunct)
          Bombini   dances   on a   cord
          'Bombini dances on a cord'
     b'.* Bombini danst   al   zijn hele   leven koord   (*SCV)
          Bombini dances   already his whole life   cord
     b". Bombini koorddanst al   zijn hele   leven   (ICV)
          Bombini corddances already his whole life
          'Bombini has been a corddancer all his life'

This provides further evidence for (30).

However, there are also some ICVs that are derived from transitives. For some of these, it is clear enough on semantic grounds that the noun is not the verb's internal argument (compare *bloemlezen* (flower-read) 'make an anthology' with *ik lees een bloem* 'I read a flower', or *steengrillen* (stone-grill) 'grill on a stone' with *ik grill een steen* 'I grill a stone'). But in some other cases the noun appears to be an argument of the verb, for instance in *stofzuigen* 'dust-suck', *beeldhouwen* 'statue-carve' and *hersenspoelen* 'brainwash'. When the detransitivization test is applied, however, it becomes clear that this is only apparently so. All these ICVs remain transitive:

(48) a.   Hij stofzuigde de kamer
          he dustsucked the room
          'He vacuum-cleaned the room'
     b.   Voor de expositie in Brussel beeldhouwde zij een monumentale bizon
          for the exposition in Brussels statuecarved she a monumental   bison
          'For the Brussels exposition she sculpted a monumental bison'
     c.   De sekte hersenspoelde al zijn leden
          the sect brainwashed   all its   members
          'The sect brainwashed all its members'

Because the interpretation of the noun with respect to the verb is completely free in ICVs, it can get an interpretation as if it were the verb's internal argument, but the examples in (48) show that in fact it is not.

Only one ICVs seems to be really problematic, namely *zegevieren* 'victory- cele- brate'. Not only is the noun a semantically plausible candidate for the verb's argument, but in this case the verb is detransitivized as well:

(49) a. Vitesse vierde   de   overwinning uitbundig
      Vitesse celebrated the win   enthusiastically
      'Vitesse celebrated the victory enthusiastically'
   b. Vitesse zegevierde   (*de overwinning)
      Vitesse victory-celebrated   (the win)
      'Vitesse won'

There is one (admittedly weaker) indication for nonargument status of the noun, though, namely a semantic one: *zegevieren* simply means 'win' and has nothing to do with celebrating anything (this in contrast to the SCV *feestvieren* 'party-celebrate'). A sentence like (50), for instance, is perfectly felicitous.

(50)   PSV zegevierde   met 3-1, maar de spelers   waren erg ontevreden
        PSV victory-celebrated with 3-1, but   the players were very dissatisfied
        'PSV won 3-1, but the players were very dissatisfied'

Apart from this potentially problematic case, it may be concluded that the prediction in (30) turns out to be correct. This then is evidence for the claim that SCVs have the complex structure in (27)-(28) in the syntactic module, whereas ICVs have no (complex) structure in this module.

6. A NOTE ON FRISIAN

In Frisian there is a productive process of forming a type of N-V compound in which the noun corresponds to the verb's internal argument. Some examples are given in (51), from Dijk (1997).

(51)   messeslypje   jerappelskilen   koekjebakke   kistesteapelje
        knife-sharpen   potato-peel   cookie-bake   box-stack

That the noun is the verb's argument in these compounds is most strikingly shown by the detransitivization test again. Although formed on the basis of transitive verbs, all these compounds are intransitives themselves (Dijk 1997: 38):

(52) a. Doede woe   (*dy grouwe hazze) graach   wyldsjitte
      Doede wanted (that big hare)   gladly   quarry-shoot
      'Doede wanted to go hunting'
   b. De perfester   autohimmele alle sneonen   (*har Volvo)
      the professor   car-washed   all saturdays (her Volvo)
      'The professor washed her car every saturday'

As the example in (52b) already shows, these compounds pose a challenge for the analysis presented above, since in contrast to their Dutch counterparts they are *in*separable. Some more examples that show that they undergo V2 as a whole are given in (53), also from Dijk (1997).

> (53) a. Heit jerappeldolt   de hiele dei
>   father potato-digs   the whole day
>   'Father is digging potatoes all day long'
>   b. Hja bôlebakt   al   jierren mei   nocht
>   she loaf-bakes already   years with pleasure
>   'For years, she has been baking loaves with pleasure'

In section 4 I argued that, in order to establish the thematic relation between verb and noun, the compound must have a complex head-complement structure. At the same time, the Complexity Constraint in (29) prohibited a structurally complex verb under C^0, with the consequence that compounds with an argumental noun cannot move to C^0 in their entirety. How are the Frisian facts in (53) possible then?[21]

We could of course say that the condition in (29) is not universal, but is parameterized, the parameter then being 'on' in Dutch and 'off' in Frisian. Apart from the fact that this would be something of an ad hoc solution, it is still problematic because in that case all other effects that are derived from this constraint (cf. Neeleman 1994) should be absent as well in Frisian. It seems that the condition in (29) is void in cases of movement of complex N-V compounds to C^0, but not in general elsewhere.

A situation in which a constraint X is violated in some particular configuration is in fact predicted to occur if there is another constraint with which X conflicts in this configuration but not otherwise, when the perspective on grammar offered by Optimality Theory (Prince and Smolensky 1993) is adopted. The constraint in (29) can then remain truly universal. Its impact in a specific language follows from its ranking in the hierarchy of constraints. Evaluation of structures with respect to the constraint hierarchy of a language proceeds as follows. The structures to be compared are first evaluated with respect to the highest-ranked constraint. The candidates that score best on this constraint (i.e. violate it the least) are then judged by the next highest constraint, and so on, until one candidate is left (or more, if there are candidates that receive equal scores on all constraints). This surviving candidate is optimal and thereby grammatical; the other ones are all ungrammatical. A consequence of this view of constraint interaction is that no constraint is necessarily surface true. A lower ranked constraint can be violated in an optimal structure when this structure scores better on a higher ranked constraint than its competitors.

As noted, this means that the difference between Dutch and Frisian can be explained if there is a constraint that conflicts with the constraint in (29) in cases of V-to-C of complex verbs. This other constraint then must be ranked higher than (29) in Frisian but lower in Dutch. In other words, if there is a constraint that, in contrast to (29), *dis*favours excorporation of the verb when the compound must undergo

V-to-C, facts as in Frisian are predicted to occur.

Now, in section 4 I argued that, in order for verb excorporation to be possible, there must first be N^0-adjunction to V^0, see (27)-(28). Thus it is clear that there is indeed a constraint that disfavours separability: economy of movement. In section 4 I already argued that the trigger for the N^0-adjunction is that, if it does not take place, (29) is violated when the complex verb undergoes V-to-C. In embedded clauses N^0-adjunction does not occur (cf. footnote 12), as it is unnecessary then with respect to (29) (since V-to-C does not take place) and bad with respect to economy of movement.

The optimality theoretic version of economy of movement is formulated as follows by Grimshaw (1997: 374):

(54)   *Economy of Movement (Stay)*
        Trace is not allowed

N-V compounds that are separated under V2 are worse with respect to (54) than compounds that are not, since in the former both N-adjunction to V and V-to-C take place, whereas in the latter only V-to-C takes place. The difference between Frisian and Dutch then follows from the constraint rankings in (55).

(55) a.   Complexity Constraint >> Stay   (Dutch)
     b.   Stay >> Complexity Constraint   (Frisian)

Although of course other consequences of the different constraint rankings in (55) must be found in order to establish them on a more firm footing, there is some independent evidence that it is the prevailing demands of Stay which makes the Frisian N-V compounds inseparable. This comes from the following observation. As already noted in section 4, if the lefthand part of a verbal compound is not the verb's argument it is possible that it is generated directly in the V^0-adjoined position, so that there is a base-generated structure as in (56).

(56)

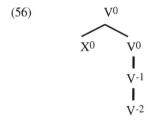

A case in point are particle verbs (see Neeleman 1994, cf. also section 2). Now, in this case there is no difference with respect to Economy of Movement whether the compound is separable or not: in both cases only V-to-C movement (of the lower V^0 and the higher V^0 in (56) respectively) takes place. If the Complexity Constraint is not inoperative in Frisian (as in a parameter approach), but just ranked below Economy of Movement (as in (55b)), then in cases where Economy of Movement does not decide the Complexity Constraint should be just as decisive in Frisian as it is in Dutch. This prediction is correct: there are separable particle verbs in Frisian just as in Dutch, as (57) shows (cf. Dijk 1997: 33). (Note that inseparable particle verbs in both languages must be syntactic simplexes).

(57) a.   It   leger blies de   brêge   op
           the army blew the   bridge up
           'The army blew up the bridge'
     b. * It leger opblies de brêge

7. CONCLUSION

I have argued that N-V compounds do not have a simple adjunction structure. Moreover, not all such compounds have the same structure. Some have no internal syntactic structure at all, while others have a structure in which at least a head position and a complement position can be distinguished. This distinction explained a correlation between the interpretation of the noun in an N-V compound and the syntactic behaviour of the compound in Dutch. It is expected that other types of compound conform to the same structure building principles and are not always simple adjunction structures either, but it remains to be seen whether empirical evidence can be provided for this in their case as well.[22]

NOTES

*   For comments and discussion I would like to thank Reineke Bok-Bennema, Geert Booij, Siebren Dyk, Jack Hoeksema, Gunlög Josefsson, Johan Kerstens, Vieri Samek-Lodovici, Mieke Trommelen, Fred Weerman, two anonymous reviewers, and audiences at

the Taalkundig Colloquium at University of Groningen, Linguistics in the Netherlands 1998 at Utrecht University, and at University of Konstanz.

1   See De Vries (1975), Geerts et al. (1984: 514), De Haas and Trommelen (1993: 443) and Ackema (1995: 101ff.) for some discussion on how to distinguish SCVs from a verb plus an NP direct object that consists only of its head N^0 and on the supposedly nonproductive nature of both types of N-V compound in Dutch. Although I believe that especially SCVs are more productive than is sometimes claimed, the question as such of exactly how productive N-V compounds are does not play a role in the discussion below; it is enough that there is a reasonable number of them from which we can draw general conclusions. See also Wurzel (1993) (on German), and note 5.

2   In general, Dutch synthetic compounds need not all have the same structure; see Booij and Van Santen (1995: 174 ff.) for discussion.

3   There is one apparent counterexample, namely the word *zittenblijver*, 'sit-remain-er' (meaning 'one who has not made it to the next grade at the end of the year'). It is unlikely that this is a derivation of a Verb Raising cluster, however, because of the main verb - auxiliary order. In the Dutch VR cluster the auxiliary precedes the main verb (although for two-verb clusters main verb - aux is an option), so we might expect **blijvenzitter* 'remain-sit-er' to be possible, contrary to fact. Instead, *zittenblijver* is presumably derived from a compound *zittenblijven* (as occurs in e.g. *zittenblijven is geen schande* 'sit-remain is no disgrace'). Although rare, there are a few V-V compounds of this form, with the lefthand verb occurring in its infinitival form; another case is *slapengaan* 'sleep-go', the nominal infinitive of which occurs in *waterdrinken voor het slapengaan helpt tegen een kater* 'water-drinking before the sleep$_V$-going helps against a hangover'.

4   Some speakers find these examples not altogether impossible. This may be caused by the fact that an alternative analysis of these cases is possible, namely as [$_N$ NP [$_N$ V N]] compounds. In many instances such an analysis is unlikely, however, namely when the V-N compound that is the righthand part of this structure does not exist, e.g. **zetapparaat* (cf. (16a)) or **stichtavontuur* (cf. (16c)). Most speakers I have asked about them agree that examples like (16) are out, certainly in those cases where the alternative analysis just mentioned is impossible.

5   The possibility of forming compounds as in (14) therefore supplies a further test to distinguish N-V strings that form an SCV from N-V strings that form VPs consisting of a bare direct object NP plus a verb in syntax (cf. footnote 1). It turns out that a number of strings that are usually not classified as SCVs do behave like them (so that, as indicated in note 1, the class of SCVs is probably bigger than often assumed).

(i)	bietenrapen	appelplukken	tafeldekken	bierdrinken
	beetsgather	applepluck	tablelay'	beerdrink
(ii)	bietenraapmachine	appelplukautomaat	tafeldektrauma	bierdrinkmeter
	beetgathermachine	applepluckautomaton	tablelaytrauma	beerdrinkmeter

Given the data in (16), the compounds in (ii) cannot involve VPs as lefthand parts. Therefore, the strings in (i), next to being possible VPs, must also have an analysis as V^0s, i.e. as SCVs.

6   This is basically the account that Neeleman and Weerman (1993) give for the mobility of the verb versus the immobility of the particle in separable particle verbs. For a detailed account of how the ECP can explain Lexical Integrity effects with respect to movement, but allows for excorporation of the head of an SCV, see Ackema (1995: 43-68). The

view that Lexical Integrity is to be derived from independently motivated syntactic principles, instead of being an absolute principle, is also argued for by Lieber (1992).

[7]   A final possibility to deal with facts like this is to give up the assumption that an element from the lexicon must always be realized either syntactically or morphologically. If uniform realization is given up, it is possible that an element from the lexicon, like an SCV, is realized syntactically under some circumstances but morphologically under others. This possibility is explored in Ackema and Neeleman 1998. It is related to the proposal in the text in that, although Lexical Integrity holds for the morphological manifestation of some construct, it does not hold for every construct that has a morphological manifestation (as assumed in the most stringent formulations of this principle). A closely related proposal is made by Ackerman and LeSourd (1997), who argue that Lexical Integrity must be weakened in this way to account for complex verbs in Hungarian, which are like their Dutch counterparts in being syntactically separable but nonetheless also a possible input for morphological derivation (thanks to Ildikó Tóth and an anonymous reviewer, who pointed out this parallel to me). In fact, Hungarian complex verbs may pose a problem for what is said in the text, in that even the nonhead (the particle) seems to be affected by syntactic movement rules here ('preverb climbing', cf. also Farkas and Sadock 1989). This might be only apparently so, if it can be argued that in such instances first the verb excorporates (as in Dutch, see below) and then the entire complex of particle plus verbal trace moves, but exploring this possibility would go well beyond the scope of this paper.

[8]   Given the descriptive character of the condition in (24) it is desirable to derive its effects from more general principles. An interesting proposal in this respect is made by Koopman (1995) who derives the difference between ICVs and SCVs with respect to V2 from independent constraints on head movement. She argues that the lefthand part of the compound must adjoin to the verb (Koopman assumes this adjunction takes place in syntax, in contrast to what is assumed here, but this is in fact not crucial to the rest of her analysis) and that, from this adjoined position, it must then further incorporate into a special 'receptor' slot of the verb. If this further incorporation takes place in overt syntax, an inseparable verb results that can undergo V2 as a whole; if it does not (i.e. if the left-hand part stays adjoined to the verb in overt syntax) excorporation is necessary. This appears to be quite compatible with the idea that SCVs are syntactically complex in a way that ICVs are not. However, since the constraint in (24) suffices for the purposes of this paper I will ignore the question whether it can be reduced to more general principles.

[9]   Although, as noted by Paulissen and Zonneveld (1988), the RHR only seems to apply with respect to the lexical category of the ICV (being, like its righthand member, a verb). In other respects, the RHR must somehow be 'blocked'. In particular, even if the righthand verb is a strong verb (showing ablaut) in isolation, the ICV as a whole must be inflected like a weak verb (or it shuns inflection altogether, cf. note 20):

(i)   a.   zuigen *zuigde zoog   b.   stofzuigen stofzuigde   ?*stofzoog
           suck   sucked sucked   dustsuck   dustsucked   dustsucked

Under an analysis in which ICVs are syntactic simplexes the RHR naturally cannot apply in any form to these verbs, so that no special explanation is necessary for why it is 'blocked' with respect to ablaut.

SCVs are never regularized in this way, which as such is not very surprising, given that in their case the verb is the same verb as the simple non-compounded one, and so keeps the inflection appropriate for this verb. It does lead to the question of how the inflection, which occurs 'outside' the compound, can be determined by the head of the compound in this way; Hoeksema (1986) and Stump (1991) propose special 'head rules' to make this possible.

10   Also, there is in fact a class of ICVs that violate 'rightheadedness', which should be impossible if they were complex. Examples are *klappertanden* 'chatter-teeth', *schudde-buiken* 'shake-belly', *stampvoeten* 'stamp-feet' and the like (cf. Weggelaar 1986). Interestingly, these are necessarily inseparable (i.e. simplex if the analysis proposed here is correct). The (b)-examples in the following are utterly impossible.

   (i) a. ze   stampvoette van   ergernis
              she stampfeeted from irritation
       b.* ze voette van ergernis stamp
  (ii) a. hij klappertandde van   de   kou
              he chatterteethed from the cold
       b.* hij tandde van de kou klapper

11   If Θ-assignment is directional (cf. Koopman 1984), we might expect VO-languages to show leftheaded V-N compounds with argumental nouns, which is not (in general) the case. In fact, in (rightheaded) N-V compounds in VO-languages that allow for such compounds the noun never seems to be the verb's argument either (see Gràcia and Fullana 1997 and Josefsson 1998 for discussion on the possible relation between noun and verb in N-V compounds in Catalan and Swedish respectively). I will not discuss this here.

12   If N^0-adjunction is blocked when another element occupies the adjunction site, then examples like (i)-(ii) provide evidence for N^0-adjunction in SCVs.

   (i) a.? dat Pires zich   suf pianospeelt
             that Pires REFL dull pianoplays
             'that Pires plays the piano so much that she becomes dizzy'
       b.* Pires speelt zich   suf   piano
             Pires plays REFL   dull piano
  (ii) a.? dat die   lui   maar   doorfeestvieren
             that those people just   onpartycelebrate
             'that those people just go on partying'
       b.* die   lui   vieren   maar   door feest / feest door
             those people celebrate just   on party / party on

Neeleman (1994) argues that resultatives (like *suf* in (i)) and particles (like *door* in (ii)) are adjoined to V^0. In the embedded clauses in the (a) examples N^0 can remain within the SCV, since V-to-C does not take place. Although marked, these examples clearly contrast with the main clauses in the (b) examples, where V-to-C is required. This indicates that N^0-adjunction to V^0 is indeed required to make excorporation of the verb possible. This adjunction apparently is blocked by the particle/resultative already adjoined to V^0, hence the ungrammaticality of (ib) and (iib). This leaves open the question why double adjunction to V^0 is impossible; see Koopman (1995) for relevant discussion.

13   The trace of the noun then ends up in a position in which it is not governed by the noun, which might seem to induce a violation of the ECP. Note, however, that we are

dealing with the trace of an argument here. If Rizzi (1990) is correct, this means head-government suffices to satisfy the ECP, and the trace is head-governed by the verbal head. The trace should also be bound by the noun to license its interpretation; given that this is an LF-requirement, binding is possible after reconstruction.

Alternatively, we can adopt Lasnik and Saito's (1992) mechanism of γ-marking and say that the trace is γ-marked by its antecedent directly after N-adjunction, before V2 takes place (note, again, that it is an argumental trace, not an adjunct trace which must wait until LF to get γ-marked according to Lasnik and Saito).

14   Note that 'lexical' in (29) is not meant as the opposite of 'functional', so a particle, which possibly is a functional lexical item, is relevant for (29) as well.

15   As an anonymous reviewer correctly points out, if syntactic derivations and morphological derivations are also compared with each other and evaluated globally, this leads to the question of why an SCV is not blocked by its syntactic counterpart (a VP consisting of verb plus NP object). This issue is discussed in Ackema and Neeleman 1998. There it is argued that a compound is indeed blocked by its syntactic counterpart, but only if the two have the same meaning. If not, a compound can be listed as such in the lexicon. Now, whereas the internal argument relation between verb and noun is the same in SCVs and syntactic VPs (as argued here), there is a subtle meaning difference between an SCV and its VP counterpart. Due to the nonreferentiality of the noun in an SCV in Dutch (cf. Hoeksema 1988, Ackema 1995), an SCV expresses a habitualized activity (cf. Dijk 1997). For instance, in *ze zijn koffiedrinken* 'they are coffeedrinking', with the SCV *koffiedrinken*, it is possible that some of the people referred to by *ze* 'they' are not actually drinking coffee, but are taking part in the social event of having a coffeebreak, along with the coffeedrinkers. This is not possible in the VP *ze drinken wat koffie* 'they drink some coffee'. Given its special meaning an SCV can be listed as such in the lexicon. (Ackema and Neeleman 1998 actually give a slightly different account for SCVs; see that paper for more discussion).

16   Rosen discusses Noun Incorporation constructions, which are not always analyzed on a par with N-V compounding (see in particular Baker 1988). Rosen supplies arguments in favour of a morphological derivation of the constructions she discusses, however (cf. also Mithun 1984, Di Sciullo and Williams 1987). In Ackema (1995) it is argued that the sole difference between Noun Incorporation and N-V compounding Dutch style concerns the possible referentiality of the noun in the former construction, which is due to the fact that bare nouns can be referential in polysynthetic languages for independent reasons (cf. Baker 1996).

17   Note that the compounds with *lopen* 'walk' and *rijden* 'ride' as righthand members are formed on the basis of the transitive variants of these verbs, as illustrated in (i)-(iii).

(i)   Die student   loopt drie   colleges tegelijk
         that student   walks three   courses at once
         'That student takes three courses at once'

(ii)   Ze   rijdt   een blauwe Saab
         she rides   a   blue   Saab
         'She drives a blue Saab (a car)'

(iii)   Ankie rijdt Olympic Bonfire
         Ankie rides Olympic Bonfire
         'Ankie rides Olympic Bonfire (a horse)'

18   In cases like these it is always the direct internal argument that is realized morphologically and the indirect internal argument that is realized syntactically, which may be explained as a consequence of the linking rules between the thematic hierarchy and morphosyntactic structure discussed in Grimshaw (1990). The indirect argument in fact appears to behave like a direct object of the complex verb, since it can be passivized, in contrast to the indirect object in a double object construction:

(i) a.   dat zij werd gelukgewenst   met haar bevordering tot generaal
          that she was   happiness-wished with her   promotion   to   general
          'that she was congratulated with her promotion to general'
     b.* dat zij een boek werd gegeven
          that she a   book was   given
          'that she was given a book'

This can be explained under the assumption that, for some reason, if the direct object is available for A-movement this excludes A-movement of the indirect object in Dutch, but if the direct object is not available the indirect object can be A-moved. This provides a uniform account of cases like (ia) (where the direct object cannot be raised to subject because it is realized as the nonhead of a compound, cf. section 2) and cases like (ii) (where the direct object is a clause, a category that resists raising to subject).

(ii)   dat de   reizigers vriendelijk worden verzocht hier   uit te stappen
          that the travellers friendly   are   asked   here   to step out
          'that the travellers are kindly requested to leave the train here'

19   For some speakers, the examples in (37) are not that bad (in which case their N-V compound counterparts can be added to the list of compounds with an argumental noun without further ado).
20   A number of ICVs resist finite inflection to a greater or lesser extent, hence the question marks in the (b") examples. For discussion of this phenomenon see Holmberg (1976), Paulissen and Zonneveld (1988), Wurzel (1993). Potentially problematic for the analysis argued for here is that in a number of cases this resistance to finite forms only occurs in main clauses, not in embedded clauses. This specific resistance to V2 might seem to indicate that the relevant ICVs are still complex in some sense. Note however that, in contrast to SCVs, the noun cannot be stranded either; ICVs of this type simply cannot occur as a finite verb in a main clause at all. In fact, even the fact whether the finite form happens to be the same as the infinitive or not can influence the felicity of the relevant examples (cf. also Wurzel 1993), see (i) (the infinitival form of the verb in (i) is *wad-lopen*). I have no account for this phenomenon.

(i) a.? dat wij met veel   plezier   wadlopen
          that we   with much pleasure shallow-walk
          'that we love to walk on the shallows'
     b.??dat hij met veel   plezier   wadloopt
          that he   with much pleasure shallow-walks
     c.? Wij wadlopen   met veel   plezier
          we shallow-walk with much   pleasure

    d. * Hij   wadloopt   met veel   plezier
        he   shallow-walks   with much pleasure

[21] Dijk (1997) argues that the noun in these compounds is not really the verb's argument. According to him, in cases of noun incorporation in Frisian the verb's internal argument is an Arb(itrary) argument that is not projected at all in syntax, similar to what Rizzi (1986) proposes for Italian object drop cases. I cannot discuss the pros and cons of this proposal here, but note that, if correct, a similar analysis would have to be adopted for the Dutch SCVs (since semantically these appear to be equivalent) and the difference in separability between the two would still remain problematical.

[22] Boertien (1997) discusses a class of prepositional compounds in English in which also a head-complement relation seems to be established, as in (i)

    (i)   outdoors, offstage, overhead, uphill, underfoot, etc.

As discussed by Boertien, these cases show the predicted head-complement order that also occurs in syntactic preposition plus complement structures. That assignment of the internal Θ-role of the lefthand preposition to the righthand noun takes place in (i) is also indicated by familiar detransitivization effects: all Ps of the type in (i) are based on transitive Ps but are intransitive themselves.

REFERENCES

Ackema, P. 1995. *Syntax below Zero*. Ph.D. dissertation, Utrecht University.

Ackema, P. to appear. *Issues in Morphosyntax*. Amsterdam: John Benjamins.

Ackema, P. and A. Neeleman. 1998. "Competition between Syntax and Morphology". Ms. University of Groningen / University College London.

Ackerman, F. and P. LeSourd 1997. "Toward a Lexical Representation of Phrasal Predicates". In A. Alsina, J. Bresnan and P. Sells (eds), *Complex Predicates*. Stanford: CSLI, 67-106.

Baker, M. 1988. *Incorporation*. Chicago: University of Chicago Press.

Baker, M. 1996. *The Polysynthesis Parameter*. Oxford: Oxford University Press.

Beard, R. 1995. *Lexeme Morpheme Base Morphology*. New York: SUNY Press.

Boertien, H. 1997. "Left-headed Compound Prepositions". *Linguistic Inquiry* 28, 689-697.

Booij, G. 1990. "The Boundary between Morphology and Syntax: Separable Complex Verbs in Dutch". In G. Booij and J. van Marle (eds), *Yearbook of Morphology 1990*. Dordrecht: Foris, 45-63.

Booij, G. and A. van Santen. 1995. *Morfologie*. Amsterdam: Amsterdam University Press.

Botha, R. 1981. "A Base Rule Theory of Afrikaans Synthetic Compounding". In M. Moortgat, H. van der Hulst and T. Hoekstra (eds), *The Scope of Lexical Rules*, Dordrecht: Foris, 1-77.

Carstairs-McCarthy, A. 1992. *Current Morphology*. London: Routledge.

Chomsky, N. 1986. *Barriers*. Cambridge, Mass.: MIT Press.

Cinque, G. 1990. *Types of A'-dependencies*. Cambridge, Mass.: MIT Press.

Cinque, G. 1993. "A Null Theory of Phrase and Compound Stress". *Linguistic Inquiry* 24,

239-297.

Coopmans, P. and M. Everaert. 1988. "The Simplex Structure of Complex Idioms: the Morphological Status of *laten*". In M. Everaert, A. Evers, R. Huybregts and M. Trommelen (eds), *Morphology and Modularity*. Dordrecht: Foris, 75-104.

Di Sciullo, A.-M. and E. Williams 1987. *On the Definition of Word*. Cambridge, Mass.: MIT Press.

Dijk, S. 1997. *Noun Incorporation in Frisian*. Ljouwert: Fryske Akademy.

Don, J. 1993. *Morphological Conversion*. Ph.D. dissertation, Utrecht University.

Evers, A. 1975. *The Transformational Cycle in Dutch and German*. Ph.D. dissertation, Utrecht University.

Farkas, D. and J. Sadock. 1989. "Preverb Climbing in Hungarian". *Language* 65, 318-338.

Geerts, G., W. Haeseryn, J. de Rooij and M.C. van den Toorn (eds). 1984. *Algemene Nederlandse Spraakkunst*. Groningen: Wolters-Noordhoff.

Gràcia, L. and O. Fullana 1996. "On Catalan Verbal Compounds". Ms. Universitat de Girona.

Grimshaw, J. 1990. *Argument Structure*. Cambridge, Mass.: MIT Press.

Grimshaw, J. 1997. "Projection, Heads, and Optimality". *Linguistic Inquiry* 28, 373-422.

Groos, A. 1989. "Particle-verbs and Adjunction". In H. Bennis and A. van Kemenade (eds), *Linguistics in the Netherlands 1989*. Dordrecht: Foris, 51-60.

Haas, W. de and M. Trommelen. 1993. *Morfologisch Handboek van het Nederlands*. Den Haag: SDU Uitgeverij.

Halle, M. and A. Marantz. 1993. "Distributed Morphology and the Pieces of Inflection". In K. Hale and S.J. Keyser (eds), *The View from Building 20*. Cambridge, Mass.: MIT Press, 111-176.

Hockett, C. 1954. "Two Models of Grammatical Description". *Word* 10, 210-231.

Hoeksema, J. 1986. *Categorial Morphology*. New York: Garland.

Hoeksema, J. 1988. "Head-types in Morpho-syntax". In G. Booij and J. van Marle (eds), *Yearbook of Morphology 1988*. Dordrecht: Foris, 123-137.

Hoekstra, T., M. Lansu and M. Westerduin. 1987. "Complexe Verba". *GLOT* 10, 61-78.

Holmberg, M. A. 1976. *Studien zu den Verbalen Pseudokomposita im Deutschen*. Lund: Acta Universitatis Gothenburgensis.

Jackendoff, R. 1997. *The Architecture of the Language Faculty*. Cambridge, Mass.: MIT Press.

Josefsson, G. 1998. *Minimal Words in a Minimal Syntax*. Amsterdam: John Benjamins.

Koopman, H. 1984. *The Syntax of Verbs*. Dordrecht: Foris.

Koopman, H. 1995. "On Verbs that Fail to Undergo V-second". *Linguistic Inquiry* 26, 137-163.

Lasnik, H. and M. Saito. 1992. *Move α*. Cambridge, Mass.: MIT Press.

Lieber, R. 1992. *Deconstructing Morphology*. Chicago: University of Chicago Press.

Marantz, A. 1984. *On the Nature of Grammatical Relations*. Cambridge, Mass.: MIT Press.

Mithun, M. 1984. "The Evolution of Noun Incorporation". *Language* 60, 847-894.

Model, J. 1991. "Incorporatie in het Nederlands". *Gramma* 15, 57-88.

Neeleman, A. 1994. *Complex Predicates*. Ph.D. dissertation, Utrecht University.

Neeleman, A. 1997. "PP-complements". *Natural Language and Linguistic Theory* 15, 43-87.

Neeleman, A. and F. Weerman. 1993. "The Balance between Syntax and Morphology:

Dutch Particles and Resultatives". *Natural Language and Linguistic Theory* 11, 433-475.

Paulissen, D. and W. Zonneveld. 1988. "Compound Verbs and the Adequacy of Lexical Morphology". In M. Everaert, A. Evers, R. Huybregts and M. Trommelen (eds), *Morphology and Modularity*. Dordrecht: Foris, 281-302.

Prince, A. and P. Smolensky. 1993. *Optimality Theory*. Ms. Rutgers University / University of Colorado at Boulder. [To appear in *Linguistic Inquiry Monograph* series].

Rizzi, L. 1986. "Null Objects in Italian and the Theory of *pro*". *Linguistic Inquiry* 17, 501-557.

Rizzi, L. 1990. *Relativized Minimality*. Cambridge, Mass.: MIT Press.

Rosen, S.T. 1989. "Two Types of Noun Incorporation: a Lexical Analysis". *Language* 65, 294-317.

Sadock, J. 1991. *Autolexical Syntax*. Chicago: University of Chicago Press.

Santen, A. van. 1992. *Produktiviteit in Taal en Taalgebruik*. Ph.D. dissertation, University of Leiden.

Sproat, R. 1985. *On Deriving the Lexicon*. Ph.D. dissertation, MIT.

Stump, G. 1991. "A Paradigm-Based Theory of Morphosemantic Mismatches". *Language* 67, 675-725.

Vries, J. de .1975. *Lexicale Morfologie van het Werkwoord in Modern Nederlands*. Leiden: Universitaire Pers.

Weggelaar, C. 1986. "Noun Incorporation in Dutch". *International Journal of American Linguistics* 52, 301-305.

Wurzel, W. 1993. "Inkorporierung und "Wortigkeit" im Deutschen". Ms. FAS, Berlin.

Zubizarreta, M. L. 1985. "The Relation between Morphophonology and Morphosyntax: the Case of Romance Causatives". *Linguistic Inquiry* 16, 247-289.

University of Groningen
CLCG
PO Box 716
9700 AS Groningen
The Netherlands

e-mail: p.ackema@let.rug.nl

Lenition in Hessian: cluster reduction and 'subtractive plurals'*

DAVID J. HOLSINGER AND PAUL D. HOUSEMAN

1. INTRODUCTION

Recent work by Golston & Wiese (1996), in the framework of Optimality Theory (Prince & Smolensky 1993, hereafter OT) has provided an new analysis of a set of unusual plural formations in Hessian German. Hessian, on the surface, appears to exhibit a case of what has been termed 'subtractive' plural marking; that is, a word-final segment is deleted in certain cases in the plural form of the noun (Hessian *hond*, *hon* 'dog', 'dogs'). Other data from Hessian and related dialects, however, show widespread and regular assimilation of the same obstruent clusters in medial position. For example, /nd/ clusters are realized medially as [n:] or [n] in Hessian words like [fɪnən] 'to find' or [unər] 'under'. The behavior of medial and final /nd/, /ld/, /rg/, /ŋg/ clusters and postvocalic /g/ in various dialects provides evidence of intermediate stages of a development which can be more accurately captured in a synchronic analysis that sees lenition as central to the development of 'subtractive plurals'. These data lead us to conclude that 'subtractive plural' formation is the result of an independent phonological process which operates without regard to morphological category.

Golston & Wiese's proposed constraint SON]PL mandates that plural nouns end in a sonorant wherever possible: it is this requirement that conditions segmental deletion in the case of the 'subtractive plural' forms. Though this constraint accurately describes plural formation in most German nouns, the pattern of cluster reduction described above leads us to question its appropriateness in the case of the 'subtractive plurals'. Instead, we propose that the subtractive plurals are conditioned by a correspondence of morphological and prosodic categories (a central proposal of Prosodic Morphology, cf. McCarthy & Prince 1995), where plurals (and other inflected forms) associate to a disyllabic foot (cf. Wiese 1996). The eventual loss of final schwa (motivated by the constraint FILL) results in a monosyllabic surface form, but one in which constraints on the appearance of medial clusters are nonetheless permitted to apply. Such interaction of phonological constraints more directly reflects the synchronic status of medial clusters and also mirrors the diachronic development of the 'subtractive plural' forms.

The organization of this paper is as follows: in section 2 we provide an overview of synchronic Hessian plural formation, paying particular attention to the 'subtractive' forms. We then give a brief account of the OT analysis in section 3 and explain how this analysis neither explains numerous apparent instances of the assimilatory phenomenon occurring outside plural formation nor the range of attested

Geert Booij and Jaap van Marle (eds), Yearbook of Morphology 1998, 159-174.
© *1999 Kluwer Academic Publishers. Printed in the Netherlands.*

plural forms themselves. Sections 4 and 5 provide additional evidence from other dialects with 'subtractive plurals' which motivates the synchronic analysis framed in terms of cluster reduction and the prosodic shape of inflected morphological forms.

2. THE HESSIAN PLURAL SYSTEM

Other than the subtractive plural forms, Hessian plural formation is similar to that of Standard German. Hessian has plurals ending in *-(e)n, -e, -(e)r,* and zero (Ø). Umlaut, alone or in conjunction with the *-e* affix, and always in conjunction with the *-er* affix, can also be used to mark plurality. As in Standard German, umlaut (vowel-fronting) is never used in conjunction with the *-(e)n* plurals. The *-s* plural form has apparently been lost in Hessian, although occasionally it shows up imported from Standard German or in loan words. In general, as Alles (1907: 363), Haas (1988: 47) and Golston & Wiese (1996: 146) all point out, the *-(e)n* plural ending has been almost entirely lost in Hessian through the loss of final *-n*. Thus, a large number of apparent *-e* plural forms are etymologically *-(e)n* plurals.

The most intriguing plural forms in Hessian, however, are the so-called subtractive plurals'. Alles identifies a number of apparent subtypes of this group in his 1907 study:

Singular	Plural	MSG Gloss	Gloss
hond	hon	'Hund'	'dog'
pond	pon	'Pfund'	'pound'
grond	grin	'Grund'	'ground'
šlond	šlin	'Schlund'	'gutter'
štand	šten	'Stand'	'situation'
vald	vɛl	'Wald'	'forest'

Table 1: Deletion of /d/ after /n/ or /l/[1]

Singular	Plural	MSG Gloss	Gloss
blog	ble	'Pflug'	'plow'
vɛg	vɛ	'Weg'	'way'
dɔg	dɔ:	'Tag'	'day'
riiŋg	riŋ	'Ring'	'ring'
gaaŋg	gɛŋ	'Gang'	'hallway'
špruŋg	spriŋ	'Sprung'	'jump'
bɛrg	ber²	'Berg'	'mountain'

Table 2: Deletion of /g/ after a vowel (sometimes accompanied by vowel shortening), after /ŋ/ or after /r/

Hessian, as mentioned, also uses zero-marking for plural forms. Below in Table 3 are just a few examples of zero-marked Hessian plural forms with stems ending in obstruents or sonorants.

Singular	Plural	MSG Gloss	Gloss
štomp	štimp	'Stumpf'	'stump'
kɔrb	kɛrb	'Korb'	'basket'
brost	brest	'Brust'	'breast'
bɑɑm	beem	'Baum'	'tree'
širm	širm	'Schirm'	'umbrella'
dɛkl	dɛkl	'Deckel'	'lid'
hoomər	heemər	'Hammer'	'hammer'

Table 3: Zero-marked plural forms

Thus, as Golston & Wiese point out, subtractive plural forms occur when the stem ends in /ld, nd, ŋg, rg/ or /Vg/, while plural forms are zero-marked in other cases. It is this (apparent) complementary distribution of subtractive and zero-marked plurals that leads them to a fundamental insight regarding Hessian subtractive plurals: the process is dependent on the phonology of Hessian and is not a new plural form. As they put it, subtractive pluralization is "predictable, not distinctive and thus does not (and could not) signal, as a morphological marker, the category plural" (1996: 149).

3. THE ACCOUNT OF HESSIAN SUBTRACTIVE PLURALS

Golston & Wiese begin their analysis by developing a set of constraints that govern the formation of plurals in both Hessian and Standard German. The first constraint they posit is one mandating retention of underlying features in surface representations:

(2)   PARSE FEAT: *Phonological features must be retained.*

Deletion of word-final /d/ does not involve a crucial violation of (2) when the preceding segment is a homorganic sonorant — in this case the feature [coronal] is retained. The following tableau reflects this for the input candidate /hond/ (where < > symbolizes the deletion of a particular segment):

/hond/	PARSE FEAT
☞ hon\<d>	
ho\<nd>	*!

The second constraint mandates the sonority of the final segment:

(3)   SON]PL: *Plurals end in a sonorant.*

Pointing to parallels in languages such as Ancient Greek, Golston & Wiese claim that Germanic languages in general prefer plurals that end in a [+sonorant] consonant. Together, PARSE FEAT and SON]PL condition 'subtractive' plural marking and zero-marking. Plural forms that already end in a sonorant satisfy SON]PL and thus are zero-marked, while /ld, nd, ŋg, rg/ or /Vg/ plural forms delete the final obstruent to satisfy (3) as long as they also satisfy PARSE FEAT. Affixation is thus the preferred strategy for nouns that end in an obstruent, when PARSE FEAT prohibits deletion of final segments. As Golston & Wiese state, "The point is that Hessian wants to have sonorant-final plurals (not subtractive plurals)..." (1996: 157).[3] The following tableau illustrates the combinatoric between these two constraints for the candidate /hond/:

/hond/	PARSE FEAT	SON]PL
hond-ø		*!
☞ hon\<d>		

The candidate [hond-ø] violates SON]PL and so loses (or is less optimal), while deletion of the coronal [d] satisfies PARSE FEAT and creates a sonorant-final and thus optimal candidate.

These constraints rest on the controversial assumption that all vowels have the place feature [dorsal], which is required to motivate deletion of /g/ (but not coronal obstruents) following vowels: [dɔg] ~ [dɔ:] 'day ~ days'. If vowels are not specified as [dorsal], the constraint PARSE FEAT would be violated in forms like [dɔ g]. However, the assumption that all vowels are [dorsal] is one not shared by all current feature geometries; Clements (1991) and Clements and Hume (1995), for example, place front vowels at the [coronal] articulator. In such a model, segmental deletion would be possible only after back vowels. We avoid this controversy by proposing that it is not place features that motivate the eventual loss of a segment but rather that a general lenition of postvocalic /g/ causes this phenomenon.[4]

The last constraint necessary to the analysis is a standard OT constraint banning vowel insertion:

(4)   FILL: *Epenthesis is banned.*

It is constraint (4) that rules out (following Golston & Wiese) candidates like [hondə], similar to the plural form found in SG, [hundə]. Hessian ranks FILL higher than SON]PL, hence selecting apparent "subtractive plurals," while Standard German ranks SON]PL higher than FILL, tolerating schwa suffixes to mark plurality.[5] The following tableau illustrates this for the Hessian candidate /hond/:

/hond/	PARSE FEAT	FILL	SON]PL
hond-ə		*!	
☞ hon<d>			
ho<nd>	*!		
hond-ø			*!

This, in essence, is the analysis proposed by Golston & Wiese to account for Hessian subtractive plural formation.[6]

3.1 *Problems with the proposed account of subtractive plurals*

Golston & Wiese's account of Hessian subtractive plural formation is one in a long line of attempts to fit these problematic data into a theoretical paradigm. One of the more recent attempts, Haas (1988), analyzes Hessian morphology (including subtractive plurals) in a generative framework. Haas points to a number of processes unique to Hessian. Of these, the most interesting for our purposes are (in his terms) /r/ to [n] assimilation (1988: 48) and /d/ to [n] assimilation (1988: 44–45). In the first case, as he states, medial /r/ undergoes complete assimilation to a following coronal nasal, a common occurrence cross linguistically, e.g. /kɔrn/ 'grain' becomes [kɔ:n].[7] Haas points out that the second case, where /d/ assimilates to [n] after a vowel, is very common in Hessian. This assimilation is optional in word-final position and in fact often does not occur there. For example, the plural form of Hessian /rend/ (SG *Rind*; '(head of) cattle') is [renər], or /land/ (SG *Land*; 'land') alternates with plurals [lɛnder] and [lɛnər].[8] In the case of /land/, however, the constraint hierarchy proposed by Golston & Wiese would incorrectly identify a 'subtractive' plural form, *[lɑn], as the optimal output, as the following tableau illustrates:

/land/	PARSE FEAT	FILL	SON]PL
land-ə		*!	
☞ lan\<d\>			
lɑ\<nd\>	*!		
land-ər		*!	
land-ø			*!

The attested forms, [lɛndər] or alternately [lɛnər], fail by violating FILL. We assume that Golston & Wiese's candidate set includes (at the very least) candidates representing *all* of the possible Hessian plural suffixes in combination with the stem, including in this case the *-er* plural affix. The class of *-er* noun plurals is quite large in both Hessian and Standard German and occurs with many nouns ending in /nd/ and /ld/, yet there is no phonological reason why certain nouns with identical consonantal structure use a strategy other than zero-marking in combination with obstruent deletion. One might argue that different constraint rankings hold for the *-er* class of plurals than for those zero-marked plurals which delete final segments, but then the proposed account provides only a detailed and complex *description* of different Hessian plurals which is not and cannot be at all predictive. It may be the case that the choice of particular affixes (such as plural *-er*) is lexically specified in Standard German and Hessian, and hence to some degree idiosyncratic.[9] But if subtractive plural formation is a strictly phonological process, as Golston & Wiese claim it is, there is no explanation (given the constraints they propose) as to how *-er* plurals could surface. To posit another (faithfulness) constraint mandating retention of *-er* in certain noun plurals is simply beside the point: affixation of *-er* or *-e* creates the environment for lenition. The so-called subtractive plurals are then the result of apocope of schwa, one of the defining characteristics of Hessian and related dialects.

This is essentially the approach taken by Haas, who analyzes the 'subtractive' case as assimilation of /d/ to [n], a rule crucially ordered before apocope of schwa. In the case of /hond/, this results in an intermediate form in the derivation, [hon:ə], from which the expected surface form, [hon], is derived. As mentioned, apocope is pervasive in Hessian and many other dialects; in fact, the *-(e)n* plural form has almost ceased to exist (cf. Alles, Haas, Golston & Wiese) due to the loss of the final [n], while most zero-marked plural forms are due to apocope: singular [bɑɑm] 'tree' alternates with plural [beem] 'trees' in Hessian, but contrasts with SG sg. *Baum* - pl. *Bäume*.

PARSE FEAT fails to capture the notion that the process is actually an assimilatory one, occurring not only in word-final position but also medially. Furthermore, in Golston & Wiese's account there is no motivation for the subtraction of homorganic segments, since (as we will now show) the constraint SON]PL is also ill-formed. SON]PL is the determining constraint for zero-marked plural forms in Hessian. As Golston & Wiese state: "Finally, there are those stems that end in sonorants. For them the best solution is to add nothing and parse everything" (1996: 156). The problem is that many sonorant-final singulars use affixation to mark plurality. Below in Table 4 are examples of sonorant-final nouns that use an affix (data from Haas and Alles):

Singular	Plural	predicted plural	SG gloss	gloss
hɑlm	hɑlm-ə	*hɑlm-ø	'Halm'	'straw'
dɔrm	dɛrm-ə	*dɛrm-ø	'Darm'	'gut'
vɑn	vɑn-ə	*wɑn-ø	'Wanne'	'tub'
pɑn	pɑn-ə	*pɑn-ø	'Pfanne'	'pan'

Table 4: Sonorant-final nouns which form the plural by affixation.

Again, the proposed analysis incorrectly predicts the output candidate [dɛrm] to be the most optimal, as a comparison with their tableau for /širm/ makes clear. Below is the tableau for /dɔrm/ singling out the candidate [dɛrm] as (most) optimal:

/dɔrm /	PARSE FEAT	FILL	SON]PL
dɛrm-ə		*!	
dɛr\<m\>	*!		
dɛ\<rm\>	*!*		
☞ dɛrm-ø			

We are thus left with no explanation as to why these nouns do not use zero-marking like the example form, /širm/.[10] Any adequate account must explain why affixation is used in some cases but not in others; the analysis cannot be considered satisfactory if the candidate set is limited to only those candidates that fit the relevant constraints. More damaging, the analysis breaks down without SON]PL as a motivation for subtraction (i.e. 'Hessian nouns subtract in order to end with a

sonorant'). One might reply that Golston & Wiese are discussing only the subtractive vs. zero-marked cases, but it is incumbent upon them to explain those cases
where *neither* strategy is used but where the conditioning environment is the same.
The point is that Hessian clearly has a number of purely phonological assimilatory
processes at work that are not used to mark the particular morphological operation of
plural formation. In addition to the empirical inadequacies, the analysis in terms of
SON]PL, by dealing exclusively with word-final assimilation, has presented a forced
account of the phenomenon which does not accurately reflect the across-the-board
nature of cluster reduction in such cases.

4. RE-ANALYSIS OF 'SUBTRACTIVE PLURALS'

In order to support our hypothesis that 'subtractive plurals' are the result of cluster
reduction and consonantal lenition rather than satisfaction of a constraint mandating
that plurals end in a sonorant, we present data from other Hessian dialects, as well as
from dialects in neighboring regions. By placing the so-called 'subtractive plurals' in
the context of a set of historical sound changes, we demonstrate that these forms are
really just one possible outcome of the interaction of several such changes. The data
to be examined come from Rhenish Franconian dialects of German in a band
stretching from the area of Upper Hesse west toward the border with the Dutch
linguistic area, spreading into some transitional dialects such as Limburgian and
Luxembourgish. Common to the entire region is the historical loss of final schwa:
in combination with the reduction of medial sonorant+stop clusters, this leads to the
development of unusual plural forms. Likewise, the realization of /g/ as a fricative or
glide in medial position is characteristic of most dialects in the region. The
subtractive plurals found in this dialect region appear to be of two types: the first, as
discussed above, results from a combination of apocope of schwa and weakening of
certain medial clusters, while a second type, found only in Limburgian Dutch, is due
to palatalization of the coronal stops when these occur in word-final position.

The degree of reduction of medial clusters is only partial in many of these
dialects, forming a glide from an original post-sonorant stop, e.g. /nd/ > [nj]. Here
and elsewhere, we find that a general lenition process affecting medial postvocalic and
intersonorant segments conditions the eventual segmental deletion characteristic of
'subtractive plurals'. In fact, many dialects show reduction of /rd/ and /lg/ clusters,
which run afoul of the deletion-through-shared-features mechanism proposed under
PARSE FEAT, and can only be explained as a lenition of the affected obstruent,
whether through a decrease in articulatory strength or an increase in sonority.

4.1. *The 'assimilation' case*

The most common case of 'subtractive plural' formation appears to be the result of
the reduction of medial /nd/, /ld/ and /rd/ clusters. Typical forms are cited for the

Hessian dialect of the Westerwald by Hommer (1915). This dialect, like all the dialects examined in this paper, has undergone apocope of schwa. Hommer cites reflexes of West Germanic *d* and *θ*, which are usually realized as [d] in Hessian, assimilating to a preceding *n*, *l* and sometimes *r* (if the *r* does not vocalize) in medial position. Forms include (following Hommer's orthography): *fønen* (SG *finden;* 'to find'), *kønɒ* (SG *Kinder;* 'children'), *bønən* (SG *binden;* 'to bind'), *rønɒ* (SG *Rinder;* 'cattle'), *fɒlən* (SG *falten;* 'to fold'), *hanəln* (SG *handeln;* 'to negotiate'), *anɒ* (SG *ander;* 'other'), *wɒrən* (SG *werden;* 'to become'), *gɒdən* (SG *Garten;* 'garden'). In final position, WGmc. *d* and *θ* are realized as *t*, except in cases where they were historically in a medial position, e.g. in certain plural nouns and other inflected forms. Examples of these reflexes in original final position include *alt* (SG *alt;* 'old'), *kalt* (SG *kalt;* 'cold'), *hant* (SG *Hand;* 'hand') and *pont* (SG *Pfund;* 'pound'). In most Hessian dialects, nouns which originally ended in [ndə], [ldə] and in some cases [rdə] appear in the singular with only the first consonant of the original cluster, such as in the dialect of Wissenbach, where we see singulars such as *en* (SG *Ende;* 'end'), *won* (SG *Wunde;* 'wound'), *šdon* (SG *Stunde;* 'hour') and *hal* (SG *Halde;* 'mound').

The notion that segmental deletion occurs in order to mark the plural of nouns is inconsistent with the appearance of the same phenomenon in adjectives and verbs with similar phonological environments. For example, in the dialect of Wissenbach, there is an apparent 'subtractive inflection' in some verbs with stems ending in /ld/, such as *hald* (SG *halt;* imperative 'stop!') but *hal* (SG *halte;* 1p. sg. 'I stop'). Subtraction of segmental material also occurs with some derivational affixes, such as the diminutive *henxe* (SG *Händchen* ;'small hand') from sg. *hand* (SG *Hand;* 'hand'). In the dialect of Ebsdorf, which is the source of much of Golston & Wiese's data, we also see derived nouns such as *joŋ* (SG *Junge;* 'boy') and *wonə* (SG *Wunde;* 'wound') lacking the final segment found in the original adjectival forms, *joŋk* (SG *jung;* 'young') and *wont* (SG *wund;* 'sore'). We thus see not only inherited forms which clearly derived from an original cluster, but also derived forms for which the underlying cluster is still attested. This necessitates an analysis which can account for both processes phonologically.

Hommer also notes that many plural forms in the Westerwald dialect exist in both their 'subtractive' and full forms, e.g. both *rønt* and *røn* are possible plurals of *rønt* (SG *Rind;* '(head of) cattle'). In the Nassau region, as recorded by Friebertshauser (1961), the nominal declension contains forms which delete a final segment as well as forms showing reduction of an underlying cluster to a glide in the same environments. For example, we see the alternations [following Friebertshauser's original orthography] sg. *wɛg*, pl. *wɛjə* (SG *Weg-Wege;* 'way'-'ways'); sg. *bɛarg*, pl. *bɛarjə* (SG *Berg-Berge;* 'mountain'-'mountains') but also sg. *doəg*, pl. *doə* (SG *Tag-Tage;* 'day'-'days') and sg. *šloəg*, pl. *šlɛ* (SG *Schlag-Schläge;* 'blow'- 'blows')). In any case, the synchronic co-occurrence of forms both with and without the glide clearly supports the hypothesis that these forms are the result of the co-occurrence of cluster reduction and apocope.

A few exceptional forms which end in underlying /g/ also deserve comment.

Systematic exception to the deletion of final /g/ can be found, but a number are recent loans such as sg. *buldog*, pl. *buldoge*, (no SG equivalent; 'a kind of tractor'). Since these would have entered a system already affected by loss of final schwa, they behave as though the /g/ is in 'true' final position, rather than an originally medial position. It thus appears, as in Standard German, with the allophone [k]. The plural is then formed by addition of schwa or by zero-marking, depending on the dialect. For the inherited forms with final [k], we disagree with Golston & Wiese and trust that the transcription of the dialect handbooks correctly reflects fortition of word-final obstruents as found in many dialects of this region. Golston & Wiese suggest that such stems have been re-interpreted as ending in /k/, for instance in doublets like sg. *kruk*, pl. *krɪk* and sg. *krog*, pl. *kre* (*SG Krug-Krüge*; 'jug'-'jugs'). Though this is a logical interpretation, it does not explain why similar forms ending in [t] (from underlying /d/) are not interpreted as ending in /t/ by the same speakers. Rather, this assumption obscures the fact that speakers of such dialects have reintroduced zero-marking as an alternative to segmental subtraction and that such processes compete within the same dialect.

4.2. The 'palatalization' case

In some dialects the palatalization of coronal stops results in forms which appear to lose segments in the plural. These are a rather different type of 'subtractive plurals' than the apparently equivalent forms examined in the case above. Johan Winkler, in his 1874 study of Low German and Frisian dialects, gives the following description of the type of palatalization found in Limburgian Dutch: "De Limburgers, en vooral de inwoners van Sittard en omstreken, spreken de *g* gewonelijk zoo zacht uit dat deze letter als *gj*, soms zelf als *j* klinkt. Buitendien hangen ze gaarne achter de *d* als deze een woord sluit een *j* ...." [The Limburgers, and especially the inhabitants of Sittard and surrounding areas, usually pronounce the *g* so softly that this letter sounds like *gj* or sometimes even like *j*. In addition, they like to hang a *j* after a *d* when it ends a word ....]

This palatalized *d* appears as a glide in some plural formations, such as sg. *andj* or *anj*, pl. *enj* (SDu. *Hand*; 'hand'), sg. *freundj*, pl. *freunj* (SDu. sg. *vriend*, pl. *vrienden* [friːndə], SG sg. *Freund*; pl. *Freunde* 'friend - friends'), giving the impression that the /d/ is being lost in these forms. The Sittard dialect has no medial assimilations of *d* to a preceding sonorant like the Middle German dialects examined in the examples above. Indeed, these plural forms do not appear to be 'subtractive' in the same sense as the Hessian forms since they are apparently the result of the palatalization of a word-final segment rather than the reduction of an originally medial cluster. If the palatalized segment is realized as a stop-glide cluster [dj], as the description and the data suggest, then segmental loss occurs not finally but medially. Such unusual plural formations are irregularly attested in the available data but seem to follow the pattern of deleting a palatalized *d* in those forms where it was historically followed by [ə]. In any case, the distribution of the palatalized *d* with respect to the glide in word-final position appears to be irregular (viz. the *andj/anj* doublet cited above), and the occurrence of 'subtractive' forms in the singular leaves little doubt that this type of 'subtractive plural' is phonologically conditioned as well.

5. LENITION, PROSODIC MORPHOLOGY AND SUBTRACTIVE PLURALS

We argue that cluster reduction, reflected in the previous analysis by the constraint PARSE FEAT, is not related to parsing of underlying place features, but to a general reduction of medial postvocalic and intersonorant stops. A number of 'intermediate' forms provided in sections 4.1 and 4.2 provide historical evidence for a gradual reduction of medial clusters, a process of consonantal lenition, rather than an all-or-nothing parsing of features. Since in many Hessian dialects, we find reductions of not only /rd/ clusters, but of /rg/ as well, that is to say, both *r* + coronal and *r* + dorsal, an analysis proposing place features as the locus of assimilation no longer appears tenable. The most important theoretical issue at hand is therefore the nature of the lenition process which reduces medial clusters and postvocalic /g/. With this established, the means by which word-final clusters can be treated as medial must be the true conditioning factor for subtractive plurals.

In cases where medial /nd/ clusters undergo weakening to [nj], as seen in section 4 above, it would appear necessary for the underlying stop /d/ to assimilate to an adjacent specification of [+sonorant]. In general, models of feature geometry do not provide an easy way to represent major class assimilations (i.e., those features which are represented either at the root node or as its direct dependents). Such assimilations are widely disputed in the literature, yet extremely common cross-linguistically. Hock (1991) provides a "weakening hierarchy" to explain this type of change, suggesting that this hierarchy is "largely defined by a combination of increased voicing and sonority" (82).

We can then explain forms in which a medial /g/, usually [ɣ], reduces to a glide between vowels in the same manner. In our analysis, as noted above, it is not the place feature [dorsal] which serves as the locus of this assimilation. Rather, the [ɣ] approaches the surrounding segments (vowels or [r]) in sonority. Unlike the PARSE FEAT constraint used to motivate assimilation of a velar segment to a preceding sonorant through feature sharing, our analysis makes no assumptions regarding the place features of vowels. What is crucial for our analysis is only that an environment can be derived in the 'subtractive plural' forms where the lenited clusters appear as phonologically medial.

We leave the phonological motivation for cluster reduction and lenition as an open question and simply propose that the following two constraints hold for Hessian (since a formulation of a more general lenition constraint is beyond the scope of the current analysis):[11]

(5)   CLUSTER CONSTRAINT: $*C_{[+sonorant]}\ C_{[-sonorant,\ -continuant,\ +voice]}$

(6)   G-REDUCTION: $*VC_{[dorsal,\ -sonorant,\ +voice]}$

These constraints allow for multiple phonotactic solutions in Hessian. In final position, both (5) and (6) can be trivially satisfied through the operation of final fortition (also called 'final devoicing'): post-sonorant voiced stops become [-voice] and pass the constraints. For (5), vocalization of the sonorant consonant in the cluster likewise satisfies the constraint. However, for non-final clusters, neither final fortition nor vocalization of the sonorant consonant is possible. In these cases, for both constraints, two phonotactic resolutions are possible: a change from [-sonorant] to [+sonorant] (attested in dialects which retain the [j] in these cases), or total assimilation of the [-sonorant] consonant to the preceding [+sonorant] segment (as found in the dialects with 'subtractive plurals').

We concur with Wiese (1996: 106-107) that, "[I]t is a noticeable fact about all noun plurals that the suffixes and schwa occur in such a way that the constraint ('a final sequence consisting of a stressed syllable plus a schwa syllable') is obeyed almost without exception. This generalization, along with others holding for adjectives and infinitives of verbs (cf. Wiese 1996: 109-113), leads us to posit a final constraint (actually, a set of constraints) which hold for all instantiations of these categories, an expression of McCarthy & Prince's (1995: 324) proposal that MCat=PCat ('the exponent of some morphological unit [is] a prosodic unit of a particular type'). In this case, we can state that inflected stems belonging to the morphological categories NOUN and ADJECTIVE must minimally comprise a FOOT (in German, a sequence of stressed plus unstressed syllable).

'Subtractive plural' nouns enter the phonological derivation such that they are associated to a disyllabic foot, and other phonological rules apply to these forms accordingly. That is to say, final fortition does not apply to stem-final consonants, which are now foot-medial, and satisfaction of CLUSTER CONSTRAINT and G-REDUCTION occurs by total assimilation. The constraint FILL prevents schwa (which, as stated previously, is uncontroversially assumed to be epenthetic in German) from surfacing, meaning that the surface form of these plurals is not a true disyllabic foot but has passed through the phonological derivation as though it were. In fact, all zero-marked nouns trivially satisfy the same mandate — only those with clusters susceptible to reduction actually show its residual effects on phonological form. The following tableau presents the derivation of [hon], the plural of /hond/, according to the proposed constraints:

/hond/	MCAT=PCAT	CLUSTER CONSTRAINT	FILL
hond-ə		*!	*
hont	*!		
☞ hon			
honə			*!

In the case of the (surface) zero-marked plurals, the difference between forms with correct and incorrect mapping of inflected stems to prosodic categories is not apparent since no other phonological processes attest to such a mapping:

/širm/	MCAT=PCAT	CLUSTER CONSTRAINT	FILL
σ | širm	*!		
φ | širm			
širm-ə			*!

Crucial for this analysis is that the specification of a certain prosodic form for all plurals is maintained on the surface as best as the constraint hierarchy in Hessian will allow. 'Subtractive plural' forms attest to this specification of a prosodic template for certain morphological categories by the operation of phonological processes which would otherwise be blocked. It is not affixation *per se* which allows for the reduction of medial clusters: this analysis avoids proposing intermediate forms in the derivation, such as an affix which triggers cluster reduction but does not appear on the surface. Instead, the correspondence between prosodic and morphological categories characteristic of certain classes of stems (i.e., plurals, inflected adjectives, and deadjectival nouns) holds for the 'subtractive plurals' as well. The introduction of FILL prevents forms in the zero-marked/subtractive category from appearing as a disyllabic foot, but all other constraints in the phonological derivation apply in the same way that they did historically.

6. CONCLUSION

We have demonstrated that Golston & Wiese's account, based on the constraints PARSE FEAT and SON]PL, is ill-suited to characterize the 'subtractive plural' formations for a number of reasons. First, that account, though accurate in its description of the majority of plural forms, does not account for the selection of affixation rather than zero-marking or segmental deletion in the plurals of several noun classes. It cannot tolerate forms which contradict proposed constraint rankings by choosing an 'incorrect' plural marker, even though all nouns taking -*er* plurals defy this hierarchy. Second, an analysis in terms of SON]PL makes an incorrect set of generalizations about the nature of subtractive plural formation; it introduces a morphological solution to a phonological problem.

Though a completely acceptable description and explanation for the type of lenition evidenced by these data remains elusive (as is apparent from the wide range of proposed accounts of lenition in the theoretical literature), we feel that lenition is, in fact, the core issue in an accurate account of Hessian subtractive plural forms. In the operation of lenition to apparently stem-final clusters, we see that a constraint on the prosodic form of plurals remains active in the grammar of Hessian, despite the presence of the constraint FILL, which prevents the zero-marked and subtractive forms from surfacing with the specified prosodic template for inflected nouns and adjectives. This analysis thus views the constraints active in the grammar of Hessian to be consistent across all inflected forms and views cluster reduction as an independent phonological process, but one which provides clear evidence of the continued correspondence of morphological and prosodic categories.

NOTES

*   We would like to thank Rob Howell, Greg Iverson, Monica Macaulay, Marcy Macken, and especially Joe Salmons, for their comments and help with this paper. Additional thanks go to participants at MCWOP 2 who offered their commentary on this paper and to Richard Wiese for his constructive criticism. We are solely responsible for any errors.
[1]   The following data are from Alles (1907: 349-352) unless otherwise indicated. We follow the phonetic transcription proposed by Golston & Wiese (1996: 147).
[2]   Data from Golston & Wiese (1996: 147).
[3]   Here the omission of -*s* plurals, a very important class of plurals (thought by many to be the default plural marker in Modern Standard German) from the analysis certainly weakens the claim that Standard German plurals also want to end in a sonorant segment. Golston & Wiese claim that -*s* has different morpho-phonemic properties: we will follow them in excluding it from our analysis.
[4]   Golston & Wiese do not discuss the use of umlaut (fronting of a, u and o) in Hessian plural forms, claiming that umlaut is "an independent phonological rule of fronting" (1996: 146). A number of the examples provided show umlaut; it is debatable whether synchronic umlaut in SG is phonological. It seems odd to talk of zero-marking when so many nouns in the corpus are also accompanied by umlaut, but this remains an area for

further research, and Golston & Wiese rightly leave it outside the scope of their analysis.

5   This can be schematized as:

Hessian:	PARSE FEAT>>FILL>>SON]PL
Standard German:	PARSE FEAT>>SON]PL>>FILL.

6   We will not discuss in depth a fourth uncontroversial constraint they posit, PARSE SEG. This constraint simply forces underlying segments to be realized on the surface.

7   There is an intermediary step in Haas' transformation where where /nn/ shortens to [n], what he terms 'Konsonantenschwächung'. There is evidence from other Hessian nouns that long consonants never show up on the surface in word-final position, for example /pann/ → [pan] for SG *Pfanne* 'pan', cf. 1988: 49. We will not discuss the vowel lengthening in these examples.

8   Also in this case we find [n] deletion in the surface form of the singular underlying form /land/ as well as lengthening of the stem-vowel: /land/ → [lann] → [laan]. Note that there is final fortition (also commonly called final devoicing) in Hessian, so that the under-lying singular form /land/ is realized on the surface as [lant]. We will not discuss vowel mutations in these examples.

9   Clearly there are good historical reasons for the particular choice of plural marker for various nouns. But Hessian, we would argue, actually shows more natural synchronic patterns of plural marking as shown by the simplification of plural markers in contrast to Standard German.

10   Golston & Wiese recognize the existence of such forms, but fail to motivate the emergence or success of such forms through the constraint process.

11   For further discussion of the representational problems inherent in a feature-geometric account of lenition and fortition, see Kaisse (1992) and Hume & Odden (1996), among others.

REFERENCES

Alles, Konrad. 1907. "Beitrag zur Substantivflexion der oberhessischen Mundarten". *Zeitschrift für deutsche Mundarten* 2, 348-351.

Clements, G.N. 1991. "Place of Articulation in Consonants and Vowels: A Unified Theory". *Working papers of the Cornell Phonetics Laboratory* 5, 77-123.

Clements, G.N. and Elizabeth V. Hume. 1995. "The Internal Organization of Speech Sounds". In J. Goldsmith (ed.), *Handbook of Phonological Theory*. Cambridge, MA: Blackwell, 245-306.

Friebertshauser, Hans. 1961. *Sprache und Geschichte des nordwestlichen Althessen*. Marburg: Elvert. (Deutsche Dialektgeographie 46).

Golston, Chris & Richard Wiese. 1996. "Zero Morphology and Constraint Interaction: Subtraction and Epenthesis in German Dialects". In Geert Booij and Jaap van Marle (eds), *Yearbook of Morphology 1995*. Dordrecht: Kluwer, 143-159.

Haas, W. 1988. "Zur Morphologie der Mundart von Ebsdorf im Landkreis Marburg-Biedenkopf". *Germanistische Linguistik* 95, 3-95.

Hock, H. H. 1991. *Principles of Historical Linguistics*. Second ed. New York: Mouton de Gruyter.

Hommer, Emil. 1915. *Studien zur Dialektgeographie des Westerwaldes*. Marburg: Elvert. (Deutsche Dialektgeographie 4).

Hume, Elizabeth & David Odden. 1996. "Reconsidering [consonantal]". *Phonology* 13,

345-376.

Kaisse, E. 1992. "Can (consonantal) spread?" *Language* 68 (2), 313-32.

McCarthy, John & Alan Prince. 1995. "Prosodic Morphology". In J. Goldsmith (ed.), *Handbook of Phonological Theory*. Cambridge, MA: Blackwell, 318-366.

Prince, Alan & Paul Smolensky. 1993. *Optimality Theory*. Technical Reports of the RuCCS TR-2, Rutgers Center for Cognitive Science.

Wiese, Richard. 1996. *The Phonology of German*. Oxford: Oxford University Press.

Winkler, Johan. 1874. *Algemeen nederduitsch en friesch dialecticon*. 's Gravenhage: Nijhoff.

Department of German
University of Wisconsin—Madison
818 Van Hise Hall
1220 Linden Dr.
Madison, WI 53706

e-mail:
houseman@students.wisc.edu
djholsin@students.wisc.edu

Nominalizations in a calculus of lexical semantic representations

ROCHELLE LIEBER AND HARALD BAAYEN

1. THE PROBLEM

The history of generative grammar has been such that exploration of the structure and meanings of words has long stayed on the back burner. With respect to the structure of words, this picture began to change in the late 1970's and early 1980's with the appearance of the first substantial works on the structure of word formation within the theory (e.g., Aronoff 1976; Lieber 1980; Williams 1981; Selkirk 1982). Following this there was a gradual increase in interest in the area of morphology that has led to a virtual explosion in recent years. A somewhat less direct trajectory has been followed in the history of lexical semantics within generative grammar. After an initial burst of activity as part of the Generative Semantics/Interpretive Semantics debate of the late 1960's, interest in general issues of lexical semantics flagged within the generative tradition, with the notable exception of the lines of work pursued by Bierwisch (1989, 1997) or Jackendoff (1983, 1987, 1990, 1991, 1996).[1]

In recent years, however, it has become increasingly obvious that issues of lexical semantics bear direct consequences for other areas of the grammar, in particular, syntax and morphology. With respect to syntax, the notion that theta roles are not primitives, but arise from the lexical conceptual structures (LCSs) of verbs is now widely accepted. Work such as that of Levin (1994) and Levin and Rappaport Hovav (1995) on lexical alternations, and Tenny (1987, 1994), Verkuyl (1989) and others on aspect attests to the importance of this line of research. Further, Lieber and Baayen (1997) argue that it is a particular combination of features in the LCSs of verbs that conditions the choice of auxiliary in Dutch. With respect to morphology, it is clear that it is useful to look at the lexical semantics of affixes; Lieber and Baayen (1993) discuss the semantic contributions of prefixes like *ver-*, *be-*, and *ont-* in Dutch to words. Lieber (1998) provides a similar approach for the English verb-forming suffix *-ize*. It is our hunch that a number of other problems that have proved recalcitrant in theories of word formation which eschew discussion of lexical semantics might benefit from analysis within a system in which more attention is paid to the representation of meaning of morphemes and words. One example is the area of inheritance of argument structure in nominalizations, where existing accounts are all problematic. We outline the problem briefly.

It has been a matter of interest for at least the past twenty-five years how to represent the similarities and differences between sentences and their corresponding nominalizations such as the items in (1):

Geert Booij and Jaap van Marle (eds), Yearbook of Morphology 1998, 175-197.
© 1999 *Kluwer Academic Publishers. Printed in the Netherlands.*

(1)   The enemy destroyed the city.
        the enemy's destruction of the city
        Daisy arrived at the station.
        Daisy's arrival at the station

In recent years, two lines of research have been pursued. One we will call the 'loose inheritance' literature, as represented by Booij and van Haaften (1988), Roeper (1987), and others, and the other the 'strict inheritance' literature as represented best by Grimshaw (1990). In the former sort of analysis, nominalizing affixes are operators of various sorts and they manipulate the theta grid or argument structure of verbal bases in a number of ways. The inheritance of argument structure may be optional. In the latter sort of analysis, there are no operations on argument structure. In nominalizations, the argument structure of a base verb is either inherited in full form or absent completely.

Our starting point is Grimshaw's (1990) treatment of the subject. Grimshaw (1990) contrasts two interpretations that occur with nominalizations formed with affixes such as *-(at)ion, -ment,* and *-al.* On the one hand, nominalizations such as *destruction* or *arrival* may have a RESULT interpretation, and on the other a PROCESS interpretation, which Grimshaw calls the COMPLEX EVENT interpretation. Grimshaw uses the following diagnostics to distinguish between the two readings. First, complex event nominals can occur with adverbs like *constant* and *frequent,* as illustrated in (2a). With such adjuncts, arguments of the nominalization are obligatory. Further, if a 'subject' is present, then the 'object' argument must be present as well, as (2b) illustrates. Similarly, if a *by* phrase is present, then the 'object' argument is obligatory (2c) (Grimshaw's examples 1990: 50-53):

(2)   a.   The frequent expression *(of one's feelings) is desirable.
      b.   The instructor's examination *(of the papers) took a long time.
      c.   The assignment *(of unsolvable problems) by the instructor

On the one hand, the result reading is compatible with determiners like *one* or *that,* or with a plural form of the nominalization. In these cases, Grimshaw claims that arguments do not occur:

(3)   a.   They studied that/one assignment (*of the problem).
      b.   The assignments (*of the problem) took a long time.

According to Grimshaw, in the result interpretation nominalizations never show the argument structure of the corresponding verb. In the complex event interpretation, however, the argument structure is obligatory. Result nouns have no argument structure in Grimshaw's analysis, whereas complex event nominalizations have obligatory argument structure.

There are a number of reasons to believe that Grimshaw's approach to the inheritance issue is not optimal. First, she deals primarily with nominalizing affixes such as *-ing, -(at)ion, -ment,* and *-al,* and only briefly with other affixes such as *-er* that create nouns from verbs. When we expand our view to these sorts of affixation – for example, in addition to agentive/instrumental *-er,* patient noun-forming *-ee,* and other affixes like *-ery* (*bakery, hatchery*) – it becomes difficult to maintain the clear dichotomy of argument structure only with complex events and no argument structure elsewhere. For example, the parallel in interpretation between (4a) and (4b), and also the apparent optionality of the argument in (4b), cannot be captured by reference to argument structure for Grimshaw:

(4) a.   Morgan drives a truck.
     b.   a driver (of trucks)

The noun involved here is neither a result nor a process nominal, but rather an agentive nominal, and 'inheritance of argument structure' is clearly not an all or nothing matter dependent upon a particular interpretation. In the case of agent/ instrumental nouns at least, the 'argument' truly seems to be optional. Further, even among the nominalizations that Grimshaw discusses, arguments do not appear really to be an all or nothing matter. With plurals of *-(at)ion* nouns, which are supposed unequivocally to be result nouns, and which therefore should show no inheritance behavior, we find phrases that look suspiciously like arguments:

(5) a.   Jan did twelve repetitions of the exercise.
     b.   We frown upon multiple submissions of an article.

For cases like these, Grimshaw appeals to the level of LCS. She claims that the phrases which look like arguments of the nominal are really not arguments at all, but instead are complements, which she defines as participants in the LCS of the verb. If we consider what true arguments are at the level of LCS, however, we find ourselves with a dilemma. Either arguments are complements, that is, participants in the LCS, or they are not. If they are not complements/participants, we might wonder why they are interpreted precisely as complements/participants are. On the other hand, if they are complements/participants, this leads to the odd result that some LCS complements get to be arguments (i.e., those in complex event nominalizations like the ones in (2)) and others do not. Either way, it becomes clear that there are interesting and important questions about 'inheritance' that need to be addressed at the level of LCS, regardless of what our theory of argument structure is. We need to go beyond Grimshaw in exploring the phenomenon of inheritance.

The works cited above which argue for some process of inheritance are more on the right track, to our, minds, but somewhat dated. They make use of a rather crude reference to the theta grid or argument structure of verbs, and also paint the contribution of the affixes with a fairly broad brush. What we believe that we need to do here is to take seriously the notion of LCS for nouns, and to see what nominalizations really do in terms of lexical semantics. It is our hope that having done this, the mechanics of inheritance will become clearer. This leads us to our formal goal in this paper.

Although a substantial amount of work has been done on the formal representation of the semantics of verbs (e.g., Pinker 1989; Talmy 1985; Jackendoff 1983, 1987, 1990), much less work has been done on the representation of nouns. Jackendoff (1991) talks about the quantificational characteristics of nouns (count vs. mass nouns, for example), and Pustejovsky (1996) makes proposals within his framework of the Generative Lexicon that allow for an interesting treatment of polysemy, and that are consistent with a computational framework, but which do not offer us the cross-categorial possibilities that we see the need for here. In the absence of clear ideas about the representation of categories other than verbs, we can have only the vaguest ideas about how the semantic representations of categories combine and affect one another. Clear ideas on cross-categorial representation are especially necessary if we are to talk about the semantics of derivational affixation, which is in many cases cross-categorial. What we need, in other words, is a larger framework in which to discuss issues of lexical semantics.

It is beyond the scope of this paper to develop a comprehensive framework for lexical semantics; we leave this task to further research. Nevertheless, what we intend to do here is to develop at least a basic proposal which allows us to specify the LCSs of both nouns and verbs and to see what happens when they combine morphologically. The framework that we are developing borrows liberally from previous ones, especially Jackendoff (1990, 1991). For example, we accept the basic framework of LCSs, although we suggest below that it is useful to decompose Jackendoff's basic functions (BE, GO, etc.) into a featural representation which leads ultimately to a classification of verbs quite different from Jackendoff's. Some of the features that we propose indeed have been discussed in various forms in previous literature (e.g., the feature [dynamic] appears with one name or another in work of Pinker (1989), Dowty (1979), Verkuyl (1972), and others). We use, as well, the idea of binding of arguments in the representations of complex derived words, an idea that has been around at least since DiSciullo and Williams (1987), and which other researchers (e.g., Booij 1988) make use of as well. Further, the notion that some features of LCS are useful across more than one lexical category is an idea that has been suggested before; for example, Jackendoff (1991) suggests that certain LCS features that account for quantificational characteristics of nouns are also useful in expressing aspectual notions in verbs.

What is new, then, in what we propose? First, as alluded to above, the specific way in which we decompose the basic functions of the verbal LCS is unique to our approach.[2] Second, we propose that our features operate cross-categorially in building the LCSs of nouns as well as verbs, and we show how this system of LCS can be useful in describing the semantic contribution of nominalizing affixes. Finally, we suggest that the system of lexical semantic representation that we need must allow for both equipollent and privative use of features: the semantic features that we propose will be binary (i.e., have a positive or negative value), but may also be present or absent, by which we will mean relevant or irrelevant in the semantic representation of various categories. We claim that it is precisely such a system that allows us to discuss the three options for inheritance that seem to be possible: full inheritance, no inheritance, or optional inheritance.

In section 2, we give a short description of the primitives that we assume, and the ways in which they allow us to rough out the LCSs of the four major lexical categories: verb, noun, adjective, and adposition. We then go on in section 3 to discuss verbs, and in section 4 to discuss nouns. Finally, in section 5 we return to the problem at hand, the representation of the LCSs of nominalizing affixes and the problem of inheritance.

2. SOME ATOMS OF LCS

We begin with the basic form of LCSs. On this point, we follow Jackendoff in assuming that the standard form of an LCS contains two basic parts, a function and one or more arguments predicated of that function (6a). We adopt Jackendoff's idea as well that LCSs may consist of a hierarchical arrangement of functions and arguments (6b):

(6) a. $[F_1 ([argument])]$
     b. $[F_1 ([argument], [F_2 ([argument])])]$

That verbs, adjectives, and adpositions are argument-taking categories is a relatively uncontroversial position. We assume, following work of Williams (1981) and Higginbotham (1985), that nouns take at least one argument as well, what Williams and Higginbotham call the "R" argument. This is typically described as a nonthematic argument which may be discharged either by co-indexation with a definite determiner or by predication. Thus far, we follow other theories.

Where we part company with Jackendoff is in claiming that the semantic functions of LCSs can be decomposed into smaller atoms of meaning, and that these atoms are typically active across more than one lexical category. We concentrate here on the most basic semantic features, claiming that the four basic lexical categories can be defined by the presence or absence of these two features in the highest semantic function of the LCS, and that the positive and negative values of these features begin to define syntactically relevant subclasses within the four basic lexical categories.

• [+/-substance]: The presence of this feature defines the conceptual category of Substances, the notional correspondent of the syntactic category Noun. The feature [+substance] denotes the presence of materiality and characterizes concrete nouns. Correspondingly, [-substance] denotes the absence of materiality; it characterizes abstract nouns. In other words, we characterize nouns as lexical units for which the distinction between concrete and abstract referents is uniquely relevant. The distinction between concrete and abstract nouns is one, moreover, that is reflected in the word structure. As pointed out by Lyons (1977: 445-446), concrete nouns tend to be monomorphemic, while abstract nouns most commonly arise through a process of nominalization.

• [+/-dynamic]: The presence of this feature defines the conceptual category of Situations. [+dynamic] lexical items correspond to Events and [-dynamic] items to States.[3] In other words, we take the fairly uncontroversial distinction between states and events as the primary characteristic of verbs.[4]

How can we use these two features to define the four major lexical categories? First, as noted above, nouns are items which bear the feature [+/-substance] as their outermost function in LCS; we will see below that this does not, however, preclude them from having the feature [+/-dynamic] as well. Verbs are the clearest case of Situations, and may be either Events or States, that is, either [+dynamic] or [-dynamic] in their outermost layer of LCS. We claim as well, however, that adjectives may also be characterized notionally as Situations, specifically as [-dynamic] Situa-tions.[5] That is, adjectives are conceptually identical to stative verbs in our system; semantically they bear the same feature, [-dynamic], in the outermost layer of their LCS, although syntactically they differ from verbs in that in English they occur only in a nonfinite form. That is, while stative verbs may occur syntactically in either finite or nonfinite forms, when used predicatively adjectives must be accompanied by a verb like *be* which bears tense features. Finally, adpositions will be defined seman-tically within the present system by the *absence* of the features [substance] and [dynamic], although they will be positively defined by other semantic features.[6] That is, we conceive of adpositions as a category of pure Relations involving neither substance nor situation. In (7) we sketch out the form of a basic LCS for an intransitive item of each category:

(7) a. Noun $[_{Substance} \text{ +/-substance } ([_{Substance} \quad])]$

      b. Verb $[_{Situation} \text{ +/-dynamic } ([_{Substance} \quad])]$

      c. Adjective $[_{Situation} \text{ -dynamic } ([_{Substance} \quad])]$

      d. Adposition $[_{Relation} ([_{Substance} \quad])]$

Note that we distinguish here and in what follows between features like [+/-substance] and [+/-dynamic] and conceptual categories like Substance, Situation, and Relation, which these features, or their absence categorize. The latter should be regarded basically as convenient mnemonics for combinations of semantic features. The four lexical syntactic categories N, V, A, and P, therefore correspond to three notional or lexical semantic categories, Substance, Situation, and Relation.

Two comments are necessary at this point. First, we point out again that the system we propose here allows for both binary and privative use of semantic features. The feature [substance] may be present or absent, as may the feature [dynamic]. Either, if present, may take the positive or negative value. While it is generally frowned upon in syntactic or phonological theory to use features in this way – such use is said to impart extra and unwanted power to the grammar – we suggest that the lexicon should be treated differently. Specifically, the issue of power does not arise in the same way with respect to the lexicon. Although we are concerned with the overall parsimony of our framework, we need a way to state that a particular semantic dimension is or is not relevant to a particular subset of lexical items. For instance, animacy is a feature that is useful for partitioning nouns, but that is irrelevant for the characterization of verbs – there are no 'inanimate' verbs. Instead of assigning verbs some featural value on some scale of animacy, we take verbs to be characterized by the absence of any featural specification for animacy. We will try to show in what follows that the ability to use features in both the binary and privative way not only pervades our system of representation at every level, but that this pervasiveness allows us to explain a number of interesting things about the lexical semantics of English.

Second, although the two features above are capable of defining the four major lexical categories, they clearly come nowhere close to characterizing those aspects of meaning which we might want to capture in the LCS for the lexicon or derivational morphology of English. In a fuller treatment of this subject (Lieber and Baayen forthcoming), we develop other features which characterize lexical functions for English and Dutch. Here, we limit ourselves to adding one feature – one that we have justified in detail in Lieber and Baayen (1997)[7] – as it will be useful in characterizing the verbal bases of nominalizations below. We caution again that the proposal we make here is just a sketch of the kind of system we think will ultimately be useful in resolving issues of lexical semantics within the generative framework.

- [+/-IEPS]: This feature stands for 'Inferable Eventual Position or State'. With this feature we try to capture the idea that for some verbs it is possible to make a specific sort of inference about the eventual position or state of the highest argument of the verb. The addition of this feature to an LCS in effect signals the addition of a Path component of meaning. If [IEPS] is absent, the notion of Path is irrelevant to the meaning of the lexical item; if it is present, a Path is relevant. Further, we can offer a precise account of the distinction between [+IEPS] and [-IEPS] in terms of the **kind** of Path they imply. Let us say that Φ is a variable that ranges over States and Places, and x is the argument of Φ. Further, let i stand for the initial State or Place, f for the final State or Place, and j...k for intermediate States/Places. Then, the addition of the feature [IEPS] to the LCS signals the addition of the semantic component in (8):

(8) $[\Phi_i(x), \Phi_j(x), ... \Phi_k(x), \Phi_f(x)]$

In other words, the addition of the feature [IEPS] signals the addition of a sequence of Places or States. Further, if the value of [IEPS] is positive, we will be able to make the inference in (9).

(9) If [+IEPS], then $i \neq f \wedge \Phi_{j,k} \notin f: \Phi_i < \Phi_j ... < \Phi_k < \Phi_f$

In plain English, if [+IEPS] is present, there will be a sequence of Places/States such that at any point between the initial and final Place/State, some progression will have taken place towards the final Place/State. If [-IEPS] is present, then we can make no inference about the progression of Places/States. The feature [IEPS] is of use in capturing classes of both verbs and adpositions. We will provide further clarification of our use of this feature in section 3 below.

Having sketched the bare minimum of semantic features which we believe that we need for our system of lexical semantic representation, we turn to a brief outline of verb classes within our framework. Following this, we will return to nouns and to the issue of inheritance in nominalizations.

3. VERB CLASSES

The features [dynamic] and [IEPS] allow us to cross-classify verbs in useful ways. Although a great deal more might be said on this subject, the classes which we outline below will be more than sufficient for our treatment of nominalizations in section 5. In fact, we elaborate on the verbal system more than is strictly necessary here, as the lexical semantics of verbs is a relatively well-studied area, and offers a good place to show how our featural approach to semantic decomposition differs from previous approaches.

The rough classification of verbs that we envision is summarized by the diagram in (10):

(10)

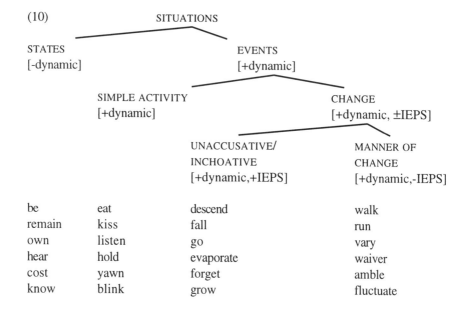

STATES [-dynamic]		SIMPLE ACTIVITY [+dynamic]	UNACCUSATIVE/ INCHOATIVE [+dynamic,+IEPS]	MANNER OF CHANGE [+dynamic,-IEPS]
be	eat		descend	walk
remain	kiss		fall	run
own	listen		go	vary
hear	hold		evaporate	waiver
cost	yawn		forget	amble
know	blink		grow	fluctuate

First, STATE verbs such as *know* and *possess* are characterized by the presence of the feature [-dynamic] in the outermost layer of their LCS. We assume the usual tests for stativity, for example that stative verbs do not occur in the progressive in English (**Daisy is knowing the answer*), or in the imperative (**Know the answer*), and so on (see Quirk et al. 1972: 94). Since the feature [IEPS], as we have defined it, signals the addition of a Path which involves a sequence of states, it is, by definition, incompatible with the feature [-dynamic]. In other words, [-dynamic] verbs denote single states, not sequences of states, and thus do not bear the feature [IEPS]. A typical two place State verb like *know* will therefore have the LCS in (11):

(11)   *know*
         [$_{Situation}$ -dynamic   ([$_{Substance}$], [$_{Substance}$])]

All other verbs will have at least the feature [+dynamic]; these together will form the class of Event verbs, all of which can occur in the progressive in English, can be used in the imperative, and so on. Referring again to Comrie's definition (1976: 49), they are verbs which "will only continue if ... continually subject to a new input of energy." Of these verbs, some will have **only** the feature [+dynamic]. This group, which we will refer to as SIMPLE ACTIVITY VERBS, lacks the feature [IEPS]. Such verbs denote Events for which the notion of a Path is irrelevant. In other words, the notion of a Path, as we have defined it, requires some change of position or state which simply does not figure in the meaning of SIMPLE ACTIVITY VERBS.[8] The LCS for a typical member of this class, *eat*, is given in (12):

(12)   *eat*
         [$_{Situation}$ +dynamic   ([$_{Substance}$], [$_{Substance}$])]

On the other hand, adding the feature [IEPS] to [+dynamic] is possible, and adds two further subclasses to our typology. The presence of [IEPS], as we have said, implies the presence of a Path component of meaning; it defines those verbs in which some change of Place or State takes place. By way of example, consider the sentences presented in (13).

(13) a. ? After having descended the ladder, John found himself to be in exactly the same place he had started from.
     b.   After having walked for five hours, John found himself to be in exactly the same place he had started from.
     c.   After John had eaten, he ate again/he felt satisfied.

(13a) is strange, because the [+IEPS] change of place verb *descend* implies a Path with non-equivalent initial and final points and a steady progression from one to the other. On the other hand, as illustrated in (13b), *walk*, a [-IEPS] change verb, does not imply anything about the relationship between the initial and final place of its argument, or about the progression from one to the other. In contrast, *eat* is a verb which lacks the feature [IEPS] entirely; as (13c) shows, it does not imply anything concerning the final position or state of its highest argument. Although many final positions or states can be envisioned, none is conventionalized as part of the meaning of the verb. We have illustrated our interpretation of the feature [IEPS] by contrasting two CHANGE OF POSITION verbs with a SIMPLE ACTIVITY verb. We can elaborate a bit more on the former verbs, which bring together a number of lexical subclasses. The first subclass of the CHANGE group contains verbs which bear the features [+dynamic, +IEPS] in the outermost layer of their LCSs. These are the verbs which have traditionally been referred to as UNACCUSATIVES (for those involving change of Place) and INCHOATIVES (for those involving change of State). For all of these verbs, the inference in (9) is possible, namely that there will be a sequence of Places or States implied by the action of the verb such that the initial and final Places/States are distinct and at any point between the initial and final Place or State some progression will have taken place towards the final Place or State. (14) contains LCSs for the UNACCUSATIVE verb *descend* and the INCHOATIVE verb *grow*:

(14) a. *descend*
$$[_{\text{Situation}} \quad \text{+dynamic} \quad ([_{\text{Substance}} \quad], [_{\text{Path}} \quad])]^9$$
$$\text{+IEPS}$$

   b. *grow* (inchoative)
$$[_{\text{Situation}} \quad \text{+dynamic} \quad ([_{\text{Substance}} \quad], [_{\text{Path}} \quad])]$$
$$\text{+IEPS}$$

The second class of [IEPS] verbs will bear the features [+dynamic, -IEPS] in their outermost layer of LCS. For such verbs, the inference in (9) does not hold. As we noted above, although a Path is relevant to the meanings of these verbs, no inference is possible about the relationship between the initial and final Places or States: the initial Place or State may be the same as the final Place or State, or not, and no steady progression between the two can be inferred. What is therefore highlighted in the meaning of these verbs is the MANNER OF CHANGE, either the manner of motion for verbs where a change of Place is involved (e.g., *walk, run, amble*) or in the manner of change of State (e.g., *vary, waver, fluctuate*). With verbs like *walk*, for example, one must change position, but no inference is possible about the nature of the path involved; one may walk in place, walk in a circle, walk back and forth, etc.[10] Verbs in the MANNER OF CHANGE class will have LCSs like those in (15):

(15) a. *walk*
$$[_{\text{Situation}} \quad \text{+dynamic} \quad ([_{\text{Substance}} \quad], [_{\text{Path}} \quad])]$$
$$\text{-IEPS}$$

b.   *vary*
   [Situation   +dynamic ([Substance], [Path])]
             -IEPS

We turn, finally, to a final class of verbs which are not included in the simple typology in (10), namely CAUSATIVES. There is a good reason why this class does not appear in our typology. All of the verbs in (10) are ones in our system which can be characterized by a single outer [dynamic] function. CAUSATIVES, in contrast, require in our system an additional [+dynamic] function and an argument outside one of the other [dynamic] functions. If this function is added to the LCS for the INCHOATIVE verb *grow*, for example, we get the CAUSATIVE variant:

(16)   *grow* (causative)
   [+dynamic ([Substance], [+dynamic   ([Substance], [Path])])]
                                       +IEPS

The causative function can of course be added to other types of verbs in English, although more often than not, this combination is not lexicalized into a single item, but rather realized by the addition of a separate lexical verb *make* (e.g., *Daisy made Morgan eat/fall/descend*, etc.).[11]

There is obviously a great deal more that must be said in a full treatment of the lexical semantics of verbs. For one thing, we have said nothing about the primitive that underlies the notion of Place we have referred to above, nor about other primitives that further divide our verb classes. We leave these interesting issues here, however, as they will not in the end impact on our treatment of nominalizations in Section 5. We will close this section, however, with the briefest of comparisons between our system of representation and that of Jackendoff (1990). Jackendoff does not explicitly divide verbs into classes, but his primitives CAUSE, BE, INCH, and GO are used in a way that makes it possible to refer to some of the verb classes that we have distinguished, but not to others. The primitive BE, for example, corresponds to our [-dynamic], that is, STATE verbs, the primitive INCH together with BE to our INCHOATIVE verbs, and the primitive CAUSE (layered on INCH-BE or GO) to our CAUSATIVE verbs. Jackendoff's system gives no direct correlates in the area of SIMPLE ACTIVITY verbs, however. He has no specific function that corresponds to [+dynamic] without [IEPS] in our model. Further, Jackendoff does not class INCHOATIVES and UNACCUSATIVES together[12] – the former having the primitive INCH and the latter GO, in his system, nor does he have any separate way of referring to what we have called MANNER OF CHANGE or of classing together MANNER OF MOTION verbs with MANNER OF CHANGE OF STATE verbs. Verbs like *walk, run*, etc. are GO verbs with a 'Manner' component for Jackendoff. He does not discuss verbs like *vary, waver, fluctuate*, which represent manner of change of State. It is beyond the scope of this article to carry out a detailed comparison of the explanatory power of the two systems. We offer this brief comparison only as a way of indicating that the two systems are not notational equivalents.

4. SIMPLEX NOUN CLASSES

Having looked briefly at the lexical categories of verbs available within our framework, we are ready now to look into a subject which has been given less extensive coverage in the literature on LCS, namely the formal representation of the LCSs of nouns. Although certain topics in nominal semantics have long been discussed in the literature on Model Theoretic Semantics (see for example, the vast literature on generics, definite descriptions, and quantification), little attempt has been made to characterize what is syntactically significant about nominal meanings in terms of LCS. Jackendoff (1991, 1996), of course, looks at quantificational aspects of nominal meaning, capturing the differences among singular count, plural count, group, and mass nouns in a featural system, but other aspects of nominal semantics have been neglected. We first seek to rectify this omission here.

We adopt here Jackendoff's term Substance for the conceptual category to which nouns generally belong. We interpret Substance as meaning 'pertaining to materiality,' and propose that this conceptual category be characterized by the presence of some value of the feature [substance] in the outermost layer of LCS. This feature allows us to express a fundamental distinction among classes of nouns, that between concrete nouns (*thing, chair, mother, child*) and abstract nouns (*war, habit, time, system*). The former nouns will bear the feature [+substance] in the outer layer of their LCS, and the latter the feature [-substance].

Next, we observe that among both the concrete and abstract classes of nouns there are those which are somehow situational in flavor, denoting states, events, or relations of some sort, and those which lack a situational flavor. Nouns which have this situational character we will assume to share something with the conceptual category of Situations, namely the quintessentially situational feature [+/-dynamic]. Situational nouns will be characterized by the feature [dynamic] and nonsituational nouns will lack this feature. Further, of nouns that have a situational character, we observe that some denote complex events, and others results, states, agents, or instruments. The former will be [+dynamic] and the latter [-dynamic]. The taxonomy that we have in mind is illustrated in (17):

(17)

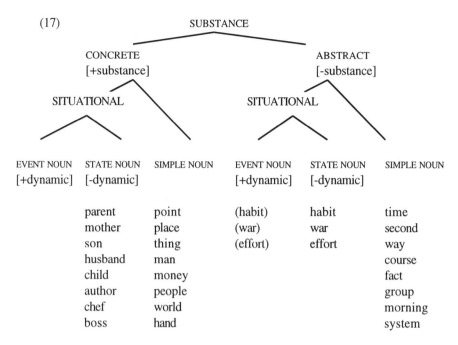

EVENT NOUN	STATE NOUN	SIMPLE NOUN	EVENT NOUN	STATE NOUN	SIMPLE NOUN
[+dynamic]	[-dynamic]		[+dynamic]	[-dynamic]	
	parent	point	(habit)	habit	time
	mother	place	(war)	war	second
	son	thing	(effort)	effort	way
	husband	man			course
	child	money			fact
	author	people			group
	chef	world			morning
	boss	hand			system

We note that our feature system once again gives rise to a combination of privative and binary oppositions for our categorization for nouns: those which are nonsituational, that is, lack the feature [dynamic], and those which are situational, for which this feature is present and which partition into [-dynamic] state nouns and [+dynamic] event nouns. We remind the reader as well of our assumption (taken from Williams 1981 and Higginbotham 1985) that nouns always take at least one argument, namely the one referred to in the literature as the 'R' argument. 'R' is not a thematic argument; as the external argument of a noun, it must be satisfied either by reference, essentially being coindexed with or bound to determiners of certain sorts, or by predication. Being bound to the definite determiner is one way of discharging or satisfying the 'R' argument. An indefinite determiner cannot discharge or satisfy 'R'. With this in mind, we can sketch LCSs for various classes of nouns.

Among the nonsituational nouns we find the most prototypical of nouns, on the [+substance] side, nouns denoting things (*dog, chair, money*), places (*world, home, hospital*), body parts (*hand, eye, foot*), and people (*man, woman*), on the [-substance] side abstract nouns such as time words (*time, year, minute*), set-dividing words (*part, kind, sort*), and others (*system, fact*):

(18) a. *chair*
      [Substance +substance ([Substance])]

b. *fact*
      [Substance -substance ([Substance])]

It seems plausible to assume that some nonsituation nouns may have a second argument as well. Among these nouns might, for example, be nouns of inalienable possession such as *leg*, where the first argument would be the external R argument of the noun:

(19) *leg*
  [$_{Substance}$ +substance ([$_{Substance}$], [$_{Substance}$])]

If the R argument is coindexed with a definite determiner, the result might be an alienable use of the noun, as in *the leg of the table*. However, we will assume that it will also be possible for the second argument of the LCS of *leg* to be co-indexed with the first, in which case the inalienable reading would arise, as for example in *Morgan's leg*.

Next, we turn to the various situation nouns. We have noted above that both [+substance] and [-substance] nouns can bear the feature [dynamic]. That is, there are concrete situation nouns – for example, people nouns like *author, merchant,* and *poet* – and abstract situation nouns – for example, *habit* and *war*. For verbs, the quintessentially situational words, we used the feature [+/-dynamic] to distinguish Events from States. We will follow the same practice with nouns, reserving [+dynamic] for nouns which have a complex event reading and [-dynamic] for nouns which do not denote complex events. As with nonsituational nouns, all situational nouns will have at least the R argument, and some will have a second argument, as well (*the merchant* vs. *the author of the book*). Representative LCSs are given in (20):

(20) a. *author*
     [$_{Substance}$ +substance   ([$_{Substance}$], [$_{Substance}$])]
           -dynamic

  b. *poet*
     [$_{Substance}$ +substance   ([$_{Substance}$])]
           -dynamic

  c. *war*
     [$_{Substance}$ -substance   ([$_{Substance}$], [$_{Substance}$])]
           +/-dynamic

  d. *habit*
     [$_{Substance}$ -substance   ([$_{Substance}$], [$_{Substance}$])]
           +/-dynamic

The LCSs in (20) illustrate a number of things about situational nouns. First, as with nonsituational nouns, the highest argument may be bound to a definite determiner, in which case the noun is referential, or it may be left unbound, in which case the noun will be used predicatively. Second, the difference between *author* and *poet* can be captured by providing the former with one more LCS argument than the latter.

We will return soon to the question of why the second argument of nouns like *author* is only optionally projected in the syntax. Finally, the LCSs in (20c) and (20d) indicate that certain situation nouns – specifically, the abstract ones – can have either a complex event or a result reading. That this is possible may not be evident to the reader; however, examples like those in (21) show that Grimshaw's diagnostics can be used to distinguish the two readings, even in simplex nouns:

(21) a.   Barbara's constant war *(with the neighbors)   COMPLEX EVENT
          Moe's frequent habit *(of biting his nails)
     b.   that war   RESULT
          one habit

As with the examples discussed in section 1, the addition of a temporal modifier like *constant* or *frequent* forces the complex event reading, and renders the expression of the full argument structure obligatory. The use of determiners like *that* or *one* highlights the result reading.

One might wonder at this point, why the same distinction in meaning is not possible with the [+substance] situational nouns; the careful reader will note that we have left that column blank in (17) above. We claim that it is no accident that we have no examples of concrete nouns with a complex event reading: it is in fact a conceptual impossibility for a concrete object also to denote a complex event. A concrete object can be an agent (*author, chef*), an instrument (*knife, awl*) or a relation (*mother*), but not an event. Concrete objects are stable across time; complex events, by definition, evolve through time. Note that the ontological impossibility of concrete event nouns shows that our features [dynamic] and [substance] are not notational variants of the syntactic category features [+/-N] and [+/-V]. Whereas any combination of [+/-N] and [+/-V] can be assigned some interpretation due to the lack of semantic content of these features, the features for which we have opted are **semantic** features, for which not all logically possible combinations are ontologically plausible or possible.

Let us finally foreshadow our analysis of nominalizations. We would like to claim that in using the feature [dynamic] to help us characterize three classes of nouns, we are doing more than simply partitioning semantic space, as it were. We are, in addition, trying to make a claim about how the meanings of nouns work. Specifically, we suggest that the use of the feature [dynamic] in nouns is marked. Nouns without this feature are the most prototypical. In terms of the simplex vocabulary of English we believe that the nonsituation nouns are also the most numerous. Further, we hypothesize that the positive value of the feature is more marked than the negative value. That is, we claim that the default interpretation for situational nouns is the result/agent/instrument reading. The most highly marked reading for nouns, the complex event reading, must be specially signalled – specifically by the obligatory presence of full argument structure, and temporal modification. In other words, extra baggage is needed with a noun to express (from the point of view of the speaker) or discern (from the point of view of the hearer) the complex event reading. Argument structure is optional with the more prototypical of nouns, obligatory with the least. We will now turn to nominalizations and see how these assumptions about prototypicality and markedness allow us to make some progress on the issue of inheritance.

5. DERIVED NOUNS AND THE ISSUE OF INHERITANCE

We have now developed enough of a system for representing the lexical semantics of simplex nouns to return to derivational morphology. First, we will determine what the LCSs of nominalizing affixes look like, in other words, what lexical semantic contribution the affix makes to the LCS of the derived word. Then we will explore the phenomenon of inheritance in various nominalizing affixes, inclu-ding *-ing*, *-(at)ion*, *-ment*, *-al*, *-er*, and *-ery*.

We begin here by noting that of the nominalizing affixes mentioned above, some will form abstract nouns and others concrete nouns. The former, among them *-ing*, *-(at)ion*, *-ment*, and *-al* will have the feature [-substance] in their LCSs. The latter include *-er*, *-ee*, and *-ery*, and will have the feature [+substance] in their LCSs. Further, of these affixes, all but the marginally productive *-ery* will be situational. As with all other nouns, nominalizing affixes will take an argument which corres-ponds to the R argument of previous literature. In addition, however, they will combine with the LCS of their bases, and their R arguments may be specified to bind one or another of the arguments of the verbal LCS with which they combine. This latter is an extension of an idea which has been used before in the literature, for example in DiSciullo and Williams (1987), and in Booij (1988).

Let us start with the [+substance] group and return to the [-substance] nominali-zations later. We will assume the lexical entries for *-er*, *-ee*, and *-ery* in (22). In (23) we show what those LCSs look like when they compose with the LCS of a verbs like *eat*, *bake*, or *employ* (all SIMPLE ACTIVITY verbs).

(22) a.   *-ery*
          [$_{Substance}$ +substance   ([$_{Substance}$], [LCS of verb])]

     b.   *-er*
          [$_{Substance}$ +substance   ([$_{Substance}$], [LCS of verb])]
                            -dynamic
          R argument binds first argument of verb.

     c.   *-ee*
          [$_{Substance}$ +substance   ([$_{Substance}$], [LCS of verb])]
                            -dynamic
          R argument binds second argument of verb.

(23) a. *eat + ery*
$$[_{\text{Substance}}\text{+substance } ([_{\text{Substance}}], [_{\text{Situation}}\text{+dynamic}$$
$$([_{\text{Substance}}], [_{\text{Substance}}])])]$$

    b. *bake + er*
$$[_{\text{Substance}}\text{+substance } ([_{\text{Substance-i}}], [_{\text{Situation}}\text{+dynamic}$$
$$\text{-dynamic}$$
$$([_{\text{Substance-i}}], [_{\text{Substance}}])])]$$

    c. *employ + ee*
$$[_{\text{Substance}}\text{+substance } ([_{\text{Substance-i}}], [_{\text{Situation}} \text{+dynamic}$$
$$\text{-dynamic}$$
$$([_{\text{Substance}}], [_{\text{Substance-i}}])])]$$

The suffix *-ery* presents the simplest case, in that it forms simple nonsituational concrete nouns denoting the places where some activity habitually takes place, of the same type as a simplex noun like *shop*. Turning to *-er* and *-ee*, it has been noted for quite some time in the literature on the argument structure of affixes (e.g. Williams 1981; DiSciulllo and Williams 1987; Booij 1988) that the suffix *-er* binds the external argument of its base verb, and *-ee* the internal argument of its base. Binding is intended to put the relevant argument out of commission with respect to the syntax. In our framework, the bound argument of the verbal base will be identified with the R argument of the affix and will no longer be available to be discharged independently. Thus the R argument of *-er* will bind the first argument of the verb to which it attaches, and the R argument of *-ee* the second. This binding pattern gives rise to the agent/instrument reading for *-er* nouns and the patient reading for *-ee* nouns.

Abstract nominalizing suffixes like *-ing*, *-(at)ion*, *-ment*, and *-al* will be treated similarly, except that they will have the feature [-substance] in the outermost layer of their LCSs. (24) gives the basic LCS for these abstract nominalizing affixes in English, and (25) an idea of what an LCS looks like when one of these, *-ment*, is composed with a verb *employ*. We note here that the overall semantic contribution of these affixes is taken to be the same. Individual items with these suffixes may be lexicalized with particular nuances of meaning that are absent in other formations with the same affix, but the general contributions of these affixes are the same, we claim.

(24)   *-ing, -(at)ion, -ment, -al*
$$[_{\text{Substance}} \text{-substance } ([_{\text{Substance}}], [\text{LCS of verb}])]$$
$$\text{+/-dynamic}$$
     R argument binds first argument of verb

(25)   *employ + ment*
$$[_{\text{Substance}} \text{-substance } ([_{\text{Substance-i}}], [_{\text{Situation}} \text{+dynamic } ([_{\text{Substance-i}}],$$
$$\text{+/-dynamic}$$
$$[_{\text{Substance}}])])]$$

The careful reader will note that the nominalizing suffixes of English fall into exactly the same categories as those we have developed for simplex nouns: *-ery* belongs to the class of [+substance] items which are nonsituational, along with simplex nouns like *house*; *-er* and *-ee* belong to the class of [+substance, -dynamic] items, along with *author* and *boss*; and *-ing, -(at)ion, -ment,* and *–al* belong to the class of [-substance, +/-dynamic] items, like *war* and *effort*. We note that just as there is no simplex noun in English which is both [+substance] and [+dynamic] (that is, a concrete complex event noun), there is no affix in English with this combination of features, and for the same reason; as we mentioned above, we believe this combination to be conceptually, and likely ontologically impossible. We note as well, that the affixes in (24) are those which exhibit either the result reading or the complex event reading, depending upon context.

We can now begin to explore the issue of inheritance. The questions must be phrased as follows in our framework. When the LCS of a verb composes with that of a noun, what happens to the LCS arguments of the verb? Is it possible to project them into the syntax? Is it necessary to do so? Or is it impossible? We would like to suggest that all three questions receive an affirmative response, but that which case obtains depends upon the class of noun the affix belongs to. Specifically, we would like to suggest that it is the privative and equipollent nature of the feature [dynamic] as it is used in distinguishing noun classes which correlates with inheritance behavior.

The first proposal that we make is that inheritance can take place only in situation nouns. Nouns which do not have the feature [dynamic] in the outermost layer of their LCS can project their own arguments, but cannot pass on the arguments of any verbs embedded deeper in the LCS. We put in this class of nouns those derived with the suffix *-ery* in English; derived words like *hatchery, brewery,* and *bakery* do not exhibit inheritance, as illustrated in (26):

(26)   * a bakery of cakes
        * a hatchery of salmon
        * a brewery of ale

All other nominalizing affixes in English, however, carry a value for the feature [dynamic]. The affixes *-er* and *-ee* belong to the class of [+substance,-dynamic] items. Although the R argument of the affix binds (and therefore puts out of commission with respect to the syntax) one of the verbal arguments, there may still be one verbal argument to be discharged. We would like to suggest that in this regard affixes with the features [+substance, -dynamic] behave no differently than simplex items with these features such as *author, parent,* and *mother*. Arguments may be projected or not; the LCS of the affix allows, but does not require projection of arguments. Inheritance from the verbal LCS is thus optional.

We turn finally to the nominalizing affixes which create [-substance] nouns. These typically have the possibility of either a result or a complex event reading (see for example, (2) and (3) above). In the former, they bear the feature [-dynamic], and in the latter [+dynamic]. Again, our treatment of simplex items in section 4 dictates how inheritance works in these two cases. We saw above with simplex items that in order for the complex reading to be signalled in this most marked of nominal categories, all argument structure must be present. Inheritance of the argument structure of the verb (and sometimes the addition of temporal modification) is thus obligatory if the speaker is to express or the hearer discern the complex event reading. With the result reading, the feature [-dynamic] in the highest layer of the LCS of the affix renders inheritance optional, but not obligatory.

It might be objected at this point that we have achieved this finer grained treatment of inheritance by virtue of a diacritic use of the feature [+/-dynamic] with nouns. In defense of our analysis, we point out first that the feature [dynamic] is independently needed for verbs (it has surfaced in many frameworks in one form or another – see references above), and our extension of the feature to simplex nouns is justified by the need to distinguish legitimate lexical classes such as situation and nonsituation nouns. Further, the possibility of privative and equipollent uses of features within our system gives rise to what seems like the proper cline of 'verbiness' among simplex nouns, from those that are most prototypical (that is, nonsituational), through those which are somewhat situational (agent/ instrument/ result nouns), to those which are most situational (complex event nouns). Any framework for lexical semantics must capture distinctions such as these somehow. The extension of this system of analysis to the arena of derivational morphology is perfectly natural, in our minds, and has the added advantage of giving a finer grained approach to the issue of inheritance.

6. CONCLUSION

We have tried to show in this paper that it is useful and interesting to develop a formalism in which the LCSs of words of all lexical categories can be represented, and that the development of this system can have positive effects for the study of morphology. Although it is beyond the scope of this paper to work out full details of the system, we have tried to sketch enough about the representation of lexical semantics that we envision to show how it can be applied to a classic problem of morphology, the inheritance of argument structure in nominalizations. Further, we have tried to show that this simple system is principled; it uses a small number of atoms to decompose the semantic functions of LCSs, and by allowing both binary and privative use of these atoms, allows economically for the description of a number of basic classes of nouns and verbs, and for extension to the lexical representations of affixes. Finally, we suggest that this system gives rise to an account of inheritance that is superior to that in Grimshaw (1990). First, we are able to link inheritance behavior in nominalized forms with the behavior of simplex nouns in the lexicon, something which Grimshaw does not attempt. Second, we are able to account for the apparent cline in inheritance patterns in a full range of nominalizations – from no inheritance at all with *-ery,* to optional inheritance with *-er, -ee,* and the result reading of *-(at)ion* and the like, to the obligatory inheritance of abstract nominalizers with complex event readings. We are thus able to extend the issue of inheritance to a wider range of data than is covered in Grimshaw (1990). The results, we believe, lead to interesting avenues for the further exploration of the semantics of both simplex and derived words.

NOTES

1   Work on lexical semantics has of course gone on in other frameworks, for example Montague Grammar (Dowty 1979), or Cognitive Grammar (Lakoff 1987; Langacker 1987, 1991). We concentrate here on the issue of lexical semantics in generative grammar, however.

2   We begin to work out this approach in Lieber and Baayen (1997), and to show how it can be useful in describing the semantic principle on which the choice of auxiliary is based in Dutch.

3   We accept here Comrie's (1976: 49) definition of the distinction between an Event and a State: "With a state, unless something happens to change the state, then the state will continue: this applies equally to standing and knowing. With a dynamic situation, on the other hand, the situation will only continue if it is continually subject to a new input of energy: this applies equally to running and to pure tone, since if John stops putting any effort into running, he will come to a stop, and if the oscilloscope is cut off from its source of power it will no longer emit sound. To remain in a state requires no effort, whereas to remain in a dynamic situation does require effort, whether from inside ... or from outside ... ."

4   Following Verkuyl (1989), we take 'processes' not to constitute a third category along with states and events. Instead, we assume that process readings arise from the interaction of events with unbounded arguments.

5   In a fuller version of this theory we will develop the idea that verbs also have a tense operator, which adjectives lack. It is beyond the scope of the present paper to develop this idea here, however.

6   As nothing in what follows hinges on the semantic features that define classes of adpositions within the system that we are developing, we will say nothing further about them here. See Lieber and Baayen (forthcoming) for a full treatment of this category.

7   Our formulation here differs in some details from that in Lieber & Baayen (1997). Specifically, we have tried to make clearer here the semantic contribution of the feature [IEPS] by elaborating on the form of the Path argument that was implicit in our earlier treatment.

8   Names like SIMPLE ACTIVITY, CHANGE, UNACCUSATIVE, or INCHOATIVE verbs, are, like the terms Relation, Situation, and Substance mentioned above, merely convenient mnemonics for combinations of features.

9   We use the notation $[_{Path}]$ here as an abbreviation for the sequence of Places/ States designated in (8), that is, $[\Phi_i(x), \Phi_j(x), ..., \Phi_k(x), \Phi_f(x)]$.

10   Note that with verbs like *walk,* however, one may **add** a Path in the form of a prepositional phrase (e.g., *to Amsterdam*). Directional adpositions like *to* will

themselves bear the feature [+IEPS] in our system.

11   An interesting byproduct of our theory, but one which we cannot explore here in depth is the result that it gives us some simple ways of characterizing both typical derivational processes in English and other languages and typical periphrastic constructions. In addition to being able to use the function [+dynamic] plus an argument to make complex predicates like *make X verb*, English also has a morphological causative: the formation of causative verbs in *-ize*, for example, involves the addition of the function [+dynamic] plus an argument to the LCS of a noun or adjective. Similarly, we can form both a periphrastic inchoative (*begin to walk, begin to eat*) or a morphological inchoative by adding the layer [+dynamic, +IEPS] to an LCS. For example, in English we can form inchoative verbs in *-en* with the addition of the function [+dynamic,+IEPS] to the LCS of an adjective.

12   We have argued extensively in Lieber and Baayen (1997) that evidence from auxiliary selection in Dutch shows these verbs to be a uniform class; all and only [+IEPS] verbs in Dutch select the auxiliary BE in the perfect.

REFERENCES

Aronoff, Mark. 1976. *Word Formation in Generative Grammar*. Cambridge, MIT Press.

Bierwisch, Manfred. 1989. "The Semantics of Gradation". In Manfred Bierwisch and Ewald Lang (eds), *Dimensional Adjectives: Grammatical Structure and Conceptual Interpretation*. Berlin: Springer Verlag, 71-261.

Bierwisch, Manfred. 1997. "Lexical Information from a Minimalist Point of View". In Chris Wilder, Hans-Martin Gartner and Manfred Bierwisch (eds), *The Role of Economy Principles in Linguistic Theory*. Berlin: Akademie Verlag, 227-266.

Booij, Geert. 1988. "The Relation Between Inheritance and Argument Linking: Deverbal Nouns in Dutch". In Martin Everaert, Arnold Evers, Riny Huybregts and Mieke Trommelen (eds), *Morphology and Modularity*. Dordrecht: Foris, 57-74.

Booij, Geert and Teun van Haaften. 1988. "On the External Syntax of Derived Words: Evidence from Dutch". In Geert Booij and Jaap van Marle (eds), *Yearbook of Morphology 1988*: Dordrecht: Foris: 29-44.

Comrie, Bernard. 1976. *Aspect*. Cambridge. Cambridge University Press.

DiSciullo, Anne-Marie and Edwin Williams. 1987. *On the Definition of Word*. Cambridge: MIT Press.

Dowty, David. 1979. *Word Meaning and Montague Grammar*. Dordrecht: Reidel.

Grimshaw, Jane. 1990. *Argument Structure*. Cambridge: MIT Press.

Higginbotham, James. 1985. "On Semantics". *Linguistic Inquiry* 16, 547-593.

Jackendoff, Ray. 1983. *Semantics and Cognition*. Cambridge. MIT Press.

Jackendoff, Ray. 1987. "The Status of Thematic Relations in Linguistic Theory". *Linguistic Inquiry* 18, 369-411.

Jackendoff, Ray. 1990. *Semantic Structures*. Cambridge: MIT Press.

Jackendoff, Ray. 1991. "Parts and Boundaries". *Cognition* 41, 9-45.

Jackendoff, Ray. 1996. "The Proper Treatment of Measuring Out, Telicity, and Perhaps Even Quantification in English". *Natural Language and Linguistic Theory* 14, 305-354.

Lakoff, George. 1987. *Women, Fire, and Dangerous Things*. Chicago: University of Chicago Press.

Langacker, Ronald. 1987, 1991. *Foundations of Cognitive Grammar, vol. 1 & 2*, Stanford, CA: Stanford University Press.

Levin, Beth. 1994. *English Verb Classes and Alternations*. Chicago:University of Chicago Press.

Levin, Beth and Malka Rappaport Hovav. 1995. *Unaccusativity*. Cambridge: MIT Press.

Lieber, Rochelle. 1980. *On the Organization of the Lexicon*. Doctoral Dissertation, MIT.

Lieber, Rochelle. 1998. "The Suffix *-ize* in English: Implications for Morphology". In Steven Lapointe, Diane Brentari and PatrickFarrell (eds), *Morphology and Its Relation to Phonology and Syntax*. Stanford, CA: CSLI, 12-33.

Lieber, Rochelle and Harald Baayen. 1993. "Verbal Prefixes in Dutch: a Study in Lexical Conceptual Structure". In Geert Booij and Jaap van Marle (eds.), *Yearbook of Morphology 1993*. Dordrecht. Kluwer Academic Publishers, 51-78.

Lieber, Rochelle and Harald Baayen. 1997. "A Semantic Principle of Auxiliary Selection in Dutch". *Natural Language and Linguistic Theory* 15, 789-845.

Lieber, Rochelle and Harald Baayen. forthcoming. *Morphology and Lexical Semantics*. Ms. University of New Hampshire, and Max Planck Institute for Psycholinguistics.

Lyons, John. 1977. *Semantics 2*. Cambridge: Cambridge University Press.

Pinker, Steven. 1989. *Learnability and Cognition*. Cambridge: MIT Press.

Pustejovsky, James. 1996. *The Generative Lexicon*. Cambridge: MIT Press.

Quirk, Randolph, Sidney Greenbaum, Geoffrey Leech and Jan Svartvik. 1972. *A Grammar of Contemporary English*. London: Longman.

Roeper, Thomas. 1987. "Implicit Arguments and the Head-Complement Relation". *Linguistic Inquiry* 18, 267-310.

Selkirk, Elisabeth. 1982. *The Syntax of Words*. Cambridge: MIT Press.

Talmy, Leonard. 1985. "Lexicalization Patterns: Semantic Structure in Lexical Forms". In Timothy Shopen (ed.), *Language Typology and Syntactic Description III:Grammatical Categories and the Lexicon*. Cambridge: Cambridge University Press, 57-149.

Tenny, Carol. 1987. *Grammaticalizing Aspect and Affectedness*. Doctoral Dissertation, MIT.

Tenny, Carol. 1994. *Aspectual Roles and the Syntax-Semantics Interface*. Dordrecht: Kluwer Academic Publishers.

Verkuyl, Henk. 1972. *On the Compositional Nature of the Aspects*. Dordrecht: Reidel.

Verkuyl, Henk. 1989. "Aspectual Classes and Aspectual Composition". *Linguistics and Philosophy* 12, 39-94.

Williams, Edwin. 1981. "Argument Structure and Morphology". *Linguistic Review* 1, 81-114.

Rochelle Lieber
English Department
Hamilton Smith Hall
University of New Hampshire
Durham, NH 03824
USA

Harald Baayen
Max-Planck-Institut für Psycholinguistik
PO Box 310
6500 AH Nijmegen
The Netherlands

A declarative approach to conversion into verbs in German

MARTIN NEEF

1. WHAT IS CONVERSION?

Among the most problematic and controversial phenomena in morphological theory is conversion. Several different analyses have been proposed in the literature which sometimes differ quite fundamentally, depending on the framework chosen. In many such frameworks the analysis of conversion demands the addition of a theoretical device that is not a natural consequence of the respective approach. In this paper, I will present an analysis of conversion within the declarative model of morphology called Word Design (cf. Neef 1996a) which allows to treat conversion as a phenomenon that is predictable from the theoretical assumptions. The analysis is restricted to German data and is not applicable straightforwardly to data from other languages for reasons that will become clear in the course of argumentation.

Before I give an outline of the Word Design model, it is necessary to clarify the understanding of the term conversion which underlies the following considerations. This is so because various mechanisms have been proposed to explain conversion, and, even more crucial, the data which shall count as instances of conversion are controversial. In my understanding, conversion is restricted to pairs of lexemes which belong to different word classes but share the same stem. Hence, a prototypical example of conversion is the English verb (*to*) *fish* converted from the homophonous noun *fish*. In German, conversion in this sense can be found as a relation between different word classes as exemplified in (1). According to Reis (1985: 396f.), the relations in (1a) are more or less productive, whereas the relations in (1b) are principally unproductive in Modern Standard German (MSG):[1]

(1) a. V → N schauen 'to look' → Schau 'show'
         A → V weit 'wide' → weiten 'to widen'
         N → V Öl 'oil' → ölen 'to oil'
     b. V → A (*none*)
         A → N gut 'good' → Gut 'property'
         N → A ernst 'serious' → Ernst 'seriousness'

Some authors (e.g. Dokulil 1968; Lieber 1992: 161; Vater 1996[2]: 95) treat umlaut and ablaut phenomena of the following kind as conversion:

(2) a. werfen 'to throw' → Wurf 'throw'
         treten 'to tread' → Tritt 'tread'
     b. Kamm 'comb' → kämmen 'to comb'
         Dampf 'steam' → dämpfen 'to muffle' (besides *dampfen* 'to steam')

These data differ from explicit derivation in that no visible affixes have been added to the stem at its periphery. These stems, however, are not faithfully preserved in the dependent word because the stem vowel has been changed (the *-en* is the infinitive marker only and therefore to be ignored when looking at conversion which belongs to lexeme formation). Following e.g. Olsen (1986: 111) and Spencer (1991: 19f.) I exclude these data from conversion and assume a quite narrow delimitation of the area of conversion. This exclusion of the data presented in (2) is not really problematic, because in German ablaut-formation is not productive any more and new umlauted verbs can only be found sporadically and unsystematically (cf. Fleischer/ Barz 1992: 305).[2] The topic of the delimitation of conversion will be taken up again in the final section of this paper.

2. DERIVATIONAL VERSUS NON-DERIVATIONAL APPROACHES TO CONVERSION

The most disputed question concerning conversion is what kind of lexeme formation process conversion is as compared to the 'normal' processes of compounding and derivation. In the generative literature, there are a lot of answers devoted to this question (cf. e.g. Lieber 1981, 1992; Kiparsky 1983; Olsen 1986, 1990; Don 1993). Since there is a strong tendency to treat all lexeme formation as concatenation, conversion is often conceived as a kind of derivation with the specific property of invoking a zero morpheme. These zeros are burdened with well-known problems (cf. e.g. Bergenholtz and Mugdan 1979a; Don 1993): are they prefixes or suffixes, how many zeros may attach to one stem, how can their lexical entries be learned? It seems that the answers to questions like these strongly depend on the theoretical framework chosen, but zeros tend to make theories unfalsifiable.

A somewhat different approach is taken by Lieber (1992: 157-165). She ascertains that three kinds of analyses have been proposed for conversion phenomena: besides derivation by zero affixes these are relisting and category-changing rules. In her attempt to reduce all morphology to syntax or phonology,[3] she rejects the category-changing option on theoretical grounds because this would introduce a purely morphological rule into her theory. The zero affix analysis fits perfectly into her approach because in this case all morphological information is tied to a (lexical) morpheme. While Lieber adopts this approach for some French conversion data, she refrains from doing so with respect to conversion in English and German because here the relevant data do not show the sort of morpho-syntactic uniformity predicted by the zero affixation analysis. Instead, she adheres to the relisting alternative. This means that items already listed in the lexicon (which contains simple morphemes and unproductively formed complex words only) can re-enter as an item of a different category. Lieber claims that this analysis does not add any new principles to her theory: "Because speakers of a language are always adding new words to their lexicons, we must assume in any theory that there is a mechanism for creating new entries in the lexicon" (cf. Lieber 1992: 159). However, relisting describes a relation between lexical items and constitutes thus a purely morphological mechanism. Moreover, defining conversion in German as principally irregular is merely an undesirable admission that the regularities within this area cannot be explained in Lieber's theory.

Since I will be able to identify some structural regularities in conversion into verbs in German, I dispense with relisting just as I dispense with zero morphemes. On the other hand, in a theory that is explicitly morphological, there seems to be no reason to refrain from the category-changing analysis. However, a category-changing rule would have to delimit the range of bases that might undergo this rule. In German, for example, there is no general rule to change the category of noun into verb because many nouns can not be used as verbs. In order to be descriptively adequate, the possible bases of this rule would have to be constrained which would make the rule very complex and unlikely to be learnable.

What all kinds of theoretical conceptions mentioned have in common is that they are derivational in nature: a directional relation from an input to an output is described in terms of rules. Following a general trend in linguistics, I will pursue a principally different strategy of morphological analysis: I will describe morphological knowledge as the knowledge of the well-formedness of a surface form (the 'output'). Within the Word Design model I will look at the target category of conversion and ask what are the conditions that guide conversion into verbs (instead of asking what derivation a base category has to go through in order to be converted into some other category). My general claim is that in principle every non-verbal stem can be used as a verb in German. There is no condition constraining the range of bases. There are, however, conditions on the side of verbs. A non-verbal stem can only be used as a verbal stem if the resulting verb is well-formed. These constraints, however, are not specific to conversion because the grammaticality of a verb is a matter that has to be dealt with independently. Thus, in order to analyse conversion into verbs, the properties a verb must have to be well-formed must be figured out. This will enable me to delimit the range of non-verbal stems that could potentially be used as a verb from those that are blocked from verbal usage, thereby revealing some regularities that have been undiscovered up to now.

In several analyses of conversion it is assumed that one of the two conversionally related morphological items be basic. This is reminiscent of the famous question of Bergenholtz and Mugdan (1979b) "Ist Liebe primär?" ('Is love primary?') concerning the directionality of conversion which is often hard to determine (cf. also Marchand 1964, 1969; Don 1993, and Eschenlohr 1997b: Ch. 3.1.2). Without going into detail I believe that this question is not problematic for an analysis interested in the speaker's competence. If conversion is a productive way to form new lexemes, this means that a new lexeme is formed on the base of a lexeme already existing in the speaker's mental lexicon. In this case, uncontroversially, directionality is invoked. On the other hand, there may be pairs of conversionally related lexemes already listed in the speaker's mental lexicon. In this case, there may be (formal, diachronic or semantic) reasons to assume one of these words more likely to be basic than the other, but in principle there is no reason to assume that this kind of dependency plays any role in the grammatical knowledge of a language user.

Relying on the seminal paper by Clark and Clark (1979) and subsequent work, I assume that there are no semantic restrictions on conversion into verbs. In order to function as a verb, the converted item has to denote an event, state or process. Typically, the meaning of the verb is connected to a prototypical or contextually highlighted aspect of the basic word, but even this is not a necessary prerequisite given metaphorical readings. There are, however, formal restrictions on conversion into verbs, at least in German. The main focus of this article is to identify formal conditions for the well-formedness of verbs which are — given an output-oriented view — relevant for conversion. To achieve this goal, I will first outline the model of Word Design and then go on to analyse the well-formedness conditions for the morphological category of infinitive within this theory. After a discussion of a phonological constraint that comes into play, I will discuss the status of the infinitive in the verbal paradigm and compare conversion to some other closely related phenomena.

3. WORD DESIGN: A SKETCH

Word Design is a declarative approach to morphology. Declarative models "characterize *what* constraints are brought to bear during language use independently of *what order* the constraints are applied in" (Pollard and Sag 1987: 8). In this constraint-based sense, these models are non-derivational and eliminate the complications of extrinsic rule-ordering. In its constraint-based character, Word Design resembles other theories like Optimality Theory (OT, Prince and Smolensky 1993) and Declaractive Phonology (DP, Scobbie, Bird and Coleman 1996). In some other respects, Word Design is different from these theories which will be discussed in the following outline.

A central topic of declarative approaches is whether constraints are rooted in UG or have to be learned from information that is available from the specific linguistic input language learners have access to. In a strict conception, OT takes all constraints to be part of UG (cf. e.g. Prince and Smolensky 1993: 3). This is necessary because in OT constraints are violable. Since constraints that are not surface-true cannot be learned from surface information alone, they must consequently be regarded as part of the genetic equipment of human beings. Several studies within this framework, however, turn out to be compelled to assume language-particular constraints. For example, Russell (1997: 119) assumes a constraint that is specific for Tagalog because it explicitly makes reference to a Tagalog morpheme. The constraint in question relies on a universal schema to create constraints, namely Generalized Alignment, but the respective constraint is specific for one language. Since this constraint is violable, the question of learnability remains unsolved.

DP takes a more coherent stand: there are universal as well as language-specific constraints (among the latter are morphemes which are conceived of as constraints), but all constraints follow the requirement to be surface-true which makes them learnable (cf. Scobbie, Coleman and Bird 1996: 688). Strictly speaking, there is no theoretical force to assume universal constraints at all in this framework. A closer look, however, reveals that constraints may be violated under specific circumstances. DP employs the notion of default. Such default constraints are not necessarily sur-face-true in this conception because there may be more specific constraints that overwrite these defaults via the Elsewhere Condition. Thus, the constraints assumed in DP are not mutually consistent despite contrary claims.

The moral of these problems seems to be that language-specific constraints cannot be dispensed with. As a consequence, it seems theoretically simpler to assume language-specific constraints only instead of employing two different modes of constraints. This hypothesis is assumed in Word Design. Consequently, constraints are not violable in this conception as a prerequisite for the assumption that they are learnable from surface information. There may be specific items that violate some constraint, but these items are then regarded as lexically marked exceptions, hence items to be learned one by one. With this assumption, Word Design is in line with Haider (1993: 50) who claims that UG does not contain any substantial information but only determines the possible structuring of any linguistic substance. Moreover, Word Design complies with Haider's (1993: 12) claim for cognitive controllability of generative models. According to that a system is cognitive controllable only if its categories stand in a continuous relation to the data. Such a relation is given only if the assumed constraints meet the condition of epistemological priority which means that they must have a discernible material equivalent in the surface forms. Based on these assumptions, Word Design claims to be a realistic model of morphological competence.

Another central topic of any morphological theory is whether the notion of morpheme is taken to be basic or not. Both OT and DP adhere to this morpheme concept. In recent years, however, several authors have put forward arguments against the morpheme as a basic unit of linguistic theory (cf. e.g. Becker 1990; Anderson 1992; Raffelsiefen 1993a; Rickheit 1993). Following this tradition, Word Design is an a-morphous approach. In particular, it is assumed in Word Design that the morpheme concept has to be split up into two discrete concepts, namely stems and affixes. Stems are part of the lexical knowledge. The mental lexicon in this concep-tion consists of lexemes only. These lexemes comprise the idiosyncratic knowledge concerning the vocabulary of a certain language. Lexemes as abstractions from surface information have three aspects: form, syntax, and meaning. Word Design is concerned with the formal side of lexemes which is conceived as stems. For example, the lexeme *Mund* 'mouth' consists of the knowledge of the non-linguistic concept MUND as the semantic part. The stem /mUnd/ can be abstracted from the knowledge of both a singular and a plural form plus knowledge of morphological regularities. The nominative singular is [mUnt], and the nominative plural is [mʏn.də]. Obvious-ly, none of these forms alone is sufficient to obtain the adequate stem representation. Thus, the notion of stem as assumed in Word Design is related to the notion of underlying representations in traditional generative grammar. The point of view in Word Design, however, is opposite: derivational approaches take underlying representations as the input and transform this input by means of a rule system into a surface form, while in the declarative Word Design model the well-formedness of surface forms is taken into account directly. One of these conditions for surface well-formedness is that a stem must be contained in each surface form. In the treatment of stems as lexical objects, Word Design is similar to OT, whereas DP takes stems to be constraints.

The most serious difference between Word Design and other generative approaches to morphology concerns the fixing of the borderline between phonology and morphology. In the context of constraint-based theories a crucial question is: given that phonological constraints hold for phonological units and syntactic constraints hold for syntactic units, then what are morphological units? The most obvious candidates would be morphemes, but since morphemes are taken to be underlying representations or lexical elements, they are not subject to constraints in surface-oriented approaches. Moreover, they are not available in Word Design as this is an a-morphous model. Another candidate would be the word. This is a problematic notion because it seems impossible to give a clear definition and, more importantly, words are not only subject to morphological, but also to phonological and semantic constraints.

Following Becker (1990) I take morphological categories to be the subject of morphological constraints. Whereas phonological constraints hold for phonological categories like the syllable or the phonological word, morphological constraints hold for categories that are specific for morphology. There are two different types of such categories: inflectional categories and lexeme formation categories. Among the inflectional categories of German are the verbal infinitive or the nominative plural of nouns. Among the lexeme formation categories are patterns like the ones represented by *Lehrer* 'teacher' or *Gehopse* 'hopping'. The notion of a morphological category is related to the notion of a lexical sub-domain in DP. Whereas in DP phonological constraints may be marked to hold for such an arbitrarily defined lexical sub-domain only (Scobbie, Coleman and Bird 1996: 698), it is assumed in Word Design that constraints that are specific for morphological categories are morphological in nature rather than phonological. Moreover, morphological categories are not part of the lexicon, but part of the morphological component of linguistic knowledge.

Obviously, morphological categories are highly language-specific. This is a natural assumption given that morphemes are also language-specific and given that this notion is partly kept within the notion of a morphological category. The main differences between the two approaches are the following:

— The morphemic approach works bottom-up. Properties of morphemes as word constituents are analysed. A fundamental problem, however, is that morphemes are not of epistemological priority: they are not the input of linguistic analysis, but the result (cf. e.g. Rickheit 1993).

— The Word Design approach works top-down and is word-based in nature.

Properties of whole words are analysed which enables to take into account especially prosodic regularities. The specific understanding of the notion 'word' in this model is that of a grammatical word (following Gallmann 1990 and Aronoff 1994). A grammatical word is a lexeme in a particular syntactic context, thus a fully inflected surface form as it appears in actual speech. Therefore, grammatical words are more likely to meet the requirement of epistemological priority.

On the formal side, lexeme formation is concerned with the well-formedness of new (or complex) stems.[4] Inflection is concerned with the well-formedness of grammatical words. This well-formedness is described by constraints that are specific for a given morphological category. These morphological constraints, which are called *design conditions* in Word Design, are not violable for instances of the respective morphological category. Just as every syllable must obey all phonological constraints that concern the unit syllable, all instances of a morphological category must obey the design conditions specific for this category.

In order to acquire morphological competence, a language user has to learn that words have specific syntactic functions in sentences. These are the inflectional categories. Moreover, s/he has to learn that words that share specific elements of form also share specific meaning components. These are the lexeme formation patterns. The knowledge of the formal properties of instances of these morphological categories first of all consists of the knowledge of the formal base. This base may be a stem as a lexical unit, or it may be a grammatical word as a surface form. Typically, an instance of a morphological category is not identical to its base but differs from this in certain aspects. These differences may e.g. consist in the addition or deletion of phonological segments or in a specific prosodic shape. The assumption that the morphological knowledge of the formal properties of instances of morphological categories consists of the formal differences of these instances with respect to their base is captured in the *Main Principle of Morphology*:

(3)   *Main Principle of Morphology*
        A grammatical word is ideally identical with the phonological realisation of its base. Violations against this principle at the end of the base are less severe than violations at the beginning of the base.

This principle is related to the faithfulness constraints in OT, but it conflates this constraint family into one principle only. Whereas in OT all constraints are violable, in Word Design only the *Main Principle* is violable and hence to be assumed to be part of UG. The rider to the *Main Principle* (which is supposed to be language-specific) takes into account that at least some languages (including German) tend to highlight the beginning of the stem sequence in a grammatical word.

Whenever instances of a morphological category differ formally from their base, this has to be stated in a design condition. In the first place, these design conditions are specific for a particular morphological category, but this does not exclude the possibility that different morphological categories may share one or another design condition (or that different languages share some design conditions). The design conditions that hold for a particular morphological category are not violable for instances of this category, and consequently, they are not ordered.

Since design conditions describe properties of the sound structure of grammatical words, they operate with phonological terms. However, they do not count as phonological conditions under the assumption that conditions of phonological well-formedness are in principle unviolated in the whole vocabulary of a language. For example, final devoicing is a phonological constraint in that it prevents voiced obstruents from appearing in the syllable rhyme, regardless of the morphological category. To end in a nasal, on the other hand, is not a general property of German words or syllables, but it is a property of instances of specific morphological categories, for example the infinitive. This will become crucial in the following analysis of conversion into verbs which will prove to be mainly an analysis of the inflectional category of the verbal infinitive.

4. CONVERSION-RELEVANT PROPERTIES OF THE INFINITIVE

4.1 *The Design Condition of Segmental Ending*

According to standard morpheme-based approaches, a German infinitive is well-formed if it is concatenated from a verbal stem plus the infinitive morpheme *-(e)n*. The letter <e> is set in parenthesis because some bases are only added with <n> (e.g. *Trommel* 'drum' — *trommeln* 'to drum'). This will become a central point in my analysis. Furthermore, the <e> is obligatory in orthography only; it is sometimes pronounced as schwa, sometimes as the syllabicity of the following nasal or of an adjacent liquid, and sometimes it is not pronounced at all. In part, this distribution depends on different language styles. The verb *malen* 'to paint' for example has all three possibilities:[5]

(4)   explicit articulation: [mɑː.lən]
        standard articulation: [mɑː.l̩n]
        colloquial articulation: [mɑːln]

In the following analysis, I will be concerned only with the level of explicit articulation of MSG. The reason for this is that a grammatical word is a possible one in German only if it has a well-formed variant at the level of explicit articulation (cf. Neef 1997a). The explicit and the standard variants mainly differ phonologically: whereas the standard variant allows syllabic consonants, the explicit variant demands that all syllable peaks are vocalic segments. The colloquial variant is characterised by a simpler grammar. For some morphological categories, for example, the difference between instances of this category and their respective base is smaller than on the other levels mentioned. This means that morphological categories can be subject to less design conditions on this lower level as compared to the higher levels. Interestingly, this set of design conditions does not vary randomly, but the design conditions that hold for a specific morphological category on a lower stylistic level form a true subset of the design conditions relevant for the same morphological category on a higher level.

In (5) I present some data to give an impression of the formal diversity of German infinitives. For the sake of convenience I give orthographical representations, with inverted commas added to indicate main stress. The analysis, however, will be concerned with the phonological representation that I will give only when necessary.

(5)	a.	sein	'to be'	tun	'to do'
		'säen	'to sow'	'hauen	'to hit'
		'malen	'to paint'	'glupschen	'to stare'
		po'saunen	'to play the trombone'	'prophe'zeien	'to prophesy'
	b.	'steigern	'to increase'	'tänzeln	'to mince'
		spio'nieren	'to spy'	klassifi'zieren	'to classify'
	c.	be'greifen	'to understand'	ver'zichten	'to do without'
		'abperlen	'to drip off'	'einkaufen	'to buy'
		'nacherzählen	'to retell'	'hinunterbewegen	'to move down'
	d.	be'aufsichtigen	'to supervise'	verge'sellschaften	'to nationalise'

These infinitives differ in prosodic structure as well as in morphological complexity. The morphemic analysis first of all captures the fact that all infinitives end in a nasal. On the surface a morpheme is nothing else than a (string of) phonological segment(s). Therefore, I reinterpret the traditional notion of affix as a design condition for particular morphological categories.

(6)   *Design Condition of Segmental Ending*
        The grammatical word must have a specific segmental ending.
        Clause: The segmental ending must be [N].

To know the morphological category of infinitive means to know its syntactic function, its formal base (which is a verbal stem) and the design conditions which are relevant. A first condition of that kind is the *Design Condition of Segmental Ending* which states that a grammatical word is well-formed as an infinitive only if it ends in a nasal. In explicit articulation, this nasal always has to be a coronal (as the default of underspecified nasals). In standard articulation, this nasal can also be pronounced as the labial nasal [m] or the velar nasal [ŋ] due to assimilation. Examples of this are the infinitives *haben* 'to have' and *welken* 'to fade' in standard articulation as ['hɑ:.bm̩] and ['vɛl.kŋ̩] respectively.

The design condition in (6) is formulated rather generally in that the formulation itself does not make reference to particular morphological categories. This is because several such categories may be subject to one and the same design condition. The 3. ps. sg. pres. for example is subject to the *Design Condition of Segmental Ending* in a different version with the clause [t] (*sie tanzt* 'she dances'), and the 1. and 3. ps. pl. pres. even obey the same version of this condition as the infinitive (*wir/ sie tanzen* 'we/ they dance'). It is conceivable that the morphological component consists of a pool where all design conditions relevant for a specific language are stored. The knowledge connected with a morphological category then consists of a reference to the design conditions relevant for this category. The design conditions themselves, on the other hand, do not know from which morphological categories they are picked. Thus, it is principally impossible to specify the domain of a design condition.

The *Design Condition of Segmental Ending* does not prohibit conversion of any non-verbal stem into a verb. It simply says: if a stem is to be used as an infinitive, it has to end in a nasal. No phonological constraint of German marks such a constellation as ill-formed. But in connection with the following morphological conditions it becomes crucial for conversion.

4.2 The Design Condition of a Unique Reduced Syllable

The *Design Condition of Segmental Ending* is not equivalent to the morphemic analysis. Whereas the latter demands that the suffix must be added to the verbal stem, the design condition in (6) simply demands the existence of a nasal in a specific position. In principle, this nasal could already be present in the stem. This analysis, however, is not sufficient because stems ending in a nasal as e.g. /din/ 'to serve' cannot be pronounced monosyllabic #[diːn] as an infinitive but only bisyllabic [diː.nən] in explicit articulation (or [diː.n̩] in standard articulation).[6] Obviously, more conditions are relevant for the morphological category of infinitive.

Here, prosodic properties come into play. In German (as in some other Germanic languages like Danish and Dutch) there exists a distinction between two syllable types. The first type contains a full vowel and bears primary or secondary stress, whereas the second type is never stressed at all, and its syllable peak is either the vowel schwa or a sonorant (including the vocalic variant of /r/ which is the usual allophone if the /r/ appears in the syllable rhyme). Following Vennemann (1991), I will refer to the former type as 'full syllables' and to the latter type as 'reduced syllables' (this type is often called 'schwa-syllables', cf. e.g. Wiese 1996). There are some differences between these syllable types concerning maximality conditions: in the rhyme a reduced syllable has one C-position less than a full syllable (cf. Becker 1998). This observation justifies the usage of the term 'reduced syllable' (which derives from diachronic analyses) in synchronic studies. Furthermore, vowels that are realised as unstressed full vowels in explicit articulation may be reduced to schwa in colloquial articulation under specific circumstances as in explicit *Käng*[u]*ru* vs. colloquial *Käng*[ə]*ru* 'kangaroo' (cf. Vennemann 1991: 212). In orthography, a reduced syllable is always indicated by the letter <e> (which can, by the way, also indicate a full vowel).

In MSG it is not enough for infinitives to end in a nasal, but they also have to end in exactly one reduced syllable. This is expressed through the following design condition (cf. Neef 1996a: 134ff.):

(7)   *Design Condition of a Unique Reduced Syllable*
        The grammatical word must end in exactly one reduced syllable.

There are two infinitives that never end in a reduced syllable, namely the very frequent ones *tun* 'to do' and *sein* 'to be'. Thus, they are lexical exceptions that do not obey the requirements of a design condition which is principally relevant for the morphological category they represent. Such exceptions are lexically marked in that the lexical entries of the lexemes in question not only comprise a listed stem but also stem variants or surface forms representing particular inflectional categories.

The *Design Condition of a Unique Reduced Syllable* does not hold for the colloquial variant of German as is indicated in (4c). Many infinitives in this variant nevertheless end in a reduced syllable as well, but for a different reason, namely if the sonority of the segments demands the existence of a reduced syllable. An example for this is *baden* 'to bathe' which can be pronounced either as ['bɑː.dən] or as ['bɑː.dn̩], but never without a final reduced syllable for phonological reasons only.

What is important for the topic of conversion is that there are no infinitives in German that end in more than one reduced syllable. This is predicted by the *Design Condition of a Unique Reduced Syllable* as a morphological condition holding for the infinitive. In Middle High German (MHG), there existed infinitives with two final reduced syllables like *trommelen* 'to drum', and the same is true for some present-day German dialects like Austrian or Swiss German or the closely related language of Modern Dutch. Moreover, many morphological categories of MSG are not subject to this reduced syllable condition. The 1. ps. sg. pres. may end in two reduced syllables as in *ich trommele* 'I drum', and in the adjectival paradigm forms can be found that even end in three reduced syllables like *goldenere*, pronounced as ['gɔl.də.nə.ʀə], 'more golden$_{nom}$'.

The *Design Condition of a Unique Reduced Syllable* is a source of blocking of conversion into verbs. In the lists that follow I only give words of the category noun that cannot be used as infinitives. The results of my analysis also hold for stems of other categories, but nouns are by far the biggest group of words in German, and the most complex phonological structure of morphologically simple words can be found in nouns. The invert lexicon of Muthmann (1988) (including about 175.000 words) contains about 60 non-derived nouns which cannot be converted into an infinitive because the resulting infinitive would have to end in two reduced syllables in order to be phonologically well-formed. Most of these nouns are non-standard in MSG in that they belong to a specific dialect or slang. I only list those examples which are more or less common:[7]

(8) a.   Kirmes 'funfair'   →   #kirmesen
          Kappes 'cabbage'   →   #kappesen

	Nippes 'knick-knack'	→	#nippesen
	Kokkolores 'nonsens'	→	#kokkoloresen
b.	Abend 'evening'	→	#abenden
	Gegend 'region'	→	#gegenden
	Jugend 'youth'	→	#jugenden
	Tausend 'a thousand'	→	#tausenden
	Tugend 'virtue'	→	#tugenden
c.	Hundert 'a hundred'	→	#hunderten
d.	Atem 'breath'	→	#atemen
e.	Tacheles (reden) 'speak frankly'	→	#tachelesen

With '#' I indicate that a word is not well-formed due to morphological reasons; phonologically all the forms in the right column in (8) are perfectly well-formed. The regular plural for *Gegend* e.g. is *Gegenden*, a form which is not allowed as an infinitive. The nouns in (8) are characterised by at least one final reduced syllable with the sonority of the final segment being less than or equal to that of the infinitive marker [N]. There is no way for these nouns to end both in the right segment and in the right prosodic constellation in order to function as an infinitive.

A conceivable strategy, though, to change these nouns into verbs would be the deletion of stem segments. In the noun *Gegend*, for example, only the final obstruent would have to be deleted to result in the seemingly well-formed infinitive *#gegen* ending both in a nasal and in exactly one reduced syllable. But this is not a possible option to form an infinitive: this morphological category always has to contain its complete base. In German, there are only two lexeme formation patterns allowing deletion regularly: the first is the formation of hypocoristic forms of names or objects ending in [i] like *Compi* to *Computer* 'computer' (cf. Neef 1996a: 278ff.; Werner 1996; Féry 1997), the second are blends like *Semantax* from *Semantik* and *Syntax* 'semantics and syntax', a productive mechanism to form dvandva compounds in German.

From the cases in (8), the noun *Atem* remains peculiar. The form *#atem* is not a possible infinitive in explicit articulation because it does not end in a coronal nasal. The form *#atemen* is not a possible infinitive because it ends in two reduced syllables. But interestingly, there exists a converted infinitive based on the noun *Atem*, namely *atmen* 'to breathe'. This is subject of the next section where *atmen* is argued to be an exception.

4.3 The Design Condition of a Potential Syllable Rhyme

Raffelsiefen (1993b, 1995: 123) makes the observation that the position of a schwa in infinitives is fixed beyond what is expectable from phonology. Focussing on the segments following the last full vowel, there is only one position the schwa may appear in, even if the phonology allows more than one position. A suitable example for demonstration is the infinitive *stapeln* 'to stack'. The consonantal segments following the last full vowel are /pln/. In explicit articulation, the infinitive has to end both in a nasal and in a reduced syllable, and it should contain no syllabic nasals and laterals (these are only allowed in standard articulation). Therefore, a schwa has to be the syllable peak of the final reduced syllable of the infinitive in question. The phonology permits the realisation of the schwa either in front of or behind the lateral ([ʃtɑ:.pəln] vs. [ʃtɑ:.plən]). The *Main Principle of Morphology* suggests that if a surface form has to differ from the realisation of its base for some reason, this difference is best indicated at the right edge of the word. Since an infinitive must end in a nasal, the preferred form should be [ʃtɑ:.plən] with the schwa following the stem segments. This phonologically well-formed string, however, is not a possible infinitive in German. The grammatical form is [ʃtɑ:.pəln] with the schwa being inserted into the stem segments. Therefore, a further design condition must be at work to demand this greater difference to the base. The following design condition is meant to capture the fact that the schwa in infinitives is always located at the same position relative to the segments following the last full vowel:

(9)　　*Design Condition of a Potential Syllable Rhyme*
　　　　Beginning with the last full vowel, the segments in the grammatical word that precede a schwa must form one potential syllable rhyme.

Crucial to this definition is the notion of a potential syllable rhyme. Without going into detail here (but cf. Neef 1996a: 60ff.), this notion can easily be given a generally intelligible reading. The central claim is that the segments that precede the schwa up to the last full vowel of the grammatical word must be pronounceable in one syllable. In the example *stapeln*, the elements in front of the schwa are pronounceable in one syllable as [.ʃtɑ:p.], but in the ungrammatical form #*staplen* this is not the case: *[.ʃtɑ:pl.] is impossible in one syllable (which is explainable in terms of sonority). The design condition in (9) does not mention an actual syllable rhyme, but a potential one. This is important because in the actual pronunciation of the infinitive *stapeln* as [ʃtɑ:.pəln] the elements in front of the schwa do not form a syllable rhyme since the /p/ is part of the syllable onset. In a potential word form, however, it could be part of the syllable rhyme opened by the last full vowel without violating any phonological constraint of German.

The *Design Condition of a Potential Syllable Rhyme* is formulated with regard to the vowel schwa and not, as could seem natural, with regard to the syllable peak of a reduced syllable for at least two reasons. First, were the vocalic /r/ within the scope of this condition, several counter-examples, such as the following, would weaken its meaningfulness:

(10)　　entjungfern 'to deflower'
　　　　gärtnern 'to garden'
　　　　klempnern 'to do plumbing'
　　　　tischlern 'to do woodwork'

Contra to the claim of many linguistic analyses and even some pronouncing dictionaries, words like these are never pronounced with a schwa in MSG, but with a vocalic /r/ as the peak of the final reduced syllable. In front of this segment, however, there is a string that is not pronounceable in one syllable in the examples given. Since the *Design Condition of a Potential Syllable Rhyme* only holds for the vowel schwa, the examples in (10) do not have to be viewed as counter-examples to this design condition.

Second, Raffelsiefen (1995: 124) remarks that there is one exception to her observation of a fixed position of the schwa in consonantal clusters in infinitives:

(11) a.   XVr•n   fahren 'to drive', schwören 'to swear', telefonieren 'to
                  telephone'
     b.   XV•rn   wiehern 'to neigh', nähern 'to approach'

Here, the X marks any string of segments, V indicates the last full vowel, and the big point marks the position of the potential schwa (according to Raffelsiefen). In Muthmann (1988), type a. is very frequent (e.g. through approximately 2600 infinitives ending in *-ieren*), whereas type b. is represented by the two examples given only. These can be argued to be exceptional (cf. Neef 1996a: 243ff.). But on the surface, again, there is no schwa in both of these infinitives which are pronounced as [vi:.ɐn] and [næ:.ɐn] respectively in explicit articulation. Consequently, they are neither true counter-examples to Raffelsiefen's claim nor to the *Design Condition of a Potential Syllable Rhyme*.

This condition has consequences for conversion into verbs. In German, there exists a number of nouns ending in schwa with a segmental cluster preceding this schwa that can not be realised in one syllable rhyme. Consequently, these nouns can not be converted into an infinitive. Muthmann (1988) contains about 200 of those (simple) nouns from which I will list some common ones:

(12) a.   Witwe 'widow'   ['vɪt.və]   →   #witwen[8]
          Zwetschge 'plum'   ['tsvɛtʃ.gə]   →   #zwetschgen
     b.   Akne 'acne'   ['ʔak.nə]   →   #aknen
          Hymne 'hymn'   ['hʏm.nə]   →   #hymnen
          Kolumne 'column'   [ko.'lʊm.nə]   →   #kolumnen
     c.   Medaille 'medal'   [me.'dal.jə]   →   #medaillen
          Kampagne 'campaign'   [kam.'pan.jə]   →   #kampagnen
          Taille 'waist'   ['tal.jə]   →   #taillen
     d.   Familie 'family'   [fɑ.'mi:l.jə]   →   #familien
          Orgie 'orgy'   ['ʔɔʁ.gjə]   →   #orgien
          Studie 'study'   ['ʃtu:.djə]   →   #studien

The nouns in (12a) have two or three obstruents in front of the schwa and the final consonant in these clusters is not less sonorous than the preceding one. Furthermore, these final obstruents are not legitimate in an extrasyllabic position (only coronal obstruents are allowed here). If the segmental combinations obey the sonority constraint including possibilities of extrasyllabicity, even clusters of four consonants are possible as in *verarzten* 'to fix up' with the relevant cluster being /rtst/. In (12b), the schwa is preceded by a nasal which itself is preceded by a consonant that is not of higher sonority than the nasal. The segmental clusters in (12c) end in the glide [j] which is restricted in its appearance in the syllable rhyme to a position immediatly following the vowel [a] or [ɔ], thus to being part of the diphthong [aj] or [ɔj]. Therefore, the given clusters may not form a possible syllable rhyme. Furthermore, the glide is of higher sonority than nasals (cf. Neef 1998a: 83). The examples in (12d) are principally identical to the ones in (12c). The only difference is that the orthography suggests a pronunciation with a full vowel instead of a glide. In fact, a word like *Studie* may be pronounced three-syllabic as ['ʃtu:.di.ə]. There are reasons to assume that this is an orthography-driven pronunciation (cf. note 11 below and Neef 1998a: ch. 7). The pronunciations given in (12) are taken to be characteristic for explicit (as well as for standard) articulation which enables to explain why these nouns can not be converted into an infinitive.

The conversion of any of these nouns into an infinitive would lead to a violation of the *Design Condition of a Potential Syllable Rhyme*. Indeed, none of these nouns exists as a converted verb. Some of them, however, can be turned into an infinitive employing a different strategy, namely to participate in the lexeme formation pattern ending in *-ier*. For *Taille* e.g. there exists the infinitive *taillieren* [ta.'ji:.ʀən] meaning 'to fit'. Note also that *to hymn*, *to study* and *to campaign* are perfect verbs in English.

However, there is one homogeneous class including the above-mentioned verb *atmen* that offends the *Design Condition of a Potential Syllable Rhyme*.[9] Muthmann (1988) lists 18 infinitives of this kind which are used in standard language plus six ones which are dialectal or obsolete; here are some of them:[10]

(13) a.	atmen	[ʔɑ:t.mən]	'to breathe'
b.	rechnen	[ʀɛç.nən]	'to calculate'
	regnen	[ʀe:k.nən]	'to rain'
c.	vervollkommnen	[fɐ.'fɔl.kɔm.nən]	'to perfect'

Raffelsiefen (1995: 147) shows that most of the infinitives of the type in (13) go back at least to MHG where they ended in two reduced syllables, thus obeying the *Design Condition of a Potential Syllable Rhyme* but violating the *Design Condition of a Unique Reduced Syllable* which obviously did not hold at that stage. Raffelsiefen found more than thirty infinitives ending in two reduced syllables that existed in MHG but vanished in MSG like †*wolkenen*ᵥ 'to be full of clouds' < *wolken*ɴ 'cloud'.

According to Raffelsiefen (1995: 151), the infinitives in (13) form a closed class;

new infinitives can no longer be formed in this way. If an infinitive is converted from a noun ending in a reduced syllable with a final nasal, the result is ungrammatical if there is a consonantal cluster not pronounceable in one syllable rhyme in front of the schwa:

(14)   Garten 'garden'   →   #gartnen
        Hafen 'harbour'   →   #hafnen
        Knochen 'bone'   →   #knochnen
        Riemen 'strap'   →   #riemnen
        Rücken 'back'   →   #rücknen

It is worth mentioning that nouns which are formally similar to the ones in (14) are not excluded from conversion into infinitives in principle. On the contrary, there are at least 26 relevant word pairs existing in MSG as listed in Raffelsiefen (1995: 145). Here are some of the relevant examples; the direction of dependency could be argued for by diachronic priority:

(15)   Flicken 'patch'   →   flicken 'to patch'
        Fohlen 'foal'   →   fohlen 'to foal'
        Rahmen 'frame'   →   rahmen 'to frame'
        Schaden 'damage'   →   schaden 'to damage'
        Schnupfen 'cold'   →   schnupfen 'to take snuff'
        Zapfen 'plug'   →   zapfen 'to tap (beer)'

Raffelsiefen argues that this again is a closed class. Her evidence is that for 22 of these 26 pairs the infinitive was formed by conversion at a historical stage when the corresponding noun did not yet end in a nasal in the nominative singular but in schwa (e.g. *graben* 'to dig' derived from MHG *Grabe* 'ditch', not from MSG *Graben* 'ditch'). Therefore, historically the relevant lexeme formation process did not concern homophonous word pairs.

However, synchronically the relation holds between homophonous words. Furthermore, I find it possible to use a noun like *Besen* 'broom' as an infinitive meaning 'to sweep with a broom' although this infinitive is not listed in German dictionaries. Moreover, there are prefixed verbs to nominal bases ending in a nasal final reduced syllable with the related simple verb being non-existent, indicating that the pattern in (15) does not form a closed class in strict terms:

(16)   Rücken 'back'   →   berücken 'to provide sth. with a back'
        Norden 'north'   →   einnorden 'to orientate'
        Bogen 'bow, arch'   →   ausbogen 'to cut archedly'
        Riemen 'strap'   →   anriemen 'to tie up with a strap'

From these observations I conclude that there are no formal reasons that prevent the use of the nouns in question as infinitives. The preference for non-nominal stems to be verbalised with a prefix or particle pattern is probably more semantic or pragmatic in nature: the possible readings of these patterns are more restricted than the readings of converted verbs (cf. Stiebels 1996: 193; Eschenlohr 1997b: 73f.). The ornative interpretation of a verb like *berücken* is clearer expressed through a verb using the prefix pattern *be-* than through a converted verb. On the other hand, there are some semantic patterns that can be expressed only through converted verbs like agentive or performative readings (cf. *gärtnern* 'to garden' or *frühstücken* 'to have breakfast' respectively). Eschenlohr (1997b: 75) concludes that conversion is productive only with respect to specific semantic patterns. According to her 'prefix/particle-preference-principle', the prefix or particle pattern is preferred to conversion if these two modes concur to express a specific semantic type.

If a noun like *Fohlen* is to be converted into an infinitive, though, it seems that the relation in question does not concern the level of stem. The verbal stem contained in the infinitive *fohlen* is /fol/ as can be seen in the past participle *gefohlt*. The nominal stem, however, seems to be /foln/ as it appears in the nominative singular form given. But there is evidence that even the nominal stem does not contain the final nasal in the group of nouns indicated in (15). If these nominal stems appear in instances of lexeme formation patterns, the nasal is missing:

(17)   Garten 'garden'   Gärtchen 'small garden'   #Gärtenchen
        Schaden 'damage'   schadhaft 'defective'   #schadenhaft
        Striemen 'weal'   striemig 'marked with weals'   #striemenig

Thus, the nominal stem is abstracted from the nominative singular form of these nouns under the exclusion of the final *-en* (cf. also Harnisch 1994: 97f. and Eschenlohr 1997b: Ch. 4.4). In this respect, this ending behaves similar to the ending schwa (cf. *Käse* 'cheese' (*käsig* 'pale'), but different to the endings *-el* and *-er* (cf. *Segel* 'sail' (*segeln* 'to sail' and *Zigeuner* 'gypsy' (*zigeunern* 'to rove' with both #*segen* and #*zigeunen* being ungrammatical). Therefore, it seems adequate to charac-terise conversion as the use of a particular stem as a stem of a different word class without formal modification.

4.4 The Syllable Peak Adjacency Constraint

Besides the morphological well-formedness conditions in (6), (7), and (9) that are in principle specific for the morphological category of infinitive, there is at least one general (phonological) condition that constrains conversion into infinitives. This is due to the obligatory reduced syllable ending of infinitives. The distribution of reduced syllables in German is not free as opposed to the distribution of full syllables. Besides the fact that a phonological word may not consist of reduced syllables only, there is a syllable contact constraint concerning the distribution of onsetless reduced syllables. Whereas two full vowels may appear inside a phonologi-cal word without other segments intervening, a reduced syllable must not follow an unstressed full vowel with no consonant intervening the two syllable peaks. This regularity is captured by the following constraint:

(18)   *Syllable Peak Adjacency Constraint* (SPAC)
         The syllable peak of a reduced syllable must not be right-adjacent
         to the syllable peak of an unstressed syllable.
         Domain: Phonological word.

An unstressed syllable is either a reduced syllable or a full syllable not bearing main stress. A reduced syllable may follow immediately the syllable peak of another syllable only if this syllable bears main stress like in *Ehe* [ˈʔeː.ə] 'marriage' or *Böen* [ˈbøː.ən] 'gusts'. The SPAC is a phonological constraint because it holds for phonological categories and not, as design conditions do, for morphological categories. Thus, it is relevant for the whole vocabulary of German.[11]

The SPAC is important for conversion into verbs since it predicts that no non-verbal stem ending in an unstressed full vowel may be used as an infinitive. This prediction follows from the reduced syllable condition on infinitives as given in (7). There is a large group of nouns prohibited from conversion into verbs due to the SPAC. All of the following nouns bear main stress on a non-final syllable:

(19) a.	Intermezzo 'intermezzo'	→	*interˈmezzoen	
	Kaffee 'coffee'	→	*ˈkaffeen	
	Kanapee 'sofa'	→	*ˈkanapeen	
	Kanu 'canoe'	→	*ˈkanuen	
	Paprika 'paprika'	→	*ˈpaprikaen	
	Taxi 'taxi'	→	*ˈtaxien	
	Turbo 'turbo'	→	*ˈturboen	
b.	Drama 'drama'	→	*ˈdramaen	dramatiˈsieren 'to dramatise'
	Gummi 'gum'	→	*ˈgummien	gumˈmieren 'to gum'
	Kommando 'command'	→	*komˈmandoen	kommanˈdieren 'to command'
	Propaganda 'propaganda'	→	*propaˈgandaen	propaˈgieren 'to propagate'
	Saldo 'balance'	→	*ˈsaldoen	salˈdieren 'to balance'

None of the nominal bases in (19) can be converted into infinitives straightforwardly which is explainable by the SPAC.[12] The nouns in b. can be used as a verb belonging to the lexeme formation pattern ending in -*ier*. This pattern does not contribute to the meaning of the verb, apart from indicating explicitly that the word is a verb. The infinitives ending in -*ieren* obey all the design conditions for infinitives, and they obey the SPAC in that the onset of the final reduced syllable is filled and in that the last full syllable bears main stress respectively.

5. THE STATUS OF THE INFINITIVE IN THE VERBAL PARADIGM

The preceding analysis offered arguments to explain why some non-verbal stems may not be used as verbs in a formally unmodified way based on the hypothesis that there is no general rule of conversion.[13] Within the declarative model of Word Design I have characterised the set of stems that may not undergo conversion by looking at the properties of the target category of conversion. In principle, every non-verbal stem may be used as a verb except those stems for which the converted verb has unwanted properties.[14] Conversion into verbs is exclusively constrained by well-formedness conditions for the morphological category of infinitive. The well-formedness of this morphological category has to be dealt with anyway, independent of the phenomenon of conversion. In this sense, conversion is not a phenomenon that requires specific theoretical devices, but it is explainable through elements that are already part of the theory of Word Design.

This summary shows an intricate relation between the notions verb and infinitive. Conversion as a mode to form new lexemes concerns the level of (abstract) stems: a non-verbal stem is used as a verbal stem without formal modification. A verbal stem, however, is only well-formed in German if it fits in the shape of the grammatical word of infinitive. This means that every verb must possess an infinitive. Thus, the infinitive has priority in the verbal paradigm. This comes as no surprise since the infinitive is the citation form of verbs. If a language user is asked to name a verb, s/he always takes the form of the infinitive. The German language has chosen the infinitive as the citation form of the verbal paradigm for several reasons:

— The infinitive is a surface form. Surface forms guarantee to be pronounceable whereas stems as abstract forms do not necessarily meet this requirement.

— The verbal stem is contained in the infinitive in an unambiguous way. On the one hand, it is always the regular stem that is contained in the infinitive. This is for example not true for the otherwise central category of 3. ps. sg. pres. (cf. Neef 1996a: 159ff.) or the 1. ps. sg. pres. that happens to be the citation form of verbs in Latin. In these latter categories, irregular stem forms may be found that do not suffice to detect the regular verbal stem (e.g. the stem /mʏs/ 'to have to' appears as [mʊs] in the 1. ps. sg. pres., the stem /ze/ 'to see' appears as [ziːt] in the 3. ps. sg. pres.). On the other hand, effects of final devoicing are avoided in the infinitive: a stem-final obstruent appears in onset position in the infinitive where the contrast in voiceness is preserved (e.g. the stem /zɑg/ 'to say' appears as [zɑː.gən] in the infinitive, but as [zɑːkt] in the 3. ps. sg. pres.).

— Finally, the infinitive is subject to the strongest restrictions to its form of the whole verbal paradigm (besides the 1. and 3. ps. pl. pres. which are homophonous to the infinitive and besides the infrequent present participle which consists of the infinitive plus a final /d/, all with the exception of *sein* 'to be'). If a stem can be used as an infinitive for formal reasons, it can be used in all other forms of the verbal paradigm as well.

This latter point can be illustrated with the ungrammatical and non-existent verb *paprikaen* converted from the noun *Paprika* 'paprika'. This verb could have the meaning 'to spice with paprika' analogous to the existent verbs *salzen* 'to salt' and *pfeffern* 'to pepper' (and identical to the existent — though marginal — irregular suffixed verb *paprizieren*). The following list contains a selection of potential forms of the verbal paradigm:

(20)   infinitive: *'paprikaen
        1. ps. sg. pres.:   *'paprikae (also: paprika)
        2. ps. sg. pres.:   paprikast
        3. ps. sg. pres.:   paprikat
        1.+3. ps. pl. pres.:   *'paprikaen
        2. ps. pl. pres.:   paprikat
        past participle: gepaprikat

Three of these forms are phonologically ill-formed because they violate the SPAC. The other forms are perfectly well-formed with respect to general phonological and category-specific morphological conditions. Yet, these forms never show up in German.[15] This shows that a verb is well-formed only if it is well-formed as an infinitive. The infinitive is the level of the determination of grammaticality of German verbs. This is an argument against Aronoff's discussion of the term of citation form (1994: 40f.) who claims that the metalinguistic notion of citation form is not necessarily significant in a theory of language where the notion of stem is central. In German, both the infinitive and the verbal stem are of grammatical significance. Therefore, a non-verbal stem may be used as a verbal stem only if it guarantees a grammatical form of the infinitive.

6. CONCLUSION

Conversion is a type of lexeme formation: a new lexeme is formed on the basis of an existing one. In this sense, a conversion relation is a directional one. A lexeme consists of three aspects: form, syntax, and meaning. In conversion, the formal part of one lexeme, viz. a stem, is used as a stem of a different word class without formal modification. Every time the stem is modified in some respect in a relation between two words of a different word class, the phenomenon is distinguished from conversion. Such modifications may be the addition, the deletion, or the metathesis of segments, or a change in prosodic structure including mere shift of stress. Whereas productive conversion may or may not form a lexeme formation pattern, morphological phenomena exhibiting a change in form are forced to constitute a lexeme formation pattern anchored in the morphological component of linguistic knowledge. This is due to the *Main Principle of Morphology*. If base and dependent grammatical word differ in some respect, this has to be stated in the list of design conditions relevant for a morphological category. Only morphological categories are connected with design conditions.

In order to serve as a lexeme formation *pattern*, some constant meaning element is necessary. Conversion into verbs in German is not a lexeme formation pattern in this sense. Converted verbs exhibit a large range of different semantic types. Thus, the meaning of a converted verb is not predictable from the form. Moreover, the meaning is not fully predictable from the meaning of the base. The meaning of the two homophonous items is only related via prototypical or contextually salient meaning aspects. In this sense, conversion is similar to nominal compounding where the meaning is also only restricted by some general semantic and pragmatic conditions (cf. e.g. Meyer 1993).

Conversion is different from another phenomenon, namely transposition on the level of the grammatical word. The following list gives some relevant examples from German (more data are given in Gallmann 1990: 51ff.):

(21) a. infinitive → noun   sagen 'to say'   Sagen 'saying'
     b. past participle → adjective verzweigt 'branched'   verzweigt
                                                               'branched'
     c. inflected adjective → noun   schöne 'beautiful$_{nom.sg.}$'   Schöne
                                                               'beauty$_{nom.sg.}$'

According to Eschenlohr (1997b: 42) these phenomena differ from (stem-) conversion by the following properties:

(22) a. they are absolutely productive
     b. they have a predictable semantic interpretation
     c. they show a low tendency towards lexicalisation
     d. their inflectional and governmental properties are caused by their basic category
     e. they are only limitedly available for further morphological processes like derivation or compounding.

In the literature it is disputed whether these phenomena belong to inflection or to word formation. Following Gallmann (1990: 61) and Aronoff (1994: 13), I prefer to use the term lexeme formation instead of word formation because derivation serves to form new lexemes as abstract lexical entries and not words in the sense of surface entities appearing in actual speech. Under this perspective, transposition is not a kind of lexeme formation because no new lexical units with unpredictable properties are formed. The properties in (22) make transposition similar to inflection. The only reason why these phenomena do not fit neatly into inflection is that they display a change of the word class. Usually, inflection is defined as not being capable of changing the word class. According to Haspelmath (1996: 50), this view seems to be the dominating one only in the second half of the twentieth century. Nowadays, only a minority of linguists believe that word-class-changing inflection exists (cf. e.g. Bybee 1985: 85; Gallmann 1990: 51; Haspelmath 1996). Gallmann (1990: 58) gives a paradigm of the verbal lexeme *lesen* containing eight verbal, six nominal and five adjectival forms. Thus, transposition may be regarded as inflection and hence different from conversion which belongs to lexeme formation.[16]

To sum up: Conversion into verbs in German is equivalent to conversion into infinitives. Conversion into verbs is possible for every non-verbal stem that can appear fully preserved as a verbal stem in a well-formed infinitive. Since the infinitive is subject to a number of morphological and phonological well-formedness conditions, the range of possible bases is restricted. If the target category of conversion is not subject to any formal conditions (which is e.g. true for nouns in German), conversion may be a fully unconstrained phenomenon, at least formally.

The results of my analysis of conversion into verbs are highly language-specific. Despite the definition of the basic notions and the *Main Principle of Morphology*, all other conditions stated are language-specific (and, moreover, in the main specific for the morphological category of infinitive). Things are likely to be different in other languages. Conversion into verbs is not necessarily identical to conversion into infinitives. In other languages, a different form of the verbal paradigm may be central for the determination of grammaticality. Furthermore, the well-formedness conditions for infinitives differ from language to language. In English for example, there are no well-formedness conditions specific for the infinitive which means that there is no morphological difference between the verbal stem and the verbal infinitive. Hence, there are no morphological or phonological conditions that could block conversion into verbs. This may explain the greater productivity of conversion in English as compared to German (which, however, is also dependent on semantic regularities). Under this perspective, there is nothing to say about conversion into verbs in a language like English.[17]

NOTES

[1]   Eschenlohr (1997b: 69) regards only N $\rightarrow$ V-conversion as productive in MSG.

[2]   For a detailed discussion of the data regarded as instances of conversion in the literature, cf. Naumann (1985), Don (1993: 1ff.), and Vogel (1996: Ch. 2).

[3]   For a sceptical evaluation of Lieber's model, cf. Neef (1994).

[4]   Analyses of lexeme formation patterns within the Word Design model are given in Neef (1996a: 254ff. and 1996b).

[5]   A fourth variant has to be distinguished which the Duden (1995[5]: 48) calls 'over-articulation'. This variant mainly follows the orthography. The verb *malen* here appears as [mɑ:.len]. Overarticulation, however, is not subject of phonology as a level of grammar because in this variant, certain grammatical regularities may be ceased to be in force (cf. section 4.4 below).

[6]   The pronunciation #[di:.ə n] is not a possible option for the stem in question because according to the *Main Principle of Morphology*, the schwa (as a difference to the base) must follow the stem except if there is a design condition demanding for something else. Altogether, I will formulate three design conditions holding for the infinitive. None of

these justifies the above constellation.

7   A complete list of these nouns and extended versions of some of the following lists can be found in Neef (1997b).

8   The attested past participle *verwitwet* 'widowed' is only used as an adjective; to my knowledge, the related infinitive #*verwitwen* does not exist.

9   There exists one more infinitive in German contradicting the design condition in question, namely *röntgen* 'to x-ray' in the pronunciation [ʀœnt.gən]. I regard this verb which is based on a proper name as an isolated exception. Interestingly, this infinitive can also be pronounced as [ʀœn.çən] in accord with the *Design Condition of a Potential Syllable Rhyme*.

10   For a complete list, cf. Neef (1997a: 24).

11   There are two areas of German grammar where the SPAC may be violated. The first are nouns of origin based on names of towns like *Jenaer* ['je:.nɑ.ɐ], the second are words containing the grapheme <i> like in *Studie* 'study'. In explicit articulation, this grapheme is pronounced as a glide like in ['stu:.djə] , but in orthography-driven overarticulation it may well be pronounced as a full vowel like in ['stu:.di.ə]. This grammatical word, however, violates the SPAC. For a detailed discussion of these problems, cf. Neef (1998a: ch. 6 and 7 and 1998b).

12   In Duden (1996²¹), there is only one infinitive that contravenes the SPAC, namely *echoen* 'to echo'. This verb, however, is most likely to occur in actual speech in the impersonal form *es echot* 'it echoes', a form that does not violate the SPAC.

13   There are some other conditions from different linguistic levels that constrain the range of conversion into verbs. For example, foreign non-verbal stems can not be used as infinitives straightforwardly, although there exists a considerable number of instances. Furthermore, morphologically complex bases by and large seem to be restricted from conversion into verbs. For some arguments accounting for these observations cf. Eschenlohr (1997a, b) and Neef (1997b).

14   The results of my analysis also hold for prefixed verbs like *bedachen* 'to roof' based on the noun *Dach* 'roof' because the recognised sources of ungrammaticality of a converted infinitive concern the right edge of the grammatical word only. It is more or less irrelevant in this respect whether a verb contains a prefix or not.

15   Admittedly, these forms never show up in German dictionaries due to the practice to list every verb in the form of the infinitive, irrespective of the form the verb has been documented in the source. In actual speech, I have the impression that verb forms to impossible infinitives hardly ever occur. An exception may be the above-mentioned *(es) echot* 'it echoes'.

16   A further related topic is polysemy. An example is the English noun *mouth*, referring either to a part of the human body or to a geographical unit (cf. Spencer 1991: 87). It is unclear whether these two readings belong to one lexeme or to two different ones.

17   This work has benefitted from discussions in the project 'Prosodische Morphologie' as part of the SFB 282 'Theorie des Lexikons', from comments by audiences in Düsseldorf (Annual Meeting of the DGfS, February 1997) and Cologne, by Irene Bartscherer, Stefanie Eschenlohr, Martin Haspelmath, Rosemary Jones, and anonymous reviewers. I am grateful to all of them.

REFERENCES

Anderson, Stephen R. 1992. *A-Morphous Morphology*. Cambridge: Cambridge University Press. (Cambridge Studies in Linguistics 62)

Aronoff, Mark. 1994. *Morphology by Itself. Stems and Inflectional Classes*. Cambridge, Mass., London: MIT. (Linguistic Inquiry Monograph 22)

Becker, Thomas. 1990. *Analogie und morphologische Theorie*. München: Fink. (Studien zur theoretischen Linguistik 11)

Becker, Thomas. 1998. *Das Vokalsystem der deutschen Standardsprache*. Frankfurt: Lang. (Arbeiten zur Sprachanalyse 32)

Bergenholtz, Henning and Joachim Mugdan. 1979a. *Einführung in die Morphologie*. Stuttgart: Kohlhammer. (Urban Taschenbücher 296)

Bergenholtz, Henning and Joachim Mugdan. 1979b. "Ist Liebe primär? Über Ableitung und Wortarten". In Peter Braun (ed.), *Deutsche Gegenwartssprache*. München: Fink, 339-354.

Bybee, Joan. 1985. *Morphology: A Study of the Relation between Meaning and Form*. Amsterdam: Benjamins.

Clark, Eve and Herbert Clark. 1979. "When Nouns Surface as Verbs". *Language* 55, 767-811.

Dokulil, Miloš. 1968. "Zur Frage der Konversion und verwandter Wortbildungsvorgänge und -beziehungen". *Travaux Linguistique de Prague* 3, 215-239.

Don, Jan. 1993. *Morphological Conversion*. Utrecht: LEd. (OTS Dissertation Series)

Duden. 1995⁵. *Grammatik der deutschen Gegenwartssprache*. Mannheim, Leipzig, Wien, Zürich: Dudenverlag. (Duden 4)

Duden. 1996²¹. *Rechtschreibung der deutschen Sprache*. Mannheim, Leipzig, Wien, Zürich: Dudenverlag. (Duden 1)

Eschenlohr, Stefanie. 1997a. "Zur kategorialen Determiniertheit von Wortformen im Deutschen". In Elisabeth Löbel and Gisa Rauh (eds), *Lexikalische Kategorien und Merkmale*. Tübingen: Niemeyer, 27-43. (Linguistische Arbeiten 366)

Eschenlohr, Stefanie. 1997b. *Vom Nomen zum Verb: Konversion, Präfigierung und Rückbildung im Deutschen*. Ph.D. dissertation, FU Berlin.

Féry, Caroline. 1997. "Unis und Studis: die besten Wörter des Deutschen". *Linguistische Berichte* 172, 461-489.

Fleischer, Wolfgang and Irmhild Barz. 1992. *Wortbildung der deutschen Gegenwartssprache*. Tübingen: Niemeyer.

Gallmann, Peter. 1990. *Kategoriell komplexe Wortformen*. Tübingen: Niemeyer. (Reihe Germanistische Linguistik 108)

Haider, Hubert. 1993. *Deutsche Syntax - generativ*. Tübingen: Narr. (Tübinger Beiträge zur Linguistik 325)

Haspelmath, Martin. 1996. "Word-class-changing Inflection and Morphological Theory". In Geert Booij and Jaap van Marle (eds), *Yearbook of Morphology 1995*. Dordrecht: Kluwer, 43-66.

Harnisch, Rüdiger. 1994. "Stammerweiterung im Singular — Stammflexion im Plural. Zum Bautyp der deutschen Substantivdeklination". In Klaus-Michael Köpcke (ed.), *Funktionale Untersuchungen zur deutschen Nominal- und Verbalmorphologie*. Tübingen: Niemeyer, 97-114. (Linguistische Arbeiten 319)

Kiparsky, Paul. 1983. "Word Formation and the Lexicon". In Francis Ingemann (ed.),

Proceedings of the 1982 Mid-America Linguistics Conference. Lawrence: University of Kansas, 3-29.

Lieber, Rochelle. 1981. *On the Organization of the Lexicon.* Ph.D. dissertation, MIT.

Lieber, Rochelle. 1992. *Deconstructing Morphology. Word Formation in Syntactic Theory.* Chicago, London: University of Chicago Press.

Marchand, Hans. 1964. "A Set of Criteria for the Establishing of Derivational Relationship between Words Unmarked by Derivational Morphemes". *Indogermanische Forschungen* 69, 10-19.

Marchand, Hans. 1969. *The Categories and Types of Present-Day English Word Formation. A Synchronic-Diachronic Approach.* München: Beck.

Meyer, Ralf. 1993. *Compound Comprehension in Isolation and in Context.* Tübingen: Niemeyer. (Linguistische Arbeiten 299)

Muthmann, Gustav. 1988. *Rückläufiges deutsches Wörterbuch.* Tübingen: Niemeyer. (Reihe Germanistische Linguistik 78)

Naumann, Bernd. 1985. "Konversion". *Zeitschrift für das deutsche Altertum* 114, 277-288.

Neef, Martin. 1994. Review of: Rochelle Lieber *Deconstructing Morphology. Word Formation in Syntactic Theory. Studies in Language* 18, 219-229.

Neef, Martin. 1996a. *Wortdesign. Eine deklarative Analyse der deutschen Verbflexion.* Tübingen: Stauffenburg. (Studien zur deutschen Grammatik 52)

Neef, Martin. 1996b. "Wortdesign: Das Wortbildungsmuster *Gehopse* und die Kopflosigkeit von 'Ableitungen'". *Zeitschrift für Sprachwissenschaft* 15, 61-91.

Neef, Martin. 1997a. "Die Alternationsbedingung: Eine deklarative Neubetrachtung". In Christa Dürscheid, Monika Schwarz and Karl Heinz Ramers (eds.), *Sprache im Fokus. Festschrift für Heinz Vater zum 65. Geburtstag.* Tübingen: Niemeyer, 17-31.

Neef, Martin. 1997b. *Conversion into Verbs: a Declarative Analysis of the German Infinitive.* Düsseldorf: Universität. (Theorie des Lexikons 95)

Neef, Martin. 1998a. *Elemente einer deklarativen Wortgrammatik.* Hürth: Gabel. (*KLAGE* 32)

Neef, Martin. 1998b. "The Reduced Syllable Plural in German". In Ray Fabri, Albert Ortmann and Teresa Parodi (eds), *Models of Inflection.* Tübingen: Niemeyer , 244-265. (Linguistische Arbeiten 388)

Olsen, Susan. 1986. *Wortbildung im Deutschen. Eine Einführung in die Theorie der Wortstruktur.* Stuttgart: Kröner. (Kröners Studienbibliothek Linguistik 660)

Olsen, Susan. 1990. "Konversion als kombinatorischer Wortbildungsprozeß". *Linguistische Berichte* 127, 185-216.

Pollard, Carl and Ivan A. Sag. 1987. *Information-Based Syntax and Semantics. Vol. 1: Fundamentals.* Stanford: Center for the Study of Language and Information. (CSLI Lecture Notes 13)

Prince, Alan and Paul Smolensky. 1993. *Optimality Theory. Constraint Interaction in Generative Grammar.* Ms., Rutgers University. (Rutgers University Center for Cognitive Science Technical Report #2)

Raffelsiefen, Renate. 1993a. "Relating Words. A Model of Base Recognition. Part 1". *Linguistic Analysis* 23, 3-159.

Raffelsiefen, Renate. 1993b. *Wohlgeformtheitsbedingungen für deutsche Wörter.* Talk presented to the 'Linguistischer Arbeitskreis', University of Cologne, 3.11.1993.

Raffelsiefen, Renate. 1995. "Potential Verbs in German: the Emergence of a Productivity Gap". *FAS Working Papers in Linguistics* 2, 122-153.

Reis, Marga. 1985. "Against Höhle's Compositional Theory of Affixation". In Jindrich
    Toman (ed.), *Studies in German Grammar*. Dordrecht: Foris , 377-406. (Studies in
    Generative Grammar 21)
Rickheit, Mechthild. 1993. *Wortbildung. Grundlagen einer kognitiven Wortsemantik*.
    Opladen: Westdeutscher Verlag. (Psycholinguistische Untersuchungen)
Russell, Kevin. 1997. "Optimality Theory and Morphology". In Diana Archangeli and D.
    Terence Langendoen (eds), 1997. *Optimality Theory. An Overview*. Oxford:
    Blackwell, 102-133.
Scobbie, James M., John S. Coleman and Steven Bird. 1996. "Key Aspects of Declarative
    Phonology". In Jacques Durand and Bernard Laks (eds), *Current Trends in
    Phonology: Models and Methods. Volume II*. Salford: European Studies Research
    Institute , 685-709. (Proceedings of the Royaumont meeting 1995)
Spencer, Andrew. 1991. *Morphological Theory*. Oxford: Basil Blackwell.
Stiebels, Barbara. 1996. *Lexikalische Argumente und Adjunkte*. Berlin: Akademie Verlag.
    (studia grammatica 39)
Vater, Heinz. 1996². *Einführung in die Sprachwissenschaft*. München: Fink. (UTB 1799)
Vennemann, Theo. 1991. "Syllable Structure and Syllable Cut Prosodies in Modern Stan-
    dard German". In Pier Marco Bertinetto, Michael Kenstowicz and Michele
    Loporcaro (eds), *Certamen Phonologicum II. Papers from the 1990 Cortona
    Phonology Meeting*. Turin: Rosenberg and Sellier, 211-243.
Vogel, Petra Maria. 1996. *Wortarten und Wortartenwechsel. Zu Konversion und
    verwandten Erscheinungen im Deutschen und in anderen Sprachen*. Berlin, New York:
    de Gruyter. (Studia Linguistica Germanica 39)
Werner, Anja. 1996. *i-Bildungen im Deutschen*. Düsseldorf: Heinrich Heine Universität.
    (Theorie des Lexikons 87)
Wiese, Richard. 1996. *The Phonology of German*. Oxford: Clarendon. (The Phonology of
    the Languages of the World)

Universität zu Köln
Institut für deutsche Sprache und Literatur
50923 Köln
Germany

e-mail: neef@uni-koeln.de

Phonological constraints on English word formation[1]

RENATE RAFFELSIEFEN

1. INTRODUCTION

In English, vowel-initial suffixation differs from consonant-initial suffixation in that it exhibits phonological effects. These include both phonologically conditioned gaps and systematic variations of the phonological structure of stem or suffix (i.e. allomorphy). Arguably both types of effects are closely related in that they allow satisfaction of phonological constraints in morphological output forms. Reference to the output rather than the input of affixation is necessary because the relevant constraints would be violated only as a result of combining the specific phonological forms of stems and affixes. I will argue that reference to output forms alone is sufficient for a description of English morphophonology if a) output forms are represented phonemically rather than phonetically and b) there are constraints which require certain features of derived words to be identical to the corresponding features in their base (cf. Benua 1995; Burzio 1994; McCarthy and Prince 1995; Raffelsiefen 1992, 1996).

While no two vowel-initial suffixes in English exhibit exactly the same phonological effects we find that all such effects can be described in terms of a few independently motivated constraints. The differences between suffixes result from different constraint rankings. The acquisition of English morphophonology can thus be described as the association of a specific constraint ranking with each suffix.

The fact that consonant-initial suffixes exhibit no phonological effects correlates with the observation that they are not integrated into the pword (i.e. phonological word) of the stem where the pword is defined as the domain for syllabification. For English, it holds then that suffixes exhibit phonological effects only when they are integrated into the pword of the stem. The observation that the pword constitutes the domain for phonological constraints in word formation does not hold cross-linguistically but rather must be considered a language-specific property of English.

In contrast to most generative work on English morphology the description presented here is limited to native word-formation because native formations obey a range of restrictions which loan words do not. This does not imply that English speakers lack intuitions regarding the relatedness between loan words. However, there is evidence that such intuitions are best described within a model of analysis for which the constraints differ from those on the synthesis of new words.

The paper is structured as follows. In section 2 I motivate the limitation of the data to native word formation. Evidence for a fundamental distinction between vowel-initial and consonant-initial suffixation in English is presented in section 3. Section 4 contains a discussion of various phonological effects in English suffixation and their analysis in terms of ranked constraints. Data which may appear to contradictthe claim that consonant-initial suffixes show no phonological effects are examined in section 5. The prosodic structure of English suffixed words is described

Geert Booij and Jaap van Marle (eds), Yearbook of Morphology 1998, 225-287.
© 1999 *Kluwer Academic Publishers. Printed in the Netherlands.*

in section 6. In section 7 I discuss the issue of abstractness arguing that only the phonemic level is relevant for the description of phonological effects in word formation. The analysis presented here is contrasted with previous work in section 8. In section 9 I present some evidence for my claim that morphological analysis is subject to specific phonological restrictions which differ from the conditions on synthesis (i.e. native word formation). In section 10 I discuss the issue of input versus output constraints in morphology and summarize the main conclusions of this paper.

2. SELECTION OF THE DATA

The description of English word formation presented below is based on native suffixation and native speaker intuitions regarding the acceptability of nonce formations. Loanwords are generally omitted from consideration which is not to deny that they can be analysed and related to other words by hearers. The omission of loanwords is motivated by the observation that the conditions for the analysis of given words differ from the conditions for the synthesis of new words (cf. section 9). When considering native coinages one should keep in mind that the phonological conditions under which a word was formed may have been obscured by subsequent historical sound changes. Consider the plural forms in (1a), which were derived in English but have subsequently been affected by historical changes like umlaut, front vowel derounding, fricative devoicing, schwa loss, etc.

(1)a. mouse]$_{SG}$ - mice]$_{PL}$ b. spouse]$_{SG}$ - *spice]$_{PL}$

man]$_{SG}$ - men]$_{PL}$ plan]$_{SG}$ - *plen]$_{PL}$

thief]$_{SG}$ - thieves]$_{PL}$ chief]$_{SG}$ - *chieves]$_{PL}$

hou[s]e]$_{SG}$ - hou[z]es]$_{PL}$ ca[s]e]$_{SG}$ - ca[z]es]$_{PL}$

While the historical stability of the plural-singular relations in (1a) shows that they are consistently recognized by English learners the nonce plural formations in (1b) show that analogous coinages are unacceptable. This sort of observation motivates a separate description of the conditions for morphological analysis (i.e. recognition of relatedness between given words) and morphological synthesis (i.e. the formation of new words). Evidence that the recognition of relatedness between the words in (1a) is subject to independent phonological constraints is presented in section 9.

Strong support for the claim that the conditions for morphological synthesis and analysis should be described separately comes from words which have undergone historical reanalysis. Consider the noun *forgiveness*, which seems to contradict the claim that the suffix *-ness* attaches only to adjectives. Significantly, *forgiveness* was originally derived from the adjective *forgiven* and subsequently underwent degemination and schwa deletion (i.e. *forgivenness > forgiveness*). Due to these phonological changes learners began to relate the noun to the verb *forgive* as is manifested by its current deverbal interpretation (i.e. 'the act of forgiving') as opposed to its original deadjectival interpretation (i.e. 'the condition of being forgiven'). However, while *forgiveness* is analysable as a deverbal noun, there is no evidence that it could be coined as such. In fact, no *-ness* suffixation based on verbs is attested and nonce nouns such as **forgetness, *forbidness* are clearly unacceptable. This example shows that words which have undergone historical reanalysis may obscure the conditions for forming new words and should therefore be omitted from consideration.

Consider next the nouns *burial* and *trial*, which are often cited as counter-examples to the claim that the noun-forming suffix *-al* combines only with iambic verbs (cf. *survival, withdrawal, rehearsal*). Neither of these nouns was coined in English by suffixing *-al* to a verb: *burial* is a reanalysis of the Old English plural form *byrgels* (i.e. OE byrgels > ME biriel > NE burial) and *trial* is a reanalysed loan word (i.e. Norman French *triel*). Although there is evidence that English learners synchronically analyse these nouns as *-al* suffixation based on the verbs *bury* and *try*, respectively, trochaic or monosyllabic verbs have never served as a base for native *-al* suffixation. There is no reason to expect that the prosodic restriction on productive *-al* suffixation to iambic bases would block the adoption of loanwords ending in [əl] which happen to lack iambic cognates in English. The conditions for both the adoption and the analysis of loanwords differ from the conditions on native word formation and should therefore be described separately.

3. VOWEL-INITIAL VERSUS CONSONANT-INITIAL SUFFIXES IN ENGLISH

In descriptions of English morphophonology two types of affixes have been traditionally distinguished: those which 'fuse' phonologically with their stem versus those which are 'neutral' w.r.t. their stem (cf. Newman 1946). For the former type, illustrated in (2a), the stress 'shifts' in accordance with English stress patterns for nouns or adjectives (i.e. antepenultimate stress if the penultimate syllable is open, penultimate stress if that syllable is closed). 'Neutrality' is illustrated by the examples in (2b).

(2)a.	médicine+al	→ medícinal	b.	áccurate+ness	→ áccurateness
	sýnonym+ous	→ synónymous		devélop+ment	→ devélopment
	márginal+ity	→ marginálity		pílot+less	→ pílotless
	móllusc+ous	→ mollúscous		frólic+some	→ frólicsome
	frágment+al	→ fragméntal		sávage+dom	→ sávagedom
	cólumn+al	→ colúmnar		éffort+ful	→ éffortful

In generative descriptions the two types of affixes are generally distinguished in terms of boundaries or levels to ensure that stress rules apply after suffixation in (2a) but before suffixation in (2b) (cf. Chomsky and Halle 1968; Siegel 1974). On those approaches the morphophonological behavior of affixes depends on class membership, which is encoded by a diacritic feature. However, as noted by Booij (1985) that behavior appears to be partly determined by the affixal shape: consonant-initial suffixes are generally neutral, whereas most vowel-initial suffixes fuse with the stem. The distinct phonological effects of the suffixes in (2) could thus be described by assuming that the pword is the domain of the English stress rule and by stipulating that vowel-initial suffixes, but not consonant-initial suffixes, are integrated into the pword of their stem as shown in (3).

(3)a. (medícinal)$_\omega$ b. (áccurate)$_\omega$ness
       (synónymous)$_\omega$ (devélop)$_\omega$ment
       (rurálity)$_\omega$ (pílot)$_\omega$less
       (mollúscous)$_\omega$ (frólic)$_\omega$some
       (fragméntal)$_\omega$ (sávage)$_\omega$dom
       (colúmnar)$_\omega$ (éffort)$_\omega$ful

Assuming that pwords constitute the domain for syllabification one should expect that stem-final consonants appear in onset position in vowel-initial suffixation[2] and in coda position in consonant-initial suffixation. Consider the different realizations of the voiceless labial stops in the near-minimal pairs in (4a) in careful pronunciation. According to Kahn (1976), voiceless stops are aspirated in syllable-initial position (cf. [pʰ]*lacenta*, *sur*[pʰ]*lus*)[3] but unreleased in syllable-final position (cf. *ti*[p'], *har*[p']).[4] If this generalization is correct the derived words in (4a) have the syllable structures in (4b):[5]

(4)a. [tʰrípʰlɔɪd] 'triple+oid' - [tʰríp'làɪk] 'trip+like'
       [pʰɪmpʰləs] 'pimple+ous' - [rʌmp'ləs] 'rump+less'
       [tʰrípʰlət] 'triple+et'- [drɔp'lət] 'drop+let'
       [kʌpʰlɪŋ] 'couple+ing' - [sæp'lɪŋ] 'sap+ling'
    b. [tʰrí.pʰlɔɪd] - [tʰríp'.làɪk]
       [pʰɪm.pʰləs] - [rʌmp'.ləs]
       [tʰrí.pʰlət] 'triple+et'- [drɔp'.lət]
       [kʌ́.pʰlɪŋ] - [sæp'.lɪŋ]

The structures in (4b) indicate that words with vowel-initial suffixes consistently obey the LOI (i.e. Law of Initials) whereas words with consonant-initial suffixes do not.[6] The violations of the LOI result from the syllabification of stem-final consonants in coda position. They thereby indicate the pword structures in (5), which show integration of vowel-initial, but not consonant-initial, suffixes.[7]

(5)   (triploid)$_\omega$ - (trip)$_\omega$ like[8]
       (pimplous)$_\omega$ - (rump)$_\omega$ less
       (triplet)$_\omega$ - (drop)$_\omega$ let
       (coupling)$_\omega$ - (sap)$_\omega$ ling

The distinct prosodic structures in (5) are natural in that only the suffixes which inherently lack a syllable onset fuse into one pword with their stem. According to McCarthy and Prince (1993) this type of condition is characteristic of prosodic morphology, in that a phonological constraint, the requirement that syllables must have onsets, dominates morphological alignment constraints (cf. section 6).

The stress shift in the words which include vowel-initial suffixes in (2) is explained under the assumptions that such suffixes are integrated into the pword of the stem and that the pword is the domain for the English stress rule. Within constraint-based frameworks this phonological effect can be partially expressed by a constraint which requires the right edge of a maximally dactylic foot to align with the right edge of the pword (for discussion and alternative approaches cf. McCarthy and Prince 1993; Pater 1995).

(6) a. F   F   b. F   F

    s w w   s w w   s w w   s w w

    (médicine)$_\omega$ (medícinal)$_\omega$ (áccurate)$_\omega$ (áccurate)$_\omega$ ness

Without stress shift the attachment of a stressless suffix like *-al* to words which end in two stressless syllables (e.g. *médicine*) would violate the constraint which restricts the size of wordfinal feet to dactyls. However, the examples in (7) show that this constraint is not obeyed in all words derived by vowel-initial suffixes:

(7)   vínegar+ish   →   vínegarish
       áccurate+acy   →   áccuracy
       ínjure+able   →   ínjurable

Not all, but only vowel-initial suffixes can induce stress shifts. The fact that the vowel-initial suffixes in (7) are consistently stress-neutral might indicate that some vowel-initial suffixes are not integrated into the pword of the stem. However, since all of these suffixes exhibit other phonological effects, their stress-neutrality is best described by ranking the constraint IDENT(S), which is stated in (8) (cf. Benua 1995; Burzio 1994; McCarthy and Prince 1995; Raffelsiefen 1992, 1996), higher than the phonological constraint which requires the right edge of the pword to align with maximally dactylic feet.[9] Identity constraints refer to certain aspects of phonological structure since there are affixes which require the identity of some, but not all, features.[10]

(8)   IDENT(S)
       A stressed syllable in a derived word must correspond to a
       stressed syllable in the base.

Unlike stress, syllabification is not affected by identity constraints in English. There are accordingly no suffixes which idiosyncratically require speech sounds occurring in a specific syllable position in the base to occur in the same position in the derived word.[11] Instead syllabification is determined entirely by its domain, the pword, and phonological constraints like the LOI.[12]

It is the aim of this paper to show that English morphophonology is most adequately described in terms of an interaction between phonological constraints, whose domain is the pword, and identity constraints which refer to the relation between a derived word and its base. Both allomorphy and gaps in word formation reflect the avoidance of constraint violations which would arise as a result of attaching an affix to a stem. The phonological effects which occur in affixation are shown in figure (9):

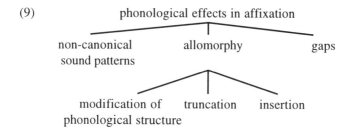

Non-canonical sound patterns refer to any segmental and suprasegmental sound structure within pwords which does not occur in underived words. Such patterns are subsumed under phonological effects in affixation because they result from the concatenation of the (unmodified) phonological structures of stems and affixes (cf. the stress patterns in (7)). The term 'allomorphy' and its hyponyms do not designate types of phonological changes but rather describe the relation between (the phonemic form of) affixed words and their base. Specifically, allomorphy indicates the low ranking of identity constraints w.r.t. phonological constraints. For example, the stress difference in the noun *ràdicálity* and its base *rádical* does not indicate that the stress has shifted in the noun (cf. *rádicality* > *ràdicálity*). Rather this difference shows that for the suffix *-ity* the constraint IDENT(S) is dominated by a constraint which requires pwords to end in a dactylic foot. In English, the most common type of allomorphy is truncation. Consonant-initial suffixes are not associated with any phonological effects.

4. CONSTRAINTS ON ENGLISH WORD FORMATION[13]

4.1 The constraint '*CLASH'

The undesirability of adjacent stressed syllables is expressed by the following constraint:[14]

(10)   *CLASH
         Two adjacent stressed syllables are prohibited. Domain: pword

The constraint in (10) is manifested by the instability of *CLASH violations. Historically, stress clashes within pwords in English tend to be eliminated by leftward stress shift (cf. (11a)), or, if that is not a possibility, by stress deletion (cf. (11b)). The shaftless arrow denotes historical sound change.

(11) a.   demónstràte > démonstràte   b.   móbìle > móbile
          recógnìze > récognìze   dándrùff > dándruff
          altérnàte > álternàte   ábdòmen > ábdomen

In word formation potential *CLASH violations arise whenever a stressed suffix attaches to a stem with final stress. As is shown by comparing the phonologically similar suffixes *-eer*, *-ese*, and *-ee* there are several ways to resolve the resulting conflict. For the suffix *-eer* stress clashes are generally avoided by restricting suffixation to words ending in an unstressed syllable (cf. the native coinages in (12a)). As a result, there exists a systematic gap for words with final stress as in (12b), including monosyllabic words as in (12c):

(12) a.   cámel+éer → càmeléer   b.   giráffe+éer → Ø
          pámphlet+éer → pàmphletéer   brochúre+éer → Ø
          múffin+éer → mùffinéer   baguétte+éer → Ø
          púppet+éer → pùppetéer   màrionétte+éer → Ø
          bállad+éer → bàlladéer   sèrenáde+éer → Ø
          prófit+éer → pròfitéer   c.   gáin+éer → Ø
          márket+éer → màrketéer   stóre+éer → Ø
          járgon+éer → jàrgonéer   cánt+éer → Ø
          pígeon+éer → pìgeonéer   dóve+éer → Ø
          wéapon+éer → wèaponéer   gún+éer → Ø
          rácket+éer → ràcketéer   fráud+éer → Ø

The claim that words with final stress do not undergo *-eer* suffixation does not preclude the existence of nouns ending in *-eer* which have cognates with final stress like those in (13a). Crucially, all of those nouns were borrowed into English as is shown in (13b) and are therefore not relevant for the description of native word formation:

(13) a.   brìgadíer - brigáde   b.   (French brigadier → E. brigadier)
          còmmandéer - commánd   (Afrikaans kommanderen → E.
                                        commandeer)
          cashíer - cash   (Dutch cassier, French caissier →
                                        E. cashier)
          frontíer - front   (Old French frontier → E. frountier)

*CLASH violations are also systematically avoided in *-ese* suffixation. However, instead of not attaching to words with final stress the suffix *-ese* avoids *CLASH violations by sacrificing stress identity as is shown in (14):

(14)   Taiwán+ése → Tàiwanése   Sudán+ése → Sùdanése
        Nepál+ése → Nèpalése   Vietnám+ése → Vìetnamése

The type of allomorphy illustrated in (14) is characteristic for the suffix *-ese₁*, which attaches to names. There is a distinct suffix *-ese₂*, which attaches to nouns and, like the suffix *-eer*, combines only with words ending in a stressless syllable. Some coinages are listed in (15):

(15)   jàrgonése, jòurnalése, compùterése, nòvelése, trànslàtionése

The suffix *-ese₂* thus avoids stress clash by not attaching to words with final stress. In contrast to the stressed suffixes mentioned so far the suffix *-ee* tolerates *CLASH violations freely. There is no tendency for this suffix to prefer bases which end in a stressless syllable, as is illustrated in (16b,c).

(16) a. cóunsel+ée → còunselée   b. seléct+ée → selèctée   c. bríbe+ée → brìbée
        abándon+ée → abàndonée   abúse+ée → abùsée   dráft+ée → dràftée
        óffer+ée → òfferée   invíte+ée → invìtée   páy+ée → pàyée
        solícit+ée → solìcitée   arrést+ée → arrèstée   híre+ée → hìrée

The observation that the suffixes *-eer*, *-ese₁*, and *-ee* differ systematically in how they respond to potential stress clashes indicates differences in constraint ranking. Consider first the suffix *-eer*, which never attaches to bases with final stress. In Raffelsiefen (1992) I argued that this type of gap reflects a dilemma: potential *-eer*-formations would be either phonologically ill-formed due to stress clash (i.e. *giràfféer*) or the stem (i.e. the derived form minus the affix) would differ from the base in the position of the main stress (i.e. *giràfféer* – *giráffe*). That is, for suffixes with initial stress like *-eer* attachment to a base with final stress will always violate either *CLASH or IDENT(S).

Consider now the question of how to ensure that no output is preferred to a candidate which violates either *CLASH or IDENT(S). The approach to gaps proposed by Prince and Smolensky (1993) is to include the input (i.e. a structure in which affixes are unattached) in the candidate set, to posit a constraint 'M-PARSE' which prohibits unattached affixes, and to rank that constraint below the constraints which cause the gap. The constraint M-PARSE is stated as follows in Prince and Smolensky (1993):

(17)   M-PARSE
        Morphemes are parsed into morphological constituents.

The gap illustrated in (12b,c) is described by the constraint-ranking in tableau (18). The input consists of the affix *-eer* and a word which satisfies its syntactic subcategorization requirements (i.e. nouns). The phonological representation of the base includes stress, which is crucial for proper evaluation w.r.t. the constraint IDENT(S). The constraint IDENT(S) ranks higher than *CLASH because the sub-optimal candidate *giràfféer*, which preserves the stress w.r.t. the base *giráffe*, is generally preferred to the candidate *gìrafféer*.

(18)

dʒəræf-íyr		IDENT(S)	*CLASH	M-PARSE
	(dʒɪrəfíyr)ω[15]	*!		
	(dʒəræ̀fíyr)ω		*!	
√	dʒəræf-íyr			*!

For words with final stress such as *giráffe*, the non-affixed candidate is optimal, because it is the only candidate which satisfies both IDENT(S) and *CLASH .[16] As a result there is a gap. For other words there is always a candidate which satisfies both IDENT(S) and *CLASH, which means that a noun can be coined:

(19)

kæmel-íyr		IDENT(S)	*CLASH	M-PARSE
	(kæ̀məlíyr)ω			
	kæmel-íyr			*!

Note that 'gap-causing' dilemmas cannot arise due to phonological constraints or identity constraints alone, but require that both types of constraints dominate M-PARSE. The phonological constraint causing such a gap would be violated as a result of affixation. The identity constraint requires identity in surface forms (cf. section 7).

For the suffix *-ese*₁, both M-PARSE and *CLASH dominate IDENT(S). This ranking accounts for the fact that for this suffix there are neither clash-related gaps nor *CLASH -violations as is shown in (20).[17]

(20)

taywán-íyz		M-PARSE	*CLASH	IDENT(S)
√	(tàywəníyz)$_\omega$			*
	(taywàníyz)$_\omega$		*!	
	taywán-íyz	*!		

The suffix *-ee* is similar to the suffix *-ese*$_1$ in that there are no clash-related gaps and it is similar to the suffix *-eer* in that it does not allow for stress-shift. It differs from both *-ese*$_1$ and *-eer* in that *CLASH -violations are allowed. These observations can be expressed by ranking both M-PARSE and IDENT(S) higher than *CLASH as is shown in (21):

(21)

əsáyn-íy		M-PARSE	IDENT(S)	*CLASH
√	(əsàyníy)$_\omega$			*
	(æ̀səníy)$_\omega$		*!	
	əsáyn-íy	*!		

The suffixes *-ee*, *-ese*$_1$, and *-eer* illustrate the three types of phonological effects in affixation presented in (9). The suffix *-ee* is the only English suffix which allows for *CLASH -violations thereby giving rise to non-canonical sound patterns. The suffix *-ese*$_1$ is the only suffix for which *CLASH ranks above IDENT(S) thereby giving rise to allomorphy. All other stressed suffixes follow the pattern of the suffix *-eer* in that they avoid *CLASH violations by not attaching to words with final stress with the result that there are gaps. The verb-forming suffix *-ize*, for example, generally resists attachment to nouns or adjectives with word-final stress as is shown by the gap in (22a):[18]

(22) a. corrúpt+íze → Ø
         obscéne+íze → Ø
         políte+íze → Ø
         ápt+íze → Ø
         cálm+íze → Ø
         bóld+íze → Ø

     b. rándom+íze → rándomìze
         fóreign+íze → fóreignìze
         rúral+íze → rúralìze
         ítem+íze → ítemìze
         líon+íze → líonìze
         mártyr+íze → mártyrìze

The claim that suffixing *-ize* to the adjective *apt* would be ungrammatical due to a stress clash (i.e. **áptìze*) is perfectly consistent with the existence of verbs like *báptìze*, *cápsìze*, or *fránchìse*, which are loan words. In fact, it is conceivable that *-ize* suffixation like *áptìze* should be considered ungrammatical even if verbs like *báptìze* were to represent the prevailing stress pattern in English.[19] This is because phonological restrictions in word-formation are affix-specific and are in principle independent of the restrictions which characterize the language as a whole. The theory does however forbid the existence of suffixes with initial stress which attach only to stems with final stress. This is because there is no universal constraint which eliminates precisely the candidates which do not have a stress clash (cf. section 10).

The claim that a description of the conditions on affixation should be confined to native coinages is also supported by the properties of *-ation* suffixation. The cognates in (23a) might give the impression that the suffix *-ation* attaches to iambic bases thereby contradicting the claim that *CLASH dominates IDENTS(S) only for the suffix *-ese₁*:

(23) a. èxplanátion - expláin b. remáin+átion → Ø
         pèrturbátion - pertúrb   distúrb+átion → Ø
         ìnspirátion - inspíre   desíre+átion → Ø
         prèservátion - presérve   desérve+átion → Ø
         èxpirátion - expíre   retíre+átion → Ø
         àdorátion - adóre   ignóre+átion → Ø
         òbscuration - obscúre   secúre+átion → Ø
         ìnvitátion - invíte   delíght+átion → Ø
         àdaptátion - adápt   adópt+átion → Ø
         cònsultátion - consúlt   insúlt+átion → Ø

However, the systematic gap illustrated in (23b) indicates that the suffix *-ation* may not attach to iambic verbs in English.[20] In fact, acording to the OED, all nouns in *-ation* which are etymologically related to iambic verbs in English are borrowings (e.g. Latin *explanation-em* > Engl. *explanation*, Latin *perturbation-em* > Old French *perturbacion* > Engl. *perturbation*, etc.).[21] In English, *-ation* suffixation is gener-ally confined to specific 'productivity niches', i.e. verbs ending in *-ate* or in the suffix *-ize*.[22] Sporadically, the suffix also applies to verbs which end in a stressless syllable. Some examples are given in (24):

(24)   bóther+átion → bòtherátion
         elícit+átion → elìcitátion
         báckward+átion → bàckwardátion
         páttern+átion → pàtternátion

The constraint ranking in (25), which has also been established for the stressed suffixes *-eer* and *-ize*, accounts for the unacceptability of the formations in (23b) while allowing for the examples in (24):[23]

(25)

rəméyn-éyšən	IDENT(S)	*CLASH	M-PARSE
(rèmənéyšən)$_\omega$	*!		
(rəmèynéyšən)$_\omega$		*!	
√ rəméyn-éyšən			*

    The fact that *-ation* attaches to stems ending in a stressless syllable far less productively than for example the suffix *-ize* might be because *-ize* subcategorizes for nouns and adjectives, which typically end in a stressless syllable, whereas *-ation* subcategorizes for verbs, which predominantly end in a stressed syllable. As a result the set of words which serve as a base for wellformed *-ize* suffixation is much larger, allowing that suffix to 'gain momentum', whereas the productivity of the suffix *-ation* is stifled.[24]

    It can be concluded then that for native formations in English IDENT(S) generally dominates *CLASH. This domination is so complete that the existence of scores of related loanwords like *expláin* and *èxplanátion*, which suggest the opposite ranking, fails to cause learners to rerank the constraints associated with the suffix *-ation*. Significantly, the only suffix for which *CLASH ranks higher than IDENT(S), i.e. the suffix *-ese*$_1$, attaches only to names. Additional evidence which indicates the exceptional status of name-based affixation will be discussed below.

    While most stressed vowel-initial suffixes are sensitive to stress clash, consonant-initial suffixes never are. Some examples are given in (26):

(26)	-líke	gódlìke, dréamlìke, péacòcklìke
	-wíse	édgewìse, clóckwìse, léngthwìse
	-fóld	twófòld, thréefòld, fóurfòld
	-hóod	chíldhòod, fálsehòod, adúlthòod
	-móst	léftmòst, tópmòst, óutmòst

The analysis of the insensitivity of consonant-initial suffixes to prosodic restrictions is discussed in section 6.

4.2. The constraint '$*L_iL_i$'

The undesirability of identical liquids within the pword is expressed by the following constraint:

(27) $*L_iL_i$
        The occurrence of identical liquids is prohibited. Domain: pword

In historical English phonology, $*L_iL_i$-violations are often eliminated, especially if they both occur in coda position (cf. Luick 1964: 1020ff, 1071). Satisfaction of $*L_iL_i$ is achieved either by deleting one of the liquids (cf. (28a) (cf. Kenyon and Knott 1953: xlvi[25]) or by substituting one liquid by another sonorant (cf. (28b,c)) ('Dial.' means 'dialectal form'):[26]

(28) a.   su/r/prise > su/Ø/prise (cf. su/r/vive)
           gove/r/nor > gove/Ø/nor (cf. gove/r/n)
           cate/r/pillar > cate/Ø/pillar (cf. cate/r/)
     b.   Dial. little> nittle
           Dial. syllable > sinable
     c.   marbre > marble (cf.German Marmor)
           purpre > purple (cf. German purpur)
           orer > laurel (cf. German Lorbeer)
           turtur > turtle
           Dial. murmur > murmel

The constraint $*L_iL_i$ is also obeyed in the phonotactics of English verbs as is illustrated in (29):[27]

(29)   grumble (*grumber, *glumble)
         splinter (*sprinter, *splintle)
         rattle (*ratter, *lattle)

In English word formation the constraint $*L_iL_i$ is generally satisfied by both the nominal and the adjectival suffix -*al*, albeit in different ways. The nominal suffix -*al* avoids $*L_iL_i$-violations by not attaching to verbs which include the liquid *l*. Examples for gaps are listed in (30). All examples satisfy the syntactic and prosodic restrictions on -*al* suffixation so that alternative explanations for their ungrammaticality can be ruled out.

(30) a. *XVl+al   *appéalal, *annúlal, *exhálal, *assáilal, *revéalal,
                   *instálal, *aváilal,*beguílal, *compélal, *compílal,
                   *concéalal, *condólal, *consólal, *contrólal, *curtáilal,
                   *deráilal, *entáilal, *distílal, *enrólal, *excélal, *fulfíllal,
                   *inhálal, *instíllal, *propélal, *preváilal, *rebélal,
                   *recállal, *repélal, *revéalal, *retáilal
     b. *XVlC$_1$+al   *insúltal, *invólval, *absólval, *assáultal, *consúltal,
                   *dissólval, *engúlfal, *evólval, *exáltal, *rebúildal,
                   *repúlsal, *resólval, *resúltal, *revóltal, *withhóldal

c. *XVlVC$_0$+al   *relíeval, *relíal, *relápsal, *relátal, *reláxal, *reláyal,
                   *reléasal, *reléntal, *deláyal, *delíghtal, *delúdal,
                   *collápsal, *colléctal, *collídal,   *belíeal,   *belíeval,
                   *belóngal

The gap illustrated in (30) can be explained only with reference to output forms.
Within a description in terms of prosodic subcategorization frames the correlation
between the *l* in the suffix, the avoidance of stems which include *l*, and the general
evidence in support of the constraint *L_iL_i illustrated in (28), (29) would appear to be
coincidental.

The four cases in which *-al* suffixation does violate the constraint *L_iL_i add
further support to the claim that the gap in (30) can be explained only with reference
to output forms. Significantly, these exceptions are systematic in that one of the
liquids does not by itself constitute a syllable node but rather forms part of a complex
onset.[28] The term 'syllable node' refers to the constituents onset, nucleus, rhyme, and
coda.

(31)   disclosal, supplial, declinal, implial

This suggests that *-al* suffixation obeys a restricted version of the constraint *L_iL_i,
which is stated in (32):

(32)   *L_iL_i'
        Identical syllable nodes consisting of liquids are prohibited.

The constraint *L_iL_i' differs from *L_iL_i in that it requires reference to syllabified
output forms. That is, the evaluation of candidates depends on the question of
whether or not liquids constitute part of complex syllable nodes in the output (e.g.
√*dis.clo.sal* versus *in.sul.tal*). The question of whether liquids are part of complex
syllable nodes in the input (e.g. *in.sult*, *in.volve*, etc.) is irrelevant for their evaluation.

To conclude, the gap in (30) is adequately described by ranking the constraint
*L_iL_i' and the constraint IDENT, which requires identity between a candidate and the
segmental and metrical structure of the base plus the affix, higher than M-PARSE as is
shown in (33). The ranking between the two dominating constraints is motivated by
the observation that violations of IDENT are even worse than are violations of *L_iL_i'.

(33)

əpíyl-əl	IDENT	$*L_iL_i'$	M-PARSE
əpíynəl	*!		
əpíyləl		*!	
√ əpíyl-əl			*

Consider next the adjectival suffix -al, which satisfies the constraint $*L_iL_i'$ not by causing gaps but by violating an identity constraint. Specifically, the liquid in the suffix must not be identical as is shown by the native coinages in (34) :

(34) a.   mole+al → molar ~ molal   b.   lobule+al → lobular
      corolla+al → corollar   nodule+al → nodular
      enamel+al → enamelar   spherule+al → spherular
      arteriole+al → arteriolar   sporule+al → sporular
      fibrilla+al → fibrillar   zonule+al → zonular
      protocol+al → protocolar   aedicule+al → aedicular

The rule of allomorphy illustrated in (34) has been adopted on the basis of Latinate loans whose stem includes an *l* such as *polar, lunar, familiar*, etc. versus loans whose stem includes no *l* like *rational, parental, general* and is mostly applied to scientific words. If both liquids are within the same syllable the rule is quite productive. However, as is usually the case with rules of allomorphy in English, true productivity is found only w.r.t. words with a specific ending, in particular nouns ending in *-ule* (cf. (34b)). In other cases, the rule applies only sporadically which gives rise to variations as is shown in (35):[29]

(35) a.   vulva+al → vulvar ~ vulval[30]   b.   column+al → columnar ~ columnal
      alga+al → algal   lamin+al → laminar ~ laminal
      lava+al → laval   dialect+al → dialectal

The data in (34), (35) indicate that an even more restricted version of the constraint $*L_iL_i'$ is needed to account for the differences between the nominal and the adjectival suffix -al. That is, for the adjectival suffix -al the domain of the constraint is the syllable, not the pword. For both suffixes the constraint against identical liquids is violated only if each liquid constitutes a syllable node. That is, the rule of allomorphy never applies in English if one of the liquids is part of a complex syllable node as shown in (36):[31]

(36)   clause+al → clausal (*clausar)
         climate+al → climatal (*climatar)
         cyclic+al → cyclical (*cyclicar)
         inflection+al → inflectional (*inflectionar)
         fluid+al → fluidal (*fluidar)
         glott+al → glottal (*glottar)

The data in (34) indicate that for the adjectival suffix -*al* the constraints IDENT(STEM), which requires the segments in the derived word to be identical to the corresponding segments in the base, $*L_iL_i'$, and M-PARSE dominate the constraint IDENT(AFFIX), which requires the output affix to be identical to the corresponding input. Since violations of the constraint IDENT(AFFIX) must be both minimal and structure-preserving (cf. section 7) the *l* is substituted by *r*, which differs only in the feature [±lateral].[32] For speakers who prefer coinages like *molal* to *molar* IDENT(AFFIX) dominates $*L_iL_i'$. For all speakers, the ranking of the identity constraints, $*L_iL_i'$, and M-PARSE differ for the nominal and the adjectival suffix -*al*. The need to associate these homophonous suffixes with different constraint rankings is further supported by the fact that the nominal suffix -*al* combines only with iambic words whereas the adjectival suffix has no such restrictions. Also the nominal suffix does not allow truncation of any stem material whereas the adjectival suffix requires truncation under certain conditions.

Not all vowel-initial suffixes show $*L_iL_i$-related effects. The agentive suffix -*er*, for example, is entirely insensitive to that constraint:

(37)   murderer, hearer, bearer, chatterer, lecturer, hirer, careerer

Consonant-initial suffixes like -*less*, -*let*, -*like* and -*ful* are never sensitive to $*L_iL_i$. Some examples for attested native formations are given in (38):

(38)   -less   goalless, wheelless, muscleless, titleless, lifeless, landless,
                  pollenless
         -let   altarlet, lakelet, lamplet, leaflet, leglet, scalelet, looplet
         -like   lifelike, fellowlike, lionlike, ladylike, snaillike
         -ful   lawful, loathful, doleful, frolicful, guileful

4.3. Additional dissimilatory constraints

In addition to the general constraint against syllable nodes consisting of identical liquids there are constraints against identical syllable nodes in specific syllable positions as is shown in (39) ('O' = onset , 'N' = nucleus, 'C' = coda, 'S' = segment). The domain of each constraint is the pword. Irrelevant structure is left unspecified.

(39) a.   SHELL[33]   b.   *ONS$_i$ONS$_i$ c.   *CODA$_i$CODA$_i$

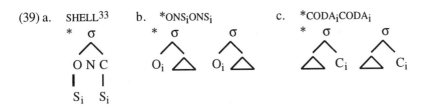

To obey the constraint SHELL, which prohibits syllables for which the nucleus is flanked by identical segments, the generally very productive suffix *-ish* never attaches to stems ending in the fricative š. Examples for gaps are given in (40b):

(40) a.   shéep+ish → shéepish   b.   físh+ish → Ø
          fármer+ish → fármerish   squísh+ish → Ø
          vínegar+ish → vínegarish   músh+ish → Ø
          cánnibal+ish → cánnibalish   rúbbish+ish → Ø

The occurrence of syllables like *shish, shash* in actual English words (cf. *hashish, shashlik*) does not affect the evaluation of potential *-ish* suffixation, which must satisfy the constraint SHELL (cf. the unacceptability of *fishish*). The gap in (40b) is described by the constraint ranking in (41). The constraint IDENT(C) requires all consonants in the derived word to correspond to identical consonants in the base. The ranking between IDENT(C) and SHELL accounts for preferences among the sub-optimal candidates in question.

(41)

fıš-ıš		IDENT(C)	SHELL	M-PARSE
	fıtıš	*!		
	fıšıš		*!	
√	fıš-ıš			*

The suffix *-ous* is similar to the suffix *-ish* in that IDENT(C) and SHELL dominate M-PARSE. Words like *biasous* are accordingly not potential *-ous* suffixation, in spite of the widespread occurrence of similar SHELL-violations in actual words (cf. *basis, census, emphasis*, etc.).[34]

(42) a.   flávor+ous → flávorous   b.   bías+ous → Ø
          tréason+ous → tréasonous   átlas+ous → Ø
          vítamin+ous → vitáminous   ménace+ous → Ø
          únison+ous → unísonous   láttice+ous → Ø

While exhibiting the same ranking among the constraints IDENT(C), SHELL, and M-PARSE, the suffixes *-ish* and *-ous* differ w.r.t. the ranking of other constraints. Native coinages such as *vínegarish* based on *vínegar* versus *carnívorous* based on *cárnivòre* show that the constraint which requires a dactylic foot to be aligned to the right edge of prosodic words dominates IDENT(S) for the suffix *-ous*, but not for the suffix *-ish*.

Additional suffixes for which IDENT(C) and SHELL dominate M-PARSE are shown in (43).[35] The examples in (43c) show that similar SHELL-violations occur among actual words.

(43) a. pístol+éer → pìstoléer   b. revólver+éer → Ø   c. (cf. career, rear)
         munítion+éer → munìtionéer   mórtar+éer → Ø

         kítchen+étte → kìtchenétte   clóset+étte → Ø   (cf. quartette,
         tówel+étte → tòwelétte   cárpet+étte → Ø   quintette)

         shórt+age → shórtage   lárge+age → Ø   (cf. judge)
         cléave+age → cléavage   wédge+age → Ø

The constraint against identical syllable onsets in adjacent syllables (cf. (39b)) is manifested in the haplology in words like *Englaland > England, eightetene > eighteen* (cf. Luick 1964: 1071). This constraint also plays a role in systematic gaps in English *-ity* suffixation. It is no coincidence that *-ity* never attaches to stems ending in *-t*. The unacceptability of the nouns in (44) is due neither to violations of subcategorizational requirements (i.e. all nouns are based on Latinate adjectives) nor to blocking by lexicalized nominalizations.

(44) a.   *acútity, *complétity, *òbsolétity, *remótity, *discréetity, *conténtity,
          *occúltity, *fáintity, *quáintity, *pàramóuntity, *exáctity, *abrúptity,
          *áptity, *inéptity, *corrúptity, *diréctity, *compáctity, *abstráctity,
          *intáctity, *corréctity, *stríctity, *dèrelíctity, *distínctity, *succínctity,
          *extínctity, *defúnctity, *disjúnctity
     b.   **covértity, **sèparátity, **affèctionátity, **quiétity, **pèrmanéntity,
          **perféctity, **consìderátity

The unacceptability of the nonce words in (44) is all the more remarkable in view of the fact that quite a few nouns end in *-tity* (cf. *entity, identity, quantity, sanctity*). The only case where *-ity* has been suffixed to a stem ending in *-t* in English is the noun *vastity*, where, crucially, suffixation does not result in adjacent identical onsets. The observation that the nouns in (44b) are particularly bad is presumably due to the fact that ONS$_i$ONS$_i$ violations are compounded by IDENT(S) violations (cf. section 7).

The fact that *-ity* never attaches to adjectives ending in *-did* as in (45a) is also expected since these are precisely the cases where *-ity* suffixation would cause adjacent identical onsets (cf. the native coinages in (45b)):

(45) a. candid+ity → Ø (*candidity) b. trepídity, squalídity, morbídity,
          splendid+ity → Ø (*splendidity)   rabídity, turgídity, pallídity,
          sordid+ity → Ø (*sordidity)   vapídity, torrídity, florídity, viví-
                                                dity, fervídity

The suffix -*ify* is like the suffix -*ity* in that ONS_iONS_i-violations are avoided by gaps. Some examples are listed in (46):

(46) a. *déafify, *tóughify, *stíffify, *béefify, *róughify
     b. **sheríffify, **plaintíffify, **dandrúffify

The suffix -*ify* is also like the suffix -*ity* in that formations become even less acceptable if they involve additional IDENT(S) violations (cf. (46b)). Such violations are allowed only for adjectives ending in -*id* (cf. *humídify, rigídify, fluídify*, etc.).[36]

The suffixes -*ee* and -*ize* differ from -*ity* and -*ify* in that ONS_iONS_i -violations are avoided not by gaps, but by 'truncation' of the word-final VC-string.[37] The examples in (47) show that truncation, which constitutes a violation of 'complete identity', applies only if necessary to prevent ONS_iONS_i-violations.[38]

(47) -ee   cohábitàte+ée → cohàbitée   délegàte+ée → dèlegàtée
            ámputàte+ée → àmputée   cónsecràte+ée → cònsecràtée
            rèhabílitàte+ée → rèhabìlitée   éducàte+ée → èducàtée
      -ize máximum+ìze → máximìze   rádium+ìze → rádiumìze
            óptimum+ìze → óptimìze   vácuum+ìze → vácuumìze
            féminin+ìze → féminìze   másculin+ìze → másculinìze
            phenómenon+ìze → phenómenìze   skéleton+ìze → skéletonìze
            áppetit+ìze → áppetìze   párasit+ìze → párasitìze

Truncation, however, is never resorted to as a means to avoid ONS_iONS_i -violations if the remaining stem consists of less than a disyllabic foot. In that case there is a systematic gap:[39]

(48) -ee rótàte+ee → Ø (*ròtée, *ròtàtée)   cóllàte+ée → còllàtée
           díctàte+ee → Ø (*dìctée, *dìctàtée)   lócàte+ée → lòcàtée
           mútàte+ee → Ø (*mùtée, *mùtàtée)   mándàte+ée → màndàtée
      -ize Híttìte+ìze → Ø (*Híttìze, *Híttitìze) Sémìte+ìze → Sémitìze
           línen+ìze → Ø (*línìze, *línenìze)   cótton+ìze → cóttonìze
           hórror+ìze → Ø (*hórrìze, *hórrorìze)   vígor+ìze → vígorìze
           Lénin+ìze → Ø (*Lénìze, *Léninìze)   Stálin+ìze → Stálinìze
           cándid+ìze → Ø (*cándìze, *cándidìze)   líquid+ìze → líquidìze

The unacceptable -*ee*-formations *ròtée, *dìctée, etc. violate a constraint IDENT (BINFT), which requires the last binary foot in the base to be preserved in the derived word. The ill-formedness of forms like *Híttìze*, *línìze*, etc. is already accounted for by the dominance of *CLASH over M-PARSE for the suffix *-ize*.[40] Additional examples are given in (49):

(49) a.   émphasis+ize → émphasìze   b.   cathársis+ize → Ø   (*cathársìze)
         epénthesis+ize → epénthesìze   ellípsis+ize → Ø   (*ellípsìze)
         sýnthesis+ize → sýnthesìze   crísis+ize → Ø   (*crísìze)
         hypóthesis+ize → hypóthesìze   scépsis+ize → Ø   (*scépsìze)

The suffixation in (49a) versus the gaps in (49b) are described by the ranking in (50):

(50)

émfəsɪs-áyz		IDENT(S)	ONS$_i$ONS$_i$	*CLASH	M-PARSE
	(émfəsɪsàyz)$_\omega$		*!		
√	(émfəsàyz)$_\omega$				
	(émfàyz)$_\omega$			*!	
	émfəsɪs-áyz				*!
kəθársɪs-áyz					
	(kəθársɪsàyz)$_\omega$		*!		
	(kəθársàyz)$_\omega$			*!	
	(kǽθərsàyz)$_\omega$	*!			
√	kəθársɪs-áyz				*

In view of the dependency of ONS$_i$ONS$_i$-violations on the segmental structure of both the stem *and* the suffix, the phonological effects presented here can be explained only by an output-oriented approach. Since each suffix is associated with an individual constraint-ranking there could exist vowel-initial suffixes which freely violate the constraint ONS$_i$ONS$_i$. An example is *-able* suffixation as is shown in (51):

(51)   -able   bribable, describable, absorbable, perturbable

Assuming that the constraint ONS$_i$ONS$_i$ is similar to the other phonological constraints considered here in that it applies within the pword and that consonant-initial suffixes are not integrated into the pword of the stem one can expect that there are no ONS$_i$ONS$_i$ related effects in consonant-initial suffixation. There is in fact no evidence for such effects as is illustrated in (52):

(52)　-ness　boniness, neatness, newness, tininess
　　　　-less　fellowless, pollenless, lifeless, landless
　　　　-ment　commitment, blemishment, movement, enamourment
　　　　-ship　marshalship, relationship, ushership
　　　　-ful　fearful, forceful, faithful
　　　　-ly　lowly, lovely, lonely, lightly, lively

4.4. Sonority constraints

The suffix *-en* differs from the vowel-initial suffixes considered above in that it attaches only to monosyllabic stems which end in an obstruent (cf. Marchand 1969: 214).[41] Examples for gaps are given in (53b, c).[42]

(53) a. tough+en → tóughen　b. éarnest+en → Ø　c. warm+en → Ø
　　　weak+en → wéaken　　módest+en → Ø　shy+en → Ø
　　　crisp+en → críspen　　básic+en → Ø　full+en → Ø
　　　brisk+en → brísken　　stúbborn+en → Ø　dear+en → Ø
　　　swift+en → swíften　　vívid+en → Ø　clean+en → Ø

From the perspective of an output-oriented approach the gap in (53b) reflects a requirement for pwords consisting solely of a trochaic foot. The gap in (53c) reflects the restriction on the sonority of onsets stated in (54):

(54)　ONS SON
　　　Syllable onsets must have sonority at least as low as a fricative.

The sonority restriction on syllable onsets referred to in constraint (54) is marked by the shaded area in table (55). Note that the allowable segments must belong to adjacent columns in the sonority hierarchy such that the rightmost column, which contains the least sonorous segments, is included.[43]

(55)　increasing sonority ←　　　　　→ decreasing sonority

Vowels	Glides	r	l	Nasals	Fricatives	Stops

According to Vennemann (1988:13ff) onsets are the more preferred the lower their sonority whereas codas are the more preferred the higher their sonority.[44] The constraint in (54) is one of a family of low sonority constraints for onsets which differ in the upper limit for the sonority. Crucially, a restriction to low sonority consonants is natural when referring to onsets, but not to codas. Therefore a description of the gap in (53c) in terms of a phonological subcategorization frame for the suffix *-en* is inadequate since it would imply that the requirement for consonants with low sonority pertained to the coda. By contrast, on an output-oriented approach the sonority restriction in question applies to onsets and can accordingly be described in terms of universal constraints. The tableau in (56) shows the evaluation of *-en* suffixation based on the adjectives *warm* and *tough*:[45]

(56) a.

wɔrm-ən		IDENT	ONS SON	M-PARSE
	(wɔr.bən)	*!		
	(wɔr.mən)		*!	
	wɔrm-ən			*

b.

tʌf-ən		IDENT	ONS SON	M-PARSE
	(tʌ́.fən)			
	tʌf-ən			*!

4.5. The constraint *VV

To avoid violations of the constraint *VV, which prohibits hiatus or onsetless syllables, certain suffixes never attach to vowel-final stems. One such suffix is *-eer*, as is illustrated by the gap in (57b):

(57) a.   músket+éer → mùsketéer   b.   bazóoka+éer → Ø
          wéapon+éer → wèaponéer   torpédo+éer → Ø
          járgon+éer → jàrgonéer   língo+éer → Ø
          slógan+éer → slòganéer   mótto+éer → Ø

The phonologically similar suffix *-ee* fails to attach only if the vowels to be combined are identical:

(58) a.   réscue+ée → rèscuée   b.   frée+ee → Ø
          dráw+ée → dràwée   sée+ee → Ø
          páy+ée → pàyée   cárry+ée → Ø
          ínterview+ée → ìnterviewée   píty+ée → Ø
          bórrow+ée → bòrrowée   énvy+ée → Ø

employ+ée → emplòyée　　　　　cópy+ée → Ø
thrów+ée → thròwée　　　　　　accómpany+ée → Ø

The suffix *-ese₁* differs from both *-eer* and *-ee* in that violations of *VV are avoided at the expense of the identity violations manifested as 'vowel deletion' or '*n*-epenthesis', depending on the moraic structure of the base. [46]

(59) a.　Chína+ése → Chìnése　　　b.　Jáva+ése → Jàvanése
　　　　Málta+ése → Màltése　　　　　Báli+ése → Bàlinése
　　　　Búrma+ése → Bùrmése　　　　Góa+ése → Gòanése

In accordance with the description of the the suffix *-ese₁* above the data in (59) indicate a high ranking of M-PARSE and phonological wellformedness constraints (e.g.*CLASH and *VV) w.r.t. identity constraints. In English, *-ese₁* is the only suffix for which the phonological constraint *VV is satisfied through 'epenthesis', i.e. a violation of the identity constraint which requires that each segment in the derived form must correspond to a segment in the base or the affix. The suffix *-ize* differs from all suffixes considered so far in that it causes truncation only if the resulting form has no stress clash. Some examples are shown in (60):

(60) a.　mémory+ìze → mémorìze　　b.　sílly+ìze → Ø (*síllìze)
　　　　jéopardy+ìze → jéopardìze　　　énvy → Ø (*énvìze)
　　　　apóstrophe+ìze → apóstrophìze　assémbly → Ø (*assémblìze)
　　　　prióriy+ìze → prióritìze　　　attórney → Ø (*attórnìze)

The suffixes *-er*, *-able* and *-ish* freely violate *VV as is illustrated in (61):

(61)　　carrier, hurrier, copier, envier, dallier, lobbyer, rallier
　　　　variable, marriable, buriable, pitiable, leviable, enviable
　　　　babyish, shabbyish, dandyish, rowdyish, fogyish, monkeyish

4.6. Some constraints which play no role in English suffixation

The cognates in (62a) are often cited in support of the claim that suffixes like *-al*, *-ous*, *-ify*, and *-ity* belong to a specific class of suffixes which trigger Trisyllabic Laxing. The cognates in (62b) are sometimes subsumed under that same rule (cf. Chomsky and Halle 1968; Myers 1987):

(62) a.　n[æ]tural - n[ey]ture　　b.　m[ɪ]mic - m[ay]me
　　　　f[æ]bulous - f[ey]ble　　　　t[ɑ]nic - t[ow]ne
　　　　v[ɪ]lify - v[ay]le　　　　　st[æ]tic - st[ey]te
　　　　prof[æ]nity - prof[ey]ne　　rabb[ɪ]nic - rabb[ay]

Vowel laxness in (62b) could also be subsumed under the 'Arab rule', which forbids long vowels if the following syllable is unstressed and has a noncoronal coda consonant (cf. Fidelholtz 1967).

The alternations in (62a) are due to a constraint on vowel length which also accounts for the absence of underived words like *c[ey]*mera* (cf. c[æ]*mera*), *[iy]*lefant* (cf. [ɛ]*lefant*). Because of the 'Arab rule' there are no words like *h[ey]*voc* (cf. h[æ]*voc*), *sh[iy]*riff* (cf. sh[ɛ]*riff*), *s[ay]*rup* (cf. s[ɪ]*rup*). However, there is no evidence that these constraints play a role in word-formation. They neither cause gaps nor 'allomorphy' as is illustrated by the native coinages in (63):

(63) a. région+al → régional   b.   base+ic → básic
         féver+ous → féverous   amóeba+ic → amóebic
         stéel+ify → stéelify   gnome+ic → gnómic
         betwéen+ity → betwéenity   phoneme+ic → phonémic

The reader may convince herself that the derived words are entirely unacceptable when pronounced with laxed vowels. The words in (62), which obey the constraints on vowel laxness in question, differ from the derived words in (63) in that they are loan words.

5. PHONOLOGICAL EFFECTS ASSOCIATED WITH CONSONANT INITIAL SUFFIXES

Are there counterexamples to the claim that consonant-initial suffixation never shows phonological effects? Consider words like *insécticìde*, *humánifỳ*, *lóngitùde* which are sometimes analysed as being derived by consonant-initial suffixes (i.e. *cide*, *fy*, *tude*) (cf. Fudge 1984; Burzio 1994[47]). The analysis of the suffixes in question as consonant-initial appears to be motivated primarily on etymological grounds. The observation that in native derivations those suffixes regularly appear with an 'insert' vowel *i* indicates that they have been reanalysed as vowel-initial suffixes in English as is illustrated in (64).[48] Phonological effects like satisfaction of the constraint $ONS_i ONS_i$ in *-icide* and *-ify* suffixation are therefore to be expected.

(64)   weed+icide → weedicide
         brute+ify → brutify
         lax+itude → laxitude

Consider next the examples in (65), which seem to contradict the claim that consonant-initial suffixes do not cause allomorphy ('<' stands for 'historically goes back to').

(65)   w[ɪ]sdom (< wíse+dom)
         bús[Ø]ness (< búsy+ness)

hán[Ø]some (< hánd+some)
wór[Ø]ship (< wórth+ship)
beáut[ə]+ful (< beáut[i]+ful)

That the phonological alternations in (65) are not properties of the suffixes can be inferred from the fact that these suffixes do not typically cause stem modification.[49] Instead these effects reflect the historical fusion of stems and suffixes into one pword shown in (66a). This process is especially common among words with high token frequency. The historical fusion of two pwords into a single pword with concomitant phonological changes can also be observed in compounds as is shown in (66b):[50]

(66) a.   (wíse)$_\omega$dom > (wísdom)$_\omega$ b.   (cúp)$_\omega$(bòard)$_\omega$ > (cúpboard)$_\omega$
       (búsy)$_\omega$ness > (búsiness)$_\omega$ (néck)$_\omega$(làce)$_\omega$ > (nécklace)$_\omega$
       (hánd)$_\omega$some > (hándsome)$_\omega$ (bréak)$_\omega$(fàst)$_\omega$ > (bréakfast)$_\omega$
       (wórth)$_\omega$ship > (wórship)$_\omega$ (shéep)$_\omega$(hèrd)$_\omega$ > (shépherd)$_\omega$
       (beáuti)$_\omega$ful > (beáutiful)$_\omega$ (fóre)$_\omega$(hèad)$_\omega$ > (fórehead)$_\omega$

In contrast to the historically fused suffixations in (65), which affect only individual words, suffixes with an initial glide are systematically integrated into the pword of the stem.

(67) a.   compóse+ure → (compósure)$_\omega$ b.   báck+ward → (báckward)$_\omega$
       expóse+ure → (expósure)$_\omega$ hóme+ward → (hómeward)$_\omega$
       depárt+ure → (depárture)$_\omega$ Gód+ward → (Gódward)$_\omega$
       rápt+ure → (rápture)$_\omega$ stréet+ward → (stréetward)$_\omega$
       eráse+ure → (erásure)$_\omega$ wáy+ward → (wáyward)$_\omega$

The suffix *-ure* exhibits two types of phonological effects. It attaches only to stems which end in an alveolar obstruent and merges with this obstruent into a (structure-preserving) palatal fricative or affricate which functions as onset (e.g. *era*[s]+[yər] → *era*[.šər]˧*era*[.žər], *compo*[z]+[yər] → *compo*[.žər], *rap*[t]+[yər] → *rap*[.čər]).[51] The allomorphy thus agrees with the evidence from syllabification which indicates that the stem and the suffix constitute one pword.[52] The native suffix *-ward* exhibits no phonological effects except for the fact that almost all suffixations consist of trochees.[53] The evidence from syllabification may seem to indicate that *-ward* is not integrated into the pword of the stem because stem-final [k], [g], [t], [d], [s], and [θ] appear in coda position although these consonants can precede the velar glide in onset position (e.g. *queen, guacamole, tweed, dwarf, swing, thwart*). However, the apparent LOI violations do not necessarily indicate intervening pword boundaries because there is evidence that the complex onsets in question are disallowed in schwa syllables in English. The evidence includes both historical cluster simplifications (e.g. *an*[sw]*er* > *an*[s]*er*, *li*[kw]*or* > *li*[k]*or*, *con*[kw]*er* > *con*[k]*er*)[54] and the synchronic syllable structure of simplexes (e.g *E*[d.w]*ard*, *aw*[k.w]*ard*).[55] While syllabification is accordingly inconclusive when determining the prosodic structure of *-ward* suffixation there is one argument from stress which suggests that *-ward* is integrated into the pword of the stem. According to the OED, the suffix is pronounced [wə d] when attached to a monosyllabic word but [wɔːd] when an unstressed syllable precedes. This type of dependency does not hold for any other consonant-initial suffix and is characteristic for stress reduction within pwords (e.g. *áltar* vs. *séminàr, hóstile* vs. *júvenìle, áuburn* vs. *tácitùrn*). It appears then that the suffixes *-ure* and *-ward* are integrated into the pword of the stem although they do not start with a vowel.

The suffix *-ry* is similar to the glide-initial suffixes but unlike other consonant-initial suffixes in that it too is integrated into the pword of the stem. The evidence for this claim is that the syllabification of the stem-final consonants is determined by the LOI as is shown by the examples in (68):

(68)   húsband+ry → husban.dry
         bígot+ry → bigo.try
         pédant+ry → pedan.try
         bándit+ry → bandi.try
         rócket+ry → rocke.try

In addition the suffix attaches only to stems which end in a trochee:

(69)   ráscalry, rívalry, révelry, rávenry, rócketry, párrotry,
         fórestry, sávagery, ímagery, freemásonry

As a result, *-ry* suffixation always yields dactyls. This output restriction highlights the relatedness between the suffix *-ry* and the vowel-initial suffix *-ery*, which attaches only to stems with final stress and thereby also yields outputs ending in dactyls. Some examples are given in (70):[56]

(70)   snóbbery, róbbery, bríbery, fórgery, físhery, fóolery, máchinery,
         scénery, gréenery, wínery, buffóonery, clównery, brávery, prúdery,
         midwífery

Assuming that all nouns in (68)-(70) are derived by the same suffix one could maintain the generalization that only vowel- and glide-initial suffixes show phonological effects. That is, one could posit a single suffix *-ery*, which requires outputs which end in a dactyl but does not require the preservation of its initial schwa. The distribution of *-ry/-ery* thus parallels the distribution of the suffix *-ence/-ency*, which is also determined by the requirement that the output form ends in a dactyl (cf. the native coinages *bellígerence, sálience* versus *cúrrency, látency*).[57] At any rate, *ry/-ery* suffixation supports the claim that the domain of phonological effects in word formation is identical to the domain of syllabification.

Consider finally the adverbial suffix *-ly*, which in some cases shows schwa-zero alternations. Significantly, in those cases the suffix is integrated into the pword of the stem as is shown by the syllabification of the derived words. Integration of this suffix into the pword of the stem is not one of its regular properties as is shown by the LOI-violations in (71):

(71) a. sim.ply (cf. simp[ə]l)   b. deep.ly
         possi.bly (cf. possib[ə]l)   superb.ly
         understanda.bly (cf. understandab[ə]l)   thick.ly

In some cases the alternations illustrated in (71a) may be related to the irregular historical schwa loss and degemination in words like †*forgivenness* in that the forms originally contained two identical consonants preceded by schwa. However, in general those alternations appear to be determined by orthographic rather than phonological structure. That is, alternations obtain only if the final rhyme in the base is spelled <le>, which includes all words derived by the suffix -*able*. Otherwise there is no allomorphy as is shown in (72b) (cf. also *roy*[ə]*lly*, *radic*[ə]*lly*, *verb*[ə]*lly*, etc).

(72) a. <simple>+<ly> → simply   b. <cruel>+<ly> → cruelly
         <possible>+<ly> → possibly   <level>+<ly> → levelly
         <subtle>+<ly> → subtly   <novel>+<ly> → novelly

The alternations in (71a) can thus be explained as the result of conventions which pertain to the relation between written and spoken forms.

Consider next the alternations in (73), which according to Wiese (1996) show that the suffixes -*ly* and -*ness* trigger schwa insertion to satisfy their preference for stem-final trochees.

(73) a. distress[ə]dly - distress[Ø]d   b. distress[ə]dness - distress[Ø]d
         amaz[ə]dly - amaz[Ø]d   amaz[ə]dness - amaz[Ø]d
         perplex[ə]dly - perplex[Ø]d   perplex[ə]dness - perplex[Ø]d
         prepar[ə]dly - prepar[Ø]d   prepar[ə]dness - prepar[Ø]d
         fix[ə]dly - fix[Ø]d   fix[ə]dness - fix[Ø]d

In contrast to Wiese I will argue that those alternations do not indicate phonological constraints on *ly*- or -*ness* suffixation but rather show that the phonological conditions for word formation can be obscured by historical sound changes. That is, the alternations in (73) result from the historical schwa loss in the adjectives[58] which occurred after the derived forms came into existence.[59] The claim that -*ness* and -*ly* suffixation prefer stem-final trochees is contradicted by the tendency to replace the adjectival stems with schwa by their schwa-less successors. Consider the examples in (74), which Walker (1826) transcribed with a schwa, which according to the OED has since been lost.[60] By contrast, there are no examples of historical schwa epenthesis in -*ness* or -*ly* suffixation.

(74)   deform[ə]dly > deform[Ø]dly   blear[ə]dness > blear[Ø]dness

resign[ə]dly > resign[Ø]dly   compos[ə]dness > compos[Ø]dness
restrain[ə]dly > restrain[Ø]dly   diffus[ə]dness > diffus[Ø]dness
confus[ə]dly > confus[Ø]dly   confus[ə]dness > confus[Ø]dness
resolv[ə]dly > resolv[Ø]dly   reserv[ə]dness > reserv[Ø]dness

The changes in (74) show that schwa loss in the adjectives has not led English learners to associate phonological constraints with the suffixes *-ly* and *-ness*, but rather has resulted in the fossilization of the derived forms which retained the schwa. Fossilization is manifested not only in the instability illustrated in (74) but also in various idiosyncracies (e.g. *prepar*[ə]*dness* is military jargon, *mark*[ə]*dness* is linguistics jargon).[61] I conclude then contrary to Wiese that the suffixes *-ly* and *-ness* neither historically nor synchronically exhibit a preference for stems ending in trochees. The schwa-zero alternations in (73) are represented most adequately by listing those words in the lexicon without positing metrical constraints on the suffixes.

Perhaps the clearest case of phonological sensitivity exhibited by a consonant-initial suffix is the tendency for the adverbial suffix *-ly* to resist attachment to adjectives ending in *-ly*. Yet, the OED lists 24 counterexamples to this generalizations. A few are listed in (75):[62]

(75)   chillily, cleanlily, friendlily, holily, jollily

Other suffixes with initial *l* show no phonological effects (e.g. *-let, -less, -ling*). The same holds for suffixes whose first consonant is less sonorous.

Granting that the status of the suffix *-ly* is unclear I conclude that only glide-initial suffixes and the suffix *-ry/-ery* exhibit regular phonological effects.[63] The fact that the initial segments in these suffixes are highly sonorous is unlikely to be coincidental in view of the fact that onsets are the less preferred the more sonorous they are (cf. section 4.4). A formal analysis of this observation is discussed in section 6. Significantly, neither *-ure, -ward*, nor *-ry/-ery* suffixation contradict the generalization that phonological effects in word formation are found only within the domain of syllabification (i.e. the pword).

6. THE PROSODIC STRUCTURE OF SUFFIXED WORDS

In the preceding section I have presented evidence that only vowel-initial and glide-initial suffixes induce phonological effects. Assuming that in English the pword is the domain for morphophonological constraints this observation is accounted for by the integration of those suffixes, but not consonant-initial suffixes, into the pword of the stem. Compare the acceptable *-like* suffixations in (76) with the unacceptable *-ize*-formations. The attested *-ize*-formations are cited to show that the unacceptability of the starred formations is not due to semantic properties.

(76)   béelìke   *stéelìze (cf. copperize)
       cówlìke   *ówlìze (cf. vulturize)
       fúrlìke   *gírlìze (cf. womanize)

The difference in the acceptability of the formations in (76) can be explained with reference to neither segmental, syllabic, nor metrical structure. Instead that difference can be described in terms of a systematic contrast in the prosodic structure of the words. Crucially, the constraint *CLASH would be satisfied in *béelìke* if the consonant-initial suffix were not integrated into the pword of the stem as is shown in (77):[64]

(77)

biy+layk		*CLASH
	$(bíy)_\omega$làyk	
stiyl+ayz		
	$(stíylàyz)_\omega$	*

How can the dependence of prosodic structure on the initial segment of the suffix be expressed in terms of constraints? Prince and Smolensky (1993) proposed that this dependency be captured by ranking the constraint ONSET, which prohibits onsetless syllables, higher than certain alignment constraints. Consider the constraint ALIGN SUFFIX, which aligns the left edge of a suffix with the right edge of a pword thereby ensuring that suffixes are not integrated into the pword of their stem:

(78)   ALIGN SUFFIX
       Align (Suffix, L, Pword, R)

Assuming that pwords constitute the domain for syllabification the integration of vowel-initial suffixes into the pword of the stem is achieved by ranking ONSET higher than ALIGN SUFFIX. [65]

(79) a.

biy+layk		ONSET	ALIGN SUFFIX
√	$(bíy.)_\omega$làyk		
	$(bíy.làyk)_\omega$		*!

b.

(stiyl)$_\omega$-ayz		ONSET	ALIGN SUFFIX
√	(stíyl.)$_\omega$àyz	*!	
	(stíy.làyz)$_\omega$		*

To ensure that glide-initial suffixes are also integrated into the pword of the stem the syllable structure constraint which dominates ALIGN SUFFIX is formulated as follows:

(80)   ONSET'
        Syllables must have a [+consonantal] onset

The restriction expressed in (80) is similar to the constraint ONS SON in (54) associated with the suffix *-en* in that it expresses an upper limit on the sonority of onsets (cf. the sonority hierarchy in (55)). It is in fact not entirely clear where that limit is. There are no suffixes with initial *r* except for the suffix *-ry*, which has been analysed as a variant of the suffix *-ery*. If *-ry* were analysed as the basic variant the upper limit on the sonority of onsets in (80) would have to be lowered to exclude the *r*. Crucially, the universal preference for syllable onsets with low sonority implies that the exclusion of *r* entails the exclusion of glides but not vice versa.

As it stands the constraint ranking in (79) does not account for the general integration of vowel-initial suffixes into the pword of the stem but results in integration only if the stem-final segment could serve as a syllable onset. The prediction would then be that vowel-initial suffixes freely attach to vowel-final bases without inducing allomorphy or gaps, which is clearly incorrect (cf. the constraint *VV in 4.5). To make the analysis work, suffixes with an inadequate onset must always be integrated into the pword of the stem, whether or not such integration actually supplies the lacking onset.[66]

The constraint ranking in (79) does not account for the prosodic structure of consonant-initial suffixes. Assuming that pwords constitute the domain for word stress, vowel reduction in (81) shows that the English suffixes differ from their German cognates in that they are not separate pwords.[67] The fact that vowels have never reduced in English monosyllabic words which used to be homophonous to those suffixes (e.g. *mess*, *bull*) follows from the pword status of lexical words.

(81)   English   German
        [ləs] '-less'   [lo:s] '-los'
        [fəl] '-ful'   [fɔl] '-voll'
        [dəm] '-dom'   [tu:m] '-tum'
        [nəs] '-ness'   [nɪs] '-nis'
        [səm] '-some'   [za:m] '-sam'
        [mənt] '-ment'   [mɛnt] '-ment'

[lət] '-let'   [lɛt] '-let'

Vowel reduction in English consonant-initial suffixes is blocked only under certain phonological conditions. In the suffix [hʊd] -*hood* (cf. the German cognate [haɪt] -*heit*) the vowel fails to reduce due to a constraint against schwa syllables whose onset is [h].[68] In the suffix -*ship* the vowel fails to reduce due to the post-vocalic non-coronal obstruent.[69] Diphthongs fail to reduce (cf. the suffixes -*like*, -*wise*[70]) as do long vowels followed by clusters (cf. -*fold*, -*most*). In such cases stress is assigned by weight, and not because those suffixes are pwords. This type of stress differs from the stress assigned to pwords in that it is inherently unstable. The suffix -*most* is pronounced [məst] in colloquial British English which perhaps indicates that the unreduced variant will eventually disappear in (at least) that variety of English. Prosodically words with consonant-initial suffixes are perhaps best categorized as clitic groups,[71] where the difference between suffixes with unreduced vowels and those with reduced vowels could be represented as in (82a) versus (82b) ('C' = Clitic group, 'Σ' = Foot).[72]

(82) a.   American English   b.   Colloquial
                                          British English

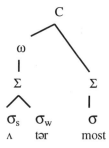 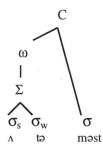

The stress on the suffix is unstable because the relevant foot is not dominated by a pword. By contrast, the righthand members of compounds have stable stress since they are dominated by a pword (e.g. (béd)ω(pòst)ω, (párcel)ω(pòst)ω).[73] Similarly, the stress on vowel-initial suffixes is stable since such suffixes are dominated by pwords as well as is shown by the examples *legalize*, *infantile*, *Japanese* shown in (83).[74] Neither English nor German consonant-initial suffixes carry main stress as some vowel-initial suffixes do:[75]

(83)

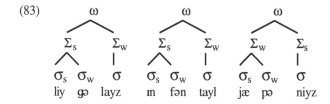

To account for stress neutrality Aronoff and Sridhar (1983) represent the suffix
-ize as a clitic, which is not integrated into the pword of the stem, in accordance with
their analysis of stress-neutral consonant-initial suffixes. However, the evidence from
syllabification shows that this analysis cannot be correct. If the suffix *-ize* were not
integrated into the pword of the stem the stem-final consonant should be
ambisyllabic, because of the rule which associates the final consonant of a pword
with the following vowel (cf. Kahn 1976).[76] Ambisyllabicity can be easily
recognized in American English because of the flapping of coronal stops regardless of
the stress on the following vowel.[77] Consider the examples *night owl* and *Pat is*
shown in (84):[78]

(84)

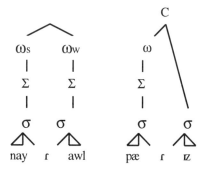

The fact that the stem-final *t* in *-ize* suffixation is never flapped shows that the suffix
constitutes neither a separate pword, nor a clitic (cf. verbs like *alphabe*[t]*ize,
magne*[t]*ize, puppe*[t]*ize*).[79] Rather the suffix *-ize* is integrated into the pword of the
stem as is shown in (83).[80] This analysis is also supported by the fact that the suffix
-ize exhibits phonological effects in word formation, in contrast to consonant-initial
suffixes.

    To summarize, the assumption that only vowel- and glide-initial, but not conso-
nant-initial, suffixes are integrated into the pword of their stem explains the systematic correlation between seemingly unrelated properties concerning syllabification,
stress, and morphophonological effects. Specifically, the analysis explains why
consonant-initial suffixes tend to undergo vowel reduction, why they form a separate
domain for syllabification (cf. the LOI violations in the words in (4)), why they do
not induce allomorphy and why they are insensitive to the phonological properties of
their base with the result that there are no gaps.

    These correlations are not universal. In German many consonant-initial suffixes
yield systematic phonological effects although the evidence from both syllabification
and stress shows that they are not integrated into the pword of the stem.[81] The suffix
-chen induces truncation of the stem-final schwa syllables *-e* and *-en*, but not *-el* and

-er. This suffix, which has an initial palatal fricative, furthermore does not attach to stems which end in a palatal or velar fricative.[82] The general rule of *g*-spirantization in coda position after the vowel *i* (e.g. *Köni*[ç] 'king'-*Köni*[g]*e* 'kings') fails when the coda in the following syllable includes a velar spirant (e.g. *köni*[k]*li*[ç] *könig+lich* 'kingly'. This rule clearly applies across pword boundaries as it also accounts for the 'blocking' of *g*-spirantization in compounds like *Köni*[k]*rei*[ç] 'kingdom' (cf. Drosdowski (ed.) 1990: 75). The suffix *-nis* does not attach to stems which end in *n* (cf. by contrast the English formations *cleanness*, *brazenness*, etc). The suffix *-lein* does not attach to stems which end in *-l* (cf. by contrast the English formations *snaillike*, *vowellike*, etc). These examples suggest that in German the pword is not the relevant domain for the dissimilatory constraints in question.[83] Why this systematic difference between English and German exists is unclear.

7. THE ISSUE OF ABSTRACTNESS

To explain the observation that certain gaps in word-formation arise to avoid stress clashes it is necessary to refer to the (surface) stress pattern of both the input and the candidates. Specifically, the evaluation of candidate forms w.r.t. the constraint IDENT(S), which requires the stress in the derived form to be identical to the stress on the corresponding syllables in the base, requires reference to the surface representation.

But just how concrete should the phonological representations be to allow one to capture the relevant generalizations? Consider again the gaps due to the constraints which ban identical segments within the phonological word (e.g. *L_iL_i, SHELL). In many English dialects liquids or stops have clearly distinct allophones depending on their position within the syllable. Recall that the *t* is aspirated in syllable-initial position, glottalized in coda position, and flapped when ambisyllabic. Similarly, the *l* is often vocalized in coda position but not in onset position in British English (cf. Wells 1982: 258ff). As a result on the phonetic level the constraint against identical segments in forms like *acutity*, *appealal*, *revolvereer*, *closetette*, etc. is not violated and therefore cannot be invoked to explain their ungrammaticality. Yet, it seems intuitively clear that the various phonetic realizations of stops or liquids in English dialects do not affect the unacceptability of those forms. It appears then that the notion of distinctiveness or structure-preservation is crucial when defining the level of abstractness which is relevant for describing phonological effects in word formation.[84]

The notion of distinctiveness is also crucial for describing the restrictions on intensive-*s* formations in English. As was noted by Stampe (1972), the prefix [s] never attaches to words with an initial voiced stop. The rule is illustrated with examples from Wright's English dialect grammar in (85):[85]

(85) a. s+voiceless stop   b. s+sonorant   c. *s+voiced stop
        s+clash → sclash   s+lounge → slounge   s+bat → Ø

s+crunch → scrunch	s+matter → smatter	s+gush → Ø
s+plunge → splunge	s+notch → snotch	s+dash → Ø
s+quilt → squilt	s+rake → srake	
s+trample → strample	s+wang → swang	

The dilemma reflected by the gap in (85c) can be described as follows. Any *s*-formation based on a word with an initial voiced stop such as *bash* would be either phonologically ill-formed (e.g. *[sb]*ash*) or the stop in the derived word would differ from the corresponding stop in the base regarding the feature voice (e.g. *s[p]ash*-[b]*ash*).[86] The two relevant constraints are stated below:

(86) a. AGREE VOICE
Obstruent clusters must agree w.r.t. the feature [±voice]. Domain: syllable
b. IDENT(F)
Corresponding consonants must have identical values for distinctive features.

The analysis of the gap in (85c) is illustrated in tableau (87):

(87)

s+bæš		AGREE VOICE	IDENT(F)	M-PARSE
	sbæš	*!		
	spæš		*!	
√	s-bæš			*

The constraint ranking in (87) accounts for the acceptability of the attested *s*-prefixations as is illustrated in (88):

(88)

s+klæš		AGREE VOICE	IDENT(F)	M-PARSE
√	sklæš			
	s +klæš			*!

The point of interest here is that there are clear phonetic differences between the acceptable formations and their respective bases. The corresponding stops in the onsets in (85a) differ with respect to aspiration (e.g. [kʰ]*lash* versus *s[k]lash*) and the corresponding sonorants in the onsets in (85b) differ with respect to voicing (e.g.

[l]*ounge* versus *s*[l̥]*ounge*). However, neither aspiration nor voicing in sonorants is distinctive in English, so the formations in (85) do not violate identity constraints. It appears then that allophonic features cannot cause gaps or allomorphy.[87]

The claim that reference to phonemic representations is not only necessary but sufficient for a description of English morphophonology might seem to be refuted by the coinages in (89):

(89)   Nix[ə]n+ian   →   Nix[ów]nian
        'Nixon+ian'   'Nixonian'
        Sieg[ə]n+ian   →   Sieg[ɛ]nian
        'Siegen+ian'   'Siegenian'
        Jord[ə]n+ian   →   Jord[éy]nian
        'Jordan+ian'   'Jordanian'

Within classic generative phonology the vowel alternations in (89) are described by positing abstract underlying vowels in the underived words. Such descriptions fail to explain how the coiners of the derived forms in (89) could identify that abstract vowel. In the examples in (89) alternations cannot play a role. Obviously the vowels are inferred from the written representations. It certainly seems plausible that the coiners of the derivations in (89) were literate. The input for word formation in (89) consists accordingly of both a graphemic and a phonemic representation as is illustrated in (90):

(90)   <Nixon> + <ian>
        níksən + iən

In native word formation the occurrence of full vowel-schwa alternations appears to be largely confined to names (cf. also *N*[ə]*pál-N*[ɛ̀]*palése*). While there are many loan words which show such alternations comparable coinages tend to be unacceptable. This indicates a high ranking of the relevant identity constraint w.r.t. M-PARSE for almost all suffixes as is illustrated by the gaps in (91b) (cf. also the examples in (44b)):

(91) a. modérnity - módern (cf. F modernité)   b. wéstern+ity → Ø (*westérnity)
       oríginal - órigin (cf. L originalis)   zéppelin+al → Ø (*zeppélinal)
       persónify - pérson (cf. F personnifier)   pígeon+ify → Ø (*pigeónify)

Coinages which do involve full vowel-schwa alternations are typically confined to certain endings as is illustrated in (92):

(92)   márgin[əl] - màrgin[ǽləti]
        géner[əs] - gèner[ásəti]
        drínk[əbəl] - drìnk[əbíləti]

Arguably the examples of word formation in (92) are not due to suffixation but rather involve 'correlative patterns' (cf. Marchand 1969). Correlative patterns are inferred on the basis of recognized relations between words as in (93a):

(93) a. Inference of a correlative pattern:

aud[éyšəs]$_A$ - aud[ǽsə ti]$_N$
sag[éyšəs]$_A$ - sag[ǽsə ti]$_N$
ten[éyšəs]$_A$ - ten[ǽsə ti]$_N$
∴X[éyšəs]$_A$ - X[ǽsə ti]$_N$

b. Application of the pattern in word formation:

Input: nug[éyšəs]$_A$
X[éyšəs]$_A$ - X[ǽsə ti]$_N$
∴nug[éyšəs]$_A$ - nug[ǽsə ti]$_N$

The inference of correlative patterns presupposes that learners have recognized relations between words which exhibit alternations in the endings but not in the initial strings. Word formation which is based on correlative patterns involves the instantiation of variables by strings which need not be independent words as is shown in (93b). This type of word formation typically shows complete productivity, which is atypical for derivational morphology.

The claim that the word formation in (93b) is based on the association of specific phonological strings is supported by the observation that nouns which involve slightly different patterns like *specious-*specity* or *pernicious-*pernicity* are unacceptable. The complete productivity of the pattern in (93) compared to the unacceptability of slightly different patterns could not be expressed if the noun in (93b) was derived by *-ity* suffixation. Instead this contrast in acceptability indicates that speakers do not associate the suffix *-ity* with phonological effects like vowel laxing, fricative depalatalization, and truncation but rather apply specific correlative patterns in the formation of new words by variable substitution. The application of the correlative pattern X[éyšəs]$_A$-X[ǽsə ti]$_N$ in word formation hence overrides the constraints on *-ity* suffixation.[88]

8. DIFFERENCES WITH PREVIOUS WORK

8.1. *Differences with descriptions in terms of affix classes*

In generative descriptions of English morphophonology affixes are typically grouped to account for the putative correlation of properties like those illustrated in (94) (cf. Chomsky and Halle 1968; Siegel 1974; Selkirk 1982):

(94) a.

	class I	class II
attach also to stems	yes	no
trigger stress shifts	yes	no
trigger segmental adjustments	yes	no

b. Class I: -ous, -al, -ity, -ize, ify, ...
   Class II -ness, -less, -ful, -hood, ish, ...

The correlations in (94) are generally associated with the origin of the suffixes: class I suffixes are mostly Latinate and class II suffixes are mostly Germanic. However, class membership is an idiosyncratic property of affixes which is not phonologically determined. There is hence no claim that the onset of a suffix plays any role in English morphophonology. Examples to illustrate the correlation of class I properties are given in (95):

(95)	stem-based	Trisyllabic Laxing	stress shift
-ous	heinous	[ɑ]minous (cf. [ow]men)	indústrious(cf. índustry)
-al	liberal	n[æ]tural (cf. n[ey]ture)	oríginal (cf. órigin)
-ity	affinity	s[æ]nity (cf. s[ey]ne)	legálity (cf. légal)
-ize	ostracìze	p[æ]tronize (cf. p[ey]tron)	ímmunìze (cf. (immúne)
-ify	edify	m[ɑ]dify (cf. m[ow]de)persónify (cf. pérson)

However, when only native word formation and additional phonological effects (notably the sensitivity of affixes to phonological properties of the stem) are taken into account the distinction between the two classes evaporates. First, it is incorrect that Latinate affixes can attach to non-words. Putative stem-based word formation is generally due to the fact that an affixed word, but not its etymological base, has been borrowed. For example, the Old French adjective *haïneus*, but not its base *haïne*, was borrowed into English with the result that Modern English *heinous* lacks a word base. Crucially, the non-existence of the word *hein* in English implies that the adjective *heinous* could not have been formed natively.

The characterization of Germanic affixation as word-based is due to the fact that borrowings happen to be exceedingly rare among words derived by Germanic affixes. However, there is a second source of putative stem-based word formation, which also affects natively derived words. That is, occasionally the base of a derived word, but not the derived word itself, becomes obsolete. Some examples from Germanic are *wistful-†wist, hapless-†hap, shabby-†shab, uncouth-†couth*. In such cases it is also misleading to state that Germanic affixes can exceptionally attach to stems since the words in question were formed before the respective bases became obsolete.

Trisyllabic Laxing plays no role in native word-formation regardless of the origin of the affix (cf. section 4.6.). By contrast, stress-related phonological effects obtain for almost all vowel-initial suffixes. However, no two suffixes show the same effects which is true even for near-homophonous suffixes like *-ee, -eer*, and *-ese* or adjectival and nominal *-al* (cf. sections 4.1, 4.2.).[89] Consider further the Latinate suffixes *-ize* and *-ify*, both of which yield verbs. Verbs derived by the suffix *-ize* systematically violate the constraint *LAPSE, which prohibits two adjacent unstressed syllables, to satisfy IDENT(S) while the opposite ranking between those constraints obtains for verbs derived by *-ify* suffixation. Some examples are shown in (96):

(96)   rádical+ìze → rádicalìze   sólid+ifỳ → *sólidifỳ
         hóspital+ìze → hóspitalìze   pérson+ifỳ → *pérsonifỳ
         cháracter+ìze → cháracterìze   hístory+ifỳ → *hístorifỳ

The suffixes -al and -ous both show a restriction to maximally ternary final feet (cf. by contrast the suffixes in (7)). However, they differ in that -al freely attaches to monosyllabic stems (cf. (97a)). That is, in terms of output forms the suffix -ous shows a preference for dactyls (cf. (97b)) whereas the suffix -al shows no such preference:

(97) a. tide+al → tídal   b. hill+ous → Ø cf. móuntain+ous → móuntainous
        tube+al → túbal   creep+ous → Ø cf. tráitor+ous → tráitorous
        tribe+al → tríbal   chill+ous → Ø cf. féver+ous → féverous
        globe+al → glóbal   risk+ous → Ø cf. házard+ous → házardous

It is hard to see how the range of stress-related effects (i.e. gaps and allomorphy) exhibited by English suffixes can be captured in terms of suffix classes. A partial solution would be to limit reference to affix classes to account for allomorphy (i.e. systematic stress shifts) and to describe gaps in terms of phonological subcategorization frames associated with each affix (cf. Inkelas 1990; Booij and Lieber 1993). However, it is widely accepted now that such an approach fails to reveal the motivation behind phonologically conditioned gaps (cf. Booij 1998 and references therein). The approach advocated here is to associate to each suffix a specific ranking for the constraints IDENT(S), *CLASH, *LAPSE, and constraints on foot size. The fact that Germanic suffixes exhibit generally no stress effects follows from the fact that they typically start with a consonant.

Descriptions of English morphonology in terms of affix-classes are inadequate not only in that they fail to capture systematic differences between Latinate suffixes. They also fail to capture similarities between Latinate and Germanic suffixes. The consonant-initial Latinate suffix -ment is similar to all consonant-initial Germanic suffixes in that it exhibits no phonological effects. On the other hand, the vowel-initial Germanic suffixes -en and comparative -er are similar to many vowel-initial Latinate suffixes in that they are sensitive to the metrical structure of their stem. The vowel-initial Germanic suffix -ish is similar to many vowel-initial Latinate suffixes in that it avoids violations of the constraint SHELL. These similarities are expressed by way of associating the suffixes with identical rankings between the constraints in question.

To summarize, descriptions of English morphology in terms of arbitrary affix-classes fail to capture the generalization that the onset of a suffix determines whether or not it exhibits phonological effects. Those descriptions also fail to express the generalization that in English phonological effects in word formation are found only within the domain of syllabification. Both generalizations are expressed by integrating suffixes with insufficient onsets into the pword of the stem and by specifying the pword as the domain for phonological constraints in word formation.

8.2. Differences with Burzio's (1994) analysis

Burzio's (1994) description of stress patterns in English suffixation differs from other descriptions in that all suffixes are metrified. In this approach, even the suffixes -*ness*, -*less*, and -*ment*, which are generally classified as stress-neutral, are systematically integrated into the foot structure of any stem whose phonological structure allows for the integration of an additional syllable. The stems in question end either in a stressed syllable (cf. (98a)) or in trochaic foot optionally closed by a sonorant or *s* (cf. (98b)). If those suffixes are not integrable they are parsed as a separate foot as shown in (98c). A final null vowel is posited to satisfy foot binarity:

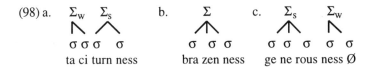

Burzio does not refer to pwords. However, on the assumption that consonant-initial suffixes are not integrated into the pword of the stem the foot structures in (98a) and (98b) are ruled out by the Prosodic Hierarchy. Instead the structures are those shown in (99), which account not only for the stress patterns but also for syllabification[90] and for the occurrence of word-internal geminates like *tacitur*[n.n]*ess*, *braze*[n.n]*ess*.

(99)

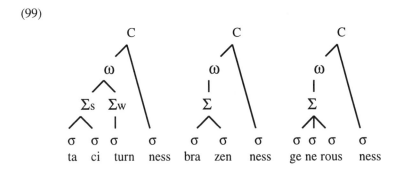

The descriptions of stress in (98) and (99) differ in two respects. According to Burzio's description the suffix constitutes a separate foot and is consequently stressed when it attaches to a stem which ends in a dactyl or a trochee which ends in an obstruent other than *s*. He does not discuss the phonological evidence for this claim but to my knowledge the suffix is invariably unstressed as expressed in (99). A second difference concerns relative prominence relations in words like *taciturnness*, which show remetrification as a result of -*ness* suffixation according to Burzio. The evidence he cites are patterns like *árbitràry-àrbitráriness, ímitàtive-ìmitátiveness,*

which he claims obtain "for many American speakers" (Burzio 1994: 240). It is unclear if such stress shifts always involve adjectives ending in *-àry* and *-àtive* and if
they correlate with a reversal of relative prominence relations in other clitic structures. At least the relative prominence pattern in (98a) appears to be generally unacceptable.

Burzio's description differs from mine not only in that all suffixes are metrified
but also in that stress effects are claimed to be predictable on the basis of the phonological form of the suffix. While such a description would go beyond the one I have
proposed he achieves this aim only at the expense of considerable abstractness.
Consider again the distinct stress effects triggered by the monosyllabic suffixes in
(100a) versus (100b), which I have attributed to the suffix-initial segment:

(100)a. accómpany+ment → accómpanyment   b. gélatin+ous → gelátinous
         génerous+ness → génerousness   médicin+al → medícinal
         cháracter+less → cháracterless
         báchelor+hood → báchelorhood

According to Burzio, stress neutrality in (100a) is due not to the presence of a syllable onset but rather to the structure of the rhyme. Specifically, he claims that *-ment*,
but not *-al* or *-ous*, can constitute a separate foot due to the final cluster. To account
for the stress neutrality of the remaining cases he claims that the suffixes *-less* and
-ness contain final geminates and the suffix *-hood* contains a long vowel whereas the
suffixes *-al* and *-ous* contain only short segments. There is no independent evidence
for those claims. Is it a coincidence that all suffixes for which abstract length is postulated to account for stress neutrality start with a consonant?

Consider next Burzio's account of some systematic differences between vowel-
initial suffixes. The stress-neutrality of the suffix *-ize* (cf. *pérsonal+ìze* → *pérsonal-
ìze*) compared to the stress shift in *-ify* suffixation (*pérson+ifỳ* → *persónifỳ*) is accounted for by claiming that *-ize*, but not *-fy*, constitutes a separate foot. However,
there is no discernible difference between the stress on those suffixes. Similarly,
stress neutrality in *-acy*-suffixation (cf. *áccurate+acy* → *áccuracy*) compared to stress
shifts in *-ity* suffixations (*légal+ity* → *legálity*) is accounted for by positing the
metrically distinct lexical representations *ity)* and *a)cy* for those suffixes, where the
right parenthesis marks the right foot boundary. Systematic differences between the
suffixes *-ic* and *-al* are accounted for by positing a null vowel before the right foot
boundary in the lexical representation of the suffix *-ic* (i.e. *icØ*) versus *a)l*). There is
no independent phonological evidence for any of these representations which calls
into question their explanatory power.[91] What prevents the linguist from positing
long segments, null vowels, or foot boundaries to account for different stress
effects?[92] What is to be gained by such a description especially with regard to a
theory of possible phonological effects in word formation?

Consider finally Burzio's account of gaps, which is similar to mine in that gaps
result when suffixation would violate either a constraint on metrical wellformedness

or a constraint which requires stress identity w.r.t. the base. Specifically he states that suffixes which require stress neutrality but cannot constitute a separate foot attach only to stems that can integrate them as a syllable. The suffixes which are allegedly subject to this restriction include the consonant-initial suffixes *-ful*, *-dom*, and *-some* (Burzio 1994: 259, 273ff), which are claimed to differ from *-less*, *-ness* and *-hood* in that they cannot constitute a separate foot.

While it is true that there are very few cases of *-ful*, *-dom*, or *-some* suffixation based on dactylic or trochaic stems which end in a consonant other than a sonorant or *s*, it is doubtful that that gap is statistically significant. Rather the rarity of such words appears to be due to the relatively low productivity of those suffixes (in comparison to *-less* or *-ness*)[93] and the low ratio of potential bases with the required phonological properties. For example, there are several hundred trochaic nouns in English which end in a sonorant compared to only about a dozen which end in a *p*. The existence of twenty *-ful*-suffixations based on trochaic stems ending in a sonorant compared to only one ending in *-p* (i.e. *wórshipful*) is therefore to be expected. The rarity of dactylic stems presumably reflects the rarity of non-Germanic bases in *-ful*, *-dom*, or *-some* suffixation.[94] Note finally that while capturing rather dubious gaps in *-ful*, *-dom*, or *-some* suffixation, Burzio's analysis fails to account for the stress-related gaps in *-ize*, *-eer*, or *-ous* suffixation.

9. PHONOLOGICAL CONSTRAINTS ON MORPHOLOGICAL ANALYSIS

In sections 2 and 3 I have argued for a limitation to native word formation when describing the conditions on the synthesis of words. In this section I will present evidence which suggests that the analysis of words, specifically base recognition, is subject to independent phonological conditions (cf. Raffelsiefen 1993, 1998). Those conditions are similar to identity constraints on word formation in that they require certain aspects of the phonemic representations of derived words and their base to be identical.[95]

There is evidence that English hearers relate irregular plural forms as shown in (1a) to the cognate singular forms only if the pairs exhibit no more than one alternation.[96] Compare the cognates in (101a), which exhibit a single voicing alternation and for which recognition succeeds, with the cognates in (101b), which exhibit an additional vowel alternation and for which recognition fails. The shafted arrow indicates morphological analysis (i.e. 'A → B' means 'B is recognized as the base of A', 'A *→ B' means 'B is not recognized as the base of A').

(101)a. shel[v]es → shel[f]   b.   st[eyv]es *   →   st[æf]
                                      'staves'   'staff'

        scar[v]es → scar[f]   cl[iyv]es *   →   cl[ɪf]
                                        †   'cliff'

        lea[v]es → lea[f]   cl[owð]es *   →   cl[ɑθ]
                                       'clothes'   'cloth'

Failed base recognition in the pairs in (101b) is manifest in semantic differentiation and the development of back-formed singulars (e.g. *stave*), the development of pluralia tantum (e.g. *clothes*), the archaization of words (e.g. *cleeves*), and the development of innovative plural forms (e.g. *staffs, cliffs, cloths*).

Assuming that the destabilization of the pairs in (101b) is due to a lack of phonologocal identity the question arises of why those pairs, but not the pairs in (101a), contain two alternations. All voicing alternations in (101) are due to either fricative devoicing in coda position or fricative voicing in medial onset position which applied at a time when the plurals were still disyllabic. At that time, the plurals were also susceptible to vowel lengthening in open syllables. That rule caused no change in the plurals in (101a) because their vowel was either already long (e.g. *leaves, houses, thieves*), or the first syllable was closed (e.g. *shelves, scarves, wolves*). By contrast, vowel lengthening affected the plurals *staves* and *cleeves*, which originally had a short vowel in open syllable. As a result the vowels in the pairs *staves-staff* and *cleeves-cliff* were no longer identical. In the pair *clothes-cloth*, the vowel alternation is due to a rule which shortened back mid vowels before the interdental fricative (cf. *broth, sloth*, etc). It is because of these purely phonological differences that the pairs in (101b), but not in (101a), developed multiple alternations and destabilized.

The data in (102) support the claim that the plurals in (101b) are no longer related to the cognate singular forms because of the number of alternations, and not because of the type (i.e. vowel alternations). The examples in (102b) are given in OE orthography, where <c'> represents the palatal voiceless affricate. All pairs in (102b), but none of the pairs in (102a), show signs of destabilization.

(102)a.	w[ɪ]men →	w[ʊ]man	b.	ae:c' *	→	a:c
	'women'	'woman'		†		'oak'
	f[iy]t →	f[ʊ]t		bre:c' *	→	bro:c
	'feet'	'foot'		'breeches'		†
	l[ay]ce →	l[aw]se		be:c' *	→	bo:c
	'lice'	'louse'		†		'book'

The crucial difference between the pairs in (102a) and (102b), all of which exhibit vowel alternations, concerns the place of articulation of the postvocalic consonant. The singular forms in (102b) have a back vowel followed by a velar stop, which, due to umlaut, was subject to palatalization in the corresponding plural forms. The result was that the pairs developed two alternations and destabilized. This phonological account of destabilization also explains a gap in the stable umlaut pairs in (102a): there are no pairs involving postvocalic velars.

The data in (102a) show that plural-singular pairs in English can remain stable in spite of developing a rare or isolated alternation (cf.*w*[ɪ]*men-w*[ʊ]*man*, *g*[iy]*se-g*[uw]*se*) whereas such pairs necessarily destabilize when developing multiple alternations. This generalization cannot be expressed in a model of morphological synthesis but shows that morphological analysis is determined by specific identity conditions. The conditions are that the relatedness between plurals and singulars in English can succeed only if either all consonants or the initial minimal word, which includes the onset and at least two moras, are identical. These conditions pertain specifically to plural-singular relations in English. Tense relations can be recognized even if they involve more than one alternation (e.g. *left-leave, taught-teach*),[97] whereas in derivational morphology, base recognition can be thwarted by even a single alternation. Compare the causatives in (103a), which are clearly related to their base verbs, to the causatives in (103b), which exhibit a voicing alternation and are no longer related to their historical base:

(103)a. warm]$_{TV}$ → warm]$_A$ b.   clo[z]e]$_{TV}$ * → clo[s]e]$_A$
                                                                    'close'   'close'

         cool]$_{TV}$ → cool]$_A$ sa[v]e]$_{TV}$ * → sa[f]e]$_A$
                                                                    'save'   'safe'

         clean]$_{TV}$ → clean]$_A$ lo[z]e]$_{TV}$ * → lo[s]e]$_A$
                                                                    'lose'   'loose'

The claim that base recognition succeeds in (103a) is supported by the fact that the causatives can be paraphrased with reference to their etymological base (cf. (104a)). This is not the case for the causatives in (103b):

(104) a. to warm the meal   b.   to close the door
          'to make the meal warm'   *'to make the door close]$_A$'
          to cool the beer   to save time
          'to make the beer cool'   *'to make the time safe'
          to clean the pipe   to lose money
          'to make the pipe clean'   *'to make the money loose'

Base recognition in derivationally related words which exhibit voice alternations does not necessarily fail as is shown by the pairs in (105):

(105)   excú[s]$_N$ →   excú[z]$_V$
         abú[s]$_N$ →   abú[z]$_V$
         adví[s]$_N$ →   adví[z]$_V$
         belíe[f]$_N$ →   belíe[v]$_V$
         relíe[f]$_N$ →   relíe[v]$_V$

The claim that the nouns in (105) are related to their etymological base is supported not only by their meaning affinities but also by the evidence from noun to verb conversion. Generally, English nouns can be converted to verbs (cf. (106a)) unless they are relatable to a base (cf. (106b)):[98]

(106) a. to culture (*cult)   b.   *to failure (→ fail)

to pity   (*pit)   *to safety   (→ safe)
to mirror   (*mirr)   *to error   (→ err)

The fact that the nouns in (105) resist conversion to verbs is accordingly indicative of successful base recognition (cf.*to excú[s], *to abú[s], *to advî[s], *to belíe[f], *to relíe[f]). While there is clear evidence then that the nouns in (105) are analysed as deverbal in spite of the voice alternation it is less clear what role that alternation itself plays in the analysis. Significantly, base recognition appears to succeed also for the cognates in (107a), which exhibit isolated alternations, as is indicated by both the semantic and morphological properties of the nouns (i.e. resistance to verb conversion as shown in (107b)):

(107)a.   intén[t]$_N$ → intén[d]$_V$ b.   *to intén[t]
          offén[s]$_N$ → offén[d]$_V$ *to offén[s]
          respón[s]$_N$ → respón[d]$_V$ *to respón[s]
          appláu[z]$_N$ → appláu[d]$_V$ *to applau[z]
          decéi[t]$_N$ → decéi[v]$_V$ *to decei[t]

In view of the non-recurrence of the alternations in (107a) it appears that the conditions for base recognition must refer to the identity of phonological structure. Specifically, the data show that base recognition for iambic nouns succeeds if the cognates exhibit identical initial minimal words.[99] It is unclear why this condition is insufficient for the analysis of the causatives in (103b). Perhaps the phonological conditions for base recognition differ for abstract nouns and causative verbs. Also the difference in the number of syllables between the verbs in (103b) and the nouns in (105) could play a role. It is further conceivable that the markedness of iambic nouns in English alerts the hearer to the likely existence of a base.[100] What seems clear is that one and the same alternation can impede the analysis of some words but not others depending on the specific conditions for base recognition.

     To summarize, the data reviewed here suggest that the phonological conditions for base recognition are identity requirements which can be relaxed because of specific properties of the input word (e.g. inflectedness, markedness in phonological form). For words which lack those properties alternations will result in failed base recognition, regardless of how frequent the alternation is (cf. voice alternations in English fricatives in (101b) and (103b)). For words which have those properties base recognition can succeed regardless of how isolated the alternations are. (e.g. the pairs in (102a) and (107a)). None of those generalizations can be expressed in a synthesis model of morphology.

10. CONCLUSIONS AND OUTLOOK

The methodological basis of this description of English morphophonology is the limitation to native word formation. This limitation is motivated by the observation that there are separate conditions for morphological synthesis and analysis.

I have presented evidence that in English only glide- and vowel-initial suffixation exhibits phonologically conditioned gaps and allomorphy. I have argued that both types of effects are related in that they serve to satisfy constraints on output forms. The observation that phonologial effects in word formation depend on the initial segment of the suffix is explained by ranking constraints to the effect that onsetless syllables (or syllables with insufficient onsets) are integrated into the pword of the stem. The generalization is then that English suffixes exhibit phonological effects only if they are fused into one pword with their stem. This generalization suggests that in English, the pword constitutes the domain for phonological constraints in word formation, which is not true universally (cf. the German data discussed at the end of section 6).[101]

While the phonological effects exhibited by English suffixation can be described with reference to a relatively small number of independently motivated constraints there is clear evidence that there are no suffixes, not even homophonous suffixes, which show the same phonological effects. Unless one is willing to sweep those systematic differences under the rug (cf. the indiscrimate assignment of those suffixes to one or two levels in Lexical Phonology) it must be concluded that the constraint ordering differs for each suffix. The acquistion of English morphophonology amounts thus to acquiring a particular ordering of (innate) constraints for each affix.[102]

The phonological constraints on word formation apply at the phonemic level and can be divided into three groups: phonological constraints (PHON), identity constraints (IDENT), and M-PARSE. For each of the three types of phonological effects in word formation (see figure (9)) a constraint from one group is dominated by constraints from the other two groups, as is shown in table 108. Phonologically conditioned gaps are largely confined to derivational morphology which suggests that for inflectional suffixes the constraint M-PARSE is generally undominated.[103]

(108) a. non-canonical sound patterns   IDENT, M-PARSE >>PHON
       b. allomorphy   PHON, M-PARSE >> IDENT
       c. gaps   IDENT, PHON >> M-PARSE

The observation that there exist phonological effects in word formation which are clearly output-oriented raises the question of whether reference to output forms suffices to describe all such effects. The answer to this question depends to some extent on the linguist's bias. Consider for example the suffix *-ous*, which prefers trochaic stems (cf. section 8). For those who believe that all feet should be binary that restriction can only be expressed with reference to input forms. However, if one feels free to make use of the complete foot inventory established within traditional metrics, that restriction can be expressed as a requirement to yield dactylic feet in output forms. Recall that reference to dactyls in output forms is needed independently to capture the distribution of *-ery/-ry* or *-ence/-ency* (cf. section 5).[104] Similarly, the fact that the nominal suffix *-al* attaches only to iambic feet is expressable in terms of output forms, but only if one is willing to refer to amphibrachs.

Consider next a case of a seemingly arbitrary segmental restriction. The English glide-intial suffixes *-ion* and *-ure* attach only to stems ending in a coronal obstruent. Significantly only these obstruents allow the resulting formations to have less sonorous and therefore improved onsets, i.e. the obstruents š, ž, č and ǰ. That is, stem-final coronals are the only consonants which assimilate with palatal glides such that structure preservation, the constraint which prohibits complex onsets, and certain identity constraints are satisfied. The identity constraints in question require the features [+obstruent], [+coronal] and [+palatal] of the output to correspond to identical features in the input.[105]

Limiting reference to output constraints is desirable because it allows for a highly restrictive theory. A few predictions which would follow from such a theory are listed in (109) and (110):

(109)

	Possible gaps	Relevant constraints
a.	Suffixes which include a liquid L_i can resist attachment to a stem which contains L_i, but they cannot select such a stem.	There is a constraint $*L_iL_i$, but there is no constraint which re-quires that words contain identical liquids.
b.	Suffixes which consist of a sequence VC_i can resist attachment to a stem ending in C_i, but they cannot select such a stem.	There is a constraint SHELL, but there is no constraint which requires that a syllable nucleus be flanked by identical consonants (cf. Vennemann 1988).
c	Vowel-initial suffixes can resist attachment to a stem which ends in a consonant with high sonority but they cannot select such a stem.[106]	Syllable onsets are the more preferred the less sonorous they are (cf. Vennemann 1988).
d	Suffixes with initial stress can resist attachment to a stem which ends in a stressed syllable but they cannot select such a stem.	There is a constraint *CLASH, but there is no constraint which requires adjacent syllables to be stressed.

(110)

	Possible allomorphy rules	
a.	Identity violations may only result in the dissimilation but not in the assimilation of (non-adjacent) liquids.	see (109a)
b.	Identity violations may only result in the dissimilation but not in the assimilation of consonants which flank the nucleus	see (109b)
c	Identity violations may only result in a sonority decrease of a consonant in onset position.	see (109c)
d	Identity violations may only result in alternating stress but not in a stress clash.	see (109d)

By contrast, a theory which also allows for constraints on input forms in terms of phonological subcategorization frames entails none of the predictions above.

The question of whether those predictions hold universally and of whether all phonological effects in word formation can be expressed in terms of output constraints is of course an empirical issue in need of further investigation.[107] Clearly, the restriction to output constraints is theoretically interesting only insofar as those constraints are independently motivated and can be assumed to be universal.[108] To ensure independent motivation I propose to admit only those constraints which play a role in sound change.[109] This condition holds for all constraints discussed in this paper. Note finally that a strictly output-oriented description requires the abandonment of the widely accepted limitation to binary feet. Hopefully this conclusion will encourage the proponents of foot binarity to reexamine the empirical basis for their assumption.

NOTES

1   In this paper I develop several ideas presented in Raffelsiefen (1992), (1993), (1996). Some of the new proposals discussed here were first presented at the Annual Meeting of the Deutsche Gesellschaft Für Sprachwissenschaft in Düsseldorf in March 1997. I thank Geert Booij, George Smith, and two anonymous reviewers for helpful criticisms. Special thanks are due to Mike Brame for many hours of discussion and to Bruce Straub for proof-reading.
2   They do not necessarily appear exclusively in onset position because of ambisyllabicity. Specifically, consonants which are preceded by a [-consonantal] segment and followed by an unstressed vowel are ambisyllabic in American English, which is true regardless of the morphological structure of the word (cf. the examples *bu*[ɾ]*er* 'butter', *wri*[ɾ]*er*

'writer', where the flap indicates ambisyllabicity) (cf. Kahn 1976).

3   According to Kahn voiceless stops are always aspirated in syllable-initial position even if the following syllable is unstressed (cf. Kahn 1976: 41ff).

4   The stops /p/ and /t/ are unreleased in syllable final position if no obstruent precedes (cf. Kahn 1976: 48).

5   For some speakers the LOI (i.e. 'Law of Initials') is dominated by a phonological constraint which prohibits complex onsets in stressless syllables. Those speakers have different syllabifications for vowel- versus consonant-initial suffixes only in the pair *triple+oid - trip+like*, but not in the remaining pairs, which involve stressless suf-fixes.

6   The Law of Initials requires all prevocalic consonants to be syllabified as syllable onsets unless the clusters in question do not occur word-initially. Since the cluster *pl* does occur word-initially (cf. *plain, plum*) this cluster should be syllabified in onset position if a vowel follows.

7   To my knowledge the assumption that only vowel-initial or glide-initial suffixes are integrated into the pword of the stem is consistent with English syllable structure. Contradicting evidence is cited by Halle and Mohanan (1985), who posit a rule of *l*-resyllabification in compounds to account for their observation that the *l* constitutes the onset of the following syllable in the compound *seal office*, but not in the phrase *the seal offered a doughnut*. This rule does not appear to be part of standard British or American English. It is odd for a rule of resyllabification to be confined to one segment.

8   It is unclear if this suffix, which was originally an independent word, still constitutes a separate pword or should be represented as a clitic. Clearly, the suffix constitutes a foot. For more discussion of the prosodic structure of suffixed words see section 6.

9   Another term for identity constraint is 'output-output correspondence constraint'. Identity constraints hold only between independent words in English and are thus closely related to the notion of the cycle developed in Brame (1974).

10   The suffix *-acy*, for instance, requires the stress but not the wordfinal VC-string of the base to be preserved as is shown by the example in (7).

11   Perhaps identity effects w.r.t. syllable structure do not exist. In that case there should be no languages in which stem-final consonants followed by a vowel-initial suffix occur in coda position to satisfy identity w.r.t. the base. To resolve this issue it is necessary to establish criteria for distinguishing suffixation from compounding. Words like English *wide-eyed, cross-eyed, clear-eyed, bug-eyed* but also German *orkanartig* 'like a hurricane', *aalartig* 'like an eel', *wolkenartig* 'like clouds' are clearly compounds although for seman-tic reasons English *-eyed* or German *-artig* do not occur by themselves.

12   For universal constraints on syllable structure, see Vennemann (1988). The condi-tions on syllabification in American English are described by Kahn (1976).

13   Some of the data discussed here and their description in terms of affix-specific con-straint rankings have also been presented in Raffelsiefen (1996).

14   Cf. Liberman and Prince (1977).

15   The quality of the first vowel is based on the spelling of the word (for a discussion of this point see section 7).

16   To eliminate candidates like *giràffenéer*, which also satisfy both *CLASH and IDENT(S), M-PARSE must be dominated by an additional identity constraint which prohibits epen-thesis.

17   Relative prominence in the winner in (20) is determined by an independent phono-logical constraint which requires that tense high vowels in word-final syllables carry main

stress.

18   The OED lists roughly 1400 *-ize*-formations. The fact that among these entries there are perhaps twenty verbs which are based on words with final stress (including monosyllabic words) still leaves a statistically significant gap to be explained. These exceptions are usually characterized by low token frequency and are typically rejected by native speakers (e.g. *?concretize*, *?Marxize*). Considering the fact that English is commonly used by non-native speakers the occurrence of such miscoinages is remarkably low.

19   Similarly it is conceivable that *-ize* suffixation like *áptìze* should be considered ungrammatical even if all other suffixes were to freely violate the constraint *CLASH (cf. the suffix *-ee*).

20   The ungrammaticality of the nouns in (23b) cannot generally be explained by blocking since several verbs lack derived nominals (e.g. *ignore, remain, secure, deserve*), whereas others coexist with potential blockers (e.g. *adaptation, adaption; perturbation, perturbance, perturbancy; accusation, accusal*).

21   The only unclear case is the noun *indentation* which, however, has a corresponding form in French (i.e. French *indentation*).

22   Cf. the notion of correlative patterns discussed in section 7.

23   Following Chomsky and Halle (1968), Pater (1995) analyses the pretonic stress in words like *còndènsátion* as an identity effect with respect to the verb *condénse*. Granted that no nouns in *-ation* are actually derived from iambic verbs in English the existence of such systematic identity effects seems unlikely. In fact, the stress patterns of the nouns in question are predictable on the basis of their segmental structure, specifically on the basis of the sonority of the segment which closes the pretonic syllable. That is, stress is most stable if that syllable is closed by an obstruent (cf. *àdàptátion, èxpèctátion, tìcktàcktóe*), somewhat stable if it closed by a nasal (cf. *còndèmnátion~còndemnátion, còndènsátion~còndensátion*), least stable if it closed by /r/ (cf. *ìnformátion, pèrturbátion*), and impossible if the syllable is open (cf. *èxplanátion, dèrivátion*). Vowel height plays a role as well as stress is most stable for low vowels (*dèmàrkátion, chìmpànzée*).

While identity effects can generally not be established for any of the *-ation* nouns which happen to have iambic cognates in English the ungrammaticality of medial stress in words like *còmpensátion* cannot be explained on purely phonological grounds. This noun, however, is based on a verb ending in *-ate* (i.e. *cómpensàte*) which means that it can be formed natively. (The relevant rule of word formation involves the correlative pattern *Xate-Xation* discussed in section 7.) The ungrammatical medial stress in *còmpènsátion can accordingly be described by a constraint which requires stress identity w.r.t. its base *cómpensàte*. (This is not to deny that sporadically loanwords can be affected by identity effects as a result of successful base recognition (cf. section 9). For example, the vowel change in *ob*[ɛ]*sity* to *ob*[iy]*sity* is certainly an identity effect in relation to the adjective *obese*.)

24   The assumption that affixes can become productive only if there is a large set of potential bases which satisfy their specific syntactic and phonological constraints accounts also for the low productivity of the suffix *-ify* in comparison to *-ize*. That is because the suffix *-ify* starts with a stressless syllable and attaches to nouns or adjectives, which typically end in a stressless syllable. As a result *-ify* suffixation would typically violate either the constraint IDENT(S) (e.g. *randómifỳ-rándom) or the constraint *LAPSE, which prohibits adajcent unstressed syllables (e.g. *rándomifỳ*). It appears then that the potential productivity of suffixes is confined by their sound shape and the canonical sound

patterns of the syntactic category they subcategorize for.

In addition, the non-coronal consonant in the suffix *-ify* conceivably also contributes to its low productivity. In consonant-initial suffixes, which are insensitive to the phonological properties of the stem, non-coronal segments seem to generally impede productivity (cf. the low productivity of the nominal suffixes *-dom*, *-ship*, compared to their rival *-ness*)

25   The examples in (28a) are American English. In British English all nonlateral liquids in coda position have disappeared. The fact that liquids in onset position have never disappeared indicates that the constraint ONSET has consistently dominated the constraint *L_iL_i in all varieties of English.

26   Consider also the sound changes in the Romance languages shown in (i), all of which 'conspire' to satisfy the constraint *L_iL_i:

(i)   Latin: arbor 'tree' > Spanish: arbol 'tree' / Italian: albero 'tree'
        Latin: marmor 'marble' > Spanish: marmol 'marble' / Italian: marmo 'marble'

27   Verbs which exhibit *L_iL_i violations are typically based on nonverbs (cf. (ia)) or are onomatopoetic (cf. (ib)):

(i)a.   label (label$_N$ → label$_V$)   b.   lull
         level (level$_N$ → level$_V$)   roar
         belittle (be+little$_A$ → belittle$_V$)   murmur

28   Following common practice the term 'onset' will be used as an alternative expression for 'head' and refer to all segments which precede the nucleus within a syllable. Vennemann (1988) restricts the term 'onset' to the first segment within the head.

29   The observation that *L_iL_i-violations are worst when they occur within a syllable accounts for the fact that the allomorph *-ar* never appears when the base ends in an *r* (cf. *culture+al* → *cultural* (**culturar*))

30   Suffix-allomorphy is especially common when the output consists of a trochee with identical syllable onsets (e.g. *bulb+al* → *bulbar*, *valve+al* → *valvar*, etc).

31   Apparent counterexamples like *nuclear* are loanwords (cf. French *nucléaire*).

32   The fact that *l* was replaced not by *r* but by *n* in the English dialect words *sinable* and *nittle* indicates a higher-ranked preference for syllable onsets with low sonority (cf. Vennemann 1988).

33   The constraint SHELL is discussed in Vennemann (1988), who notes that SHELL-violations are worse if the syllable shell includes additional speech sounds. The constraint SHELL differs accordingly from the other syllable-based dissimilatory constraints in that it does not refer to identical syllable nodes.

34   For the suffix *-ous* SHELL-violations are sporadically avoided at the expense of other constraint violations. For example, the native coinage *gaseous*, which is based on *gas*, is pronounced either [gæšəs], thereby violating IDENT(C), or [gæsiəs], thereby violating the constraint which prohibits epenthesis.

35   The productivity of these suffixes is typically subject to semantic restrictions as well. The suffix *-eer*, for example, attaches most productively to nouns denoting weapons.

36   This generalization might be incorrect as those *-ify*-suffixations could also be derived without violating IDENT(S) from the nouns *humídity*, *rigídity*, *fluídity* by truncation. This

is clearly a possibility since for each *-ify*-suffixation the corresponding noun in *-ity* is attested earlier.

37   The fact that constraint satisfaction is achieved by truncation is remarkable since truncation implies a stronger violation of identity constraints than seems necessary. That is, the ONS_iONS_i-violation in **maximumize* could also have been avoided by modifying just a single feature (cf. *maximunize, maximubize*, etc.). Interestingly, truncation in English always affects a word-final VC_0 string (e.g. *-um, -on, -in, -is, -ate*).

38   The noun *evacuee*, which is related the verb *evacuate*, is not a counterexample to this claim since it is borrowed from French *évacué*: In English word formation, truncation does not apply in comparable verbs (cf. *evaluate+ee* → **evaluee, situate+ee* → **situee*). Cf. also truncation in *-ese₁*-suffixations as in *Lebanon+ese* → *Lebanese* versus *Pentagon+ese* → *Pentagonese, Aragon+ese* → *Aragonese*.

39   *Ese₁*-suffixation differs from *-ee* or *-ize* suffixation in that ONS_iONS_i-violations are generally preferred to gaps (cf. *Húnán+ése* → *Hùnanése*).

40   Recall that M-PARSE dominates *CLASH for the suffix *-ee* (cf. *kìssée, pàyée, thròwée*, etc.)

41   Marchand's claim that in the last two hundred years the suffix has only attached to stems ending in *-t* or *-d* is not correct (cf. Marchand 1969). Counter-examples listed in the OED include the formations *blithen, closen, coarsen, crispen, densen, grossen, largen, pinken, richen, steepen*. Perhaps it is significant, though, that none of these formations has gained currency.

42   The OED lists three counter-examples to the gap in (53c): *dullen, palen, dimmen*. However, each of these verbs is described as 'rare' and is documented with only one citation.

43   The implicational relations considered here are also the subject of Prince and Smolensky's formal analysis of sonority preferences within syllables (cf. Prince and Smolensky 1993: 140f). Unfortunately those authors fail to distinguish syllable onsets and syllable codas when discussing those preferences, but just refer to syllable margins.

44   Vennemann's precise formulation is that a syllable head is the more preferred the greater the Consonantal Strength of its onset and that a syllable coda is the more preferred the less the Consonantal Strength of its offset, where the term 'onset' refers to the first speech sound in the syllable head and the term 'offset' refers to the last speech sound in the syllable coda (cf. Vennemann 1988: 13, 21). These preferences are manifested both in structure-preserving historical changes such as the spirantization of the glide [w] in German (cf. [w]*all* > [v]*all*) and in allophonic processes such as the aspiration of voiceless stops in onset position in English compared to their unreleasedness in offset position (cf. Vennemann (1988: 13ff)).

45   Verbs like *soften, hasten, fasten*, etc. may suggest that the constraint IDENT needs to be modified to the effect that only the first post-vocalic consonant in the base must be preserved. However, new coinages like *swif[t]en* argue against such a modification. Alternations in cognates like *soften-soft* are best analysed as the result of the historical rule of *t*-loss between a fricative and a syllabic sonorant (cf. *of[t]en* > *of[Ø]en, cas[t]le* > *cas[Ø]le*), which is irrelevant for describing constraints on *-en*-suffixation.

46   The initial syllable in each noun in (59a) is bimoraic while the initial syllable in each noun in (59b) is monomoraic. This account presupposes that the velar glide in *G*[ow]*a* is syllabified in onset position and hence does not contribute to syllable weight. For the suffix *-ese₂*, hiatus is avoided by avoiding suffixation altogether.

47   Burzio's description of English stress differs from other descriptions in that he rejects the notion of stress-neutrality, which also applies to consonant-initial suffixes. The relevant data are discussed in section 8.2.

48   Clearly, vowel 'insertion' in (64) could not be motivated on metrical grounds since the vowel appears regardless of the stress contour of the base. For illustration consider native -(i)cide derivations such as *hérbicìde* (cf. *herb*), *parénticìde* (cf. *párent*), *insécticìde* (cf. *ínsèct*), *èlefánticìde* (cf. *élephant*), *pàrasíticìde* (cf. *párasìte*).

49   Citing the example *beautiful* Halle and Mohanan (1985: 67) claim that the rule of stem-final tensing does not apply before the suffix -*ful*, giving rise to the alternation *beaut*[i]-*beaut*[ə]*ful*. However, according to both Jones and Gimson (1977) and Kenyon and Knott (1944) the alternation in question is not typical for the suffix -*ful* (cf. the pairs transcribed with identical vowels like *fanc*[ɪ]-*fanc*[ɪ]*ful*, *merc*[ɪ]-*merc*[ɪ]*ful*, *plent*[ɪ]-*plent*[ɪ]*ful*, *dut*[ɪ]-*dut*[ɪ]*ful*). The fact that *beautiful* is the only -*ful*-suffixation which is transcribed with a stem-final schwa in both dictionaries is certainly due to the high frequency of the adjective *beautiful* compared to those other -*ful* derivations.

50   There is some evidence that the consonant-initial suffixes originally constituted separate pwords (cf. section 6). It is not always clear if the fusions in (66a) result from the loss of internal pword boundaries as is illustrated in (66b), or if they occurred after the decay of the pwords which historically dominated the suffixes and hence involve the prosodic integration of a clitic as is presumed in (66a).

51   As is shown by these examples the question of which palatal fricative or affricate is yielded by suffixation is subject to variation. The suffix -*ion*, which is almost never used in native word formation, shows the same phonological effects (e.g. *òbsoléte+ion* → (òbsolétion)$_{(\omega)}$).

52   Sequences consisting of an alveolar obstruent and a palatal glide necessarily involve pword boundaries (cf. *brigh*[t][y]*ellow*, *cour*[t][y]*ard*).

53   The words *heavenward* and *netherward* are exceptions to this generalization.

54   There is an alternative explanation for *w*-loss in cases where the schwa historically corresponds to a round vowel. That is, *w* may have disappeared before the vowel reduced to schwa due to a constraint against clusters consisting of round glides and round vowels (e.g. [sw]*ord* > [s]*ord*, [tw]*o* > [t]*o*).

55   Since its historical base became obsolete (i.e. †*awke*) the adjective *awkward* is generally perceived as a simplex. Unfortunately there are very few simplexes which allow one to study the strictly phonological constraints on the syllabification of the relevant clusters in unstressed syllables.

56   The fact that the suffix *ry/-ery* never attaches to words ending in -*r* indicates that the constraint against identical syllable nodes in adjacent syllables dominates M-PARSE. The suffix also fails to attach to words ending in -*y*, which indicates a constraint against identical syllable nuclei in adjacent syllables (e.g. **carryry*, **pityry*, **envyry*).

57   The preference for dactyls also accounts for the fact that words like *áffluency*, *cómpetency*, *pértinency*, *cónsequency*, etc. have become obsolete in English whereas words like *décency*, *úrgency*, etc. persist.

58   Wiese claims that the complex words in (73) are based on participles. However, neither the suffix -*ness* nor the suffix -*ly* attach to participles as is shown by the unacceptability of words like **boughtness*, **talkedness*, **bakedly*, **eatenly*, etc. The claim that the suffixes -*ness* and -*ly* are based on adjectives in (73) is supported by the facts that the respective bases can appear in prenominal position (e.g. *the distressed teacher* vs.

the bought car) and that they are gradable (*very distressed*, *quite distressed* vs. *very bought*, *quite bought*).

59   The alternations in (73) have come into existence because schwa loss in trochees was not phonologically conditioned but rather involved a series of analogical changes. Those changes were initiated by the (phonologically conditioned) schwa loss in dactyls (cf. Luick 1964: 508ff), which led to alternations in the form of the participle suffix (e.g. *detérmin*+[Ø]d versus *confús*+[ə]d). The observation that schwa subsequently disappeared in that suffix (unless its loss would have resulted in a cluster of homorganic stops (*guard*[ə]d *> *guard*[Ø]d), but not in phonologically similar endings (e.g. *wick*[ə]d, *nak*[ə]d, *wretch*[ə]d, *dogg*[ə]d), indicates the analogical conditioning of schwa loss in trochaic participles. This conditioning did not apply in adjectives, which were historically derived from participles, which led to the alternations in (i).

(i)   a.   diffus[Ø]d$_{PART}$ - diffus[ə]d$_A$ (> diffus[Ø]d$_A$)
           prepar[Ø]d$_{PART}$ - prepar[ə]d$_A$ (> prepar[Ø]d$_A$
           distress[Ø]d$_{PART}$ - distress[ə]d$_A$ (> distress[Ø]d$_A$)
      b.   suppos[Ø]d]$_{PART}$ - suppos[ə]d]$_A$
           alleg[Ø]d]$_{PART}$ - alleg[ə]d]$_A$
           learn[Ø]d]$_{PART}$ - learn[ə]d]$_A$

The data in (ia) illustrate the subsequent loss of the schwa in the adjectives which is due to analogical leveling w.r.t. the schwaless participles or perhaps to innovative conversions based on such participles. (Adjectival forms like *diffus*[ə]d, *prepar*[ə]d, *distress*[ə]d are marked as 'poetic' in the OED). Adjectives in which the schwa has remained are typically lexicalized as is illustrated in (ib). The alternations shown in (73) indicate that the leveling illustrated in (ia) did not simultaneously affect all derivations based on the adjectives.

60   Some speakers still prefer the fossilized forms with schwa. The judgements are generally not very clear since none of these words are used in colloquial English.

61   The native speakers I have consulted have expressed an intuition that the suffix in those expressions is *-edness*. Conceivably, such a fused suffix has developed by reanalysis for those speakers (cf. the German suffix *-igkeit*) and can be used to coin new words. The only attested case is the noun *well-formedness* (and, by analogy, *ill-formedness*), which like *markedness* is also linguistics jargon according to the OED. The suffix *-edness* is clearly not part of ordinary English. There is no evidence for a reanalysed fused suffix *-edly*.

62   In a detailed study Bauer (1992) concludes that *-ly*-suffixation to adjectives ending in *-ly* is of limited productivity. He also argues that in these cases productivity is affected more strongly by the morphological than the phonological structure of the base.

63   This generalisation does not apply to the suffix *-wise*, which also starts with a glide. The suffix *-wise* is not integrated into the pword of the stem as is shown by LOI violations in words like *cloc*[k.w]*ise* (cf. in[.kw]*ire* 'inquire'). The suffix *-wise* was originally an independent word which like other so-called 'semi-suffixes' appears to still constitute a separate pword (cf. Marchand 1969: 358).

64   Of course, it is also conceivable that the constraint M-PARSE dominates *CLASH for the suffix *-like*, but not for *-ize*. That account misses a generalization, however, since all consonant-initial suffixes freely violate *CLASH whereas all vowel-initial suffixes except for

-ee avoid vioations of *CLASH.

65   The function of pwords as domain for syllabification is expressed by the following two constraints, which align the edges of pwords with syllable boundaries (cf. also the discussion of the LOI violations discussed in section 2 (cf. (rump.)$_\omega$*less*, not *(rum.p)$_\omega$*less*)):

(i)   ALIGN PWORD
        Align(Pword, L, σ, L)
        Align(Pword, R, σ, R)

The constraint ALIGN PWORD follows from the Prosodic Hierarchy and rules out candidates like (stíy.l)$_\omega$*ize*. The question of whether and under what conditions the Prosodic Hierarchy is violable in principle is a matter of debate. For example, how strong is the evidence for feet which span pword boundaries or for resyllabification across pword boundaries and what are the consequences for prosodic representation? In English the Prosodic Hierarchy consistently holds in the lexicon. Assuming that ALIGN PWORD implies just that each segment within a pword must be associated with a syllable within that pword this constraint is also not violated by the ambisyllabicity resulting from the association of pword-final consonants with the syllable of a following vowel-initial word (cf. note 76).

66   A similar issue arises for Nespor and Vogel's (1986) analysis of Italian prefixes. The authors propose that all consonant-final prefixes are integrated into the pword of the stem. This analysis suggests that the constraint ONSET or the constraint NOCODA, which prohibits segments in the syllable coda, dominate a constraint which aligns the right edge of a prefix with the left edge of a pword. However, when attaching to consonant-initial stems the integration of consonant-final prefixes never serves to satisfy ONSET and in many cases also fails to satisfy NOCODA (e.g. *com+piacere* 'please', *sub+dolo* 'underhand') which raises the question of how integration of consonant-final prefixes can be formally described in such cases. In Vogel's (1994) analysis of the prosodic structure of Italian prefixes the distinction between consonants and vowels plays no role (cf. also Peperkamp 1997).

76   The only German consonant-initial suffixes which have undergone vowel reduction and thus do not constitute separate pwords are *-chen* and *-sel*. These exceptions are perhaps not accidental. The suffix *-chen* differs from other German suffixes in that its initial consonant is a palatal fricative, which is not allowed in word-initial position. The constraint in question is violated only in names and recent loanwords in northern standard NHG (e.g. *China* 'China', *Chemnitz* 'Chemnitz', *Chemie* 'chemistry'). Plausibly, as a result of the violation of this phonotactic constraint the suffix *-chen* cannot be parsed as a pword. The suffix *-sel* is a reduced variant of the suffix *-sal* (i.e. [zaːl]), which does constitute a pword. Some conditions under which reduction took place are discussed in Wilmanns (1896: 272). The suffixes *-chen* and *-sel* are perhaps best represented as clitics (cf. the discussion of the English consonant-initial suffixes at the end of section 6).

68   As a result of this constraint there are variant pronunciations like *máy*[hè]*m* or *máy*[ə]*m*, but not **máy*[hə]*m*. The constraint against the sequence [hə] also accounts for the stability of penultimate stress in words like *inhérent, cohérent, abhórrent* (cf. *réferent, ígnorant, pértinent*) and the stability of final stress in words like *cóhòrt* (cf. *cóncert, yógurt, cómfort*). Interestingly the sequence [hə] is allowed in pword-initial position in

English (cf. ([hə]mogenous)$_\omega$ 'homogenous', ([hə]lucinate)$_\omega$ 'hallucinate'. Failure of vowel reduction in the suffix -*hood* thus supports the claim that consonant-initial suffixes are not pwords.

69   If followed by a non-coronal obstruent vowels reduce only if they are preceded by a stressed light syllable (e.g. [ǽrəb]- [éyrǽb] 'Arab', [bíšəp] 'bishop'- [pársnìp] 'parsnip'). The suffix -*ship* is never preceded by a light syllable with the result that the vowel cannot reduce.

70   Conceivably, these two suffixes differ from other English consonant-initial suffixes in that they are still analysed as a separate pword. Both -*like* and -*wise* suffixation originated historically as compounding whose respective rightmost member continue to exist as independent words. Also the meaning of those words can still be recognized in the suffixes -*like* and -*wise*, respectively. These properties distinguish the suffixes -*like* and -*wise* from other English consonant-initial suffixes.

71   The claim that the prosodic integration of clitics can depend on the question of whether they have an onset is also supported by the Dutch consonant-initial third person singular pronoun *hij* [hɛi], which differs from the equivalent vowel-initial pronoun *ie* [i] in that it is not integrated into the pword of its (preceding) host (cf. Booij and Lieber 1993).

72   The structures in (82) do not conform to the Strict Layer Hypothesis proposed in Nespor and Vogel (1986) since prosodic categories are not necessarily dominated by categories on the next higher level. Evidence against that version of the Strict Layer Hypothesis is discussed in Ladd (1986, 1996), Vogel (1994), Selkirk (1995), Peperkamp (1997).

73   The fact that consonant-initial suffixation in English typically originated as compounding indicates that the reduction exhibited by the suffixes in (81), (82) is due to a successive decay of prosodic structures: the decay of the pword and subsequently the decay of the foot. It appears that the German cognates of the consonant-initial suffixes in (81) continue to be dominated by pwords.

74   Of course a foot which is dominated by a pword can also be unstable. However in such cases instability is governed by independent conditions which determine the wellformedness of word-internal stress contours (cf. the loss of stress due to the constraint *CLASH illustrated in (11b)).

75   This is because consonant-initial suffixes historically started out as the righthand member of compounds, which exhibited a strong-weak stress pattern (cf. (árm)$_\omega$(chàir)$_\omega$, (lámp)$_\omega$(pòst)$_\omega$, etc.). The decay of the prosodic structure in the suffix thus started out with the loss of the pword category, with the subsequent loss of the foot category in English. The decay of prosodic structure always presupposes that the category in question is labeled weak. Cf. also note 81 for the German data.

76   It is unclear whether or not ambisyllabicity of pword-final consonants must be considered a violation of the Prosodic Hierarchy on the phonetic level (cf. note 65). At any rate the association of such consonants with the coda before a stressed vowel is clearly indicative of an intervening pword boundary. Also this type of Prosodic Hierarchy violation satisfies the condition that syllabification rules are only structure-building, but may not change structure (cf. Steriade 1982). None of these properties hold for phonetic resyllabification across pword boundaries as proposed in Nespor and Vogel (1986), Kang (1992), Hannahs (1995).

77   The effect in question occurs also across word boundaries in phrases like [hɪræl] 'hit

A1'.

78   I leave open the question of how to represent the highest node in compounds.

79   The possibility that the *t* is syllabified exclusively in onset position and also occupies the final position in the pword is ruled out by the Prosodic Hierarchy (cf. also notes 65 and 76).

80   Stress neutrality in *-ize* suffixation is represented by ranking IDENT(S) higher than the constraint *Lapse, which prohibits sequences of stressless syllables.

81   Cf. *-lich*-suffixations like *tä*[k.l]*ich* 'daily', in which the syllable boundary clearly precedes the suffix although the cluster *kl* is a wellformed syllable onset in German. The evidence from stress entirely correlates with the evidence from syllabi-fication and shows that consonant-initial suffixes are not integrated into the pword of the stem. Stress often falls on the word-final syllable in German (e.g. *radikál* 'radical', *Elefánt* 'elephant', *Seminár* 'seminar'), but this is never the case when the final syllable belongs to a consonant-initial suffix (i.e. *entzíffer+bàr* 'decipherable', *Mútter+schàft* 'motherhood', *áufmerk+sàm* 'attentive', *Müh+sàl* 'tribulation'). In German the stress-pattern of words with consonant-initial suffixes corresponds thus to the stress pattern of compounds (i.e. strong weak), which further supports the claim that such suffixes usually form separate pwords in German.

82   The relevant constraint is satisfied by '-*el*-insertion' (e.g. *Dách+chen* 'roof'- *Dächelchen* 'little roof').

83   According to the Prosodic Hierarchy, which requires that feet are properly contained within pwords, consonant-initial suffixes which are not integrated into the pword of the stem cannot exhibit stress-related phonological effects. Specifically such suffixes cannot be associated with output constraints on foot structure where the foot includes material from both the stem and the suffix. A putative counter-example to this generalization is cited by Féry (1997), who claims that *-chen* suffixation favors final trochees in the output forms. The evidence for this claim are regular truncations in *-chen* suffixation like *Ófen+chen* → *Öfchen* 'little stove', *Áffe+chen* → *Äffchen* 'little monkey'. However, the fact that only the string *-ən*, but not *-əl* or *-ər*, delete indicates that truncation is motivated not by metrical constraints but by rhyme dissimilation here. There are even cases of regular *-əl*-insertion to avoid clusters of velar fricatives in output forms (cf. the preceding note). Truncation of word-final schwa as in *Áffe+chen* → *Äffchen* 'little monkey' is not motivated by a preference for trochees either as it also applies in compounds like *Auge+Apfel* → *Áugàpfel* 'eye apple', *Birne+Baum* → *Bírnbàum* pear tree', *Erde+Beben* → *Érdbèben* 'earth quake', etc.

84   The level in question corresponds roughly to the output of the lexicon in Lexical Phonology. Clearly the relevant representations must include word stress in English, but not necessarily syllable structure, which may account for the absence of identity effects in syllable structure (cf. the discussion in section 3).

85   The fact that intensive *s* never attaches to words with an initial fricative reflects an OCP constraint against fricative clusters. The absence of *s*-prefixations based on vowel-initial words is discussed in note 107.

86   To rule out the form *[zb]*ash* the constraint AGREE VOICE could be replaced by a constraint which requires that all obstruent clusters are voiceless. The domain of that constraint is the syllable as is shown by the occurrence of heterosyllabic voiced obstruent clusters (cf. *le*[zb]*ian*). As was noted by Kahn (1976) English words which include tautosyllabic voiced clusters are always bimorphemic (e.g. *le*[gz] 'legs', *bi*[dz] 'bids'). The oc-

currence of such voiced clusters therefore indicate that identity constraints dominate the constraint which requires that all obstruent clusters are voiceless.

87   Are there counter-examples to the condition that identity constraints can only affect distinctive features? In her analysis of truncated forms like English [lær] 'Lar' from [læ.ri] 'Larry', Benua (1995) argues that identity effects can also pertain to 'allophonic properties' of words. Generally the vowels [æ] and [ɑ] are in complementary distribution before [r]. The vowel [æ] appears before heterosyllabic [r] (e.g. [kæ.ri] 'carry') and [ɑ] appears before tautosyllabic [r] (e.g. [kɑr] 'car'). The appearance of [æ] rather than [ɑ] before tautosyllabic [r] in the truncated form is accordingly clearly an identity effect. However, the question not asked by Benua is whether or not this identity effect is possible only in in case the relevant vowels do contrast in other environments (e.g. [kæm] 'cam' vs. [kɑm] 'calm'). If such a correlation existed the truncation data would be unproblematic because the identity constraints would pertain to phonemic representations. If not it should be investigated whether or not phonetic identity effects are found only in truncation and if so why truncation differs from other word formation rules.

88   Additional examples are X[éyšən]-X[èyt], X[əfəkéyšən]-X[əfày], X[əzéyšən]-X[àyz], X[ǽləti]-X[əl]. Significantly, the notion of subcategorization plays no role in word formation based on correlative patterns. Such formations should therefore not be cited as evidence in support of restrictions on input forms (cf. section 10).

89   As was shown in section 4.1. an adequate description of the systematic differences between the phonologically similar suffixes -eer, -ese₁, and -ee alone would call for the positing of three distinct levels which precede the 'neutral' level. Note further that the suffixes which exhibit the same stress-related effects as -eer differ in other phonological effects. To account for these differences additional levels would have to be posited. In fact, an adequate description of the systematic aspects of English morphophonology would require a separate level for each vowel-initial suffix in addition to a level for all consonant-initial suffixes.

90   Cf. LOI violations in words like *rum*[p.l]*ess*, which consist of a single foot according to Burzio.

91   Cf. Ross (1972) for a critical discussion of the abstractness in Chomsky and Halle's (1968) description of English stress.

92   Actually, reference to any of these abstractions does not allow for a description of the systematic differences in the stress patterns between -ee, -eer, and -ese affixation. Burzio claims that such 'auto-stressed' suffixes are exceptional in that it is not possible to account for their stress behavior on the basis of their phonological form. By contrast, I have argued that the suffixes -eer and -ese are similar to other English suffixes in that they avoid violations of the constraint *CLASH.

93   Perhaps, the low productivity of the suffixes -ful, -dom, or -some is partially due to the labial consonants (cf. note 24). The fact that -less is much more productive than -ful appears to be due also to semantics. For example, the existence of *pilotless* but not **pilotful aircraft*, *ticketless* but not **ticketful travel* is apparently due to semantic rather than phonological restrictions on -ful-suffixation contrary to Burzio's analysis.

94   The same explanation applies to -hood suffixation, which is also rarely based on dactyls, although that suffix can constitute a separate foot on Burzio's account.

95   The observation that semantic stability in the relation between cognates is determined by phonological identity conditions constitutes the basis for the morphological analysis model developed in Raffelsiefen (1993, 1998). Semantic stability is taken to in-

dicate successful base recognition, because of the assumption that each word must be interpreted in terms of its (recognized) base. The phonological determination of semantic stability suggests that base recognition proceeds in two stages. First, for a word A base candidates are generated on the basis of strictly phonological criteria and second these candidates are evaluated w.r.t. their semantic compatibility with the context in which A was encountered. If a base B is recognized for a word A, then A is interpreted in terms of B with the consequence that the words show strong semantic similarities. If base recognition fails a word is interpreted only w.r.t. the context in which it has been encountered with the consequence that the semantic relationship to its etymological base is prone to destabilize.

96   For more discussion and additional examples, see Raffelsiefen (1998).

97   While the conditions for the recognition of tense relations are clearly looser than the conditions on the recognition of plural-singular pairs, onset identity is probably required. The evidence is that tense relations destabilized whenever the onsets became nonidentical (cf. the alternation in the pair [r]*ought**→ [w]*ork*, which arose because metathesis 'fed' w-deletion before *r* in *wrought*). Unfortunately, the evidence is not conclusive since onset alternations are rare in English.

98   For a different account of noun to verb conversion in terms of affix classes see Kiparsky (1982). None of the generalizations discussed below are captured by Kiparsky's analysis.

99   Provided that the initial syllables in those words have reduced vowels it is precisely the respective last consonant which can be omitted without making the words unpronounceable in English (i.e. without violating phonological wellformedness conditions in pwords).

100   The claim that the phonological conditions for base recognition are relaxed if a word exhibits phonological properties which signal to the hearer that the word is derived is also supported by the data in (i):

(i)a. growth → grow   b.health *→ heal   c. breadth → broad
    flight → fly   stealth *→ steal   depth → deep
    height → high   filth *→ foul   width → wide
    truth → true   dearth *→ dear   length → long
    warmth → warm   birth *→ bear   strength → strong

The relatedness of the cognates in (ia), which show no alternations, is systematically recognized as is shown by the stability of the meaning relations. The cognates in (ib) and (ic) have developed vowel alternations, because the stem vowel is followed by two consonants in the suffixed words, but by a single consonant in the corresponding bases. Due to the vowel alternations base recognition fails in the pairs in (ib), which has led to semantic drift. The systematic recognition of the relatedness in the pairs in (ic), which also exhibit vowel alternations, is due to the violations of sonority sequencing exhibited by the final clusters. These violations alert the hearer to the morphological complexity of the nouns with the result that the phonological conditions for base recognition are relaxed to the effect that vowel identity is not required (cf. Raffelsiefen 1998).

101   The generalisation that phonological effects in English word formation occur only within pwords is not entirely true for prefixation. Specifically, the final consonant in the prefix *iN-* assimilates to the stem-initial sonorant or stop across pword-boundaries. There

is clear evidence that *iN-* is not integrated into the pword of the stem as is shown in Raffelsiefen (1993: 97ff). There it is proposed to account for assimilation in terms of not the prosodic but rather the segmental representation of that prefix.

102 Booij (1998) rejects affix-specific constraint rankings because he considers such a grammar implausible from the point of view of language acquisition. However, assuming that constraints are innate and given that the number of both affixes and the constraints associated with each affix is rather small learnability might not pose a problem. As is shown in this paper the empirical evidence for affix-specific constraint rankings in English is rather strong.

103 Inflectional affixes which exhibit phonologically conditioned gaps are rare but they do exist. In Swedish there is an agreement suffix *-t* which marks neuter adjectives. This suffix does not attach to adjectives which end in a long voiced alveolar stop as is illustrated in (id). The forms in question are avoided altogether according to Norstedts Stora Svenska Ordbok (1988).

(i)	a.	en söt flicka	'a sweet girl'	ett sött barn	'a sweet child'
	b.	en trött flicka	'a tired girl'	ett trött barn	'a tired child'
	c.	en glad flicka	'a happy girl'	ett glatt barn	'a happy child'
	d.	en rädd flicka	'a fearful girl'	Ø	('a fearful child')

The insight that the gap in question requires reference to constraints rather than rules was first expressed in Eliasson (1981).

104 If dactyls were disallowed one would have to posit prosodic subcategorization frames to the effect that the disyllabic suffix *-ery* attaches to monosyllabic stems (cf. *bríb+ery*, *róbb+ery*, etc) whereas the monosyllabic suffix *-ry* attaches to disyllabic stems (cf. *ríval+ry*, *rével+ry*, etc). Such an approach would obviously fail to express the relevant generalization.

105 The features [+obstruent] and [+coronal] are matched by the corresponding feature values in the stem-final consonant. The feature [+palatal] is matched by the corresponding value in the affix-initial glide.

106 According to Booij (1998) the Dutch suffix *-aar* occurs after stems which end in schwa followed by /r,l,n/, which in fact are the most sonorous consonants according to Zwicky (1972). However, the segmental restriction to those sonorants presumably just follows from the restriction to stems which end in schwa syllables since with few exceptions no consonants other than /r,l,n/ follow schwa in word-final position. That is, in terms of output forms the stressed suffix *-aar* is associated with both *CLASH and IDENT(S), but not with a constraint on the sonority of syllable onsets.

107 A particularly problematic case for output constraints is the rule of negative *s*-prefixation in Italian. In general the prefix attaches as long as the resulting cluster does not violate Italian phonotactics (cf. Muljacic 1969) and seems thus a prime example for output constraints (cf. (ia) versus (ib)). However, the prefix also fails to attach to vowel-initial stems as is illustrated in (ic). The examples in (i) are adopted from Scalise (1984: 48):

(i)a.	fortunato - sfortunato	b.sano - *ssano	c. umano - *sumano
	'lucky' 'unlucky'	'healthy'	'human'
	leale - sleale	sensibile - *ssensibile	onesto - *sonesto
	'loyal' 'disloyal'	'sensitive'	'honest'

gradevole - sgradevole   sicuro - *ssicuro   educato - *seducato
'pleasant' 'unpleasant'   'secure'   'well-mannere'

The gap in (ic) is hardly arbitrary since the same restriction applies to intensive *s*-prefix-
ations in English. What is wrong with attaching a single consonant to a vowel- initial
stem? Intuitively, the problem is that such a consonant would be somehow 'pre-empted' by
its phonological function, i.e. to serve as a syllable onset, and therefore could no longer
function as a morphological marker. On this view the explanation of the gap is
output-oriented but it is unclear how the constraint in question should be formulated.
[108] Assuming that the constraints in (109) are innate the relevant phonological effects
are expected to occur cross-linguistically. For example the constraint $*L_iL_i$ is manifested
in phonological effects in many languages which are not genetically related to English.
The Khalkha-Mongolian suffix *-u:r* denotes tools (e.g. *xana* 'to bleed'-*xanu:r* 'lancet', *ölgö*
'to hang up'-*ölgü:r* 'knot'. When the base contains an *r* the suffix is *-u:l* instead (e.g. *bari*
'to grasp'-*bar^{i}u:l* 'handle') (cf. Poppe 1951: 33). The Georgian suffix *-ur* derives adjectives
from nouns (e.g. *xalxi* 'people'-*xalxuri* 'popular', *jaǧli* 'dog'-*jaǧluri* 'canine'). When the
base contains an *r*, the suffix is *-ul* instead (e.g. *gmiri* 'hero'-*gmiruli* 'heroic') (cf. Aronson
1982: 95). The Lezgian suffix *-ra* marks the oblique stem (e.g. *lam* 'donkey'-*lamra*, *luk'*
'slave'-*luk'ra*). The *r* is not preserved in a stem-final cluster *r*C (e.g. *werč* 'hen'-*wečra*) (cf.
Haspelmath 1993: 63, 77).
[109] This restriction is inspired by Vennemann's preference laws for syllable structure
which are largely motivated by historical sound change (cf. Vennemann 1988).

REFERENCES

Aronoff, M. and S.N. Sridhar. 1983. "Morphological Levels in English and Kannada; or
    Atarizing Reagan". In J. Richardson, M. Marks and A. Chuckerman (eds), *Papers from
    the Parasession on the Interplay of Phonology, Morphology and Syntax*. Chicago:
    Chicago Linguistics Society, 3-16.
Aronson, H. I. 1982. *Georgian. A Reading Grammar*. Columbus Ohio: Slavica Publishers,
    Inc.
Bauer, L. 1992. "Scalar Productivity and *-lily* Adverbs". In G. Booij and J. van Marle
    (eds), *Yearbook of Morphology 1991*. Dordrecht: Kluwer Academic Publishers, 185-
    191.
Benua, L. 1995. "Identity Effects in Morphological Truncation". In J. Beckman, S.
    Urbanczyck and L. Walsh (eds), *Papers in Optimality Theory*. University of
    Massachusetts Occasional Papers in Linguistics 18. Graduate Linguistics Student
    Association, Amherst, Massachusetts, 77-136.
Booij, G. 1985. "Coordination Reduction in Complex Words: a Case for Prosodic Phono-
    logy". In H. van der Hulst and N. Smith (eds), *Advances in Nonlinear Phonology*.
    Dordrecht: Foris, 143-159.
Booij, G. 1998. "Phonological Output Constraints in Morphology". In W. Kehrein and R.
    Wiese (eds), *Phonology and Morphology of the Germanic languages*. Tübingen:
    Niemeyer, 141-163.
Booij, G. & R. Lieber. 1993. "On the Simultaneity of Morphological and Prosodic Struc-
    ture". In S. Hargus and E. Kaisse (eds), *Studies in Lexical Phonology*. San Diego:

Academic Press, 34-44.

Brame, M. 1974. "The Cycle in phonology: Stress in Palestinian, Maltese and Spanish". *Linguistic Inquiry* 5, 39-60.

Burzio, L. 1994. *Principles of English stress.* Cambridge: Cambridge University Press.

Chomsky, N. and M. Halle. 1968. *The Sound Pattern of English.* New York: Harper and Row.

Drosdowski , G. (ed.). 1990. *Duden Aussprachewörterbuch: Wörterbuch der deutschen Standardaussprache.* Mannheim, Wien, Zürich: Dudenverlag.

Eliasson, S. 1981. "Analytic vs. Synthetic Aspects of Phonological Structure". In D.L. Goyvaerts (ed.), *Phonology in the 1980's.* Ghent: E. Story-Scientia, 483-524.

Féry, C. 1997. "Uni und Studis: die besten Wörter des Deutschen". *Linguistische Berichte* 172, 461-489.

Fidelholtz, J. 1967. *English Vowel Reduction.* Ms. Cambridge: M.I.T.

Fudge, E. 1984. *English Word-stress.* London: George Allen and Unwin.

Halle, M. and K.P. Mohanan. 1985. "Segmental Phonology of Modern English". *Linguistic Inquiry* 16, 57-116.

Hannahs, S. 1995. "The Phonological Word in French". *Linguistics* 33, 1125-1144.

Haspelmath, M. 1993. *A Grammar of Lezgian.* Berlin; New York: Mouton de Gruyter

Inkelas, S. 1990. *Prosodic Constituency in the Lexicon.* Doctoral dissertation, Stanford University 1989. (Reprinted by Garland, New York)

Jones, D. and A.C. Gimson. 1977. *Everyman's English Pronouncing Dictionary.* Fourteenth ed.. London, Melbourne and Toronto: J.M. Dent and Sons Ltd.

Kahn, D. 1976. *Syllable-based Generalizations in English Phonology.* New York: Garland Press.

Kang, O. 1992. *Korean Prosodic Phonology.* Doctoral dissertation, University of Washington.

Kenyon, J.S. and T.A. Knott. 1944. *A Pronouncing Dictionary of American English.* Springfield, MA: Merriam.

Kiparsky, P. 1982. "Lexical Morphology and Phonology". In I. Yang (ed.), *Linguistics in the Morning Calm.* Seoul: Hanshin, 3-91.

Ladd, R. (1986) "Intonational Phrasing: The Case for Recursive Prosodic Structure". *Phonology Yearbook* 3, 311-340.

Ladd, R. 1996. *Intonational Phonology.* Cambridge: Cambridge University Press.

Libermann, M and A. Prince. 1977. "On Stress and Linguistic Rhythm". *Linguistic Inquiry* 8, 249-336.

Luick, K. 1964. *Historische Grammatik der Englischen Sprache.* Oxford: Basil Blackwell. (Originally published between 1914 and 1940 by Bernhard Tauchnitz Verlag, Stuttgart.)

Marchand, H. 1969. *The Categories and Types of Present-day English Word Formation.* Second ed. München: Beck.

McCarthy, J. J. and A. S. Prince. 1993. *Prosodic Morphology I: Constraint Interaction and Satisfaction.* Ms., University of Massachusetts, Amherst and Rutgers University, New Brunswick.

McCarthy, J. J. and A. S. Prince. 1995. "Faithfulness and Reduplicative Identity". To appear in René Kager, Harry van der Hulst and Wim Zonneveld (eds), *Proceedings of the OTS/HIL Workshop in Prosodic Morphology.* Cambridge: Cambridge University Press.

Muljačič, Z. 1969. *Fonologia generale e fonologia della lingua italiana.* Bologna: Il Mulino.

Myers, S. 1987. "Vowel Shortening in English". *Natural Language and Linguistic Theory* 5, 485-518.

Nespor, M. and I. Vogel. 1986. *Prosodic Phonology.* Dordrecht. Foris.

Newman, S.S. 1946. "On the Stress System of English". *Word* 2, 171-187.

Norstedts Stora Svenska Ordbok. 1988. Second ed.. Förlagsaktiebolaget OTAVA, Keuru.

Pater, J. 1995. *On the Nonuniformity of Weight-to-Stress and Stress Preservation Effects in English.* Ms. McGill University.

Peperkamp, S. 1997. *Prosodic words.* The Hague: Holland Academic Graphics.

Poppe, N. 1951. *Khalkha-Mongolische Grammatik.* Wiesbaden: Franz Steiner Verlag.

Prince, A. and P. Smolensky. 1993 *Optimality Theory: Constraint Interaction in Generative Grammar.* Ms. Rutgers University and University of Colorado, Boulder.

Raffelsiefen, R. 1992. "A Nonconfigurational Approach to Morphology". In M. Aronoff (ed.), *Morphology Now.* Albany, NY: State University of New York Press, 133-162.

Raffelsiefen, R. 1993. "Relating Words. A Model of Base Recognition. Part 1". *Linguistic Analysis* 23, 3-159.

Raffelsiefen, R. 1996. "Gaps in Word Wormation". In U. Kleinhenz (ed.), *Interfaces in Phonology.* Berlin: Akademie Verlag, 194-209.

Raffelsiefen, R. 1998. "Semantic Stability in Derivationally Related Words". In R.M. Hogg and L.van Bergen (eds), *Historical Linguistics 1995, Vol. 2.* Amsterdam/Philadelphia: Benjamins, 247-267.

Ross, J.R. 1972. "A Reanalysis of English Word Stress (part I)". In M. Brame (ed.), *Contributions to Generative Phonology.* Austin: University of Texas Press.

Scalise, S. 1984. *Generative Morphology.* Dordrecht: Foris.

Selkirk, E. 1982. *The Syntax of Words.* Cambridge, Mass.: MIT Press.

Selkirk E. 1995. "The Prosodic Structure of Function Words". In J. Beckman, S. Urbanczyck and L. Walsh (eds), *Papers in Optimality Theory.* University of Massachusetts Occasional Papers in Linguistics 18. Graduate Linguistics Student Association, Amherst, Massachusetts, 439-469. (Also published in J. Morgan and K. Demuth (eds). 1996. *Signal to Syntax: Bootstrapping from Speech to Grammar in Early Acquisition.* Mahwah, NJ: Lawrence Erlbaum Associates, 187-213).

Siegel, D. 1974. *Topics in English Morphology.* Garland. New York.

Stampe, D. 1972. *How I Spent my Summer Vacation.* Doctoral dissertation, Ohio State University.

Steriade, D. 1982. *Greek Prosodies and the Nature of Syllabification.* Doctoral dissertation, MIT.

The Oxford English Dictionary. 1993. Second ed.. Oxford: Oxford University Press

Vennemann, T. 1988. *Preference Laws for Syllable Structure and the Explanation of Sound Change.* Berlin, New York: Mouton de Gruyter.

Vogel, I. 1994. "Phonological Interfaces in Italian". In M. Mazzola (ed.), *Issues and Theory in Romance Linguistics: Selected Papers from the Linguistic Symposium on Romance Languages XXIII.* Washington, D.C.: Georgetown University Press, 109-126.

Walker, J. (1826) *A Critical Pronouncing Dictionary, and Expositor of the English Language.* London and Leipsic [Leipzig].

Wells, J.C. (1982) *Accents of English I: an Introduction.* Cambridge: Cambridge University Press.

Wiese, R. 1996. "Prosodic Alternations in English Morphophonology: a Constraint-based Account of Morpheme Integrity". In J. Durand and B. Laks (eds), *Current Trends in Phonology: Models and Methods, volume 2.* Salford: European Studies Research Institute, University of Salford, 731-756.

Wilmanns, W. 1896. *Deutsche Grammatik.* Zweite Abteilung: Wortbildung. Strassburg: Verlag von Karl J. Trübner.

Zwicky, A. 1972. "A Note on a Phonological Hierarchy in English". In R.P. Stockwell and R.K.S. Macaulay (eds), *Linguistic Change and Generative Theory.* Bloomington: Indiana University Press, 275-301.

Freie Universität Berlin
Institut für Englische Philologie
Gosslerstraße 2-4
D-14195 Berlin
Germany

Review of Packard (1998): *New approaches to Chinese word formation*[1]

RICHARD SPROAT

1. INTRODUCTION

As Packard notes in the preface to this volume, Chinese is a language with "no grammatical agreement, little morphophonemic alternation and no inflection" (p.xii), so one might be tempted to ask: why a nearly 400-page book on Chinese word formation? In fact, as the contributors to this volume amply demonstrate, there is no question that Chinese has morphologically complex words; indeed, it has had them for many millenia. And there is likewise no doubt that the formation of morphologically complex words is, again as Packard notes, both "interesting and worth investigating".

This book is a collection of ten papers by Chinese specialists of various backgrounds and theoretical predilections. The topics include word formation in Ancient and Classical Chinese, the syntax and semantics of Chinese verbal compounds, the nature of Chinese compounding, the definition of the notion of 'word' in Chinese, Mandarin lexical phonology, and lexical semantics and Chinese thematic structure.

A recurrent theme throughout the book is the definition of word. As we have noted, this is the topic of some of the contributions, but it in fact arises in most of the chapters. Of course, the question 'what is a word?', is one that plagues morphologists studying any language: *seven* is surely a word in English, but what about *twenty seven*: is that one word or two? For those who would answer that *twenty seven* is clearly a word, how about *one hundred and twenty seven*? Or *three million, two hundred and forty nine thousand, one hundred and twenty seven*? Where does one draw the line? But the problem of definition is much worse in Chinese for a number of reasons. First Chinese, on the face of it, would appear to lack the kinds of lexical phonology that help distinguish words from non-words in other languages. Similarly, it seems not to possess much in the way of inflection, which again, in other languages, can be a useful cue to wordhood. Finally, the writing systems of most of today's languages use spaces to delimit word-sized units. While a string of symbols surrounded by whitespace does not always correspond to what morphologists would argue to be a word, at least such orthographic words serve as a starting point for morphological discussions, and at least there can be little doubt that literate speakers of such languages have some notion of what a word is. In Chinese, of course, the situation is different, since Chinese writing does not use spaces to delimit morphologically complex entities of any kind. Thus linguistically naive Chinese speakers have no (conscious) notion of word, and even in Chinese linguistic studies the concept of word is quite recent. Thus while this volume is useful and timely for many reasons, in my view its single most important contribution is that it collects into

Geert Booij and Jaap van Marle (eds), Yearbook of Morphology 1998, 289-309.

one place various concrete proposals on what constitutes a word in Chinese, and how to establish whether a given polymorphemic construction is a word.

The remainder of this review will discuss each of the eleven chapters (Packard's introduction, plus the ten contributions), in the order in which it appears in the book.

2. PACKARD: INTRODUCTION

Packard's introduction, in addition to introducing the other papers in the volume, also serves to introduce two other topics. The first of these is the question of complex words in Old Chinese, a topic also addressed in the contributions by Feng, and Baxter and Sagart. The second is a brief history of 20th century linguistic views of word formation in Chinese.

Available evidence suggests that Chinese originally was a truly 'monosyllabic' language, with each word consisting of a single syllable. There was morphology, but it involved various kinds of phonological changes, plus 'sub-syllabic' affixation, neither of which altered the monosyllabicity of the base. Thus we have, for example, *derivation in 'going tone'*. Middle Chinese had four tonal categories, namely level, rising, going and entering,[2] and words could be derived from other words by converting to going tone from one of the other three tonal categories. For example, the words *mai*$_{rising}$ 'buy' and *mai*$_{going}$ 'sell' were related in this manner (this particular alternation surviving into Modern Chinese). According to Baxter and Sagart, this Middle Chinese tonal alternation derived from an old Chinese subsyllabic suffix *$-s$, which was eventually lost and replaced by going tone. Yet another kind of monosyllabic derivation involved 'fusion words': thus *$pieu$ 'not' and *ti 'it' would fuse into *$piuet$ 'not it'.

The earliest evidence of polysyllabic morphologically complex words involves full and partial reduplications, and 'splitting' of formerly monosyllabic words. Thus full reduplications such as *$siao$ 'little' becoming *$siao$-$siao$ 'very little', were found in Old Chinese, just as they are in Modern Chinese. Partial reduplication involved either repeated onsets, and distinct rimes, or (partially) repeated rimes and distinct onsets: examples such as *$sjet$ 'cricket' becoming *$sjet$-$sjuet$ 'cricket' (Modern Mandarin *xīshuài*) are typical. The *morphological* function per se of partial duplication is rather unclear, though it may indeed have been in part to expand "one syllable into two for purposes of clarity" (p.9). Finally, splitting involved breaking a syllable involving a complex onset, into two syllables with a common rime pattern: thus *$dzlied$ 'clover' becoming *$dz'ied$-$lied$. Again it is not clear that this had a morphological function per se.

Syllabic affixation and compounding became the primary means of forming morphologically complex words by the Han dynasty (206 BC-206AD), as the subsyllabic affixes that had been used in older forms of the language were eroded. As we shall see from Feng's article, the evidence is compelling that compounding as a morphological process was very active by the Han period. But for early Chinese the consensus appears to be that compounding was quite limited, and one is inclined to wonder why (and indeed whether) this was true. Compounding and (syllabic) affixation are common and productive in Modern Chinese, and disyllabic forms comprise something like 67% of word *types* in Modern Chinese text (Suen 1986); yet disyllabicity, and the lexical processes that support it seem to have been almost absent in Old Chinese, if one is to believe the evidence that has been adduced.

There are basically two views on why monosyllabicity eroded. The first, and perhaps more traditional view is 'phonology-driven': Old Chinese allowed much more complex syllables than later Chinese, and as the syllable structure simplified over time, phonological distinctions were lost. These losses, which could affect communication, had to be compensated somehow: thus Chinese words started to become polysyllabic.[3] The alternative view, due to Cheng (Cheng 1981), is that disyllabism became necessary because of the increasing complexity of Chinese society and thus a sociolinguistic need to expand the vocabulary; for Cheng, the phonological simplification was a secondary and later phenomenon.

Packard's second topic, as we have noted, is a concise history of 20th century views on word formation in Chinese. He divides the views into five more-or-less chronologically ordered periods. These are:

1.   The 'character-affix' period (approximately 1900-1920's), where views on Chinese morphology were heavily influenced by Western work on highly inflected languages.

2.   The 'sentence-grammar' period (1920's-1940's) where word structure was seen as being a microcosm of sentence structure.

3.   The 'inflection' period (1950's) where, in the PRC at least, complex Marxist sociolinguistic reasoning, plus close political ties with Russian linguists in the Soviet Union, made it fashionable to apply the concept of inflectional morphology to Chinese.

4.   The 'syntax' period (1960's-1980's), which was in part characterized by an interest not so much in the structure of words, but in how words syntactically relate to one another.

5.   The contemporary period, wherein one sees a rejuvenation of interest in morphology per se, and in the application of increasingly sophisticated models of word formation to Chinese.

The taxonomy aside, the most useful aspect of this review is the fact that Packard pulls together citations to over thirty works on Chinese morphology spanning the last ninety years or so. It is invariably impossible to find this kind of information conveniently together in one place, unless someone has taken the trouble to collate the various pieces. The field owes Packard a debt of gratitude for investing this effort.

3. BAXTER/SAGART: WORD FORMATION IN OLD CHINESE

Appropriately enough, the main portion of the book starts with a discussion of word formation in the earliest forms of recorded Chinese. Now, the first problem one faces in Chinese, which one does not face in a great many other early recorded forms of languages is the fact that the writing system generally fails to represent in any consistent fashion any of the morphological alternations under discussion. That is, whereas in preclassical Greek (including forms recorded in the Linear B script) one could find direct evidence in the written form for particular forms of affixes, in Old Chinese, all affixes are of necessity reconstructed.

Nonetheless, while there is no *direct* evidence of affixational processes, indirect evidence can be found in commentaries on Classical Texts starting in the sixth century AD (i.e. about 800 years after the period being reconstructed), which gave fairly precise indications of how problematic homographs were to be pronounced in different contexts. Thus *zhé/shé* (Mandarin pronunciation) was marked by Lu Deming (583 AD) as being pronounced with the onset of *zhī* and the rime of *shé*[4] in one instance meaning 'break off', and with the onset of *shí* and the rime of *shè* in another meaning 'die young [= be broken off]'. Assuming a Middle Chinese reconstruction for *zhī+shé* and *shí+shè* as *tsyi+zyet* and *dzyi+syet*, respectively, we arrive at the Middle Chinese pronunciations *tsyet* and *dzyet* for 'break off' and 'die young'. The Middle Chinese voicing alternation is then hypothesized to come from an Old Chinese alternation involving a prefix, reconstructed as *N- (see further below), and we arrive at the forms *tjet* and *N-tjet* for Old Chinese.

Baxter and Sagart discuss a number of different affixation processes, including *N- (semantics unclear), *k- (in part forming concrete countable nouns out of verbs), *t- (often forming a derived mass noun), *-s (deadjectival or deverbal noun-forming suffix that is responsible for the going tone derivation previously mentioned), and the infixes *-j- (function difficult to establish) and *-r- (collective, or iterative marker). These affixes survive into Modern Standard Chinese only as fossilized alternations between forms that were at one time apparently related, though the claim is made that the verbal /kə/ prefix (forming verb forms with the reading 'do X a little') found in Modern Shanxi dialects may be a remnant of the Old Chinese *k- prefix. Also discussed are reduplication and compounding: note that here, unlike the case of affixation, we have direct evidence from the written language, since the pieceparts of reduplicated constructions or compounds were written as separate characters.

To get a flavor for the kinds of reconstructions involved, it is worth taking a closer look at a couple of the affixes. Consider the *N- prefix which is involved in alternations such as the following (OC = reconstructed Old Chinese form; MC = reconstructed Middle Chinese form; MM = Modern Mandarin):

OC	MC	MM	
prats	pæjH	bài	'ruin'
N-prats	bæjH	bài	'go to ruin'
krep	kɛp	jiá	'clasp'
N-krep	hɛp	xiá	'narrow'
tsʰang	tshang	cāng	'storehouse'
N-tsʰang	dzang	cáng	'conceal, store'

What was the exact form of the prefix? This is unknown, but evidence from Chinese loan words in Yao (p.71, fn.11] suggests that it was at least some kind of nasal. It is certainly not implausible that a nasal prefix could have had the voicing effect that it supposedly had in middle Chinese: exactly the same thing happened in Irish, where the nasal consonant mutation (called 'eclipsis') caused voicing of voiceless obstruents.

Consider now the suffix *-s. Some alternations are given below:

OC	MC	MM	
m-ljɨŋ	zying	chéng	'mount, ride'
m-ljɨŋ-s	zyingH	shèng	'chariot [=something ridden']]
drjon	drjwen	chuán	'transmit'
drjon-s	drjwenH	zhuàn	'record [=something transmitted]'
goʔ	huwX	hòu	'thick'
goʔ-s	HuwH	hòu	'thickness'
hlot	thwat	tuō	'take off clothing';
hlot-s	thwatH	tuì	'exuviae [=something taken off]'
tsjap	tsjep	jiē	'connect'
tsjap-s	tsjejH	jì	'connection'

The Old Chinese -s eventually became *H* in Middle Chinese, which in turn evolved into the going tone. The -s is, according to Baxter and Sagart, the easiest suffix to establish for Old Chinese: certainly it appears to have been quite productive, given the number of pairs of alternants that Baxter and Sagart list. However what is not clear – or at least is not made clear by this discussion – is what motivates the particular phonetic form of the suffix. Grant that there was an alternation in Old Chinese that eventually resulted in what Packard terms derivation in going tone: why did the form of that suffix have to be -s?

In general, the particular forms and, in many cases, functions of the various morphological processes in Old Chinese are necessarily hypothetical. We simply have no direct evidence of the pronunciation of words in the relevant period, and the most relevant language-internal evidence comes from linguistic commentaries written by people living 800 years after the Old Chinese period, speaking a form of the language (Middle Chinese) that we must also reconstruct. What seems clear, however, is that Old Chinese did have affixational morphology of a kind that has been all but lost in the modern Chinese languages.

4. CHANG: V-V COMPOUNDS IN MANDARIN

This paper treats V-V compounds – consisting largely of verbs that are commonly termed 'resultatives' (cf. the papers by Li and by Starosta et al.) – within a lexical argument structure framework inspired by Lieber (1983). It will be recalled that Lieber's analysis was intended to explain various English compounds involving a noun and a verb, cases like *rat catcher*, *pick pocket* or *handweave*, making use of her well-known *percolation conventions*, plus the constraint that the verb must link all internal arguments within its projection. Thus in *rat catcher*, the internal argument of *catch* is satisfied within the compound (obligatorily so, since the verbal projection does not go outside the compound); whereas in the verb *handweave*, it can be satisfied outside the compound (*she handweaved the material*), leaving *hand* free to be interpreted as an adjunct. Lieber has little to say about V-V compounds, however, because English lacks many of these. For the few cases that exist like *freeze-dry*, the thematic structure of both verbs seems to be identical, and Lieber posits that the argument structures are simply shared in the compound verb. In contrast to English, V-V compounds abound in Chinese, and in most cases the argument structures of the two verbs are not identical.[5] Nonetheless, Chang proposes to adapt Lieber's percolation principles to analyze these constructions.

Chang starts with a taxonomy of V-V compounds into five types – confusingly distinct from the four-way classification she later uses – depending upon how the argument structures of the two component verbs ultimately get assigned to the compound's NP arguments. For instance her fifth type, illustrated by (1a) combines two intransitive verbs into a transitive construction; whereas her third type (1b) are the well-known ambiguous cases involving one transitive (in this case *qi* 'ride') and one intransitive:

(1) a.   ta ku-shi-le shoupa
          he cry-wet-PERF handkerchief
          'He cried so much that his handkerchief became wet.'
     b.   ta qi-lei-le ma
          he ride-tired-PERF horse
          'He$_i$ rode the horse until he$_i$ was tired'
          'He rode the horse until it was tired'

The formal presentation of the model that Chang is assuming is brief. She seems to propose, straightforwardly enough, that in a case like *chi-bao* (eat full) 'eat until one is full', the argument structure of *chi* (*agent [theme]*), is linked up in such a way with the argument structure of *bao* (*theme*), so that the complex verb has the argument structure *agent-theme [theme]*, where the second theme linked to *agent* is from *bao*;[6] this is consistent with the analysis presented in Li's paper later in the volume, as well as Li's earlier paper (Li 1990), which is oddly barely cited here.

In the fourth section of the paper, Chang discusses implications of the analysis, and here a new and clearer four-way taxonomy based on argument structure is presented (AG = 'agent of first verb'; TH = 'theme of first verb'; TH2 = 'theme of second verb'):[7]

Type	Argument structure	Example	
I	AG-TH2 [TH]	chi$_i$-bao$_j$	'X eat$_i$ Y until X full$_j$'
II	AG [TH2]	ku$_i$-shi$_j$	'X cry$_i$ until Y wet$_j$'
III	AG [TH-TH2]	tui$_i$-dao$_j$	'X push$_i$ Y until Y fall$_j$'
IV	AG-TH2 [TH]	qi$_i$-lei$_j$	'X ride$_i$ Y until X tired$_j$'
	AG [TH-TH2]	qi$_i$-lei$_j$	'X ride$_i$ Y until Y tired$_j$'

Thus, type IV is simply Type I combined with Type III.

Chang uses this taxonomy to explain a number of grammatical properties of the different V-V classes. Thus for instance, verbs in only a few of the categories can function as middles. One can say *fan rongyi chi-bao* (rice easy eat-full) 'rice is filling' (Type I), but not **shoupa rongyi ku-shi* (handkerchief easy cry-wet) (Type II).[8] This is explained by appealing to the idea (attributed to Carrier and Randall) that middles require a direct internal argument. According to Chang, the direct internal argument must uniquely come from the first verb, so that while Type I qualifies for middle formation, Type II does not. Passives behave the opposite of middles: Type I **fan bei chi-bao le* (rice PASSIVE-PARTICLE eat-full PERF), but Type II *shoupa bei ku-shi le* (handkerchief PASSIVE-PARTICLE cry-wet PERF) 'the handkerchief was made wet by (someone's) crying'. One of the functions of the passive is to suppress the agent. In a Type II verb, the agent can be suppressed without affecting other roles since the agent is not linked to another role; on the other hand for Type I, AG is linked to TH2, so that if one were to try to suppress the agent, one would be left with a 'dangling' theme.

The last section of the paper briefly discusses two syntactic constructions similar to the V-V compounds which were the topic of this paper. The first of these is the serial verb construction, such as *dao cha he* (pour tea drink) 'pour tea to drink'; the second is the syntactic resultative, discussed at greater length in Li's paper.

5. DAI: SYNTACTIC, PHONOLOGICAL, AND MORPHOLOGICAL WORDS IN CHINESE

This paper, which is based in part on the author's PhD dissertation (Dai 1992), outlines the various notions of word as they apply to Chinese, and enumerates some tests for determining the wordhood of a given constituent. After an introduction of three familiar notions of word – syntactic, morphological, phonological – and a brief overview of the history of the notion of word in Chinese, Dai outlines evidence for the relevance of the three categories of word to Chinese.

The evidence presented for the notion of syntactic word seems oddly chosen. In an expression like *xiu qiche* (repair car) 'repair the car', it is Dai's intention to show that *xiu* 'repair' is maximally a V^0, and thus that Chinese has a notion of 'minimal unit to which syntactic rules can refer'. This he does by demonstrating that *xiu* can be isolated from its object *qiche*, and by a few other tests. Fair enough, but while *xiu* is surely a word, how do we know that it is also not some non-zero projection of V? To do that one would need to show that an obviously phrasal construction *cannot* inhabit the position that *xiu* inhabits, something that it ought to be possible to show.

Phonological wordhood is argued to be relevant to a handful of putatively word-internal phonological rules. One of these is final elision, which deletes the rime of a prosodically weak syllable after another syllable. This only applies within words, so that we get *tamen* 'they' (second syllable weak) becoming *tam*, but not *ta meng* (he mask) **tam*.[9] Finally, in defense of morphological words, Dai presents a brief review of specific instances of previous work arguing for the lexical status of certain constructions in Chinese.

The bulk of the remainder of the paper presents seven sufficient tests for deciding whether a particular sequence of morphemes constitutes a word in Chinese. If a constituent passes any one of these tests it cannot be a bound morpheme and so in principle could be a word. The tests are:

1. Syntactic independence
2. Movement
3. Pronominalization
4. Filling a slot in a syntactic construction
5. Deletion
6. Modification
7. Expansion

Many of these are obvious enough and require no explanation. *Modification* refers to phrasal modification with a modifier in *de*: in *X-de Y* where *X* is the modifier, *Y* cannot be a free morpheme.[10] *Expansion* refers to the prohibition on inserting phrasal material in the middle of *XY* if either *X* or *Y* is a bound morpheme.

6. DUANMU: WORDHOOD IN CHINESE

The next paper in the volume also deals with wordhood in Chinese, though Duanmu's topic is more narrowly focussed than Dai's. Duanmu focusses on bare modifier noun (MN) constructions, such as *da gou* 'big dog'; that is, MN constructions that lack the particle *de*. He argues that these, and their iterative derivatives ([M[MN]], [M[M[MN]]]), etc., are words in Chinese. Like Dai, Duanmu lists a set of syntactic criteria for determining wordhood in Chinese, some of which he ultimately rejects, and others which he adopts. The tests that he adopts all converge on the conclusion that MN constructions are words.

Having dealt with the syntactic arguments, Duanmu turns to the core of his analysis, namely phonological arguments for the wordhood of MN constructions. His central argument is that there is abundant metrical and tonal evidence in Chinese for distinguishing words from phrases, and that this evidence yields yet another type of converging evidence for the wordhood of MN constructions. The majority of the discussion centers on tone-association domains in Shanghai, with a small discussion of Mandarin at the end. Of course Shanghai and Mandarin are different languages, so it may not seem justified to draw conclusions about wordhood in Mandarin, from the behavior of cognate constructions in Shanghai, or vice versa. But in using cross-dialectal evidence in Chinese, Duanmu is at least consistent with common practice, as he notes.

As Duanmu also discusses elsewhere (most recently Duanmu 1997), Shanghai has a process whereby non-initial tones in a domain are deleted, and the tone associated with the initial syllable spreads across the domain. The span of the domain is evidently metrically determined. In monomorphemic tetrasyllabic words (e.g., transliterated foreign names) one finds two binary domains – $(AB)(CD)$ – but in trisyllabic words one finds a single ternary domain: (ABC). In Duanmu's analysis these facts are handled by assuming a left-to-right binary foot construction over the domain, with stray syllable adjunction conjoining the stray syllable C to the binary foot to the left in (ABC). Foot construction is cyclic, and in rightbranching lexical constructions like *[lā [tsʰo ve]]* (cold fry rice) 'cold fried rice', where one would predict the domain structure $(A(BC))$, one in fact finds (ABC). This is due to Stress Class, which feeds Foot Merging, which effects the removal of the second foot.

Phrasal and lexical domains behave differently with respect to tone domain formation. In particular *[tsʰo ve]* (fry rice) as a nominal ('fried rice') forms one domain, whereas when it is a verb phrase ('fry rice') it is two domains. This is handled by assuming that while lexical stress is leftward, phrasal stress is rightward in Chinese, as it is in English. Stress Class applies in either case, but Foot Merging can only remove destressed feet on the right (i.e, the righthand foot in lexical domains), not on the left (i.e., lefthand foot in phrasal domains), since Shanghai feet are trochaic. Duanmu then proceeds with a demonstration that simple and complex MN constructions behave as words with respect to domain formation, whereas M-*de*-N constructions are phrasal.

The final section of the paper deals with a few residual issues such as stress in

personal names; and *de*-omission in cases like *wo ba* 'my father' (cf. *wo de ba(ba)* (I
DE father) 'my father'), where omission of the *de* does not appear to turn these constructions into words: but as Duanmu notes, *de*-omission is not very widespread.

7. FENG: PROSODIC STRUCTURE AND COMPOUND WORDS IN CLASSICAL CHINESE

The centerpiece of the collection is Feng's lengthy discussion of compound words in
Classical Chinese, drawn from the author's PhD dissertation (Feng 1995}. The question that Feng addresses is simple: why was there a marked increase in the use of
compounding between the Old Chinese of Mencius (c. 372-289 BC), and the Chinese
of one of his Han Dynasty commentators (Zhao Qi, c. 107-201 AD)? This is of
course the age-old question that Packard raises in the introduction to the volume: why
did Chinese cease to be monosyllabic? Feng's answer is rather novel.

First of all, Feng does of course need to establish that there was such an increase
in the use of compounding. We must again have a criterion for deciding that a
construction *is* a compound. Clearly the phonological and syntactic criteria that are
used in Modern Chinese do not apply to Classical Chinese, for the simple reason that
we do not know enough about the phonology of the language, and there is no
foolproof way to test syntactic properties such as whether the two parts of a putative
compound are inseparable from one another (cf. the *expansion* criterion discussed
previously). Feng therefore uses a semantic criterion, since at least it is known what
Classical constructions, as well as their individual parts, meant. His criterion is as
follows: let A' denote the meaning of A. Then a construction $[AB]$ is a compound if
$[AB]' = A'$ or $[AB]' = B'$ or $[AB]' = c$, for some other meaning not compositional of
A and B. Thus, in the first two cases one part of the compound simply contributes
no meaning; an example is *ju-ma* (cart horse) 'cart', where 'horse' contributes no
meaning. The third case is the more familiar case of exocentricity: *tian-xia* (sky
below) 'Emperor' (or, more normally, 'world'). Of course these are rather restrictive
criteria since compounds can, after all, be compositional. We may therefore assume
that Feng's counts of compounds in Classical Chinese are undercounts.

The core of Feng's analysis of the development of Han compounds is a comparison of Mencius and Zhao Qi's commentary thereon. One finds that in many cases
a monosyllabic (single-character) expression in Mencius is translated by a disyllabic
expression in Zhao Qi; thus *guo* 'mistake' in Mencius is glossed as *miuwu* 'mistake'. More generally one can ask how many two-syllable lexical expressions there
were in Zhao Qi, how many of these came from monosyllabic expressions in
Mencius, how many were carried over from earlier disyllabic expressions, and how
many corresponded to no expression in Mencius – i.e., were introduced by Zhao Qi
in an extended gloss of Mencius. One can also ask how many of the two-syllable expressions in Zhao Qi are compounds on Feng's definitions. Feng's conclusion from
his data is that there was a marked increase in the number of disyllabic expressions in
Zhao Qi's text (a total of 169) over the original Mencius, the single largest group

(43%) being the cases where single-character terms in Mencius are translated as two-syllable terms in the later text. Thus there is apparent evidence for an increase in the use of morphologically complex (two-character) expressions by the Han dynasty. Furthermore, many of the two-character terms in Zhao Qi are not compounds on Feng's rather stringent definitions. Anticipating his later proposal, Feng suggests that this may hint at the true reason for the increase in compounding: the true reason may not be that compounding became more favored, but rather disyllabicity. Indeed, the development of compounding and disyllabicity are somewhat independent, Feng later argues.

Feng critiques the traditional 'functional' explanation that we have met with already: briefly again, phonological contrasts were lost in the transition from Old to Classical Chinese, and these lost contrasts had to be supplemented by making the words distinctive in other ways, one way being replacing older monosyllabic constructions with polysyllabic ones. One criticism that Feng levels is that while certain distinctions were indeed lost, others were simply transformed into other contrasts: cf. the change of final *-s* into the Middle Chinese *-H* noted in the discussion of Baxter and Sagart. Another criticism relates to coordinate compounds like *bi-jian* (clumsy-lousy) 'lousy', which in Zhao Qi translates Mencius' *jian* 'lousy'. Since *bi* contributes little to the meaning of *bi-jian*, this is a reasonable candidate for being a functionally motivated formation, under the assumption that the original Old Chinese pronunciation of *jian* was sufficiently distinctive to be unambiguous, but that this phonological distinctiveness was subsequently lost. But this functional explanation ought to predict that such compounds are in the majority, something which Feng argues not to be the case.[11]

What then happened between Old and Classical Chinese? Evidently the number of disyllables increased, but why was that? Later classical textual criticism suggests that the reason may have been prosodic: Feng cites several passages by Kong Yingda (574-648 AD), a Tang Dynasty commentator, who seems to cite prosodic reasons for why certain constructions were written the way they were written. For example *gaoyang zhi pi* (lamb-sheep's skin) 'sheep's skin' cannot be the semantically identical *yang zhi pi* because that would not be 'balanced'.

Taking Kong's intuition in part as his basis, Feng makes the claim that the development of disyllabicity in Classical Chinese was for prosodic reasons: specifically, while Old Chinese allowed syllables ascomplex as CCCMVCCC (M = 'medial'), by Middle Chinese of 800 AD the syllable complexity had reduced to maximally CVC, or in other words the same complexity as one finds in some Modern Chinese languages such as Cantonese.[12] Presumably the syllable structure of Han Dynasty Chinese was more complex than that of 9th century Chinese, but less complex than that of Old Chinese. Feng's thesis is that this simplification of syllable structure made syllables monomoraic, and hence incapable of functioning as a minimal word – which on commonly-held assumptions must be bimoraic. (Feng actually expresses the generalization in terms of minimal foot formation, but the two descriptions are equivalent.) Thus loss of phonological contrast is the basic cause in Feng's analysis, as in the 'functional' analysis, but for an entirely different reason.

The remainder of the paper deals with various issues, including grammatical evidence for the importance of disyllabic feet in Classical Chinese, and the syntactic origins of compound constructions.

Feng's analysis is ingenious, yet there is an issue here that he does not adequately address. The loss of bimoraicity would appear to be a categorical shift, and yet there is no categorical shift in the amount of disyllabicity. True, Feng refers in several places to a 'sharp increase in compounding' during the Han Dynasty, as if a veritable 'Cambrian explosion' of compounding occurred during that period. But he presents no evidence for this conclusion, over the equally plausible conclusion that there was simply a gradual increase in the percentage of disyllabic forms between Mencius and Zhao Qi. Of course, a gradual increase *might* be expected on Feng's analysis under the following scenario. Presumably the loss of complex syllables did not happen all at once: rather, one assumes that some complex syllable types simplified before others. Perhaps the first syllables to simplify are the ones that first entered into novel disyllabic forms; and so on as further syllable types simplified. Perhaps, but it is up to further research to determine that this was the case. Over and above that, there is the problem that even in Modern Chinese languages, monosyllabic CV words abound, and the situation was no different in Classical Chinese. Evidently these must be violations of the prosodic requirements, and an explanation is needed on why these violations are allowed.

It is interesting to observe that the 'functional' explanation that Feng rejects neither predicts a categorical change, nor does it predict that monosyllabic forms should have been outright eliminated.

8. HUANG: CHINESE AS A HEADLESS LANGUAGE IN COMPOUNDING MORPHOLOGY

Huang studies 24,000 disyllabic compounds from the Mandarin Daily Dictionary (*Guoyu Ribao Cidian*), plus some data from Hakka and Taiwanese (source unspecified), and concludes that "Chinese is a headless language in its morphology since neither the rightmost nor the leftmost member uniquely determines the category type of a compound" (p.279).

This conclusion is reached by observing that one is able to predict with significantly better than chance accuracy the category of a disyllabic compound given the category of *either* the lefthand or the righthand member. For righthand members it is 0.755, for lefthand members 0.652. Thus there is no fixed head position in Chinese compounds, therefore they are headless. Now observe the definition of head that Huang is presuming: an element in a compound that shares the same category as the whole compound may be considered a head. Note that semantics does not enter into the issue:[13] in *jingxi* (capital opera) 'Beijing opera' either *jing* 'capital' or *xi* 'opera' may be considered the head merely because they are both nouns. Given this rather unusual definition, part of the reason the predictability is as high as it is, is due to the large number of XX compounds – i.e. compounds where both elements are the same category in this collection (or indeed in any such collection). By my calculation, 12,249 out of 23,986 compounds (51%) are either NN, VV or AA. So fully half of the compounds in the data could, on Huang's definition, equally well have their heads on the right or the left. The frequency of XX constructions confounds the results. For example, 7,384 NX compounds are nouns, out of a total of 8,222 NX compounds of all categories. From this Huang observes that 7384:8222 = 0.898 of compounds with N on the left are nouns. But of these 7,384, 6,910 are NN, meaning that the vast majority are consistent with the more traditional view that the head is on the right. In a similar vein, 1,854 out of 5,857 (0.317) AX compounds are adjectives, but of these, 1,609 are AA.

The decision to focus on disyllabic compounds is also questionable, to my mind. After all, as has been noted elsewhere (e.g., in Duanmu's paper) compounds can be built up of many constituents, and thus be significantly longer than disyllabic. As Starosta et al. discuss later in this volume, all long compounds in Chinese (which are invariably nouns) are rightheaded. Of course there was a pragmatic reason for Huang's focus: disyllabic compounds are the only class of compounds for which one can expect to find a large sample in a Chinese dictionary. Unfortunately, though, they are arguably not very representative of productive compounding morphology in Chinese (see, e.g., Dai 1992).

Huang ends the paper by comparing the claimed headlessness of morphology in Chinese, with the evident headedness in syntax. In particular VP's are leftheaded, whereas APs and NPs are rightheaded. Of course in more traditional notions of headedness in Chinese compounds it would be observed that, contrary to Huang's conclusions, there is actually a significant parallel between phrases and compounds. Compounds headed (in a more traditional sense) by nouns and adjectives have their heads on the right; and compounds headed by verbs – in particular, VO constructions like *chi-fan* (eat rice) 'eat' – have their heads on the left.

9. LI: THE UNIFORMITY OF THETA ASSIGNMENT HYPOTHESIS

Baker's Uniformity of Theta Assignment Hypothesis (UTAH) (Baker 1988) – the claim that "identical thematic relationships between items are represented by identical structural relationships between those items at the level of D-structure" – has been a guiding principle for much work on grammatical relations in the Principles and Parameters framework. Li examines two roughly synonymous resultative constructions in Chinese, illustrated in (2), and argues that unlike the syntactic resultative in (2a), the morphological resultative (2b) is a compound formed of two verbs in the lexicon:

(2) a.   youyou ku-de Taotao feichang fan
           Youyou cry-DE Taotao extremely impatient
           'Youyou cried so that Taotao became extremely impatient.'

  b.   youyou ku-fan-le Taotao le
       Youyou cry-impatient-PERF Taotao PERF
       'Youyou cried so that Taotao became extremely impatient.'

Hence these two constructions, while having identical semantic relationships, do not
apparently stem from the same structural relationships at D-structure. This would appear to be prima facie evidence against the UTAH, but Li does not want to go that far
since the semantic relations in question are "probably not thematic in the sense Baker
uses the term" (p.286). Rather Li takes the more conservative position that one
should not take the UTAH for granted as applying to semantic relations of all kinds
and that "each extended application of this hypothesis beyond Baker's original work
should be accompanied by sufficient justification" [ibid].
    Li starts with an analysis of the syntactic resultative of the type in (2a). The
basic structure is argued to be as in (3), where the CP is embedded:

  (3)   youyou ku-de [$_{CP}$ Taotao feichang fan]
          Youyou cry-DE Taotao extremely impatient
          'Youyou cried so that Taotao became extremely impatient.'

As it turns out, however, the CP is a weak island, a point which requires an explanation. Li proposes that the correct structure is actually as in (4), where the *de* is a preposition that has been incorporated into the matrix verb.

  (4)   youyou ku-de$_i$ [$_{PP}$ t$_i$ [$_{CP}$ Taotao feichang fan]]
          Youyou cry-DE Taotao extremely impatient
          'Youyou cried so that Taotao became extremely impatient.'

Since PP is categorially different from the CP it contains, the latter is a weak island.
    In the next section Li introduces the resultative compound constructions as in
(2b), and notes some important similarities between them and the syntactic causatives. In particular both constructions assign Causer and Causee readings to NPs and
both, surprisingly, allow argument inversion:

  (5) a. youyou zhui-lei-le taotao le
           Youyou chase-tired-PERF Taotao PERF
           1. 'Youyou chased Taotao and as a result Taotao was tired',
           or
           2. 'Taotao chased Youyou and as a result Taotao was tired'
       b. youyou zhui-de taotao tai-bu-dong tui le
           Youyou chase-DE taotao lift-not-move leg PERF
           1. 'Youyou chased Taotao and as a result Taotao couldn't move his legs',
           or
           2. 'Taotao chased Youyou and as a result Taotao couldn't move his legs'

Then Li turns to the differences between the two constructions, which as he argues "can easily be accounted for if the compound is formed in the lexicon and occurs in the sentence like a single verb" (p.296). There are three such differences, but for the sake of brevity, we will only review one here.

The resultative compound example in (5a) in fact has a third reading, namely (3.) 'Youyou chased Taotao and as a result Youyou was tired'. The equivalent reading for the sentential resultative in (5b) is unavailable: *'Youyou chased Taotao and as a result Youyou couldn't move his legs'. The lack of the third reading in the sentential case is explained by James Huang's theory of generalized control. The structure is as in (6):

(6)   youyou zhui-de taotao [CP *pro* tai-bu-dong tui le]

Here, according to the generalized control theory, the *pro* must be controlled by the closest available NP, namely *taotao*. Hence only *taotao* can be interpreted as being the one who couldn't move his legs.

If the resultative compound were formed 'in the syntax' via incorporation, one would expect that here too the third reading would be unavailable. Instead, Li proposes (consistent with his earlier 1990 analysis) that the resultative compounds are formed in the lexicon. The argument goes as follows. *Zhui* 'chase' has two theta roles to assign, *lei* 'tired' one. *Lei's* theta role may be associated with, and thus assigned with, either theta role of *zhui*. And *zhui's* theta roles may be assigned in either order to the subject and object. This results in four possible theta assignments, of which the last is ruled out for reasons that Li explains:

Subject	Object	Interpretation of (5a)
CHASER+TIRED	CHASEE	3
CHASER	CHASEE+TIRED	1
CHASEE+TIRED	CHASER	2
CHASEE	CHASER+TIRED	–

Thus, while resultative compounds share important properties, including semantic relations, with syntactic resultatives, they are also different in ways that are most consistent with the view that the former is a lexical construction, and the latter syntactic. Hence, at the very least one would have to say that the UTAH does not apply to these examples.

One thing that Li does not discuss at all is the motivation for considering lexical resultatives to be compounds composed out of two verbs. The final paper in this volume (see Section 12), directly challenges this assumption, claiming instead that the resultative portion (e.g., the *lei* 'tired' in *zhui-lei* 'chase so that one becomes tired'), is really a derivational affix. But this point is really orthogonal to Li's concern in this paper, since it could well be the case that from a semantic point of view lexical resultatives are identical to a syntactic construction consisting of two verbs, whereas from a morphological point of view the 'verb' denoting the result is in fact merely an affix. In fact, that would not be surprising at all: Baker himself cites many examples where a verb or some other unbound form shows up as an *affix* when incorporated. Given that Chinese lexical resultatives are not formed by incorporation, one might, I suppose, even more expect that the resultative 'verbs' in question might really be affixes. If nothing else, Baker's work, and subsequent work in that framework, has taught us that the morphological expression of a function, and the function itself, are two quite separate things.

10. PACKARD: A LEXICAL PHONOLOGY OF MANDARIN CHINESE

Packard's own contribution to the volume is a continuation of his previous work on the lexical phonology and morphology of Mandarin (Packard 1990, 1992}. Here he focusses on the phonology, and in particular on the interaction of the rule of Third Tone Sandhi with various reduction rules of Mandarin. The facts of the phonology, he claims, are consistent with, and therefore support his previous lexical morphology account.

As far as I can tell, Packard's treatment of the facts of lexical phonology is different only in a few details from his previous treatment. Basically the problem to be accounted for is the following. Mandarin Third Tone Sandhi is an obligatory rule that changes a (low) third tone into a (rising) second tone when it precedes another third tone: thus *lao3shu3* 'rat' becomes *lao[2]shu3*, where the '[2]' indicates the sandhied tone. Yet there are certain classes of construction where it apparently fails to apply, and these are treated by Packard. To take just one example, reduplicated kinship terms like *jie3jie0* 'older sister' fail to have sandhi, even though in this case the underlying form is *jie3jie3*, and the '0', or 'neutral' tone is obligatorily introduced later. These contrast with reduplicated third-tone classifiers like *ben[2]ben0* (volume volume) 'every volume', which may have neutral tone on the second copy, but *must* have sandhi on the first. In keeping with the style, if not the exact details of Packard's previous treatments, *jie3jie3* is formed at Stratum I and assigned non-head stress; non-head stress blocks sandhi at Stratum IV; and then neutral tone is introduced postlexically. On the other hand classifier reduplication (*ben[2]ben0*) happens at Stratum II, where the constructions receive *head* stress, which triggers sandhi at stratum IV; again neutral tone is introduced postlexically.

Now, here is a simpler analysis. In *ben[2]ben3* tone sandhi applies lexically (not on a particular stratum, but simply on a lexical cycle), and neutral tone formation optionally applies postlexically. For *jie3jie0* we can assume that there is a kinship terminology tonal contour of the form 3-2 that is assigned to the word: *jie3jie2*. Note that this contour is available for kinship, and other familiar naming terms of all tonal categories except tone one (high level tone): thus one finds *li4xuan2* (a name), but *xuan3xuan2* as the reduplicated familiar naming term of the second tone-two morpheme. In fact Packard is incorrect about the neutral being obligatory in cases like *jie3jie0*: it is not obligatory, but when it does not occur then one *must* have the pattern *jie3jie2*, with the tonal contour we have identified. This tonal contour then explains the lack of sandhi: there is no environment for the first third tone to change.

Essentially the same argument was made in our previous critique of Packard's stratum-ordered analysis of Mandarin (Sproat and Shih 1993), and in general many of the arguments we made there seem to carry over straightforwardly to this new paper. The interested reader will no doubt want to peruse Packard's present and earlier paper, along with our already published critique, and form their own opinion.

11. ROSS: COGNATE OBJECTS AND THE REALIZATION OF THEMATIC STRUCTURE IN MANDARIN CHINESE

This paper deals not with word formation per se, but with lexical semantics. Ross seeks to explain why in English one can say things like (7a) whereas in Mandarin the verb must have a semantically weak or empty cognate object as in (7b):

(7) a. When do we eat?
     b. women shenmo shihou chi fan?
         (we what time eat food)

The core proposal – which is developed within a Jackendovian model of thematic structure – is that the theta structure of Mandarin activity verbs entails a Theme, and Theme cannot be suppressed, unlike the case of English. Thus Mandarin activity verbs must have an object to assign the Theme role to.

This seems straightforward enough, except that there are some activity verbs, like *zou* 'walk', or *pao* 'run', which have a Theme, but where this role is arguably assigned to the subject. Nonetheless, these verbs require a cognate object:

(8)   wo zou lu
         (I walk road)
         'I walk'

The explanation for this runs roughly as follows. Verbs like *zou* 'walk' differ on the one hand from motion verbs like *lai* 'come' in that the latter class are achievement verbs, and it is the attained endpoint that is salient. On the other hand, *zou* differs from stative verbs like *gao* 'high, tall', in that it is not stative. For Ross, the function of the transitive structure for *zou* 'walk' and *pao* 'run' is to mark them as activity verbs and thus to "clearly distinguish them from stative verbs and achievement verbs of motion and to identify them with other activity verbs" (p.340).

In addition to providing an explanation for obligatory cognate objects, Ross also proposes an analysis for Mandarin subject postposing constructions – cases like *lai ke le* (come guest PERF) 'guests have arrived', which explains its restriction to a small class of motion verbs.

12. STAROSTA/KUIPER/NG/WU: ON DEFINING THE CHINESE COMPOUND WORD

The last paper in the volume deals again with compounds. Two issues are examined, namely headedness in Chinese compounds, and the resultative 'compounds' of the form VR, where V is a verb and R is a result. In both cases the authors compare traditional sinological conceptions of what compounds are with modern linguistic views, the general conclusion being that "in the study of Chinese word formation, care needs to be taken with the extent to which linguists rely on traditional analyses" (p.347).

The first topic – headedness in compounds – is straightforwardly treated. In disyllabic compounds it is complex to determine the headedness and in some cases one apparently must say that they are exocentric: cf. Huang's chapter. But longer compounds, all of which are nouns in Starosta et al.'s data, are unequivocally right headed. Thus one might better look at longer compounds to see what the true generalizations about Chinese morphology are, rather than focussing on disyllabic compounds, which is of course fully in keeping with my earlier critique of Huang's paper. Of course, one must be careful not to overstress the point. There are a great many disyllabic compounds which are well-behaved with respect to their head placements. Even some left-headed ones are not ill-behaved: VN constructions such as *zoulu* (walk road) 'walk' are appropriately headed once one considers the parallels between VN compounds and VP's, which are also left-headed in Chinese. But there is no question that there is a great deal more idiosyncracy among disyllabic compounds than among longer constructions.

The second topic deals with the status of VR resultatives such as *da-kai* (hit open) 'to open'. Are they compounds or not? In particular are they composed of two free verbs as traditional analyses would have it, or is the R part (*kai* 'open', in this example) really a bound form, and hence probably a suffix.[14] Starosta et al.'s basic point is that for many of the resultative elements, if they occur at all as a separate verb, they often do so with a quite different meaning from their meaning as a resultative. Thus, for instance *zou* means 'walk' as a separate verb, but has the meaning of 'away' in constructions like *pao-zou* (run-away) 'run away'; *xia* means 'descend', but it functions more like the English particle 'down' in cases like *chi-xia* (eat-down) 'swallow, finish one's food'.

Starosta et al. presume that VR constructions are handled by derivational rules of the Word-and-Paradigm variety, though not many details of this analysis are given, lamentably. Much of the latter portion of the section on VR constructions is devoted to comparing the suffixal analysis with a VV analysis such as that of Li (1990). As Starosta et al. point out, in treating the R as a V, Li must struggle with the fact that there are often too many theta roles floating around. Under the suffixal analysis, this is not a problem, since there are no theta roles per se with the suffix. Of course, one still has to account for the fact that in well-known examples like *qi-lei* (ride-tired) 'ride until tired', the resultative *lei* seems to behave as if it has a theta role to assign (in this case either to the subject or the object), something that Li's analysis is specifically designed to explain. Naturally this could be handled in the suffixal account too, and ultimately the discussion would reduce to the issue of which approach is more ex-planatory and which more stipulatory, an issue I will stay away from here.

13. FINAL NOTE

Having treated the scholarly aspects of this book, I will end with a couple of comments on production quality. Since the book retails at US$185.35, it is fair to ask what kind of physical production one gets for one's money. The printing, paper and binding are of course the same as in other books in the *Trends in Linguistics* series by Mouton de Gruyter, which is to say good, though not exceptional for such an expensive series of books. In this book I found a number of typos, without explicitly looking for them, including an obvious one in the table of contents which lists an *Indroduction* by Packard, as well as a less obvious though more potentially misleading one in Table 2 on page 318, where the tones of *liǎngben* 'two volumes' (with sandhied tone on the first syllable) are listed incorrectly (*liàngben}*) in a couple of places. There were quite a number of other small typos of this nature which I will of course not bother to list here, but the overall impression I got was that a little more care might have been taken in the copy-editing phase.

NOTES

1   I thank Chilin Shih for a number of useful comments on this review.

2   These are translations of the traditional Chinese names, and should not be interpreted as denoting any specific phonetic properties of the tones.

3   As we shall see, Feng's view can be understood as a creative twist on this traditional phonology-driven account.

4   This traditional method of indicating pronunciations is termed *fanqie*.

5   This assumes that there actually *are* two verbs, as opposed to a verb plus an affix, which is what Starosta et al. later argue at least for the resultative constructions.

6   I say "seems to propose", because, unfortunately, the diagram that is supposed to illustrate the model – (18) on page 87, is almost impossible to interpret. I am inclined to suspect though that this must be a copy-editing problem: see Section 13.

7   Again, Li later gives a similar classification.

8   However, as Chilin Shih notes (p.c.), the passive equivalent of (i) in (ii), which is presumably parallel in syntactic structure to **shoupa rongyi ku-shi*, is perfectly acceptable:

(i)   ta ku-hong-le yanjing
        he cry-red-PERF eye
        'He cried so much that his eyes became red.'

(ii)   yanjing rongyi ku-hong
        eye easy cry-red
        'Eyes are easy to make red from crying.'

9   Unfortunately, as Dai himself notes, the prosodic weakness criterion would already explain this case – since *meng* is strong, without appealing to word status, so it is unclear what these examples show. Also, as Chilin Shih notes (p.c.), the phenomenon is far from general, even for the affixes where it may apply: thus, alongside *tamen* (3rd-Person PL) 'they' one finds *pengyou+men* (friend PL), but here reduction of *men* is impossible: **pengyoum*.

10   Why this is a separate test is not clear: it is really just an instance of test 4.

11   The data that Feng uses to support this, from Cheng (1981), are oddly chosen though, as they come from a study of the distribution of compounds in Confucius. Since Confucius lived more than 100 years *before* Mencius it is hard to see how the percentages of compound types in his writings could have much relevance for the question that Feng is addressing, namely the development of the language *after* Mencius.

12   Note, though, that many Modern Chinese languages allow glides between the onset and the rime, and one assumes Middle Chinese was the same in this regard.

13   Huang *does* discuss semantic issues – for Hakka and Cantonese – very briefly, and claims to have found that even from a semantic point of view, compounds are headless. But few details of how the analysis was performed are given, so that the results seem to me to be irreplicable.

14   I note for the record my disagreement with Starosta et al.'s assumption that compounds must be constructed out of free forms. While this is a common assumption, in Chinese at least it is not obviously correct. Indeed, as we took great pains to show in Sproat and Shih (1995), there are compound-like formations in Chinese that are formed productively out of bound morphemes: an example is *bai-yi* (white-ant) 'termite', where *y i* 'ant' is not a free form. We argued that such constructions must be considered compounds because there is really very little else they could be.

REFERENCES

Baker, Mark. 1988. *Incorporation: a Theory of Grammatical Function Changing.* Chicago: Chicago University Press.

Cheng, Xiangqing. 1981. "Xianqin shuangyinci yanjiu" [A study of Disyllabic Words in Pre-Qin]. In Xiangqing Cheng (ed.), *Xianqin Hanyu Yanjiu* [Studies of Pre-Qin Chinese]. Shandong: Shandong Jiaoyu Chubanshe, 41-113.

Dai, John X.-L. 1992. *Chinese Morphology and its Interface with the Syntax.* Ph.D. thesis, The Ohio State University, Columbus, OH.

Duanmu, San. 1997. "Recursive Constraint Evaluation in Optimality Theory: Evidence from Cyclic Compounds in Shanghai". *Natural Language and Linguistic Theory* 15, 465-508.

Feng, Shengli. 1995. *Prosodic Structure and Prosodically Constrained Syntax in Chinese.* Ph.D. thesis, University of Pennsylvania.

Li, Yafei. 1990. "On V-V Compounds in Chinese". *Natural Language and Linguistic Theory* 8, 177-207.

Lieber, Rochelle. 1983. "Argument Linking and Compounds in English". *Linguistic In-*

quiry 14, 251-286.

Packard, Jerome. 1990. "A Lexical Morphology Approach to Word Formation in Manda-rin". In G. Booij and J. van Marle (eds), *Yearbook of Morphology 1990*. Dordrecht: Foris, 21-37.

Packard, Jerome. 1992. "Why Mandarin Morphology is Stratum-orderd". Presented at the Fourth North American Conference on Chinese Linguistics, University of Michigan, Ann Arbor.

Sproat, Richard and Chilin Shih. 1993. "Why Mandarin Morphology is not Stratum-ordered". In G. Booij and J. van Marle (eds), *Yearbook of Morphology 1993*, 185-217.

Sproat, Richard and Chilin Shih. 1995. "A Corpus-based Analysis of Mandarin Nominal Root Compounds". *Journal of East Asian Linguistics* 4(1), 1-23.

Suen, Ching Y. 1986. *Computational Studies of the Most Frequent Chinese Words and Sounds*. Philadelphia: World Scientific.

Bell Laboratories
Room 2D 430
600 Mountain Avenue
Murray Hill, NJ 07974

e-mail: rws@bell-labs.com